S0-BZL-714

Founders as Fathers

Founders as Fathers

The Private Lives and Politics
of the American Revolutionaries

LORRI GLOVER

Yale UNIVERSITY PRESS

NEW HAVEN AND LONDON

Published with assistance from the Louis Stern Memorial Fund.

Copyright © 2014 by Lorri Glover.

All rights reserved.

This book may not be reproduced, in whole or in part, including illustrations, in any form (beyond that copying permitted by Sections 107 and 108 of the US Copyright Law and except by reviewers for the public press), without written permission from the publishers.

Yale University Press books may be purchased in quantity for educational, business, or promotional use. For information, please e-mail sales.press@yale.edu (US office) or sales@yaleup.co.uk (UK office).

Designed by James Johnson.

Set in MT Bell Standard type by Integrated Publishing Solutions, Grand Rapids, Michigan.

Printed in the United States of America.

Library of Congress Cataloging-in-Publication Data

Glover, Lorri, 1967–. Founders as fathers : the private lives and politics of the American revolutionaries / Lorri Glover.

pages   cm

Includes bibliographical references and index.

ISBN 978-0-300-17860-9 (clothbound : alk. paper)

1. Founding Fathers of the United States—Family relationships.   2. Founding Fathers of the United States—Biography.   3. United States—Politics and government—1775–1783—Biography.   4. United States—Politics and government—1783–1809—Biography.   I. Title.

E302.5.G65 2014

973.3092'2—dc23

[B] 2014014623

A catalogue record for this book is available from the British Library.

This paper meets the requirements of ANSI/NISO Z39.48-1992 (Permanence of Paper).

10 9 8 7 6 5 4 3 2 1

Contents

Illustrations follow page 134

Acknowledgments

Writing this book, like any other, was at once a grueling ordeal and a wonderful adventure, made bearable on the one hand and fulfilling on the other by what eighteenth-century folks called "friends": people who looked out for me, smoothed my path, and generously shared their expertise, connections, and support. I was also lucky enough to draw on the kindnesses of friends in the twenty-first-century meaning of the word, and more often than not my benefactors became my buddies and vice versa. The academic and the personal, the public and the private blurred in my life, too, then.

Matt Schoenbachler and Craig Friend have been friends in both senses for twenty years now. Matt, always my most valued critic, read the entire manuscript and, as ever, gave me the best advice about improving it and the clearest perspective on it. Craig read the early chapters with his trademark rigor and thoughtfulness. This project benefited enormously from our editorial partnerships and from his inspirational example. Bruce Wheeler started out as a mentor, became a friend, and is now a writing partner. He took time from his many projects to read mine with his remarkable blend of capaciousness and precision. Ami Pflugrad-Jackisch and I can never remember exactly how we met, only that we became fast friends at some gathering at a Southern Historical Association conference. I tried out some of the early ideas for this book at a talk I gave at Ami's invitation, and she later provided me excellent counsel on revising the manuscript. In between, we enjoyed many fun breaks from academic conferences and as many scholarly conversations over dinner. Jeff Norrell first told me I should and could write this book, and, since he'd always been right down to that point, I decided to believe him. He remained an inspiration through the whole process. And I would never have written anything without the encouragement and influence of Larry Nelson, whose imprint words cannot describe.

Jon Kukla's writing is a model for our craft, and so I was exceedingly happy when he made time to read the manuscript and share his deep understanding of Virginia history. And Thomas Foster graciously swapped manuscripts with me, which meant I both got an advance reading of his newest (wonderful) book and the benefit of his deft reading of mine. Jen Popiel and Kathy Marty also read the whole manuscript—and the much longer, earlier draft—and helped me sharpen my ideas and prose.

The archivists and docents and curators I met while researching this project were, to a one, encouraging and helpful. I must, however, single out Karen Gorman and Edith Poindexter at Red Hill and Mark Whatford and Susan Anthone at Gunston Hall, for going above and beyond. Karen Gorman made sure I was able to attend an eighteenth-century-style lunch on the grounds of Patrick Henry's last estate during my visit, and Edith Poindexter gave—impromptu—probably the single best tour I've ever been on. Anyone writing about the founding era and certainly about the founders must thank the heavens for the digitization projects that have made the editorial projects of men like Thomas Jefferson, George Washington, and James Madison, immediately accessible and, now, free. To echo one of the revolutionaries, we live in an age of wonders.

Saint Louis University has been an exciting academic home. Since joining the faculty in 2009, I've had the great good fortune to work for two deans, first the late Don Brennan and currently Michael Barber, both deeply committed to the scholarly mission of SLU and unfailingly encouraging of all my endeavors. I am profoundly grateful for the generous support of the College of Arts and Sciences, which gave me the time, financial resources, and academic environment to write this book. The History Department at SLU has had two fine leaders in the past five years, both of whom are exemplary scholars and honorable people.

Michal Rozbicki warmly welcomed me to the department and inspired me by the example of his work. Phil Gavitt is boundlessly encouraging and supportive. In addition to Phil and Michal, I have the privilege of working alongside other historians at the top of their game who challenge me to be my best, including Flannery Burke, Torrie Hester, Hal Parker, Silvana Siddali, and Katrina Thompson. Silvana, Flannery, and Katrina read the book proposal and gave me sage advice and heartening encouragement when I needed it most. Katrina, Torrie, and I were making the same writing journey at the same time; sharing work with them kept me motivated, and I'm happily indebted to them, as writers and friends. Financial support from SLU included graduate research assistants, and I relied on Joshua Mather, Christopher Schnell, and Ivy McIntyre for more research aid, fact-checking, and editing than I really want to admit. Josh also compiled elaborate genealogies of these complex families that I turned to countless times. I'm sure I managed to sneak back in some of the errors Chris and Ivy corrected, despite their best efforts. Ivy, Josh, and Chris were also part of a terrific graduate student cohort that included Kristi Roberts, Luke Ritter, Scott McDermott, Stephen Kissel, Ian McPherson, and Jeff Dorr. They all enriched my experiences at SLU and this book. And Chris Pudlowski holds us all together, working hardest of all. I'm thankful for her presence in the department and all the guidance she's given me since my first day at SLU.

I consider it a minor miracle that I somehow landed in the same job as Stefan Bradley and Jen Popiel, much less that I get to call them friends. I admire them both very much, academically and personally, and I am thankful for all the things they have taught me, in word and deed. The Women's and Gender Studies Program at SLU is the most intellectually vibrant community I've ever been a part of, and I am grateful for the example set by and the friendship of leaders in the program, especially Penny Weiss, Georgia Johnston, and Elisabeth Perry.

My parents were uplifting and patient when I begged off family visits to keep writing. Dick Kreckler kept me fed at my favorite breakfast spot ever, Macklind Deli. Rowena McClinton, Nancy Schurr, and Christy Fry offered compassion, distractions, empathy, and perspective—and always exactly when I needed it.

Warm thanks must go to my agent, Geri Thoma, who believed in the project and found it a wonderful home at Yale in the skilled editorial hands of Christopher Rogers, who has been a tremendous friend to this book. It is far stronger (and mercifully shorter) for Chris's careful guidance. I greatly appreciate, too, the thoughtful advice offered by the anonymous reviewer for Yale University Press; the hard work of Christina Tucker and Erica Hansen to shepherd the book toward publication; and the spot-on copyediting of Laura Jones Dooley.

Dan Smith discussed, traveled, read, consoled, edited, and celebrated. He is my best friend, in every sense and for all time.

Introduction

After the "father of his country" was laid to rest in December 1799, the United States Congress turned to his longtime friend and a fellow Virginian, Representative Henry "Light-Horse Harry" Lee, to offer a eulogy on behalf of a grateful and grieving nation. Hundreds of such eulogies were delivered that winter, in cities and communities across the country. As Americans heard the sad news of George Washington's death, they organized solemn civic commemorations and elaborate mock funerals, starting in mid-December and running through the following 22 February, which would have been Washington's sixty-eighth birthday. Of all the orations, though, Lee's is the most enduring. Lee predicted that Washington's reputation would outlast monuments and nations, that his life story would remain an inspiration for mankind "until love of virtue cease on earth." George Washington deserved that immortal renown, Lee proclaimed, because he was "first in war, first in peace, and first in the hearts of his countrymen." But that phrase—so familiar in our collective memory—is incomplete. For Henry Lee continued, past that dependent clause of his sentence, to a larger point he wished to make: "he was second to none in the humble and endearing scenes of private life."[1] This book is, at heart, about the unexplored story behind Lee's phrasing: the part of the founders' lives that became famous, the part that has been forgotten, and how the two—public and private, politics and family—were indelibly linked in the revolutionary age.

1

We begin in Virginia, for the story of the creation of the American Republic is in a large measure the story of Virginia. The plantation masters who presided over the largest, oldest, and most influential of England's North American colonies were used to their word holding sway; they instinctively preferred to take the lead and were loath to yield power to (or take criticism from) other men. To be sure, political radicalism emerged in the streets of Boston in the 1760s; by the mid-1770s it had spread so far throughout the mainland of British North America that colonists undertook a continent-wide war against their king. Along the way, Virginia's leading revolutionaries worked with lawyers, intellectuals, and politicians from all the colonies. And, much to their dismay, the self-styled gentlemen-patriarchs realized in the perilous years before Independence and during the Revolutionary War that they needed to partner with artisans, farmers, shopkeepers—men they casually referred to as the "lesser sort." But designing a government and society to replace the colonial order American patriots overthrew in 1775–1776— that mammoth task was taken up by a small cohort of Virginians.

The values that moved the revolutionary generation from rebellion to a republic, the ideas that laid the foundation for an independent country, the documents that created the United States government and guide it still, in the third century after its establishment—these came principally from men occupying the great houses of Virginia, men like George Mason, Patrick Henry, Thomas Jefferson, James Madison, and, of course, George Washington.[2]

Throughout the revolutionary age, these Virginians loomed large over their fellow Americans. "We all look up to Virginia for examples," John Adams told Patrick Henry in the precarious and fateful summer of 1776. And they answered with exemplary service. Virginians rose to shepherd the rebellion against England, to command the Continental Army, to lead early continental governments. They designed the first bill of rights and constitution for the breakaway states, the Declaration of Independence, and the US Constitution. In the early constitutional era, Virginians exerted disproportionate authority over the US Congress and federal judiciary, and they dominated the presidency for thirty-six years, interrupted only by Adams's single term. By the 1810s marvel for the Virginians' service had turned to envy, and gratitude to frustration. Politicians feared there was, in fact, a Virginia conspiracy afoot and even floated the idea of a constitutional amendment to "wrest the sovereignty of the union out of the hands" of Virginians, whose reputation for political primacy lasted long after their real power faded.[3]

In the middle of his stirring eulogy, Henry Lee mentioned the "end" of George Washington's life, then immediately corrected himself: "An end, did I say? His fame survives." And it survives still, alongside widespread recognition of the revolutionaries' momentous political innovations and improbable military exploits, their fractious and fitful efforts to design a working government, and their fierce resolve in the face of political setbacks and partisan fallings-out.[4]

For all the historical fame they earned, though, a key element of their lives, one essential for truly understanding their Revolution, is often forgotten: their families. Before they even thought about being founders, these men were Virginia planter-patriarchs, fathers in their small corner of the British Empire. Our modern definitions of fatherhood and family are very different from theirs. In the plantation culture of colonial Virginia, a respectable father not only raised dutiful children and secured his household's finances but also provided for extended kin, ran a thriving estate, mastered slaves, and even served in political office. Families and households were fluid especially because death did to their families what divorce often does to ours; stepparents and half-siblings were commonplace. Orphaned children were routinely taken in by their uncles and older brothers; young men seeking career guidance took up residence on the estates of successful relatives for months and years at a time; widows lived with siblings and aunts and uncles. In the day-to-day lives of dutiful gentry fathers—including men who became the most famous founders—educating the children in their households and protecting their inheritances got conflated with making wise planting decisions, controlling slaves, and serving in public office. Fatherhood was, then, complicated and wide-ranging—and, it turns out, central to the political careers of Virginia's leading revolutionaries.

To a large degree, these Virginians became founders *because* they were fathers, responsible, in their minds, for the well-being of their communities, the wealth and power of their relatives, the preservation of social order and civic justice. They were founders *while* they were fathers, struggling after the 1760s to balance competing, inviolable claims on their time. And *how* they headed their families shaped and was shaped by their leadership of the American Republic.

Not for nothing, then, were these men called, in their own age as in ours, "founding fathers." The term is not mere alliteration or metaphor. A familial context underlay the revolutionary generation's civic ideals and political actions. It is not possible to fully understand these founders' zeal for liberty, sacrifice, and virtue—words casually invoked today but that had explicit and existential meaning in the eighteenth century—apart from their family values and domestic experiences. It was no coincidence that in both their households and the public square these men exercised independence and worried about guiding posterity. Nor was it an accident that race and gender divided both their experiment in republican government and their families. The values cultivated in their plantation households shaped the founding documents written by these Virginians and the essence of the revolution they led.

At the same time, the founding fathers' political actions had profound (if unintended) domestic consequences. As they aged, these men witnessed their families and their Revolution change in ways they never intended. Aware that both the fate of their civic experiment and the continuation of their families' prominence depended on the rising generation, they watched their descendants with equal parts vigilance and alarm. They were often justifiably distressed at what they saw. By the time Virginia's domination of the American Republic began to wane in the 1810s and 1820s, the family lives of these men and their fellow Americans had undergone sweeping changes. They and their children grappled with the often troubling ramifications of the revolution in values that reshaped families every bit as much as government, including the erosion of deference and the seductive and often chaotic lure of individualism.[5]

Founders as Fathers explores these connections between family values and revolutionary politics in the lives of the principal architects of the American Republic, the Virginians who first charted the course of our nation: George Mason, Patrick Henry, George Washington, Thomas Jefferson, and James Madison. The story begins in the colonial households that nurtured this cohort, follows them through their revolution in politics and family life, and ends with the transformed world they bequeathed their descendants in the early nineteenth century. It reveals that we cannot fully understand the revolutionary generation or the country they forged without going home with them, exploring the most intimate parts of their lives, and appreciating the plantations and kin groups and slave quarters over which they presided. In short, we must meet these founders as fathers.

CHAPTER 1

The Last Colonial Patriarchs

A t first glance, Virginia planters seem like highly unlikely candidates for fomenting a revolution. In our mind's eye, men like George Washington, Thomas Jefferson, and Patrick Henry always appear as "founders." But they were first and foremost planters; they made their livings from agriculture and spent their formative years on plantations, their lives defined by family, neighbors, and slaves. Virginia's leading men presided over that localistic and agricultural world, as they said, "like patriarchs of old."[1] In addition to their decidedly provincial, planter-centered perspectives, they were deeply loyal to Britain and cavalier about political duties.

Personally, the men who partnered (or conspired) to create an independent America—Jefferson, Washington, and Henry, along with George Mason and James Madison—were as different as could be. Thomas Jefferson achieved renown in diplomacy, politics, education, philosophy, and agriculture. But not even his greatest admirers would describe him as an impressive orator. In formal settings Jefferson worried about stumbling over his words, so much so that he used diacritical marks to help him read the draft of the Declaration of Independence aloud to the Second Continental Congress. He also had an annoying habit of humming to himself. Conversely, Henry was an undistinguished statesman and, Jefferson later gossiped, a lazy lawyer, but his oratory dazzled even his sharpest critics. Mason, never given to profuse praise, concluded, "He is by far the most powerful speaker I ever heard."[2] Madison, though possessing the most brilliantly rigorous mind of the age, spoke so softly that people had to lean in to hear him—perhaps a canny move if he had intended it, which he did not. Washington knew his intellectual limits enough to hold his tongue, which, in time, contributed to his air of gravity. His friend Mason, conversely, said what he thought, regardless of the outcome. "I would not," he told his son, "forfeit the approbation of my own mind for the approbation of any man, or all the men upon earth."[3] They looked wildly different, too. Henry was tall and wiry and vacillated between patrician and homespun, depending on his audience. Mason was shorter and rounder, and though he complained constantly about his health, most contemporaries thought of him as robust (they perhaps conflated his disposition and his health). And then there was the lanky redhead Jefferson, and his best friend and physical opposite, the diminutive intellectual Madison. Rounding out the odd brotherhood was the statuesque, dashing Washington.

As they worked to build a new nation in the 1770s and 1780s, their stark differences in temperament and breadth of talents made them a formidable—if sometimes fractious—lot. They could act together as brilliant and indefatigable allies, unless their agendas diverged, in which case they turned into vicious adversaries who knew exactly how to exploit one another's weaknesses.

For all their differences, on the eve of the American Revolution these Virginians shared in common nearly everything that mattered in their world. Though at different stages of life and on different paths, they wanted the same thing, which was what all well-to-do men from Virginia wanted: to be respected as patriarchs. Patriarchal power, expressed through mastery of a family, a plantation, and the social order, lay at the center of their identity. Exercising that authority was a duty they inherited from their fathers. If they succeeded in preserving their estates and the family's good name, they could bequeath that legacy to their own sons. Office holding followed family lines. Politics was a vital, though part-time obligation of the colony's well-bred (or shrewdly married) planter-patriarchs. A good patriarch—the highest aspiration of a Virginia gentleman—balanced rearing children, building wealth, mastering slaves, protecting kin, leading households, and governing. All of these duties derived from their wide understanding of what family meant and what responsible fathers did.

Family, class identity, and power formed an unbroken circle in colonial Virginia. Patriarchs regarded themselves as caretakers: judiciously growing their inheritance to preserve a patrimony for their heirs. They belonged to an old and inviolable arrangement, inheriting and bequeathing wealth and power within their families and, ultimately, for the greater good of society. They saw their principal duties as familial—broadly defined—and their status as organic. At heart, then, their position in Virginia did not differ fundamentally from that of the king in England; they were linked in a great "chain of being" as patriarchs over worlds large and small.

Without appreciating the families and gentry culture in which this cohort grew up, it is not possible to truly understand their behavior as heads of households in a tumultuous age and as leaders of a radical revolution. We begin, then, by meeting the progenitors of Virginia's, and to a large extent America's, revolution where they lived. Family was *the* central, transcendent institution in their lives, shaping their identities and vision of the world until events in the 1760s and 1770s redirected their futures in ways unimaginable just a few years before. To their great surprise, this generation turned out to be the last of the colonial breed.

In 1763, twenty-year-old Thomas Jefferson wrote his friend Will Fleming about his dreams for the future. Jefferson had recently finished his studies at the College of William and Mary, and he was reading law with George Wythe, the most distinguished legal mind in Virginia. Wythe provided his students not only the benefit of his storied legal prowess but also entry into Williamsburg's inner circles of power, and Jefferson's striking intellect made him a welcome addition to the scene, including at the royal governor's mansion. The young student, understandably, saw a bright future for himself.

Young Jefferson had high hopes in 1763: he imagined that he and Fleming would buy neighboring plantations and get married to prominent local women (Will to Sukey Potter and Thomas to Rebecca Burwell). Once established in their homes, the two friends would become partners in a two-horse carriage that they would use to "practise law in the same courts, and drive about to all the dances in the country together." Riding the circuit with Will, owning a plantation with Rebecca, and enjoying a happy social life was, Thomas proclaimed, "the cleverest plan of life that can be imagined."[4]

He had good cause to envision that sanguine future. Though as a teenager he had lost his father, Peter Jefferson, Thomas still had the family advantages necessary to claim the rank of a Virginia patriarch. Peter had been a successful surveyor and planter, served on county courts, and speculated—with great success—in land. Jane Randolph, his mother, belonged to one of the colony's most prominent families. The couple owned thousands of acres of rich land and led a refined lifestyle at Shadwell, their home, and Tuckahoe, the estate of William Randolph, Jane's kinsman and Peter's best friend, where they resided for many years, raising Randolph's children along with their own.

Jefferson knew his family's wealth and connections had brought him to Williamsburg, and that achieving the status of a gentleman and patriarch would continue to depend on family. He grew to manhood imbibing a worldview that pervaded English America: social hierarchy was organic, just, and family-based. Rank depended in large measure on birth; lineage was identity. Slave laws codified the most rigid dimensions of this inheritable social order. White women's legal status—or, more to the point, the absence of a legal status under the doctrine of coverture—was of the same piece. The "lesser sort" of white men—those lacking sufficient land, family connections, and reputations to claim gentry status—learned their place as well. A raft of laws reminded them lest they try to forget. Sartorial statutes even policed clothing, with the "lesser sort" forbidden from wearing certain fabrics and colors.

But even with those family advantages, if Thomas Jefferson wanted to guarantee his reputation as a worthy patriarch, he would have to excel: in his career, at those dances, with a woman. His understanding of how colonial Virginia worked fueled his concern for finding the right kind of wife. Rebecca Burwell was smart, charming, pretty, and an orphan raised by her uncle, William Nelson, a rich and powerful politician. Wooing a reputable woman like Rebecca, Thomas knew, would advance

his standing. Career success would likewise depend on carefully cultivated connections, hence his enthusiasm to live near and work with Will
Fleming.

Though he didn't say it in his letter to Fleming, slave mastery was
also essential to Jefferson's imagined future. Slaves tended the carriages
and horses that lawyers used to ride the circuit. They readied the clothes
for the dances and, of course, provided the labor that subsidized the lifestyles of Virginia's gentry. Throughout his young life, slaves had daily
attended to Jefferson's needs. His first memory, in fact, was of being
handed to a slave, who sat him on a pillow and rode him on horseback to
Tuckahoe.[5] In his world, racial power was another inheritance, like land,
money, and family ties. He would have to work hard to make the most of
those advantages, though, if he hoped to join the ranks of the first men
of Virginia.

George Mason IV was born and bred a Virginia planter-patriarch.
He descended from a long line of men whose plantations
thrived on Virginia's Northern Neck, along the Potomac
River. So certain was his family's claim to power that George IV had the
luxury of resenting the occasional intrusions on his time made by serving in the House of Burgesses; he resisted calls to public office from time
to time, but he could not escape them altogether. Gentlemen like Mason
believed that they took care of the "lesser sort" and upheld social order
by submitting to political service. While rising men like Thomas Jefferson scrambled for positions that signaled their arrival into Virginia's
inner circle, George Mason, secure in his land and his family's reputation, preferred whenever possible to remain at Gunston Hall, where he
could, as he wrote to his friend George Washington, "sit down at his
Ease under the Shade of his own Vine, & his own fig-tree, & enjoy the
Sweets of domestic Life!"[6]

The Mason family story was typical of Virginia's gentry, built on
land, marriage, ambition, and luck. The first George Mason—great-
grandfather to the revolutionary leader—migrated to Virginia in the
early 1650s, and he settled on the Potomac River, in Indian country that

he and like-minded farmers struggled to turn into a profitable extension
of the Virginia colony. He succeeded in carving an estate out of the wil-
derness and gave his first-born son both that land and his name. George
Mason II was a canny land speculator and proficient planter. He married
well, twice, into prominent Chesapeake families. As was the Virginia
way, George II turned his family connections and economic success
into political power. In the 1690s he took a seat in the Virginia House
of Burgesses, where, duplicating his father's priorities, he spent most of
his political capital lobbying for frontier defense measures. The first
two George Masons understood that the fate of their families depended
on land—acquiring it, policing it, and producing lucrative commodities
on it.

George Mason III (born in 1690) kept those family traditions alive.
He bought more and more land in Virginia and Maryland and followed
his late father into public office, first as sheriff of Stafford County and
then, in 1715, into the House of Burgesses. This George Mason was also
as lackadaisical about his political obligations as he was ambitious for
land. During his tenure in the Burgesses (1715–1726), he was formally
reprimanded for being absent. He preferred to focus on his diversifying
business interests—planting, land speculation, and shipping goods on
the Potomac—and his family. He married well, to Ann Thomson, one of
the two heiresses of a powerful royal appointee. Inheriting their father's
estate made Ann and her sister sought-after brides in Virginia's marriage market, attractive to ambitious men like George Mason III.[7]

Ann and George's first child was born in 1725, and, predictably,
named George IV. Reflecting his parent's landholdings, he and his two
siblings, Mary and Thomson, were all born on different plantations.
When George III died in 1735, Ann Mason found herself with three
small children, ages two through nine, to raise. Most Virginia widows
chose to remarry, but Mason took another course. She became a skilled
planter, financial manager, and land speculator. She made sure her children dressed their status: ruffled linen shirts for the brothers and fashionable petticoats for Mary. But she also adeptly managed her household
without accruing debts.[8]

Kin helped Ann Mason with those fatherless children, a practice
rendered commonplace in the colonial era by Virginia's unhealthy envi-

ronment. In George Mason's case, John Mercer, his uncle and father's business partner, stepped in. Mercer was rich and well-read; he owned a library of some fifteen hundred volumes. Ann and John oversaw George's education, which was not simply scholastic. As his Uncle Mercer explained, a good tutor should teach a boy to "be particularly careful of his Religion, morals, & behavior, in short he should be a gentleman."[9]

George Mason IV was not an easy man—forthright to the point of gruff, relentlessly uncompromising, intolerant of others' failings—but he was a respected one according to the values of his age. In his twenties and early thirties he amassed vast holdings in Prince William and Fairfax Counties in Virginia, Charles County, Maryland, and Analostan Island. With all those hundreds of acres, he acquired scores of slaves. He looked out for his young relatives and, as his mother taught him, watched his money. In 1750 he married sixteen-year-old Ann Eilbeck. Her father, William Eilbeck, was not only a longtime family friend and business ally, but also one of the richest men in Charles County. And he had but one heir: Ann. (Apparently his father's example showed Mason the advantage of courting a woman whose rich father had no sons.) Mason learned, like his ancestors, that social rank and political power had a mutually reinforcing relationship: gentlemen needed to perform public obligations while political service affirmed gentry status. Following the script for a Virginia gentleman, George took a term on his vestry, served on the local court, and won election to the House of Burgesses in 1758. The next year he and Ann moved into Gunston Hall, where they raised nine children and buried three others.[10]

By his mid-thirties George Mason had made the most of the advantages he enjoyed because of his family, and so rightly claimed the status of a Virginia gentleman. He turned his and Ann's inheritances into a vast estate, some seventy-five thousand acres spread across Virginia and Maryland and onto the southern frontier. He was widely respected for his intellect, and though not temperamentally suited for politics, powerful. He loved foxhunting, horseback riding, and horse racing—the sports of Virginia patriarchs. Ann kept Gunston Hall beautifully appointed, and the couple socialized with the best families in northern Virginia. Her household duties would have been onerous, but she could pass the most difficult jobs—cleaning up after sick children, cooking meals, changing diapers—to her slaves. Slavery purchased every part of their lifestyle. Their son John later bragged, "My Father had among his Slaves—Carpenters, Coopers, Sawyers, Blacksmiths, Tanners, Curriers, Shoemakers, Spinners, Weavers & Knitters, even a Distiller. His woods furnished Timber and Plant for the Carpenters and Coopers—and charcoal for the Blacksmith; his cattle killed for his own Consumption or for Sale, supplied skins for the Tanners Curriers & Shoemakers—and his Sheep gave wool and his Fields produced cotton & Flax for the weavers and Spinners—and his orchards fruit for the Distiller."[11] A colonial planter-patriarch could have achieved no more.

Mason's friend and neighbor George Washington settled into the same lifestyle, on a nearby plantation, at nearly the same time. The Washingtons, like the Masons, traced their Virginia history back a century, to the 1657 arrival of brothers John and Augustine, but the family owed its prominence principally to the women these first migrants and their sons married. John, the great-grandfather of George Washington, wed the daughter of a prominent Maryland family. By 1668, he owned over 5,000 acres in Virginia's Northern Neck. George's father, Augustine, inherited 1,100 acres of that family estate and shortly married a woman who added 1,750 more. When Augustine's first wife died in 1729, he again married advantageously, to a twenty-one-year-old heiress named Mary Ball.[12]

Mary Ball's first son, George, received only a modest education, a fact that embarrassed him throughout his life. Still, he learned well as a boy the essential lessons to act the part of a gentleman-patriarch. His father died in 1743, when George was barely eleven, and he found support from his older half-brother, Lawrence, and his wife, Anne Fairfax. Anne descended from the most prominent family in all of Virginia; the Fairfax holdings exceeded a staggering five million acres, including vast tracts of fertile land between the Potomac and Rappahannock Rivers and running as far west as the Shenandoah Valley. Having no sons of their own, Anne and Lawrence doted on George, buying him the most fashionable clothing, teaching him music and dance, and connecting him with Anne's father, Colonel William Fairfax.[13]

Around age fourteen, Washington used the English translation of a French conduct book to define for himself "Rules of Civility and Decent Behaviour in Company and Conversation." His 110 exacting rules covered everything from eating to hygiene, facial expressions to attire. Humming and excessive laughing in public were to be studiously avoided, as was crossing legs, biting fingernails, picking ticks and lice, blowing on soup to cool it, and raising one eyebrow higher than the other.

Washington's guidebook bore two particular imprints of the colonial age: restraint, of the sort he manifested in physical comportment, and rank, conveyed through interactions with others. According to his guide, the "better bred and quality of the person" the more deference owed (no. 26). Men sat according to rank (nos. 28 and 106); walked to the left side of a social better, "but if three walk together, the mid place is the most honourable" (no. 30); and if asked a question by "those of higher quality . . . stand upright, put off your hat, & answer in few words" (no. 85). Number 37 stipulated: "In speaking to men of quality, do not lean nor look them full in the face, nor approach too near them, at least keep a full pace from them."[14] As a young man, Washington performed the gentlemanly part beautifully: he looked handsome in the saddle and rode confidently, danced elegantly, and charmed women. That last matter was especially important, since Washington knew that his best chance at quickly amassing a large estate lay in an advantageous marriage.

Martha Dandridge Custis was a twenty-seven-year-old widow when she began to accept George Washington's romantic overtures. She was not just any young widow, though she was one of the richest women in Virginia. Her first husband, Daniel Parke Custis, had been twenty years her senior when he wed Martha, herself descended from a leading family. Daniel Custis died seven years into the marriage without a will. Martha was left with two young children and a splendid inheritance: an estate valued in excess of £23,000—nearly $3,000,000 in today's money—that included over seventeen thousand acres and 250 slaves. On top of that, Martha was smart, vivacious, optimistic, and resourceful. When Daniel died, she took over his business interests. "I now have the Administration of his Estate & management of his Affairs of all sorts," she informed a London merchant. She handled those affairs with a savvy confidence unusual for women of her era. She had her pick of men, then, and many suitors far wealthier and more prominent than the one she chose.[15]

Martha met George shortly after he returned from the Ohio Country, where he had spent the better part of five years trying to defend Virginia's western lands. He brought home a reputation for military prowess and personal valor. The dashing war hero and the charming rich widow married in January 1759. As the newlyweds and Martha's two children, four-year-old John Parke Custis, called Jacky, and Martha, nicknamed Patsy, not yet three, made their way to Mount Vernon, George sent exacting orders to his overseer and slaves: the house was to be thoroughly cleaned, tables and staircase polished, beds made, fires tended, and fresh eggs gathered.[16]

George immediately took over the finances, not only Martha's third of the Custis estate but also the two-thirds reserved for Jacky and Patsy. Though Martha was certainly capable of continuing her management, eighteenth-century Virginians thought that settling estates with lawyers and transacting business with foreign merchants was men's work. George therefore directed all of her London contacts to start addressing their letters to him.[17]

As they settled into their new home, the couple spent like mad, bent on acquiring the things that would signify their status and, apparently, thinking little about their long-term finances. Their primary London agents, Cary and Company, sent to Mount Vernon an astounding array of goods in the first years after their wedding: cloth, ribbon, leather, lace; shoes, jackets, and hats for the whole family; exotic foods such as anchovies, capers, almonds, and mangoes; endless household items including brushes, scissors, chimney pieces, axes, and hinges; elegant furniture, glasses, dishes, and curtains. The lists went on and on and on. In less than three years they ran through nearly all of Martha's inheritance from Daniel Custis.

The Washingtons must have cut quite a figure in the Northern Neck. He ordered a new sword belt, made of red Moroccan leather. For her came salmon-colored taffeta with a satin flower inlay for a new coat, perhaps adorned with the pearl-edged ribbon sent in the same shipment. She could wear the luxurious coat with her white silk hose, black satin shoes, and the best kid gloves London could offer. The couple wore corduroy from India, linen from Ireland, lace from Brussels.[18]

The exquisitely dressed newlyweds soon found themselves in the same boat as most of the Virginia gentry (though not the Masons, for they lived within their means): enjoying a luxurious lifestyle while drowning in debt to English factors, or agents.[19]

Washington, though temporarily extravagant, proved an excellent steward of his Virginia lands. Like George Mason, he speculated in land with great success. He was also an adept planter who experimented creatively with scores of crops, always seeking a more robust and profitable yield. He wisely diversified his businesses beyond planting, breeding livestock and running a successful fishing business on the Potomac. Or, to be accurate, he directed his slaves to undertake those endeavors.

Washington's writings from the 1760s reveal the same priorities as Mason's. Washington's biographers, understandably intent on revealing his contributions to building the American nation, often slight how thoroughly provincial Washington was as a young man. In the 1760s and early 1770s he was no nationalist in waiting; he saw himself as a Virginian and planter. He, like Mason, served on the local vestry and in the Burgesses, but colonial governance held little fascination for either man. Politics mattered principally as a means to secure their real priorities: money, land, and family status.[20]

The two friends preferred to spend their time on family and business concerns, which increasingly overlapped in their comfortable corner of Virginia. Mason and Washington both owned shares in the Ohio Company, and they served on the Truro vestry and the Fairfax courts. They bought neighboring pews at the Pohick Church and occasionally speculated together on land. George Mason hired tutors to come to Gunston Hall, including a dance instructor, and Patsy Custis attended classes there. Washington sought Mason's advice about a teacher for Jacky Custis.[21]

Once the Washingtons got their spending in check, the only striking difference between the two estates was that the Masons raised a house full of children at Gunston Hall, whereas there would be none born at Mount Vernon. Martha was well within her childbearing years when they wed, and she seems to have easily conceived in her first marriage (four times in seven years). She and George had a loving marriage, and gentry families did not choose childlessness. So the most reasonable conclusion is that the "father of his country" technically could not have been. Many biographers speculate that Washington was left infertile after a bout with smallpox that he contracted during a 1751 trip to Barbados with Lawrence. More recently at least one historian has been willing to entertain the equally plausible, if far less popular, idea that Washington was impotent.[22] In any event, George and Martha doted on Jacky and Patsy. Though she loved children, Martha was healthier and more vibrant for not bearing more. If George felt disappointed at producing no offspring, he never said as much. Rather, he seemed in the early 1760s to have settled into a happy life with Martha.

Not yet thirty years old, Washington's vision of his future was sunny if unexceptional: "I am now I believe fixd at this Seat with an agreable Consort for life and hope to find more happiness in retirement than I ever experienced amidst a wide and bustling World."[23]

On the eve of the American Revolution, George Mason and George Washington were all that Virginians imagined men should be, whereas James Madison remained still a boy. It would be two more decades before he met his true partner in politics, Dolley Payne Todd, the woman who, a contemporary said, "relieved him of much Bile—and rendered him much more open and conversant than I have seen him before."[24]

The youngest of this cohort of Virginia founders, Madison shared the most in common with Mason, the oldest. He too was the firstborn son and namesake of one of his county's leading planter-patriarchs. For years after he rose to national prominence he continued to sign his name "James Madison, Jr." Each man inherited vast tracts of land, both were gifted intellectually, and neither was ideally suited for leadership, though for different reasons. Mason was frank, often stubborn, and refused to suffer fools. Madison was every bit as sure of his ideas, but he was soft-spoken to the point of diffidence and he did not mix well in company. Like Mason, he obsessed over his health; both men verged on the hypochondriacal. But unlike the quick-tempered Mason, Madison was praised throughout his life for his gentle spirit, which could disguise his fierce resolve. Both his neighbor James Barbour and his longtime personal slave Paul Jennings agreed: neither ever saw James Madison "in a passion." Coupled with his unparalleled work ethic and relentless reasoning, Madison's calm demeanor made him a formidable force—in time. But on the eve of the American Revolution that destiny lay far in the young man's future. It was not at all clear in the early 1770s whether he could even fill his father's shoes in Orange County.[25]

The Madisons had been in Virginia since the middle of the seventeenth century, amassing land and family prestige. James Madison Sr. had been an only child, and he lost his father when he was just nine years old. After he came of age, James Madison Sr. inherited a large estate, which he expanded through astute business deals and an advantageous marriage to Nelly Conway, rich daughter of a prominent planter-merchant. James Madison Sr. soon became the largest landholder in Orange County, and he raised his children in the high style of a Virginia gentleman. Private tutors came to Montpelier to train young Jemmy and his siblings. One of those tutors saw the boy's special talents and recommended in 1769 that he go to Princeton, then known as the College of New Jersey, so that he might fully cultivate the outstanding mind he evidenced in his studies. (William and Mary was too Anglican to suit James Madison Sr.) Eager to encourage his namesake's success, James Sr. happily made the investment. James Jr. studied with well-to-do and talented young men from throughout British America and readied himself to compete for renown back home. In retrospect, it is easy to infer that the Princeton experience pulled Madison from the parochial Virginia perspective pervasive among his contemporaries. But it hardly seemed that way at the time. What the Madisons saw in the short-term was that their son's indefatigable intellectual curiosity and his feeble constitution formed a poor partnership. He finished college early, graduating in 1771, and stayed on for more intense study, but at a steep cost to his health. He returned to Montpelier in 1772 to recover. In the meantime, lacking any real responsibilities or practical outlet for his academic pursuits, he tutored his younger siblings, as any leisured and dutiful Virginian would have done.[26]

James Madison Jr. showed little interest in imperial-American politics while at Princeton. He did write his father about the collapse of New York's nonimportation agreement, but there is exceedingly little in his college letters to predict the future career he undertook. He worried a great deal, as did most young men of his age, about making a name for himself, and after returning home, he commiserated in letters to a college friend, William Bradford, about their "first entrance on the Theatre of Life." It was, James knew, essential that he capitalize on his family roots and his Princeton education. He longed for greatness but predicted it would elude him. "I am too dull and infirm," he wrote Bradford, "to look out for any extraordinary things in this world." He did not, he added, "expect a long or healthy life." He was profoundly wrong. But in 1772, twenty-one-year-old James Madison still wondered how he would ever become a worthy Virginia gentleman.[27]

P atrick Henry had no such self-doubts. As a young man, Henry lacked James Madison's leisured wealth, Thomas Jefferson's capacious intellect, and George Mason's vast estate, but he more than made up for those deficiencies by polishing his talents to a high sheen. He also benefited from the family tradition of shrewd marriages. The fortuitous marriage of his father, John Henry, to a rich widow fueled the family's initial rise to prominence. Colonel John Syme, a member of the Virginia Burgesses, was a friend of the Henry family, and when John Henry arrived in the colony in 1727, Syme welcomed him into his home. When the colonel met an untimely death in 1731 his young protégé comforted the attractive widow Syme, who, a visitor to her home noted, "seem'd not to pine too much for the Death of her Husband."[28] They soon wed. Sarah Syme Henry brought to the relationship six thousand acres of land in Hanover County, along with kin connections to merchants, land speculators, and some of Virginia's most illustrious families. She also had a son, John Syme Jr., who was raised on Studley Plantation in Hanover County alongside her children with John Henry, the brothers William and Patrick, and their seven sisters.

Patrick Henry acquired only a modest formal education. His parents were not especially wealthy but certainly had funds enough to send him to William and Mary. Yet, unlike James Madison or Thomas Jefferson, Patrick Henry seemed little inclined toward academics, and so his father made another choice. In 1751 he sent the fifteen-year-old to work as a clerk for a Hanover County merchant and learn that business. The following year, John Henry set up Patrick and William in their own company, which they shortly ran into the ground. Fortunately, Patrick Henry proved better at the business of marriage than commerce. While still a teenager, he wed Sarah Shelton, a sixteen-year-old whose dowry included three hundred acres of land along with several slaves. John Syme Jr., meanwhile, inherited Studley Plantation and married the wealthy widow Mildred Meriwether, which further advanced the family's standing.[29]

Though well connected, Patrick Henry still needed to capitalize on his family ties. He briefly ran one of Sarah's father's businesses, Hanover Tavern, where he honed his social skills before determining that his best course might lay with the law. His pursuit was decidedly casual, even given the informality of legal education in that age. He spent between one and six months studying on his own before journeying to Williamsburg to be examined by the colony's leading legal minds. Brothers John and Peyton Randolph had both studied at Middle Temple. They joined George Wythe and Robert Nicholas on the examining panel. The men, to put it mildly, were underwhelmed. Wythe refused to support Henry, and the others did so reluctantly, after concluding that he "was very ignorant of law" but seemed "a young man of genius & did not doubt he would soon qualify himself."[30]

And so he did, with a quintessential mix of family connections and personal talent. Henry's first legal clients included his father-in-law, uncle, cousin, and brother-in-law. Despite his unimpressive mastery of the law, no one surpassed him in oratorical brilliance and homespun logic. When he succeeded with his relatives' cases, they recommended him to their friends. At the same time, Henry expanded his landholdings, speculating with his half-brother, John Syme Jr., and his brother-in-law William Christian, a member of the House of Burgesses married to Anne Henry.[31] Patrick Henry was always buying land, and as his family grew—he eventually fathered sixteen children with two wives—so did his commitment to supplying each son a large estate and each daughter a lucrative dowry.

Aside from land, Henry cared less about the accoutrements of gentility than most of his contemporaries. He bartered his legal services in exchange for practical items: cider, sheep, animal skins. The largest house he ever owned, Scotchtown, was thirty-six by eighty-four feet and surrounded by 960 acres. It was plain, hip-roofed with eight rooms, and lacking in the architectural flair that Thomas Jefferson and George Washington insisted on in their homes. His friend and brother-in-law Samuel Meredith characterized Henry's furniture as "of the plainest sort, consisting of necessaries only; nothing for show or ornament." What Scotchtown earned, as opposed to how lovely it looked, revealed Henry's priorities: he bought the home in 1771 for £600 and sold it seven years later for £5,000.[32]

By the 1760s Henry justifiably saw himself as a worthy patriarch. He presided over an ever-expanding estate, household of children, and community of slaves, who worked his lands to secure his wealth. Samuel Meredith complimented Henry's devotion to his larger family, which was essential for any respected gentleman: "He interested himself much in the happiness of others, particularly of his sisters." Henry smoothly bridged gentry and country society. He rode in a fine carriage and wore a powdered wig. He also loved to hunt with his poorer neighbors and make music. His son-in-law praised Henry for having "a remarkable faculty of adapting himself to his company. . . . He would be pleasant and cheerful with persons of any class or condition."[33]

While less self-consciously refined than some of his contemporaries, Henry cemented his position at the top of Virginia's hierarchy in December 1763 through a singular talent. Outside Hanover County, he was a relative unknown until he defended the county that winter in the "Parson's Cause." The case centered on King George's veto of an act of the House of Burgesses to restrict clerical salaries. It no doubt advantaged Henry that his father was the presiding judge. But he showcased in that controversial and widely publicized trial the incomparable oratorical skill that made him famous. When Henry addressed the jury, every person in the courtroom was, eyewitnesses reported, "taken captive; and so delighted with their captivity, that they followed implicitly, whithersoever he led them, that, at his bidding, their tears flowed from pity, and their cheeks flushed with indignation." In 1765 the grateful citizens of Hanover County sent Henry to the House of Burgesses, where an ambitious law student hoping to capitalize on his own talents marveled at Henry's gift. Still on the outside and working to get in, Thomas Jefferson listened from the chamber door of the Burgesses to "torrents of sublime eloquence" from Patrick Henry.[34]

❖ ❖ ❖

What do these men's stories tell us about what it took to become a Virginia patriarch? That earning the highest status in colonial society required a combination of luck, skill, and strategy, and that family, as eighteenth-century Virginians broadly defined it, lay at the heart of all three.

By the spring of 1776, revolutionary leaders began to seriously consider the idea that hereditary monarchy—and with it the entire notion that power derived from the chance of birth—might, as Thomas Paine so plainly put it, "not bear looking into."[35] But that was a new and controversial proposition. Colonial North Americans had long seen family membership as the foundation of identity. Family did not mean only the conjugal unit; it spread outward to include affinal and consanguinal kin even as it defined the parameters of each individual's world. For some unlucky Virginians, that circle was tighter than for others. Slaves and white women were born into a particularly circumscribed place. Sex—or, rather, perceptions of innate, unalterable frailties predicated on sex—outweighed lineage in the case of white women. They had no property rights, no legal claim over their children, no assured control over their estates or even their own wages, no civic identity at all. Still, their lot was vastly better than that of the African American men and women held in perpetual bondage—a status Virginia laws mandated as inheritable.[36]

For white men of the middling and gentry classes, the connection between family and rank was a bit more complicated. Lineage was essential, but not definitive. Cultivating natural talents and affecting the actions of a gentleman mattered, too. A male might be descended from a prominent family and, because of his actions, be denied political power and social affirmation as a gentleman. Conversely, an especially talented man of middling rank might attract the patronage of an established patriarch—or, better still, the affections of a well-connected woman— and thus join the families that ruled Virginia.

Young George Washington, the first son of a second marriage whose half-brothers divided most of their father's patrimony before he came of age, understood this experientially. Washington lacked a large inheritance and distinguished formal education. But he knew that, aided by his relatives, he could build on his talents and rise through Virginia's ranks. By meticulous attention to his "Rules of Civility," he could perform the part of a gentleman and win the respect of his social betters.

Washington's "Rules of Civility" reduced to a size manageable for a teenager the advice offered in wildly popular conduct guides that crossed the Atlantic in the eighteenth century.[37] The focus of these writers centered on physical comportment and sociability, and the takeaway of the endless suggestions was simple: men acquired status by performing. The payoff, in the case of colonial Virginia, was not simply respect from one's peers and betters—though that was a matter of profound consequence. Gentlemen also won desirable wives, secured business connections, and acquired political power. No one succeeded more at cultivating a proper character than George Washington. Biographers often remark that the whole of his professional life was an act of will, a determination to live a scripted part: valorous commander, disinterested politician, virtuous chief magistrate.

While on the surface this cultivation of conduct and character might seem individually determined—each man making himself— family connections, in fact, were essential. Relatives mentored young people in the art of conduct. Both Washington and Jefferson learned how to dance and appreciate music from female relatives. George Mason and James Madison's fathers hired tutors to train them from a young age in dance and oratory, Greek and Latin. As was customary in Virginia, the best education was more ornamental than practical.

Scions of Virginia's first families did not need to worry about physically working for a living or building a career or an estate from scratch. Patriarchs passed down to their children land and slaves so that they could maintain the lifestyle to which they were born; bequeathing financial stability was central to fatherhood. But since reputations were more precarious than property, they advised their sons on social graces more than professional accomplishments. James Madison's graduate work at Princeton, for example, did little to enlarge his standing in Orange County. His name and estate mattered far more. Upward mobility, in the case of moderately well-off families like the Washingtons and Jeffersons, depended on building ties to more established families. Jefferson later reflected on that distinct Virginia social order, where "certain families had risen to splendor by wealth and the preservation of it from generation to generation." Those families maintained their rank "on the grounds of their forefathers" and allowed only occasional "changes in station" based on personal bonds.[38]

The best chance at making one of those "changes in station" came through marriage. Marriage formed the cement of colonial Virginia society, making the gentry one "great tangled cousinry."[39] Wealth, property, business connections, and power were at stake in courtships. Making a great match required the good fortune of the right lineage, skillful cultivation of talents, and a shrewd strategy.

Marriage was far too important, then, to leave to the whim of youthful infatuation. Other interests did not, of course, *preclude* love. George and Martha Washington clearly loved each other. They both addressed their letters to "my dearest" and longed to be reunited whenever separated. Similarly, everyone who knew Thomas and Martha Jefferson saw how deeply they loved one another. His inconsolable depression after her death in 1782 is legendary. George Mason was also devastated when Ann passed away. Three years after her death he told a long-lost friend, "I was scarce able to bear the first Shock; a Depression of Spirits, & setled Melancholly followed, from which I never expect, or desire to recover."[40] But none of these men indulged in foolish passion when choosing a wife, nor did Patrick Henry or, much later, James Madison. Quite the contrary, Jefferson, Washington, and Madison wooed affluent widows with extensive connections to influential families.

George Mason and Patrick Henry each twice wed women who brought to the marriages property, slaves, and advantageous kin ties.

The most established Virginia families policed courtships to counter the threat of downward mobility. Cousin matches and sibling exchange marriages, in which siblings from one family married siblings from another, were commonplace. Such matches consolidated rather than fragmented estates. Families taught women that they needed to be even more cautious than men. If a woman married down—as Martha Custis did with George Washington—she needed to see something very special in her future husband to justify that risky investment.

Although a vital tool in building Virginia's gentry class, marriages could be remarkably precarious. "'Til death do us part" was often a stunningly short time in eighteenth-century Virginia. Early modern medical knowledge posed no match for the disease-ridden deathtrap that was much of the colonial South. Because of the endless perils of ceaseless pregnancies, women fared even worse than men.[41] Death eroded traditionally structured families so that many children grew up in homes without one parent and often with a stepparent and half-siblings. When remarriages did not occur quickly, fatherless boys in particular needed to seek out mentors and patrons, as Washington and Mason did in their youth. Households were thus fluid, and extended, blended families the norm. Patriarchs had to negotiate inheritances, emotional rivalries, and sometimes estrangements in their ever changing households.

So, colonial Virginia families were, to say the least, complicated. Remarriage, cousin marriage, orphanhood and adoption, step- and half-siblings—to say nothing of the mixed-race relatives in many families—yielded genealogies that defy linear structure. The recycling of names—to honor and reinforce connections to relatives—exacerbates the problem of charting family ties. George Mason was not only the fourth in his family line to share that name. He gave it to his firstborn son, who in turn gave the same name to his first son. In fact, six of George Mason IV's children named sons George, and five named daughters Ann. No fewer than ten of Patrick Henry's grandchildren were named Patrick.

The complexities wrought by death did not, however, weaken the centrality of family to colonial life. By lingering a bit over Martha and Thomas Jefferson, we see how complicated families could become and yet how instrumental kin ties were in the structure of colonial society and the destinies of ambitious patriarchs. John Wayles, Martha's father, married and buried three wives in fifteen years, which left him with four young daughters to raise and no sons to inherit his land. The daughters, Martha and her younger half-sisters Elizabeth, Tabitha, and Anne, were quite close, especially Elizabeth and Martha. (That sibling attachment did not extend to their other half-sisters, the daughters of the slave Betty Hemings.) The white Wayles sisters grew up in gentry style at the family plantation, The Forest, and because they had no brothers, knew they would split their father's estate on his death. Ambitious Virginia gentlemen knew it, too. The sisters shrewdly kept their assets in the family. Elizabeth married Francis Eppes, a cousin of her half-sister Martha. Martha married Bathurst Skelton, who was the younger brother of her second stepmother's first husband. Tabitha and Anne married brothers, Robert and Henry Skipwith, in a sibling exchange marriage. After Bathurst died, Martha married Thomas Jefferson and took her half-sister Sally Hemings to Monticello. Several years after Martha died, Thomas fathered children with Sally.[42] It was a "tangled cousinry" indeed, defined both by the randomness of death and the calculations of wealth, and greatly complicated by race.

Thomas Jefferson grew up at Tuckahoe Plantation alongside Thomas Mann Randolph, who was left under Peter and Jane Jefferson's care when his widower father, William Randolph, died in 1745. The two boys were essentially fictive brothers, and the parentless Randolph was doubtless a comfort when Jefferson lost his father at age thirteen. A few years later, Jefferson headed to Williamsburg, and he came into his inheritance in 1764, at age twenty-one. He was already building Monticello when he met the widow Skelton. They fell deeply in love, and soon married their fortunes. When John Wayles died eighteen months after their wedding, Thomas claimed Martha's share of the estate: eleven thousand acres of land and more than a hundred slaves, including several children John Wayles fathered by Betty Hemings.[43]

The Jefferson siblings, like the Wayles sisters, knew how to marry wisely. Thomas's sister Lucy wed a first cousin, Charles Lewis, in 1769, and eleven years later his younger brother Randolph married Charles's sister, Anna Lewis—a neat trick of simultaneously effecting a cousin *and* an exchange marriage. Such moves conserved rather than fragmented family assets, of both the financial and the social sort.

Family ties also opened access to professions and political power. Law, one of a handful of gentry careers in this era, provides a good example of the centrality of familial connections. Before the Revolution men became lawyers the same way they became merchants or military commanders: through a patron-client relationship predicated on kinship and friendship. The best-connected young men studied with George Wythe in Williamsburg. Others, like Patrick Henry, made the most of less prestigious ties and personal talent. Henry did not need to know much about the law to succeed at the local bar, so long as his relatives supported him and he captivated jurors.

Political office holding worked the same way. Once they achieved the social standing of a gentleman, men usually moved into family-centered political offices. The local vestry, county court, and then the House of Burgesses was the customary path, although a particularly talented man like Patrick Henry might skip a step or two. Colonial government was often a family affair: many men served alongside their brothers, fathers, in-laws, uncles, nephews, and cousins.

Ironically, the men who led the Revolution and devoted years of their lives to public service thereafter did not, before the 1770s, particularly care for politics except as it reflected on their families. And they surely did not see government as a full-time or lifelong career. Planter-patriarchs wanted the recognition and power that came with political positions, and sometimes they found an office advantageous to family ambition. But mostly they held office because such service signified their and their family's status and because their neighbors and relatives expected as much of them.[44]

Economic self-sufficiency was a more dominant concern. For most Virginia patriarchs their prized financial independence rested on running a plantation. Landownership was paramount in their culture, which explains why established men like Mason and Washington speculated so often in land and bought as much property as they could afford. Tobacco had long been the Chesapeake's signature crop. It cast so long a shadow over Virginia that the province was often called a tobacco colony. People paid their taxes in tobacco, and gentlemen calculated their status according to their success in the market. So, it is no surprise that planters meticulously honed their proficiency at tobacco cultivation, which could be extraordinarily complicated. Bringing a lucrative tobacco crop to market, from seed to hogshead, could take the better part of fifteen months, and a host of things could go wrong along the way. Weather was a particularly vexing factor, but also plants had to be carefully chosen, storehouses well maintained, English factors judiciously cultivated—the list went on and on. Successful planters like Washington and Mason skillfully diversified their economic interests so as to better weather the boom-bust cycle of the tobacco market and make the most of their lands to the best advantage of their families.[45]

No plantation succeeded without slave labor. Indeed, slaves were so pivotal to every part of the plantation enterprise that colonial Virginia's leading men could scarce have imagined a world in which they did not hold dominion over slaves. Racial power was elemental to their worldview.

Power was the principal dynamic at play inside planter households as well. Colonial patriarchs expected to command the respect and obedience of their children—and their neighbors expected to see as much. Fathers controlled children through the implicit and sometimes explicit threat of withdrawing resources and affections and, in dire cases, inheritances. For colonial fathers, the stakes of failing to maintain an ordered household ran very high, for society read the actions of descendants as a direct reflection of a man's ability to lead. There was, as well, reciprocity in those power relationships. Fathers owed a financial obligation to dutiful children: daughters received inheritances that made them attractive brides, and sons got land and slaves. A man who squandered his assets failed his children, and he was no man at all. So, men's rank depended not just on family ties but also on the conduct of children. And sons' and daughters' future prospects rested on the approval of fathers, who controlled family assets.[46]

Ideally, an able planter would preside over an ordered and independent estate peopled by dutiful children and diligent slaves, which, in turn, would earn him the respect of his neighbors and a place at the head of society, where affirmed patriarchs would preserve order and secure the standing of their families. And all would be right in their small corner of the world.

I n the late 1760s and early 1770s, while international events threatened Anglo-America, Virginia's future revolutionaries remained preoccupied by what had consumed planter-patriarchs for decades: pursuing family wealth and land acquisitions and skillfully managing plantations. On the eve of the American Revolution, George Washington, George Mason, and Patrick Henry ranked among the most securely established patriarchs and at the pinnacle of Virginia society. All three men, like their contemporaries at the same stage in life, saw family assets as their main responsibility. Henry's papers are sparse, but Washington and Mason filled their writings in the 1760s and early 1770s with planting concerns. They experimented with new crops, worried about the capabilities of overseers, pressed for government protection of their western lands. Both men managed their estates with remarkable diligence. Mason was so hands-on that he corresponded with workmen refinishing a cellar at Gunston Hall about the best mortar to keep out cockroaches.[47] Nothing in Mason or Washington's correspondences from this period forecast the remarkable life awaiting each man just around the corner. Like most of Virginia's late colonial gentry, they worried about indebtedness to English businessmen. But these concerns centered on family finances, not the philosophy of rights.

Before 1774, the crises that most upset members of this cohort were not imperial but familial. And at each household, anxiety was more than justified.

After George Washington married Martha Custis, he intended to be a responsible stepfather to her young children, but Jacky Custis sorely tested his capabilities. Hoping to provide Jacky with the formal education he himself lacked, Washington sent him to a local boarding school, promising the tutor that he was a fine boy who might be "a little rusty" in Greek. Aptitude, however, was the least of Jacky's problems. Burying two children before her second marriage and caring for her chronically sick daughter, Patsy, made Martha so anxious a mother that she could scarcely bear to be apart from Jacky, much less discipline him. Jacky also knew, even as a young boy, that his father had left him such a large fortune that he would never need to work. The results were predictable.[48]

Despite his parents' best efforts, Jacky seemed the exact opposite of the idealized man that George had described in his "Rules of Civility." When he went off to King's College (today Columbia University) in 1773, he bragged to Martha about his apartment, which included a large parlor, two studies, six chairs, two tables, and a separate room for his slave, Joe. While scarcely mentioning his studies, Jacky lingered over the welcome his status earned him from the faculty. He dined with them regularly, "a liberty," he boasted, "that is not allow'd any but myself." Reflecting the colonial propensity for rank, Jacky reported that "there is as much distinction made between me & the other students as can be expected."[49]

George Washington, who, according to custom took the lead in guiding Jacky in his teenage years, noticed another sort of distinction: Jacky proved a prodigious ne'er-do-well. He failed at every part of college life except socializing. And that led to another humiliation in the spring of 1773, when Jacky made premature marital overtures to Eleanor Calvert, a descendant of Maryland's founding family. An embarrassed George Washington had to write Eleanor's father and gingerly explain that Jacky's "youth, inexperience, and unripened Education, is, & will be unsuperable obstacles in my eye, to the completion of the Marriage." Benedict Calvert graciously agreed, and a full-blown scandal was avoided, but George and Martha's troubles with Jacky were hardly over.[50]

Washington knew that Jacky was setting himself on a wrong course, but being a stepfather limited, at least in his own mind, the degree to which he could forcefully intercede. And the boy's enormous birthright lay beyond Washington's control, so he could not threaten disinheritance. When Jacky abruptly quit college, Washington explained to a university administrator that he had long hoped that his stepson would become a responsible man but saw now that "these hopes are at an end." When Jacky pushed to leave school, Martha acquiesced and George felt trapped. "I have yielded," he conceded, "contrary to my judgment, & much against my Wishes to his quitting College."[51]

More grievous still was the death of Patsy Custis in the summer of 1773. Patsy had suffered from seizures most of her life, and they worsened with age. Washington cherished his stepdaughter, buying her imported toys and dolls when she was a girl and stylish clothes and dance lessons as she matured. Being a girl, she was mostly Martha's responsibility; respectful and sweet-natured, she brought none of the disappointments that shadowed her brother. As her seizures escalated in frequency and violence, her parents hired the best doctors, to no avail. In mid-June, with relatives and neighbors gathered at Mount Vernon, seventeen-year-old Patsy was making friends with Nelly Calvert, who, despite Washington's delicate negotiations with her father, had not left the romantic scene. Patsy was, her adoring stepfather explained, "in better health and spirits than she appeared to have been in some time," until shortly after 4:00 p.m. on 19 June, when she suffered a fatal seizure. George and Martha were by her side as she slipped away and sent reeling by the loss. Martha fell into "the lowest ebb of Misery." George canceled all his travel plans and tabled his business interests to mourn his daughter and care for his inconsolable wife.[52]

Death afflicted Gunston Hall that same year, and George Mason's devastating loss was pivotal to the political roles he played—and declined—after 1773. Ann Eilbeck Mason, as a good eighteenth-century woman, was the center of her family's "domestic Happiness." She bore twelve children during twenty-two years of marriage, and as was all too common in the colonial South, her last pregnancy, twins, proved fatal, both to her and to the infants. She died from childbirth complications in March, leaving nine children—her oldest was not yet twenty—and a grief-stricken widower. George Mason wrote a loving tribute to Ann in the family Bible understandably idealizing both her character and her death. According to him, she was kind, honest, cheerful, and steadfastly dedicated to family. Ann's greatest heartbreak, as she accepted her mortality, lay in being torn from her husband and children. It was a lesson in priorities that George took to heart.[53] Her death also left him the single father of nine children. His eldest daughter, Nancy, managed the household as best she could, and neighbors visited regularly and watched the younger children when Mason needed to travel from home. While he praised Nancy's ability to oversee his "little domestic Matters, with a Degree of Prudence far above her Years," he knew how much his children needed him. He had no intention of forgetting the lesson of Ann's death or failing his family.[54]

The Henry family faced their own tribulations in the early 1770s. Patrick and Sarah moved their burgeoning family to Scotchtown Plantation in 1771. It was the finest home that Patrick Henry would ever own, overlooking a fertile estate with an English garden adjacent. Visitors described the residence as "spacious," "charmingly situated," and "delightfully well-ordered." Though it was neither a particularly beautiful nor elegantly furnished house, it suited the ambitious lawyer and his large family. And, conveniently, it had a big basement.[55]

As Patrick's star rose, Sarah entered into a downward spiral that left her, literally, locked in that basement. By the late 1760s, she was suffering from mental illness, probably worsened by what we today would understand as post-partum depression. Between 1767 and 1771, she delivered three children, and she already had three others. Nothing she wrote during those years has survived, but it's not difficult to imagine her situation. After seventeen years of marriage, she had six children to raise: sixteen, fourteen, eight, four, two, and a newborn. Her husband was preoccupied with his career and often away. Shortly after the birth of her last child, Edward, she went hopelessly insane. Rather than endure the mortification of sending Sarah to the mental hospital in Williamsburg—such illnesses were considered shameful in that age—Patrick kept her confined to a storage room in the Scotchtown basement. The ceiling was low and the window too small to fit through. Slaves attended Sarah, making sure she did not harm the children. Doctors offered no remedy, and at times she was straitjacketed. She died, perhaps by her own hand, in February 1775. But, for all practical purposes, Patrick Henry had been a single father for several years prior, relying heavily on household slaves and his eldest daughter, Martha.[56]

During those same years in Albemarle County, Martha Jefferson was also suffering, though from physical rather than psychological wounds. When they married, she and Thomas were young and passionately in love; she bore their first child in late September 1772, barely nine months after their wedding. Nine months after delivering that baby, Martha was pregnant again, creating a pattern that would persist for the rest of her life: six children in ten years. Her health worsened with each delivery, and four of the children died; grief layered on physical debility. Thomas also took responsibility for two sisters with mental deficiencies, Elizabeth and Anna, and he struggled to manage this complicated, ailing family and a financially fraught estate.

James Madison, because of his stage of life—he was single, financially dependent on his father, and just twenty-two years old in the spring of 1773—escaped responsibility for the kind of turmoil that roiled Mount Vernon and Gunston Hall, Scotchtown and Monticello in the early 1770s. His parents were in good health and Montpelier was solvent. Freed from any work by the family slaves and his father's wealth, Madison attended to his siblings' studies while worrying that he would not live a long or distinguished enough life to merit the name of a Virginia gentleman.

Madison alone among this cohort had the luxury of fretting about the future as an abstraction. For the others, the hard realities of life had already set in, alongside the many rewards and responsibilities of being a powerful man in colonial Virginia.

As they grappled with such domestic tragedies, Virginia's ruling class still imagined themselves as part of a larger imperial family, bound together by commitments no less inviolate than their duties to their own relatives. England was the mother country, the king a father, and New York and South Carolina "sister colonies" overseen by citizen brothers. These planter-patriarchs loved that family and could not imagine leaving it, for it was the foundation on which their social order, family wealth, and identity rested. Yet they were equally clear about certain matters; as George Mason insisted, "We owe to our Mother-Country the Duty of Subjects but will not pay her the Submission of Slaves."[57]

In a remarkably short time in the middle of the 1770s, North Americans' defense of their rights as Englishmen transformed into a military contest with Britain and a radical critique of hereditary monarchy and, with that, the rejection of the whole notion of an ordered colonial family. But none of that was clear even as late as 1773. James Madison Jr. could not have known, as he lingered long hours over his books upstairs at his father's mansion, how essential those studies would eventually be to a new nation. As he cleaned up after his frustrating prodigal stepson, George Washington did not yet see that Jacky Custis's messes would soon fade into the background of his life. George Mason was certain, though dead wrong, that his greatest legacy would be the motherless children he raised at Gunston Hall.

Historians typically date the beginning of the revolutionary era to 1763 and the innovations in imperial policy after the signing of the peace treaty that put a formal end to the French and Indian War. England emerged from that war with a staggering debt of no less than £122,000,000 and perhaps as much as £137,000,000. The annual interest alone, somewhere in the neighborhood of £5,000,000, was impossibly high.[58] Persistent fighting against Indian nations in the trans-Appalachian west and the consequent hemorrhaging of money only exacerbated the empire's financial predicament. London leaders saw little choice: Britain could either restructure its finances or risk its survival. So, the king and his advisers reasoned, shouldn't the American colonists—the least-taxed people in the empire—pay their fair share?

But it is only in retrospect that the Proclamation of 1763 and parliamentary programs like the Stamp Act seem so fateful. In the 1760s and early 1770s Virginia patriarchs, though intermittently angered by imperial policy innovations and increasingly politicized, still imagined that they would preside over a world like their fathers and their fathers' fathers.

It was not to be: this generation of Virginians turned out to be the last of the colonial patriarchs. As young men this cohort followed the rules to rise as far as their vision could carry them: running plantations, leading families, and performing civic duties in their small corner of the British Empire. But just as they began to settle into the genteel lives their lineage and talents afforded them, the colonial world began to unravel. So, Thomas Jefferson never rode the circuit with Will Fleming,

George Washington set aside his planting experiments, and James Madison abandoned his cloistered studies. The American Revolution pulled them from their parlors and plantations, from their parochial destinies onto the stage of international politics—and, in time, history. After 1775 these erstwhile provincial patriarchs found themselves leading that Revolution while struggling to be at once founders and fathers.

CHAPTER 2

Independence

John Mason was born in 1766 and so only a small boy when he watched the leading men of Virginia gather in his family parlor to debate how best to counter what they saw as their government's increasingly corrupt policies. And yet these meetings left a powerful impression on George Mason's fourth and favorite son: "Among the first things I can remember, were discussions and conversations upon the high-handed and tyrannical conduct of the King towards his colonial subjects of this country." Though still a child, John understood the perils posed by the conversations his father led: "Universal was the idea that it was treason and Death to speak ill of the King." The boy imbibed this mixed message of disdain for the king's policies and deference to his person. "I even now," John Mason recalled in his late sixties, "remember a Scene in the Garden" of the Mason family's closest neighbors, where they had gone for a Sunday visit. Socializing quickly gave way to politics, and the children listened to the grown-ups' "many complaints and distressing forebodings as to this oppressive course toward our Country" before running off to play. John, imitating his father and showing off for his friends, "cursed the King, but immediately begged and obtained the promise of the others not to tell on me."[1]

The boy was mimicking his father in more ways than one. George Mason resented London's seemingly arbitrary imposition of taxes, as did growing numbers of his fellow Virginia planter-patriarchs. He and his neighbors used incendiary language to voice their outrage. Given

George Mason's sometimes caustic temperament, it is easy to imagine his children overhearing him curse George III. And yet resentment of and even resistance to imperial authority was one thing, revolution quite another. In December 1770, George Mason flatly dismissed the idea of American independence: "The wildest Chimera that ever disturbed a Madman's Brain has not less Foundation in Truth than this Opinion. The Americans have the warmest Affection for the present Royal Family; the strongest Attachment to the British Government & Constitution . . . there are not five Men of Sense in America who wou'd accept of Independence if it was offered."[2]

And yet in five short years George Mason would reverse that strident opinion and craft the foundational argument justifying that "wildest Chimera" and ending the North Americans' long-standing allegiance to the "Royal Family." The idea of breaking away from the British Empire came remarkably quickly, though not easily. Only ten years after the first efforts to resist imperial economic policies, a bloody war broke out between England and its mainland American colonies. It took another eighteen months after the battles at Lexington and Concord before colonial leaders could fully reconcile themselves to the radical notion of independence. George Mason and an interconnected cohort of Virginia gentlemen helped propel that shift, and then they explained to the world their audacious conviction that they knew better how to govern themselves than the learned leaders in Parliament and even King George III himself.

In his *Notes on the State of Virginia*, Thomas Jefferson offered a succinct explanation of the perceived violations that, to his mind and that of his fellow revolutionaries, forced American independence:

> The colonies were taxed internally and externally; their essential interests sacrificed to individuals in Great-Britain; their legislatures suspended; charters annulled; trials by juries taken away; their persons subjected to transportation across the Atlantic, and to trial before foreign judicatories; their supplications for redress thought beneath answer; themselves published as cowards in the councils of their mother country and courts of Europe; armed troops sent among them to enforce submission to these violences; and actual hostilities commenced against them. No alternative was presented but resistance, or unconditional submission. Between these could be no hesitation. They closed in the appeal to arms.[3]

From the patriot perspective, this fairly well captured the immediate grievances against Britain between the Stamp Act Crisis of 1765 and the outbreak of war in Massachusetts ten years later. Ironically, Americans arrived at independence through a patriotic pursuit of English rights. Eighteenth-century Englishmen, regardless of where they lived, enjoyed certain inviolate civil liberties: taxation through representation, participation in elective government, trial by jury, and freedom from martial law. Conscientious citizens safeguarded those rights against abuses of power. In the wake of the "violences" Jefferson enumerated, a growing number of North Americans felt duty-bound to defend their rights—as English citizens and for the good of the larger empire—even to the point of an "appeal to arms."[4]

But independence had a much broader meaning and far more complicated history than can be understood by focusing on the military contest over sovereignty. After all, as John Adams insisted, "The Revolution was effected before the war commenced. The Revolution was in the minds and hearts of the people."[5]

For the Virginians who became the architects of American independence, the fracturing relationship with the mother country in 1765–1775, the armed overthrow of imperial authority during the Revolutionary War, and the Revolution in "minds and hearts" that occurred along the way cannot be fully understood apart from their family values. Family provided the framework for understanding and then redefining the colonial-imperial relationship between 1765 and 1775. At the outset of the Revolutionary War, paternal duty inspired these leaders and helped them motivate their countrymen. The break with England in 1776—the very act of independence—was, of course, political. But ideas about family dynamics, class order, gender, and race infused these men's conception of independence and thus the treatises they designed to publicly proclaim American sovereignty.

Even as the founders turned to family to frame their political cause, they were also turning from it. The time-consuming work required to craft an independent republic rivaled and even jeopardized men's leadership of their families, which forced them to make hard new choices between family and politics. In 1775–1776, Virginia's leading patriots learned a powerful lesson: in a republic of citizen brothers, family and politics would not fit together nearly as seamlessly as they had in the colonial world, in which every person had a clearly defined place in the imperial family.

English Americans, no less than their contemporaries in the Old World, defined themselves as members of a larger political, imperial family, subjects of a father-king. Family was also the basis of colonial social order and the model for colonists' other relationships. This was thrown into bold relief in Virginia where the "better sort" of men amassed land and slaves to preside over (ideally) self-sufficient plantation estates and thus situate themselves as patriarchs over their households and their small part of the empire. Colonial Virginians understood their civil rights in precisely the same terms as their domestic lives and family estates: they should be dutiful caretakers of a legacy, passed from one generation to the next. A successful patriarch preserved his family birthright, whether land or liberty. He would not stand idly by and allow his legacy and his heirs' future to be stolen. So, as they struggled to make sense of the rapidly changing events of the 1760s and 1770s, Virginia's revolutionary leaders reflexively turned to family.

The first significant conflict between England and its North American subjects erupted in 1765, over the imposition of the Stamp Act. In towns from Massachusetts to the Carolinas, mobs hanged tax collectors in effigy, performed mock funerals for the act and the despised royal officials attempting to impose it, and destroyed the hated stamped paper. Such vigilantism, orchestrated by the newly formed Sons of Liberty, intimidated tax collectors into resigning and nullified the law. (The very name Sons of Liberty revealed at once the familial framing of colonial opposition and the end members sought.) Parliamentary leaders, stunned by the colonists' outsized reaction, repealed the unenforceable Stamp Act and quickly passed the face-saving Declaratory Act, asserting England's sovereign right "to make laws . . . to bind the Colonies and people of America . . . in all cases whatsoever." England retained unquestioned dominion over its American subjects—at least in the short term.[7]

No matter how vociferous opponents of the Stamp Act got, they never seriously considered leaving the imperial family in 1765–1766. Patrick Henry galvanized the opposition in Virginia with his incendiary "Caesar-Brutus" speech. But the most memorable part of that address, in which he proclaimed, "If this be treason, make the most of it," has in historical memory overshadowed real events. Mortified members of the Burgesses upbraided Henry, who apologized for allowing "the heat of passion" to make him say more than he intended; he adamantly asserted his loyalty to George III.[8]

Still, the colonists could not easily forget the hurtful violations of the mother country and the truths about the imperial family that the Stamp Act laid bare. They turned again and again to the long accepted parent-child metaphor to understand their fraught relationship with England. While continuing to accept their status as children within the empire and so subject to the governance of the mother country, colonial leaders resented the (perceived) cruelty of the parent state that broke the family trust.[9]

A few months after passage of the Declaratory Act, George Mason wrote a group of London merchants a letter that perfectly illustrated the powerful familial metaphor that would often be employed in the coming decade. "The Epithets of Parent & Child," he began, "have been so long applyed to Great Britain & her Colonys." But, he complained, "we rarely see anything, from your Side of the Water, free from the authoritative Style of a Master to a School-Boy."

Mason continued his blistering letter by affecting the haughty attitude of British parents patronizing their American children: "Pray be a good boy for the future; do what your Papa and Mamma bid you . . . and then all your Acquaintance will love you, & praise you, & give you pretty things." But, Mason mimicked, "if you are a naughty Boy, & turn obstinate, & don't mind what your Papa & Mamma say to you, but presume to think their Commands (let them be what they will) unjust or unreasonable . . . and pretend to judge for yourselves, when you are not arrived at the Years of Discretion, or capable of distinguishing between Good & Evil; then every-body will hate you, & say you are a graceless & undutiful Child; your Parents & Masters will be obliged to whip you severely."

While he embraced the familial construction of the imperial-colonial relationship, Mason charged imperial leaders with profoundly misunderstanding the problems that were damaging those ties. The colonists were not wayward children but mistreated heirs, as loyal & useful Subjects as any in the British Dominions," who had, in their resistance to the Stamp Act, "been only contending for their Birth-right." Reflecting the conviction among American colonists that they were full and dutiful members of the imperial family, Mason called on what he termed "our fellow-Subjects in Great Britain" to remember "that we are descended from the same Stock with themselves, nurtured in the same Principles of Freedom; which we have both suck'd in with our Mother's Milk: that in crossing the Atlantic Ocean, we have only changed our Climate, not our Minds, our Natures & Dispositions remain unaltered; that We are still the same People with them, in every Respect."

This assertion of fraternity and legitimacy—and the condemnation of parental cruelties—continued throughout Mason's letter. "We claim Nothing," he insisted near the close, "but the Liberty & Privileges of Englishmen, in the same Degree, as if we had still continued among our Brethren in Great Britain: these Rights have not been forfeited by any Act of ours, we can not be deprived of them, without our Consent, but by Violence & Injustice." Mason argued that in defending their English rights in 1765, British Americans acted as good stewards of a treasured patrimony: "We have received them from our Ancestors, and, with God's Leave, we will transmit them, unimpaired to our Posterity."[10]

Their suspicions raised in 1765–1766, North Americans did not wait long before they saw the next signs of corruption in the imperial family. The colonists resurrected all the complaints and tactics employed during the Stamp Act Crisis to counter the Revenue Act of 1767 (the first of a series of acts frequently called the Townshend Duties). Again they would need to stand together to defend their birthright as Englishmen.

Even as they confronted these crises, Virginia political leaders were still inclined to think first of their own domestic responsibilities. For them, civic leadership had always been a part-time familial duty, an obligation that reflected a man's significance and enabled him to protect his family assets and social standing. Seldom did politics detract from a patriarch's primary obligation to oversee family estates. In the 1760s, however, political controversies began to rival family time, calling men into service and away from their homes.

George Mason and George Washington knew that their preeminence in Fairfax County mandated they help formulate a response to the Townshend Duties, but both remained preoccupied with domestic matters that year, and they struggled to balance the competing claims on their time. Mason was loath to leave Gunston Hall. His and Ann's burgeoning family now included seven children, and she was pregnant again. He accordingly refused to stand for election in the Burgesses in 1767. Washington did serve, though Patsy Custis's health often took precedence over his attendance. He was absent in April 1768 when the Burgesses formally protested the Townshend Duties. Absence, though, did not mean indifference. At Gunston Hall, Mason set to work on a proposal calling for a colonywide boycott of certain English goods. On 18 May 1769, Washington presented Mason's work to the Burgesses. It was a pivotal moment in Washington's career, when he first left the backbenches of the Burgesses and emerged as a leader of colonial resistance to imperial policies.[11]

Virginia's leading men conceived of their new political activism as temporary and necessary to fulfill their duties as planter-patriarchs. Because of unjust taxes, Washington commiserated with Mason, "many families are reduced, almost, if not quite, to penury & want." Drastic times called for drastic measures. Virginians, Washington concluded, had no choice but to oppose the laws by boycotting English goods. Otherwise they risked losing forever "the liberty which we have derived from our Ancestors." Mason heartily agreed: "Our Sister Colonies all expect it from us, our Interest, our own Liberty & Happiness, as well as that of our Posterity, everything that is near & dear to us in this World requires it."[12]

As Virginians joined the continent-wide resistance to the Townshend Duties, traditional planter values shaped their opposition. Virginians had to work harder at forging interdependence within their ranks, as that ran counter to the ideals of planter independence. And they were more skittish about working with the "lesser sort." In Boston and New York, farmers, silversmiths, shopkeepers, and shoemakers cooperated with merchants and lawyers on the boycotts. The gentry architects of Virginia's nonimportation association likewise advertised for "all Gentlemen, Merchants, Traders, and other Inhabitants of this Colony" to participate. But they did not encourage radicalism in the streets of Williamsburg or Richmond the way John Hancock and Sam Adams did in Boston. And even though they understood that boycotting could not succeed without widespread participation, elites did not imagine any long-term sharing of real power with the "lesser sort" of Virginia men.[13]

While elevating themselves to a position of equality with their brothers throughout the empire, Virginia leaders viewed the 1765–1770 crises squarely in the context of their long-standing colonial social order—with themselves on top. Even as they coordinated boycotts dependent on broad-based support, Washington and Mason believed that their defiance of parliamentary power rested on political deference in Virginia. Or, as Mason put it, "Let the principal Gentlemen but set the Example, they will be quickly followed by the Bulk of the People."[14]

The power of reputation in Virginia's interrelated gentry circles afforded Mason and Washington their best recourse against elite men who violated the 1769 nonimportation pledge. Mason recommended that "the Sense of Shame & the Fear of Reproach must be inculcated, & enforced in the strongest Manner" against anyone disinclined toward boycotting. He wanted men to know that the wrong political move put reputations and family power at risk. "We shou'd resolve," he argued, "not to associate or keep Company with them in public Places, & they should be loaded with every Mark of Infamy and Reproach." He even called for the names of violators to be published in the newspapers so that they would be "stigmatized as Enemys to their Country." To be clear: in the summer of 1770, avowedly loyal English subjects declared their neighbors, who by rejecting nonimportation actually upheld English laws, "Enemys to their Country."[15]

Despite all of this inflammatory rhetoric, at no time in the tumultuous 1760s did Virginia's leading men—or anyone in America, for that matter—expect defiance to separate them from the mother country. Mason numbered among the most strident critics of imperial policy, but he remained convinced that when "Justice & Harmony" were restored—and in his view they would inevitably be restored—American colonists should welcome the chance to mend their relationship with their mother country, where their best interest lay. "Supplying our Mother-Country with gross Materials, & taking her Manufactures in Return is the true Chain of Connection between us," Mason reasoned, and that relationship was based on "a constant Reciprocation of Interest."[16]

Mason (and other leading intellectuals and politicians) repeatedly employed that language of reciprocity when writing about the imperial-colonial relationship in the 1760s. He sought "mutual Confidence and Harmony" between the provinces and the imperial center and reasoned that reciprocally beneficial trade relations and the common defense of English liberties were in "the Interest both of *Great-Britain* and *America*."[17]

Mason, the intellectual leader of the Virginia gentry after the Stamp Act Crisis, was inadvertently moving toward a profound reevaluation of the connection between the parent state and citizens in North America. Even as he declared fealty to England, Mason wanted the relationship to be defined by partnership, which was antithetical to the very nature of colonialism. The father-king could never abide that redefinition of the imperial family—a clear fact that a man of Mason's intellect should have known, had he been prepared to think through the full implications of his rhetoric. But breaking with England remained simply inconceivable, and so he could not yet quite bring himself to see what was self-evident.

The same contradictions were evidenced in the House of Burgesses in May 1769. On first learning of the passage of the Townshend Duties, Virginia's legislature, in the English tradition and along with other colonies, petitioned for redress. By the spring of 1769, it was abundantly clear that Parliament had no intention of abandoning Townshend's program or, in most cases, of even answering the petitions out of North America. The Burgesses took another tack. Patrick Henry was representing Hanover County and Thomas Jefferson was a first-time delegate. They worked alongside George Washington. George Mason remained at Gunston Hall, but his brother Thomson served. On May 16 the Burgesses passed a series of decrees, beginning with this one: "That the sole right of imposing taxes on the inhabitants of this his Majesty's colony and dominion of Virginia, is now, and ever has been, legally and constitutionally vested in the House of Burgesses." At the same time, the Burgesses wanted to assure George III "of our inviolable attachment to his sacred person and government and to beseech his royal interposition, as the father of his people." Virginians remained "faithful subjects . . . ever distinguished by their loyalty, and firm attachment to your Majesty." And so, "with hearts filled with anguish, by such dangerous invasions of our dearest privileges, we presume to prostrate ourselves at the foot of your Royal throne, beseeching your Majesty, as our king and father, to avert from your faithful and loyal subjects in America those miseries."[18]

The persistence of such deferential language ran counter to Virginians' insurgent assertions. George III may have remained their "king and father," but Virginians and their "sister colonies" also recast their relationship with the larger empire when they rejected the Declaratory Act and cooperated to thwart the Townshend Duties—most notably in denying England's right to set tax policy in its economic subsidiaries, the American colonies.

Looking back it is possible to glimpse in the heated conflicts of the 1760s the beginning of the end of English America as well as the hierarchical and organic worldview that had so long defined colonial life. The language of Virginia gentlemen shaped their actions, and those actions had consequences: for the structure of imperial-colonial government, the relationships between gentlemen and nonelites, and the connections between fathers and sons. Virginians living through these rapidly changing events could not yet perceive those consequences, but they soon would.

A new political culture, operating under dynamics at odds with the organic hierarchy of the colonial world, was beginning to emerge. Even as they professed fidelity to their father-king, Virginians edged toward a civic order defined by fraternity. In order to preserve their family fortunes and pass on a legacy of liberty to their children, they insisted, the sister colonies needed to stand together against the unjust policies of the mother country. Leaders emphasized the maturation of the North American provinces, the passage from childhood to maturity, and the equality and conditionality of fraternal ties. Still, in the 1760s they were not ready to decide which political family mattered most or to see that they might not be able to live simultaneously in both.

Family remained the metaphor for defining the imperial-colonial relationship, even if the Virginians could not settle on the exact nature of their familial bond. Sometimes the upset colonists concentrated their criticism on the father-king and his unjust treatment of his American subjects—couched in deferential language and attributed principally to corrupt ministers who misled George III. At other times they focused on the fraternal and sororial bonds linking colonists to one another and to British subjects throughout the empire. In the late 1760s they vacillated back and forth, depicting themselves sometimes as afflicted subordinates and at other times as defiant equals.

One thing was clear: the mother country's plans were failing, including at the most basic level of arithmetic. By 1770 the Townshend Duties had yielded less than £21,000. Meanwhile, British businessmen had lost perhaps £700,000 because of the nonimportation agreements. In April, taken aback by so successful a trade war waged by the North American colonies, Parliament repealed all the Townshend taxes, save the one on tea. This set the stage for the next major crisis between England and its North American holdings and the beginning of the end of that relationship. In 1773 the tea tax triggered yet more extralegal resistance, most famously in the Boston "Tea Party," which in turn, provoked the Coercive Acts of 1774.[19]

"We are now," Lord North warned, "to establish our authority, or give it up entirely."[20] And move to establish it the prime minister did, closing the port of Boston, shutting down the Massachusetts Assembly, and replacing the colony's civilian governor with a military commander. Colonists termed these measures "intolerable," and though the laws punished Massachusetts alone, the outrage reverberated far outside New England. Virginia's gentlemen did not look kindly on the Bostonians' destruction of the East India Company's tea. To them, the spectacle smacked of lawlessness and the mob. But Britain's outsized reaction to the regrettable actions of Boston's Sons of Liberty could not be abided. In Williamsburg, the Burgesses tried to proclaim their solidarity with Massachusetts. Instead, the royal governor dissolved the legislature. Delegates reconvened, extralegally, at Raleigh Tavern and informed King George III that they were "clearly of opinion, that an attack made on one of our sister colonies, to compel submission to arbitrary taxes is an attack made on all British America."[21]

After the spring of 1774, the familial language of the colonial-imperial relationship, so often vacillating and contradictory, lurched toward the fraternal. Virginia's leading men returned to their home counties to raise support for their Massachusetts brethren, which Washington saw "as the cause of America." Still disapproving of the mobs in the Boston Tea Party, he immediately added a caveat: "not that we approve their conduct in destroying the Tea."[22] In Fairfax County, in early July, Mason and Washington conferred while Mason drafted the Fairfax Resolves. They met at Mount Vernon on 17 July to revise Mason's work; the next day Washington chaired the meeting of the county's freeholders, which passed the Fairfax Resolves. Thirty other counties passed similar decrees, but Mason's was the most important: it was Mason who called for a Continental Association and the enforcement of a general boycott of English goods.[23]

Mason's resolutions revealed Virginians' rejection of their long-standing place in the English imperial family and proclaimed their status as "Friends and Brethren" of their fellow Americans. The document included the simple and shocking assertion that "the Inhabitants of the american Colonies are not, and from their Situation can not be represented in the British Parliament." Consequently, "the legislative Power here can of Right be exercised only by our own Provincial Assemblys or Parliaments." Now Virginians were apparently denying England's right not only to tax but to govern its colonies. Mason added a qualifier to that last line: "subject to the Assent or Negative of the British Crown." But it is hard to imagine how, realistically, such a check might work. In an especially egregious mischaracterization of colonial history, Mason insisted that, despite the long-standing sovereignty of the American colonies, their legislatures had, in the past, "to avoid Strife and Contention with our fellow-Subjects . . . always Chearfully acquiesced" to trading agreements. Now, the Americans expected, indeed demanded, to be "treated upon an equal Footing with our fellow Subjects."[24]

But "equal Footing" had its limits in Virginia; it would not, the ruling elites imagined, extend beyond their own ranks. Many Virginians outside the political class shared elites' convictions about imperial authority, even as they continued to defer to planter-patriarchs. For example, the citizens of Hanover County took it upon themselves to write their representatives, Patrick Henry and his half-brother John Syme Jr., to show their unwavering support for Massachusetts. The letter started with a qualification based on their rank: "The sphere of life in which we move hath not afforded us lights sufficient to determine with certainty, concerning those things from which the troubles at Boston originated." They allowed as how, unlike their social betters, they might not perceive all the nuances concerning the uproar in New England. But they understood what was most important: "If our sister colony of Massachusetts Bay is enslaved, we cannot long remain free."[25]

The up-and-comer Thomas Jefferson, meanwhile, authored a stunning reassessment of the imperial-colonial relationship in August 1774. Rejecting entirely the deferential language employed in the House of Burgesses as late as 1769, Jefferson wrote his essay, "Summary View of the Rights of British America," as he put it, "divested of those expressions of servility which would persuade his majesty that we are asking favors and not rights." Jefferson wrote as if addressing the king of England, who, he reminded his audience, "is no more than the chief officer of the people, appointed by the laws . . . and consequently subject to their superintendance." Jefferson lectured George III that "kings are the servants, not the proprietors of the people" and called on him to stop "sacrificing the rights of one part of the empire to the inordinate desires of another: but deal out to all equal and impartial right."[26]

In elevating himself to a position of critiquing George III, Jefferson captured the radical turn that some Americans were beginning to make by the summer of 1774. He also wove into the essay a daringly revisionist history of colonial America, akin to George Mason's, depicting the colonies as independent of England from their origins. The settlements were secured, he maintained, not through the efforts of the mother country, but by the colonists themselves: "Their own blood was spilt in acquiring lands for their settlement, their own fortunes expended in making that settlement effectual. For themselves they fought, for themselves they conquered, and for themselves alone they have right to hold." England, meanwhile, had directed from the sidelines, and from time to time "intermeddled with the regulation of the internal affairs of the colonies." At times, including during the French and Indian War, Jefferson noted, England provided military help, as it often did for allied countries. The colonists, Jefferson claimed, "never supposed that, by calling in her aid, they thereby submitted themselves to her sovereignty. Had such terms been proposed, they would have rejected them with disdain." Americans, it seemed, had always been and would continue to be the authors of their own fates.

As he would do two summers later, Jefferson then turned to enumerating grievances against the king himself, or as he put it—in a remarkably condescending tone—"we next proceed to consider the conduct of his majesty . . . and mark out his deviations from the line of duty." The Virginia planter and sovereign monarch of Britain were close to the same age. In 1774, Jefferson turned thirty-one, George III thirty-six. But those comparable ages belied a world of differences. This level of audacity—that a farmer from the hinterlands of North America would even think of upbraiding the man who, by divine design, ruled a global empire—stunned even the friends of America in London.

Jefferson's essay, though controversial in 1774, predicted the emergent transformation in American self-consciousness that would redefine politics and family over the coming years, making authority both at home and in the public square ideally rest on merit, reason, and consent. The new civic family would consist of American brothers, matured beyond reflexive submission and bound by choice, not birth. Most important, governing was to be a privilege, not a right. Lest anyone misunderstand the relationship of America to the empire, Jefferson closed where he had started: "These are our grievances," he explained, "which we have thus laid before his majesty with that freedom of language and sentiment which becomes a free people, claiming their rights as derived from the laws of nature, and not as the gift of their chief magistrate."

What did Jefferson want in the summer of 1774? What relationship did he foresee working between the Americans and Britain? Like George Mason, Jefferson saw his country, which at that time he interpreted as Virginia, as on a par with England, two equal parts of an imperial family. And he wanted, or at least he claimed to want, "to establish fraternal love and harmony thro' the whole empire."

In April 1775 the contest over words and consumer behavior and family dynamics turned violent in the farming towns of Lexington and Concord, Massachusetts. George Washington left Mount Vernon on 4 May 1775, to lead the Virginia delegation to the Second Continental Congress. He carried his military uniform with him. Soon thereafter, in the extralegal state government Virginians created, Patrick Henry blasted the cruel father-king who, through "a long series of oppressive acts has proved himself the tyrant instead of the protector of his people," which left Virginians "absolved of our allegiance to the crown."[27] George Mason's "wildest Chimera" was happening.

⬥   ⬥   ⬥

The early stages of the military contest did not alter the centrality of family to our cohort's worldview nor deter their quest for "fraternal love and harmony" with Britain. Family remained a central component of Virginia leaders' political and military actions in 1775 and 1776, even as they joined the radical turn toward armed conflict with their government and, then, fifteen months later, pursued political independence.

Family dutifulness was crucial to Virginia leaders trying to garner support for the patriot cause among their neighbors. This was not simply manipulation, for they personally envisioned their cause as a paternal obligation. George Mason played a pivotal role in organizing Fairfax County's militia, and like so much else in his political career, he framed this action in familial terms. *Posterity* afforded him a particularly compelling way of motivating his neighbors to action. He called on the men of his home county to remain "firmly determined, at the hazard of our Lives, to transmit to our Children & Posterity those sacred Rights to which ourselves were born." Mason repeated this generational call to action in an April 1776 letter to George Washington, who was by then commanding the Continental Army. He hoped that if they could not soon return to their happy domestic lives they would "bear our present & future Sufferings, becoming Men determined to transmit to our Posterity, unimpair'd, the Blessings we have received from our Ancestors!"[28]

Revolutionary leaders also depicted the costs of war in familial terms. Once combat commenced, the death of each soldier made the likelihood of reconciliation more and more remote. George Mason was adamant on this score: "Can they restore the Husband to the widow, the Child to the Parent, or the Father to the Orphan? . . . The Die is cast—the Rubicon is passed—and a Reconciliation with Great Britain . . . is impossible." Both private correspondences and published tracts echoed this refrain. Virginians were appalled at British efforts to incite Americans, including prisoners of war, "to bear arms against their families, kindred, friends, and country." And even more horrifying: British commanders were "encouraging, by every means in their power, our savage neighbours, and our more savage domesticks, to spill the blood of our wives and children."[29]

In particular, decisions made in late 1775 by Virginia's royally appointed governor, Lord Dunmore, mortified leading white Virginians. Not only did Dunmore formally offer freedom to any enslaved man who fled his patriot owner, he also organized those African American loyalists into a military company. Indeed, the governor called on black men to help "in reducing this Colony to a proper Sense of their Duty to His Majesty's Crown and Dignity." Virginia patriarchs idealized order and harmony, both in their households and more broadly in society. If they led ably, they imagined, they would preside over a stable society—especially in regards to race. At home they would command the respect and dutifulness of their dependents: wives, children, wards, even slaves. The war with Britain thus posed an existential threat to everything Virginia planter-patriarchs held dear: their families and social order as well as their rights and lives.[30]

The legacy that British oppressions might inflict on future generations fairly consumed these leaders, and they repeatedly invoked their duty to "ages yet unborn," both in promoting support for the military and as they fitfully made their way toward independence. Richard Henry Lee, writing Patrick Henry from the Second Continental Congress in April 1776, raised the issue of independence and pressed the responsibility of Virginians in particular: "Ages yet unborn, and millions existing at present, must rue or bless that Assembly, on which their happiness or misery will so eminently depend. Virginia hath hitherto taken the lead in great affairs, and many now look to her with anxious expectation, hoping that the spirit, wisdom, and energy of her councils, will rouse America."[31]

In the summer of 1776, these Virginians did take "the lead in great affairs" as they met the challenge leveled by Thomas Paine to "begin the world over again."[32] The creed that embodied their noblest aspirations built on long-standing English political traditions and reflected the diverse and distinctive social and economic character of North America. The text balanced Boston radicalism with South Carolina conservatism, esoteric theoretical tracts with "Common Sense." Historian Pauline Maier has artfully recovered the lineage of the Declaration of Independence and the grueling writing by committee that finally produced a text agreeable to the fractious Second Continental Congress.[33] Rehearsing that story here is unnecessary. But, like so much else of the Revolution, this signal document cannot be fully understood without considering the family values of the Virginia planters who conceived it.

George Mason and Thomas Jefferson outlined the philosophical consequences of independence, and they principally designed the political rationale for it. For them, independence was not simply an abstract political construct. It had very concrete meaning, inextricably connected to their domestic lives, especially their identity as heads of households and masters of slaves.

All the leading figures in Virginia politics owned slaves—scores if not hundreds of slaves—whom they depicted as charges in their households, under their patriarchal oversight, and even as members of their families. Their contact with and command over slaves was constant; they lived, in the most intimate ways, the stark divide between freedom and slavery. Every day they saw unchecked exploitation and the complete absence of rights. Mason needed only to open the doors of Gunston Hall or Jefferson to stroll through the picturesque gardens of Monticello to witness the unceasing denial of freedom. The English writer Samuel Johnson famously wondered, "How is it that we hear the loudest yelps for liberty among the drivers of negroes?" The short answer: because they knew whereof they spoke. Furthermore, because unfree labor made Virginia planters rich and leisured, they could study philosophy and law, cultivate their particular genius, and devote themselves to government service. Slaveholding bought them the time and education to become intellectuals, and slavery taught them that it might be possible for all (free, white) men to be equal. After all, in colonial Virginia white men would never be enslaved; African American slaves constituted the permanent underclass.[34]

So, when they considered the post-1763 imperial policies that challenged their economic autonomy and other prized rights including trial by jury and representative government, Virginia's planter-patriarchs understood those actions as antithetical to liberty—and, then, reflexively as attempts at enslavement. In the steady refrain of this cohort, Patrick Henry insisted, "There is no retreat but in submission and slavery!"[35]

Such language imbued these men's public addresses and the documents that came out of the governmental bodies they led. From the Stamp Act Crisis forward, Virginia leaders bitterly complained about their "enslavement." Virginia's 1769 Nonimportation Agreement was typical. Supporters stood together against "the evils which threaten the Ruin of themselves and their posterity, by reducing them from a free and happy people to a Wretched & miserable State of Slavery." Five years later the Fairfax Resolves struck the same note: "Tho' we are it's [England's] Subjects, we will use every Means which Heaven hath given us to prevent our becoming it's Slaves."[36]

Personal writings varied little from this characterization. George Washington warned in 1774 that bowing to the Coercive Acts would "make us as tame, & abject Slaves, as the Blacks we Rule over with such arbitrary Sway." Their only choice was to fight for their rights. He repeated that conviction in a letter to his friend George William Fairfax the following year. Washington regretted "that a Brother's Sword has been sheathed in a Brother's breast." But he saw only two options: "The once happy and peaceful plains of America are either to be drenched with Blood, or Inhabited by Slaves. Sad alternative! But can a virtuous Man hesitate in his choice?"[37] Patrick Henry echoed that same conviction in his "Liberty or Death" speech in March 1775. In one of the most famous passages, Henry asked, "Is life so dear, or peace so sweet, as to be purchased at the price of chains and slavery?" "Our chains are forged," he warned. "Their clanking may be heard on the plains of Boston!"[38]

Over and over and over again, Virginia's revolutionary leaders depicted their struggle against Britain as at once a defense of liberty *and* a fight against enslavement. If Americans failed or, worse still, were seduced into giving up, they would meet a dreadful end. And, they would be inflicting that same terrible fate on their children.

This was not a rhetorical device; fears about enslavement reflected these men's simultaneous utter dependence on and growing contempt for slaveholding. As early as 1765, George Mason complained of the insidious effects of slavery in Virginia: "One half of our best Lands in most Parts of the Country remain unsettled, & the other cultivated with slaves; not to mention the ill effect such a Practice has upon the Morals & Manners of our People." Patrick Henry likewise condemned slaveholding as an "abominable practice" that Christians should feel ashamed to tolerate. He judged slaveholding "a species of violence and tyranny" antithetical to the teachings of the Bible, to just political principles, and to basic humanity. He conceded that he could manufacture no valid excuse for the fact that he owned slaves: "I will not, I cannot justify it."[39]

Their concern, though, centered not on their slaves but rather on their white families. Jefferson lamented the "unhappy influence on the manners of our people," especially the white children of slave masters like himself: "The parent storms, the child looks on, catches the lineaments of wrath . . . and thus nursed, educated, and daily exercised in tyranny, cannot but be stamped by it."[40] Jefferson's draft of the Declaration of Independence contained a long (purged) passage condemning the slave trade. He feared there and in his private writings the just retribution of enslaved men and women. He was hardly alone. Without exception, Virginia's leading founders condemned slavery, even as they passed up every chance to end it, both in legislative halls and in their own households. None of this cohort, except George Washington—and then only in his will—ever planned to separate themselves from an institution that they defined as cruel, unjustifiable, and antithetical to what they said they loved most: liberty.

The reason for their inaction was clear: to do more would have destroyed their power as planter-patriarchs and devastated their family wealth. Such men imagined that their identity as genteel and capable patriarchs required them to protect a patrimony of land, money, and rank—which depended on perpetuating slavery. When confronted about the hypocrisy of slaveholding in a free republic, either by others or in their own minds, Virginia's founders repeatedly pointed to family—to their relatives' estates, social standing, even survival—to explain away their inaction. When it came to questions of slavery, then, protecting their white families always finished in front of their political principles.

Family values infused other aspects of these men's thinking about the move toward independence as well. They were deeply fearful about losing the estates they inherited and built for their relatives' futures. To be affirmed as a man in elite Virginia society required economic autonomy. Gentlemen were presumed to master self-sufficient households and plantations and to preserve them for the next generation; otherwise they lost their claim to genteel manhood and political power. Their consequent zeal for financial independence left Virginians particularly aggrieved by their indebtedness to English factors, whom they charged with predatory business practices. Their supposed friends in England had, Virginia planters complained, forsaken what should have been a mutually beneficial partnership in favor of exploitative tax innovations. This came on top of English merchants having flooded American markets in the 1760s with consumer goods as tobacco prices plummeted by 75 percent. The Virginians' personal finances gave them the motivation and the language to identify with radical political ideas in the 1770s.[41]

George Washington's disdain for the indebtedness signified by the Stamp Act certainly reflected his domestic situation. He might well have been writing about his and Martha's shopping habits rather than the import-export relationship between Virginia and London when he observed, "Many of the Luxuries which we have heretofore lavished our Substance to Great Britain for can well be dispensed with. . . . Great Britain may then load her Exports with as Heavy Taxes as She pleases but where will the consumption be?"[42] Washington was hardly alone. With a few exceptions—particularly savvy men like George Mason—in the 1760s and 1770s the planter class of Virginia saw their prized financial independence undermined by their immersion in Atlantic credit-based markets. Tax innovations only exacerbated the problem and the Virginians' resentment of the mother country.

Their experience with Atlantic markets and the coming of war made Virginians all the more committed to protecting their most reliable family asset: land. During the Revolutionary War George Washington repeatedly cautioned his stepson, who, grown to manhood, preferred to be called Jack, to avoid selling land he inherited from his late father. "Land," Washington insisted, "is the most Permanent Estate we can hold, & most likely to increase in its value." The worth of the property Jack Custis proposed to sell off in the summer of 1778 would, Washington calculated, rise even more in value "when our Independancy is established, and the Importance of America better known." When that day might come, he could not predict. But he knew one thing for certain: paper money taken in wartime for land would "melt like Snow before a hot Sun."[43]

So, although much changed in 1775–1776, these Virginians' core family values—owning land, commanding slaves, growing estates, and protecting relatives—endured, shaping their reactions to the rapidly and radically changing political climate. At the same time, though, intellectual and political leaders could no longer hold at bay a frustrating new conflict between family and politics.

F amily and politics had always fit together so smoothly. As Virginia patriarchs, members of this cohort expected to acquire political power because of their family ties and to pursue political means to serve familial ends. Throughout the colonial era they held offices as an extension of their social and familial rank and to the occasional advantage of their relatives. Trips to the colonial capital to conduct government business took up little family time; wives and children sometimes traveled to Williamsburg with delegates to the House of Burgesses. But even if men went alone to the capital or to participate in militia musters or to sit on county courts, such duties seldom felt truly burdensome. Certainly the offices did not run for months and years at a time. Rarely were a man's finances—to say nothing of his life—put in jeopardy.

But in 1775–1776, the stakes rose fast and steep. The outbreak of war brought unprecedented burdens of service: commanding military forces, governing a state under siege, designing a new nation. Men like George Mason, George Washington, and Thomas Jefferson faced tough choices. What should they do when the demands of defending their country and crafting new governments collided with their domestic duties? Could they be both *good fathers* and *virtuous founders*?

To begin to understand the new competing pulls of family and politics, a trip to Gunston Hall is in order. In 1773 George Mason seems, at a particularly contemplative moment, to have anticipated what lay ahead. He had faced hard choices during the 1760s and managed to prioritize his family while also contributing to civic life. But such a balance could not so easily be struck in the mid-1770s. Right after Ann Mason died in March 1773, George wrote his will. Though he lived another two decades, he never revised that document. Apparently all of Mason's political achievements over the ensuing years did not change his mind about the advice he gave in that will: "I recommend it to my sons, from my own Experience in Life, to prefer the happiness of independence & a private Station to the troubles and Vexations of Public Business." Sometimes, he conceded, "Public Business" could not be avoided. In a stunningly prescient commentary, Mason continued: "If . . . the Necessaty of the times shou'd engage them in Public Affairs, I charge them, on a Fathers Blessing, never to let the motives of private Interest or ambition to induce them to betray, nor the terrors of Poverty and disgrace, or the fear of danger or of death deter them from Asserting the liberty of their Country, and endeavouring to transmit to their posterity those Sacred rights to which themselves were born."[44]

A "Necessaty of the times" came for Mason in the summer of 1774. He went to Williamsburg to help coordinate Virginia's response to the crisis in Boston, but his thoughts remained at home. Martin Cockburn and his wife were the Masons' closest neighbors, and they looked after the children in George's absence. The Masons and Cockburns were, John Mason explained, a part of each other's families and shared "the most intimate & constant and friendly intercourse." George wrote Martin not two weeks into his stay in Williamsburg: "I begin to grow heartily tired of this town and hope to be able to leave it some time next week. . . . I beg to be tenderly remembered to my children."[45]

His wealth, political experience, and intellectual talents combined to make George Mason a natural choice to serve in the First Continental Congress, which met in Philadelphia in September and October 1774. He had even argued for the need for such a body in the Fairfax Resolves. But traveling to Philadelphia was another matter entirely from trips to Williamsburg. It meant making politics a full-time job, with precedence over family. Mason worked closely with the Virginia delegation going to the Continental Congress, and he even spent the night at Mount Vernon with Patrick Henry and Edmund Pendleton before they and their host left to join the rest of the Virginia delegation for the journey to Philadelphia. But while they all headed north, Mason returned to his "private Station" at Gunston Hall.[46]

As Mason anticipated in his will, it was not always possible to avoid political "troubles and Vexations." In 1775, he tried to decline a seat in the Virginia Convention by reminding his Fairfax neighbors about his family life: "I entreat you, Sir, to reflect on the duty I owe to a poor little helpless family of orphans to whom I now must act the part of father and mother both, and how incompatible such an office would be with the daily attention they require."[47] But that appeal failed. When his neighbors persisted, Mason's sense of civic duty made him leave Fairfax County to fill the seat vacated by George Washington, the newly appointed commander of the Continental Army. In August of that same year Mason was "personally applied to by more than two thirds of the Members" of the Virginia legislature to serve in the Second Continental Congress. He begged them not to name him, but twenty proceeded to do so anyway. When he balked, Patrick Henry and Thomas Jefferson weighed in, reminding Mason that the patriot cause sorely needed him. By repeated appeals to family duty Mason did avoid going to Philadelphia in 1775, but, he complained to Martin Cockburn, "my getting clear of this Appointment has avail'd me little." He was soon called to join the Committee of Safety, "which," he groused, "is even more inconvenient & disagreeable to me than going to the Congress. I endeavour'd to excuse myself . . . but was answer'd by an universal NO."[48] (The Committee of Safety governed Virginia whenever the Convention, which was designing the state constitution, was not in session.)

Revolutionary politics might have headed toward full-time work, but that did not mean that fathers, even ambitious and faithful patriots, eagerly chose politics over family. George Mason came and went to Williamsburg in the next few years, serving in the Virginia Convention in 1775 and 1776 and then in the newly formed House of Delegates after 1777. But he successfully evaded attending the Continental Congress by insisting, "My own domestic affairs are so circumstanced as not to admit of my continued absence from home."[49]

Mason willingly served Virginia in ways that did not compromise his duty to his motherless children, but he was exceedingly loath to do more. Though he drafted Virginia's Declaration of Rights and played a central role in organizing militia companies and designing the first state constitution, family remained George Mason's first priority after 1775, just as it had been before. He simply would not leave home for long periods because his numerous family of children required "constant attention."[50] Other considerations, of course, factored into Mason's reluctance to take on more prominent roles. He simply did not like and did not want to be around some men; he obsessed over his health. But if his children afforded Mason an excuse, which they doubtless did in some instances, it was one that resonated with his contemporaries. Successfully pleading his paternal duties reflected the degree to which men of his station understood prioritizing family life.

Though absent from office, Mason made his presence felt in the words and ideas that birthed a nation. In April 1775, the same month the Revolutionary War commenced, Mason used the occasion of annual elections in Fairfax County to articulate his beliefs, in language strikingly familiar to most Americans today: "All men are by nature born equally free and independent. To protect the weaker from the injuries and insults of the stronger were societies first formed; when men entered into compacts to give up some of their natural rights, that by union and mutual assistance they might secure the rest. . . . Every society, all government, and every kind of civic compact therefore, is or ought to be, calculated for the general good and safety of the community."[51]

Mason refined those ideas about republican government and the nature of a just society at Gunston Hall, in the large first-floor family room that doubled as his study and overlooked his beautifully manicured grounds. From the rear exit of the house, wide gravel paths separated

four symmetrical gardens, bordered by immaculately maintained box-
woods. Further in the distance lay earthen mounds, constructed, as was
nearly everything in Mason's sight, by slaves and designed so that he
could keep watch over his wharf and fields. Just steps from his study,
Mason could enjoy breathtaking views of his vast estate, the Potomac
River, and Maryland's shore. During the daytime, if the weather was
good, he took periodic breaks to "walk for a considerable time wrapped
in meditation, and return again to his Desk."[52]

The pristine landscaping would have offered Mason a stark contrast
(and no doubt welcome reprieve) from his rowdy household. Ann had
borne twelve children in twenty years. The infant William died in 1757,
and the twins born in 1772, Richard and James, did not survive, either;
Ann passed away soon after their tortured delivery. Nine children remained at home, and though they were tragically without their beloved
mother, they were fortunate to have an especially dedicated father. The
upstairs at Gunston Hall was laid out on a long hallway, with small bedrooms running along both sides and filled with children, from the baby
of the family, Thomas, who was barely five years old in 1775, to the
young adults (and namesakes) George and Ann, whom they called
Nancy. George Mason raised them with occasional help from neighbors
and, of course, the constant aid of household slaves. He did not take a
new wife, nor did he send the children to live with female kin, the two
most common options of widowed fathers in early Virginia. He kept
them at home and left them only occasionally.

Still, public obligations sometimes pulled the other way, and the
Mason children saw that their usually attentive father could, when
"deeply engaged" in revolutionary politics, be emotionally absent even
when physically present. As a grown man, John Mason recalled that he
and his siblings knew not to disturb their father when he was writing at
his desk or walking through his thoughts outside. While it is hard to
imagine that nine children didn't occasionally violate that rule, it was
still a firm memory in John's mind half a century later. George faithfully
broke from his work to eat dinner with his children, but in the height of
the crisis of 1775–1776, he was, John remembered, sometimes so distracted that he would inquire about one of his absent daughters "who
had perhaps been gone a week to visit some Friend of which he had

known but forgotten."[53] Even remaining at home, then, offered no sure way to balance family and politics in the height of the Revolution.

Though Mason worked at Gunston Hall as much as possible, the formal adoption of a declaration of independence and constitution for the new state of Virginia had to be conducted in Williamsburg. So Mason once again reluctantly left his children to join the Virginia Convention in May 1776. He was friends with Richard Henry Lee, who was representing Virginia in the Second Continental Congress, and admiring of Patrick Henry, whom he had met two years earlier in the now defunct House of Burgesses. Mason thought Henry "the first man upon this continent, as well in abilities as public virtues." Otherwise, he was mostly unimpressed by the men populating Virginia's legislature. The committee appointed to draft a plan of government was, he told Lee, "overcharged with useless Members." "We shall, in all probability have a thousand ridiculous and impracticable proposals," Mason concluded.[54]

Retrospect draws our eyes to Philadelphia, but the real drama of 1776 started in Virginia, where Mason took the lead in designing the government and set to work drafting a bill of rights. Though initially skeptical of his colleagues, Mason collaborated with several experienced legislators as well as with a new delegate, a slight twenty-five-year-old intellectual from Orange County, James Madison. Madison was especially keen on ensuring religious freedom; it was this issue that politicized him.[55] The Convention heavily edited parts of the text, including what Madison contributed, but the heart of the finished product reflected Mason's ideas and language. The other states followed Virginia's lead in the summer of 1776, just as the Virginians followed Mason's.

Mason divided his time between Williamsburg and Gunston Hall as his ideas spread to Philadelphia and beyond. Thomas Jefferson remained in Philadelphia in the summer of 1776, a member of Virginia's dwindling Continental Congress delegation. More and more responsibilities fell his way, including chairing the committee that did for the newly imagined United States what Mason did for Virginia: legitimize independence. Jefferson borrowed from Mason in terms of both ideas and language. Seven other states, including Pennsylvania and Massachusetts, also imitated Mason's work. And all the while, he never left Virginia.[56]

Mason and Jefferson understood the profundity of their work, and they even anticipated the sweeping historical significance of the events of the summer of 1776. But at the time, both men weighed their political work against their familial obligations, and they were extraordinarily eager to dispense with politics and make their way home.

A s was commonplace among the Virginia gentry, Thomas Jefferson spent much of the first years of his marriage intermittently engaged in politics. Martha and Thomas understood that the duties of a gentleman of his standing sometimes required service on the county courts and in the Burgesses. But by 1775 the scope of political participation had been transformed and was no longer what they had bargained for. Now the stakes were global and potentially life-threatening. And the seat of power moved from familiar Williamsburg to faraway Philadelphia. It was not so easy or desirable for a young mother to make the trek to Pennsylvania. So, in June 1775 when Thomas left Williamsburg for Philadelphia to join the Continental Congress, Martha remained at home with three-year-old Martha and baby Jane. That September, Jane died at Monticello, and though Thomas briefly came home, he soon returned to Philadelphia. Martha went to stay with her half-sister, Elizabeth Eppes, who had also lost a child. Thomas wrote faithfully but complained to his brother-in-law Francis Eppes, "I have never received the scrip of a pen from any mortal in Virginia since I left it, nor been able by any enquiries I could make to hear of my family."[57]

The couple was reunited just after Christmas 1775, which brought another pregnancy. With each one, Martha's health worsened, and Thomas was reluctant to leave her. But he did return to politics in 1776. It always seemed an impossible choice. Which inviolable duty could he abdicate? And what would be the cost of the decision?

As Jefferson labored over the Continental Congress's justification for independence, family matters weighed heavily on his mind. Martha was getting sicker and sicker, and as his work neared completion Thomas begged to be relieved of his post. He later burned all Martha's letters, but it is not difficult to imagine the kinds of things a pregnant and ailing woman, raising one child and grieving the death of another, might have told an absent husband to speed his return. "The situation of my domestic affairs renders it indispensably necessary that I should sollicit the substitution of some other person here in my room," Thomas wrote Edmund Pendleton, head of Virginia's provisional government. He did not feel comfortable explaining "the private causes which render this necessary" but was emphatic about his need to get home.[58] While Martha's worsening condition grieved him, Jefferson would not abrogate his public duty, even for what he feared was a life-and-death matter. The political stakes were simply too high. Without Virginia's support, he reasonably feared, the entire patriot cause might be lost. He would not leave until he knew for certain that Virginia would be represented in the Congress, and Richard Henry Lee was in no hurry to get back to Philadelphia. Lee's wife was sick as well, and he was disinclined to abandon his mate so that Jefferson could attend to his. At the end of July, an anguished Jefferson wrote Lee directly: "For god's sake, for your country's sake, and for my sake, come. . . . I am under a sacred obligation to go home."[59]

The morning of 3 July 1776 began an excruciating day for Thomas Jefferson. As he had the day before, he endured what he characterized as "mutilations" to his draft of the Declaration of Independence. The Congress moderated his language in numerous places and purged entirely his long critique of the slave trade. Other delegates tried to console Jefferson and convince him the changes were for the better. He would have none of it. When the revisions were done, he hand-copied the two versions and mailed them to his friends, so that they could judge for themselves "whether it is the better or worse for the Critics."[60]

Meanwhile, 250 miles southward, Martha Jefferson was having her best day in months. Francis Eppes wrote Thomas on 3 July with the happy report that she "is perfectly recover'd from her late indisposition, and except being a little weak, is as well as ever she was." Martha's brutal pregnancy had ended in a miscarriage sometime in late June, while Thomas was begging to be replaced in Congress.[61]

As soon as another Virginian arrived in Philadelphia, Jefferson rushed home. With Martha's health no longer in peril, his thoughts soon returned to political service, but not on the national stage. This

time, he took Martha and their daughter with him, moving the family to
Williamsburg, where he served in the Virginia legislature.

More than any other Virginian—arguably more than any
other American—George Washington decided after 1775
to sacrifice his family life to fulfill his civic duty. He became
the "father of his country" in no small measure because he, more than
any among this cohort, sometimes reluctantly but always consistently
chose his country over domestic life.

Most of George Washington's peers moved in and out of political
offices in 1775–1776. Thomas Jefferson, working with John Adams and
Benjamin Franklin in Philadelphia, grappled with the rationale for declaring independence from England. In Virginia, Mason, Henry, and
Madison undertook the practical and daunting task of designing a new
kind of state.

But a military contest would have to be won if those ideas were to
have any hope of survival. And here again, a Virginia patriarch led the
way. The qualifications John Adams enumerated when he nominated
George Washington to head the Continental Army, along with Washington's response, reveal the character of the revolutionary age. Washington, proclaimed Adams, was "a Gentleman from Virginia . . . whose
Skill and Experience as an Officer, whose independent fortune, great
Talents and excellent universal Character, would command the Approbation of all America." He was exactly the kind of man required to lead
a volunteer force while inspiring respect and allegiance from his fellow
citizens. As the comportment of a gentleman in that age required,
Washington responded with modesty and disinterest: he reluctantly accepted the appointment while reminding the Congress "that I this day
declare with the utmost sincerity, I do not think my self equal to the
Command."[62]

General Washington immediately understood the domestic costs of
his new post. His first thoughts were of Martha. "Far from seeking this
appointment," he assured her, "I have used every endeavour in my power
to avoid it, not only from my unwillingness to part with you and the

Family, but from a consciousness of its being a trust too great for my Capacity." But, he explained, "it was utterly out of my power to refuse this appointment without exposing my Character to such censures as would have reflected dishonour upon myself." While preparing to be apart from his beloved wife for how long he could not predict, he wanted her to know that "I should enjoy more real happiness and felicity in one month with you, at home, than I have the most distant prospect of reaping abroad, if my stay were to be Seven times Seven years."[63]

This, the earliest extant letter of George to Martha, voiced a steady refrain of their lifelong correspondence. He wanted to remain with her at Mount Vernon, focused on their shared domestic concerns, but he felt inescapably pulled into public service. Troubled at the prospect of leaving Martha at Mount Vernon—not least of which because he feared a British raid on his home and, so, for her life—he wrote his brother-in-law, Burwell Bassett, to encourage him and Nancy, Martha's sister, to keep an eye on Martha. He said he felt "great uneasiness at her Lonesome Situation." That same day he wrote Jack Custis (unsuccessfully, it turned out) to encourage him to watch out for his mother and "keep up her spirits."[64]

Martha was uneasy herself. She confessed to a friend, "I shudder every time I hear the sound of a gun." But, she quickly added, she tried to keep those fears to herself, for they served no helpful purpose. Martha Washington was optimistic; she believed that "the greater part of our happiness or misery depends upon our disposition," and she always resolved "to be cheerful and to be happy in whatever situation I may be." She was also resourceful and experienced at managing on her own; her first husband's death taught her skills that served her well during the Revolutionary War. It was not easy, of course, but Martha Washington was as prepared for the challenges that lay before her as any woman in that era could have been.[65]

Whatever anxieties the couple felt, George Washington never seriously considered making the choices that George Mason or Thomas Jefferson made. He accepted that he could not be at once the head of the army and of his own household. His family would have to adjust. Martha would have to take greater responsibility for Mount Vernon and relatives help out as needed. Washington's entry in the military also forced Jack Custis to grow up and become his own man, a serious matter Washington hoped to impress upon the decidedly unserious Custis. Washington wrote the twenty-one-year-old the very day he officially received his commission, "You must now take upon yourself the entire management of your own estate, it will no longer be in my power to assist you."[66] Washington had neither the time nor the inclination to continue to protect Jack from himself. And the emergent understanding of what would make a man worthy, which hung on self-determination, made him disinclined to intercede.

Both Washington's letter to Jack Custis and his command of the Continental Army revealed the degree to which family and civic life were being revolutionized in 1775–1776. On the battlefield, the general proudly led, he said, a "patriotic band of Brothers" fighting for the abstract concepts of liberty and independence. And at home he left dependents to care for themselves and each other without a patriarch to guide them.[67]

Independence became, in the minds of American patriots, necessary to escape the destruction of liberty at the hands of corrupt politicians in London and to ensure that the British Americans would not be enslaved by the cruel ambitions of power-hungry royal insiders. But independence would also be fraught. Our Virginia cohort knew this firsthand, having been rendered independent in their families much earlier than they wanted. Before Mason, Jefferson, and Washington came to preside over plantations, each had lost his father at a young age. Mason's father drowned in a ferry accident when George was only ten years old. Washington's father died shortly after George turned eleven, and Jefferson was fourteen when he lost his father. Jefferson never forgot how it felt to have "the whole care and direction of my self . . . thrown on my self entirely, without a relation or friend qualified to advise or guide me."[68] Their personal experiences made these men at once daring and careful—qualities that served them well in the challenges they faced as leaders of the Revolution and American nation.

Rejecting British authority meant that a new republican political family—in rhetoric and reality—rose to fill the place of the old colonial order. The colonies grew up and so needed to leave the "mother country." American "brothers" wrested their rights from an outdated, patriarchal colonial power, embodied in the corrupt father-king. Revolutionaries put the matter to their skeptical neighbors: "To know whether it be the interest of the continent to be independent, we need only ask this easy, simple question: Is it the interest of a man to be a boy all his life?"[69]

But independence was not to be entered into lightly. These men and their revolutionary compatriots imagined themselves as seizing a rare, momentous, and fragile moment. (The language that seems so inspiring and prescient today was, in the eighteenth century, incredibly reckless.) Mason insisted that "North America is the only great nursery of free-men, now left upon the face of the earth. Let us cherish the sacred deposit. . . . In all our associations; in all our agreements let us never lose sight of this fundamental maxim—that all power was originally lodged in, and consequently is derived from, the people. We should wear it as a breastplate, and buckle it on as our armour." Thomas Paine evoked that same sense of specialness, of holding both history and destiny in their hands: "Every spot of the old world is overrun with oppression. Freedom hath been hunted round the globe. Asia and Africa have long expelled her. Europe regards her like a stranger, and England hath given her warning to depart. O! receive the fugitive, and prepare in time an asylum for mankind."[70]

The nature of the government they planned to live under made their independence from England all the more precarious. In this new "nursery of freedom" and "asylum for mankind" a brotherhood of republican citizens would govern themselves, choosing leaders according to merit, not by the accident of birth.

Inventing the most transcendent of all the familial metaphors of their age, Americans picked a Virginian to lead their new family of independent citizens. From the late 1770s until his death in 1799, Washington was widely celebrated as the father of the American Republic, "at whose birth he presided, whose infancy he nourished, over whose childhood he watched with a parent's care and solicitude, and which he never left till it had attained the strength of manhood."[71] Washington's paternity was not biological or destined by providence or randomly determined by birth. He was father by the considered choice of his fellow citizens. Washington's authority derived from his virtuous example, his ability to inspire rather than compel. Such republican power starkly contrasted with that of kings and aristocrats, signifying the radicalism of the age and the defining the character of the American Republic— values that did not long remain in the public square.

CHAPTER 3

Sacrifice

T he Revolutionary War pushed the obligation of sacrifice to unprecedented heights, a phenomenon embodied most completely by George Washington, whom Americans quickly hailed as the "father of his country." Washington's wartime sacrifices— whether weighed by duration, magnitude, personal peril, or consequence—outstripped those of his patriot brethren. His command of the Continental Army made him the highest-profile man in America. It also required the greatest sustained service: year after year he longed for but never saw Mount Vernon. Delegates to the Continental Congress and legislators and governors of states, in contrast, faced term limits and so moved in and out of those (less dangerous, more flexible) offices. Even the most committed statesman could never match his sacrifices. And Washington, unlike the Revolution's political leaders, did not have the option of quitting. By the time of the Battle of Trenton in December 1776, he was already so universally identified with the young country that the man and the movement merged. Americans celebrated his birthday, alongside the Fourth of July, as the two signal American holidays. Parents soon began to name children after him, writers to dedicate their books to him, and towns to adopt his name.[1] Understanding Washington's centrality to the patriot cause, Continental Army officers upbraided him for entering the fray at Monmouth in 1778. As the Marquis de Lafayette reminded him, had Washington been killed, "there is no officer in the army who might fill that place" and so "the American cause itself would perhaps be entirely Ruined."[2] Washington resented that governmental failures to support the war financially prolonged it, and he criticized his countrymen who quit public offices out of self-interest. Still, he remained steadfast in the darkest days of combat.

The cost of that seemingly infinite capacity for service—and the fame that went with it—was steep, and paid not only on the battlefields of the Revolutionary War but also at home. Washington continually worried that his efforts on behalf of the patriot cause pulled him away from relatives he loved and needed to protect. On receiving his commission to head the Continental Army in the summer of 1775, George wrote Martha that he had reluctantly accepted the appointment despite "my unwillingness to part with you and the Family." At the same time, his personal ambition and sense of civic responsibility overrode that reluctance to leave home.[3]

For Washington and the men who joined him in the long military contest, sacrifice was their watchword; service jeopardized their livelihoods and lives. The risks were only marginally less perilous for the architects of independence: at stake lay their fortunes and reputations, and, if British forces had their way, perhaps their lives as well. Sacrifice was also a foundational tenet of republican government. In the political structure idealized by patriot leaders, citizens surrendered their own self-interest to pursue the greater common good.

But the revolutionaries did not simply understand sacrifice as an abstract political concept or a consequence of military service; they lived it with their families. Patriots left their homes for governmental and military posts in hopes of securing a better future for posterity. That choice forced their relatives to sacrifice, too, which sometimes checked their enthusiasm for putting republican principles into action. Even the most prominent of Virginia patriots were intermittently unwilling to sacrifice family wealth and status for American independence. They were sometimes skittish about shifting their domestic duties onto other members of their families, especially as the war dragged on. And they downright refused to abandon their mastery over African American slaves—and the wealth and power slave ownership accrued to their relatives—even when they themselves clearly saw that their racial order could not be reconciled with their political ethics.

Caught between the traditional demands of patriarchs and the compelling prospect of creating an independent republic, leading Virginians were forced to make tough choices during the war years. Which would they privilege: public service or family duty?

Sometimes they followed Washington's example and made a calculated sacrifice to advance the Republic, even at great cost to their domestic responsibilities. That was what Thomas Jefferson did when he left an ailing Martha in Virginia to serve in the Continental Congress in 1776. Soon after Martha Jefferson died in 1782, Thomas agreed to represent America in France, leaving in Virginia his two younger daughters, Mary (who was always called Polly as a child and Maria after her adolescence) and Lucy, and placing the eldest, Martha, in a convent outside Paris. He later sent for Polly, who stopped in London, where she was met by Abigail Adams, wife of the American ambassador. Adams reproached Jefferson when she discovered that the nine-year-old had lived so long apart from her father that she did not recognize him: "I shew her your picture," Adams explained. "She says she cannot know it, how should she when she should not know you."[4] Patrick Henry stayed closer to his Virginia home during the Revolution, traveling only to Philadelphia for a term in the Continental Congress. But he was often in Williamsburg (the capital of Virginia until 1780, when it moved to Richmond) on state business and away from his mentally troubled first wife, Sarah. In 1774, while Patrick focused on lobbying for a continent-wide response to the Coercive Acts, Sarah was confined to their basement. She died in 1775, the same spring that her husband gave his famous "liberty or death" speech before the House of Burgesses.

At other times, Virginia's leading men refused public office, choosing to put their family needs first. Thomas Jefferson retreated from politics on several occasions when he and Martha tended to dying children. He was fined in 1778 for failing to show up at the legislature and castigated by his friends for his dereliction. After serving as governor in 1779–1781, he again left politics to be a full-time husband and father. Here he followed Patrick Henry's example. After three years in the grueling job as governor (1776–1779), Henry moved his entire family to a remote corner of the state and refused even to serve on the local vestry. And to the dismay and even disgust of his overburdened friend General

Washington, George Mason rejected numerous calls to hold national office. He condemned efforts in 1784 by his neighbors to change his mind "as an oppressive and unjust Invasion of my personal Liberty." If he could "arrange my own Domestic Concerns in such a manner as to enable me to leave my Family," he promised he would "most cheerfully let the County know it."[5]

This cohort knew that respectable men needed to be dutiful and self-sacrificing. Most were also highly ambitious. They wanted personal renown and a lasting legacy and saw in the Revolution a ripe chance to secure a prominent place in history. But the war years tested them: the stakes escalated higher and higher, as service required distant travel and long absences from home. Being a patriot leader, as opposed to a colonial patriarch, consumed a tremendous amount of time and threatened the forfeiture of wealth and reputation. It even put lives at risk. So, as the war dragged on, men like Jefferson, Mason, and Henry had to decide: What would they sacrifice? Family time and fortune for political service? Or reputation and power for family?

It was not hyperbole but rather a clear statement of fact that Americans wagered "our lives, our fortunes, and our sacred honor" on the shaky proposition of independence. Implementing their radical political ideals articulated in the Declaration of Independence required military triumph over Great Britain, which at the outset of the war was the most powerful nation in the West, possessing the world's largest navy and an awe-inspiring army of professional, experienced, well-funded soldiers. By 1778, Britain had stationed nearly fifty thousand soldiers in North America. And the British hired some thirty thousand mercenaries from the German states to help prosecute the war. The fledgling Continental Army consisted of a fraction of that number of men, and they were commanded by inexperienced amateurs. To say they were undersupplied would be kind. On paper, it seemed fairly impossible for Britain to lose.

Quite apart from the fearsome challenge posed by the British army and navy, the list of internal obstacles ran depressingly long: disease, deprivation, desertion, camp violence, drunkenness, hoarding, and an overall lack of adequate discipline and competence. Servicemen enlisted for short terms and were often parochial, refusing to fight when the conflict spread to different regions. And that was just among patriot supporters. Loyalism and apathy combined to make patriots a minority in some locales. Some among the "lesser sort" in Virginia developed their own ideas about independence—including from elite authority—and refused to follow the social script that called for deference to the state's gentlemen. The tumult of war made maintaining control over Virginia's slaves extraordinarily difficult, especially in the wake of Governor Dunmore's 1775 offer of freedom to African American men in exchange for military service to the crown.[6]

From the very start of the war, then, it seemed clear that the sacrifices required to lead the army would be myriad and relentless, with a decidedly uncertain outcome. In his youthful "Rules of Civility," Washington had set for himself the goal of always being a man of his word. "Undertake not what you cannot Perform," he wrote, and "be Careful to keep your Promise." And so, understandably doubting whether he was up to the audacious task, Washington assumed command of the Continental Army in 1775 with trepidation. In a letter to his brother John, he likened it to being "Imbarked on a wide Ocean, boundless in its prospect, & from whence, perhaps, no safe harbour is to be found."[7]

We know, in retrospect, that Washington found not only a safe harbor but success beyond his capacity to imagine. Yet it is worth lingering over what that "wide Ocean" meant in 1775. Taking command of the Continental Army made George Washington, in the eyes of the British government, the chief traitor in North America. The list of possible results of his leadership was short and depressing. He might somehow prevail. But that unlikely outcome was also the only positive one. He could die in combat or succumb to camp disease or get killed by friendly fire or be cut down by insurrection in his own ranks. British forces might capture and execute him. He could fail so abysmally as to lose his command and with it his reputation and perhaps his property. Economic chaos and a British occupation might conspire to rob him of his wealth, even if he survived. So, in addition to his life, Washington also wagered his good name and his family estate, which were, in his world, what made a man. Washington intuited the tremendous financial hazard that awaited him and his family as he took leadership of the army. Still, determined to preserve the part of his reputation over which he had some control—and reflecting the attitudes of colonial elites—Washington refused a salary. In trying to preserve his honor by this act of self-sacrifice, he risked Mount Vernon. At war's end, he admitted, "I made no money from my Estate during the nine years I was absent from it and brought none home with me."[8]

Other servicemen, regardless of their military rank, likewise risked their lives, fortunes, and honor, and they too feared the perilous consequences of military service. Volunteering to fight for liberty allowed a man to demonstrate his character and thus earn respect for his family. It also threatened the lives of soldiers and sailors, whose deaths would leave behind suffering families. In a typical letter, a young lieutenant named Samuel Cooper warned his wife that he could not predict the exact dangers he would face on the battlefield or what his fate might be. "But," he comforted himself by vowing, "it Shall never be Said to my Children your father was a Coward."[9] On George Washington's watch, twenty-five thousand servicemen, including Lieutenant Cooper, never made it home to their families.

What drove men to stake their lives on such a lopsided war? As they decided to fight Great Britain and create republican governments, Americans repeatedly invoked a core set of values, including liberty, virtue, independence, equality, and sacrifice, to explain their actions. They saw these principles as both the building blocks of a republic and the foundations of American character. The volunteer military became for them the first and most important way to reveal that character, especially the essential quality of self-sacrifice.[10] In the eyes of many of his contemporaries, the commanding general of the Continental Army embodied the best of America, especially in his willingness to put the greater good ahead of personal interests and even, in wartime, personal safety. And from the American perspective, the survival of the patriot military in the face of seemingly insuperable odds confirmed their belief in the special destiny of their republic.

Despite clear-eyed understanding of the uphill campaign they faced, many Virginians felt optimistic at the outset of the war, sharing with other American patriots a conviction of inevitability of their cause. Richard Henry Lee captured the dominant sentiment when he wrote Washington in the fall of 1775 that, despite continuing British offensives against patriot forces, "It is impossible that vice can so triumph over virtue, as that the Slaves of Tyranny should succeed against the brave and generous Assertors of Liberty, and the just rights of humanity."[11]

George Washington recognized, from dearly bought experience, the gulf between such rhetoric and the hard realities of the military contest. Americans loved to talk about sacrifice, but they were not very good at making it. Which explains why even as his renown grew to near sanctification, General Washington fell into despair. He confided to one relative in September 1776, "If I were to wish the bitterest curse to an enemy ... I should put him in my stead. ... I see the impossibility of serving with reputation ... yet I am told that if I quit the command inevitable ruin will follow. ... In confidence I tell you that I never was in such an unhappy, divided state since I was born."[12]

Washington's letter gave voice to what Americans learned experientially in the early years of the war: living their high-minded ideals, particularly sacrifice, was going to be far more difficult than anyone, including the commander-in-chief of the Continental Army, imagined. British troops vastly outnumbered the chronically ill-equipped Americans, who understandably feared facing down the world's preeminent military. But the main problem before Washington's army was not a lack of soldiers or shortcomings in their courage and resources. Rather, political failures compromised troop strength and burdened the fledgling forces, extending the hell of the war. The Continental Congress ran the country, such as it was, during most of the war, and though it was populated by dedicated men, its structure was ill-conceived for the task. General Washington quickly discovered that Congress, in denying itself the power Americans found so corruptive under the British system—the authority to tax—had crippled its ability to prosecute the war. In the late 1770s the American cause, born out of a defense of English liberties, teetered on the brink of failure because of a decision to reject models of English power. This left General Washington in an untenable position: "I believe I may with truth add, that I do not think that any Officer since the Creation ever had such a variety of difficulties and perplexities to encounter as I have."[13]

Washington was grieved to discover that all too rarely did men who ran the states share his willingness to sacrifice for the greater good. Throughout the late 1770s state legislatures, including Virginia's, proved endlessly stingy and chronically slow when it came to sending money to Congress. The political newcomer James Madison shared Washington's contempt for the inactions of states. "The vicissitudes which our finances have undergone," he concluded, "are as great as those of the War."[14]

It was heartbreaking for Washington to witness the depths to which tightfisted Americans allowed his troops to descend. During the terrible winter at Valley Forge, General Washington wrote back home to Governor Patrick Henry, painfully describing the "melancholy prospect before us." The situation was "more deplorable than you can easily imagine . . . For several days past, we have experienced little less than a famine in Camp; and have had much cause to dread a general mutiny and dispersion."[15] In early January 1779, Jack Custis, serving in the Virginia House of Delegates, complained to Washington of the excruciatingly slow pace of the legislative process. Washington's reply revealed the toll chronic state legislative inaction and a vacillating public had taken on him: "I really am not, nor shall I, I believe, be again surprized at any thing; for it appears to me that idleness & dissipation seems to have taken such fast hold of every body that I shall not be at all surprized if there should be a general wreck of every thing."[16]

Things looked no better in the Continental Congress. While serving in 1780, James Madison witnessed the costs of failing to sacrifice for the common cause. Within days of arriving at Congress, Madison bluntly concluded that if the states persisted in their refusal to appropriate adequate funds for the war effort, "we are undone." The list of obstacles Madison described to Thomas Jefferson, then governor of Virginia, ran depressingly long: "Our army threatened with an immediate alternative of disbanding or living on free quarter; the public treasury empty; public credit exhausted . . . Congress complaining of the extortion of the people; the people of the improvidence of Congress, and the army of both."[17]

After the war moved south, Virginians—those in Congress, on the front lines, and in the state capital—were aghast at the reticence of their "sister" states to come to their aid. As one disgusted man put it, "Virginia freely contributed when her sister States were in distress—why is she left not only to struggle for her self under many difficulties, but required to bear the burthen of the whole Southern War?"[18]

Through the late stages of the war Washington corresponded with George Mason to commiserate over the dire straits of the patriot movement. The "present distresses" seemed, he insisted, "so great and complicated, that it is scarcely within the powers of description to give an adequate idea of them. . . . We are without money, & have been so for a great length of time, without provision & forage except what is taken by Impress—without Cloathing—and shortly shall be (in a manner) without Men. . . . The history of this War is a history of false hopes, & temporary devices." Washington believed that winning the war required nothing short of "an entire new plan." The starting point: a permanent and reliably funded military, followed by a redesign of government. Echoing Madison's bleak assessment, Washington concluded that without real and immediate change "our efforts will be in vain."[9]

For generations, Chesapeake patriarchs had taught their sons that leadership required sacrifice. Young gentry men learned to put aside personal predispositions and put on the character of a gentleman: to lead households; to serve on county courts, on vestries, and in the colonial militia; to be good stewards of family land and businesses. In this way, a male achieved public affirmation of his manhood and his family enjoyed respectability and security. Before the 1770s, though, a patriarch's political duties typically complemented rather than conflicted with domestic life. But during the war years, the public sacrifices of patriot leaders grew deeply personal. The war thus laid bare the difficult choices Virginia's founders made when called on to sacrifice their reputations, wealth, and family duties to save their political ideals.

S acrifice for the war was not, then, an abstraction but a painful, personal ordeal. This cohort of Virginians took their sacrifices, their contributions, and their peer's judgment very personally. As they worked on an enterprise with such grave meaning—including their own estates and lives—they also formed deep attachments as well as intense rivalries. The most notable among these was the fifty-year friendship between Thomas Jefferson and James Madison, forged in 1779–1781, while Jefferson was governor of Virginia and Madison served the state on the Executive Council and in the Continental Congress. They quickly came to admire each other, and over the course of their lives they shared over twelve hundred letters. Their attachment, Madison wrote in his old age, "was never interrupted in the slightest degree for a single moment."[20] Conversely, Jefferson and Patrick Henry became bitter rivals during the war. Even Henry's death did not inspire Jefferson's forgiveness: he gave scathing interviews to Henry's first biographer in a bid to undermine his historical legacy, disparaging him as "rotten hearted."[21]

Virginia had always been, for elites, a small, interrelated place, including for our cohort. For example, Patrick Henry first met Thomas Jefferson in 1759 at the home of Martha Washington's uncle. In 1780 John Marshall, a George Washington protégé, started reading law at William and Mary under the guidance of George Wythe and Bishop James Madison, James Madison's cousin, at a school officially supervised by Wythe's former student, Governor Thomas Jefferson, and with Bushrod Washington, George's nephew, and Spencer Roane, Patrick Henry's future son-in-law, as classmates.[22]

The Revolution politicized those traditional bonds as it raised the stakes of politics: personal relationships now shaped the fate of Virginia and America. It was, then, a deeply personal letter that George Washington, four years into the grinding brutality of a war with no end in sight, wrote George Mason, urging him to reconsider his prioritizing of family duty over political service. Despite all their idealization of sacrifice, Washington complained, Americans had given in to war weariness and turned inward, fretting over their own financial predicaments and the parochial interests of their states. Worse still, some leading Virginians simply withdrew from public office, leaving the Republic teetering on the brink of failure.

In Washington's view, the very men who should have been most deeply invested in the patriot cause had chosen family and local aims over the desperate call to national duty. "I cannot refrain lamenting," he not so subtly chided Mason, "the fatal policy too prevalent in most of the states, of employing their ablest Men at home in posts of honor or profit." Suffering from a paucity of virtuous men sharing a national vision, congressional leadership had devolved into fractious and petty self-interestedness and lost sight of "matters of great national moment at this critical period."[23]

In his plea for sacrifice, Washington beseeched Mason and others who had chosen domestic interests over the infant nation's common good: "No man who wishes well to the liberties of his Country & desires to see its rights established, can avoid crying out where are our Men of abilities? Why do they not come forth to save their Country? Let this voice my dear Sir call upon you—Jefferson & others—do not from a mistaken opinion that we are about to set down under our own Vine and our own fig tree let our hitherto noble struggle end in ignominy."[24] Washington intentionally chose those words, "our own Vine and our own fig tree." It was a phrase repeatedly invoked in his and Mason's correspondence, and it signified for them, and for Virginia gentry generally, the idyllic and independent plantation homes they all dreamed of heading and that their political actions—and inaction—now jeopardized.

The founding fathers appear in our mind's eye to have been thoroughly captivated, consumed even, with politics. But it was not reflexive and not easy for the fathers in this generation to sacrifice family for politics. Certainly they were convinced of the necessity of winning independence and defending the American Republic. And they were personally ambitious—stunningly so in some instances. One could not attain the kind of immortal fame they sought simply by responsibly raising children, but patriarchs had to maintain ordered households of accomplished descendants. So, a balance needed to be struck.

George Washington, in his consistent privileging of the greater civic good over his domestic affairs, stood on one end of the spectrum and his friend George Mason on the other. In April 1776 Mason wrote Washington to congratulate him on a "glorious & important Event"— the retaking of Boston. Mason understood that his friend's military exploits "will render General Washington's Name immortal in the Annals

of America." But Mason, while respecting Washington's renown, neither sought it for himself nor particularly idealized it. Rather he hoped
for Washington to be able to resume the family-centered life that both
men had prized in the past: "May God grant us a return of those halcyon
Days; when every Man may sit down at his Ease . . . & enjoy the Sweets
of domestic Life!"[25]

Mason never wavered in his veneration of "the Sweets of domestic
Life," though he wholeheartedly identified with the patriot cause. He
was a long-standing colonel in the state militia and served on the Fairfax County Committee on Safety. He worked hard both to build a government for Virginia and to procure supplies and recruits for the war
effort. His sons joined the military and, to their father's gratification,
served valiantly. But there were clear limits to the Mason sons' contributions, at least in their father's eyes. Henry "Light-Horse Harry" Lee
offered William a staff position, but George Mason declined on his behalf. Mason was unambiguous about the future he imagined for his son:
"I have ever intended him for civil and private life; his lot must be that of
a farmer and country gentleman." He did not allow his younger sons to
enlist until they finished their education, and he saw to it that his namesake, George, quit the service when he developed "a violent Rheumatic
Disorder."[26] Mason also consistently put up boundaries to his own willingness to sacrifice, which frustrated his fellow Virginians. To their cha-
grin, he did not accept a national appointment—or leave Virginia—
until he attended the Constitutional Convention in 1787.

Even the most zealous advocates of the Revolution—patriots as
dedicated as Patrick Henry and Thomas Jefferson—discovered in the
war the limits of their willingness to sacrifice their families' needs. Henry
became the first governor of the new state of Virginia in 1776, a service
that represented a profound sacrifice: of his family concerns, his law
practice and livelihood, and, if things went as they likely would, perhaps
his life. "I feel my mind filled with anxiety and uneasiness to find myself
so unequal to the duties of that important office to which I am called by
the favor of my fellow citizens at this truly critical conjuncture," he told
leaders of Virginia's new government.[27]

Knowing the weight of the office, Governor Henry stayed in his post
for three years (all that was allowed under the state constitution). So

popular was he that no one was nominated to oppose him in 1777, and in 1778 the Virginia Assembly did not even need to take a vote. In his second-term acceptance letter Henry voiced the high-minded ideals that he tried to live up to during his governorship: "The good of the commonwealth shall be the only object of my pursuits, and I shall measure my happiness according to the success which shall attend my endeavours to establish a public liberty."[28]

Like George Washington, though, Patrick Henry found sacrifice difficult to inspire in others. As governor he presided over nearly chronically low enlistments and inadequate military funding, which he took very personally. Because it was Governor Henry's duty to ensure that Virginia met its quota of soldiers and requisitions for the Continental Army, he had occasion to write often to General Washington. Almost always this meant giving bad news. In March 1777, for example, Henry had to explain, "The recruiting business of late goes on so badly, that there remains but little prospect of filling the six new battalions from this State, voted by the Assembly." He was even more frank with Richard Henry Lee, a delegate in the Continental Congress, whom he informed that same week that the "lies of deserters and the want of necessarys" had raised "fatal objections to the continental Service."[29]

Serving as governor wore down Patrick Henry's health, his goodwill toward his fellow citizens, and his willingness to sacrifice for the patriot cause. He left office exhausted and disgusted; he wrote his successor, Thomas Jefferson, to wish him well, but his letter gave no cause for optimism. Henry saw little in Virginia's political culture that might inspire confidence. Corruption and self-interestedness seemed pervasive. And even without such character deficiencies afflicting the citizens, the economy was in a free fall. Henry warned Jefferson that he "feared that our body politic was dangerously sick." As to civic virtue, he concluded, "our countrymen are not capable."[30]

After he finished his frustrating tenure as governor, Henry rather easily shed the burdens of public service and retreated to the sanctuary of family. Lest anyone doubt his determination to retire, he moved nearly as far from the seat of power as he could, to Leatherwood plantation in Henry County (named in his honor), which lay well over two hundred miles southwest of Williamsburg. He carried with him a large and extended family, to which he rededicated himself. In the summer of 1777 the widower Henry had begun to court Dorothea Dandridge. Dorothea descended from two of Virginia's leading families: besides the Dandridge line, her mother was a Spotswood, daughter of one of Virginia's most successful colonial governors. She was only twenty-two when she married Patrick, the same age as his eldest daughter, Martha Henry Fontaine. Henry was already a grandfather by Martha when Dorothea bore their first child in 1778. In time, she would deliver ten children, one about every other year for the rest of Patrick's life. In 1779 the Henry clan trekked to Leatherwood: Dorothea, then pregnant with a second baby; Martha Henry Fontaine and her toddlers; Patrick's minor children by Sarah; and Patrick's sisters. Local men quickly elected their newest and most famous resident to the vestry and county court, but Henry declined the positions, preferring instead to concentrate on protecting his estate and the many members of his household. A year later he returned to the Virginia Assembly, but his next significant political office would wait until 1784, after peace with Britain, when he agreed to become governor again.[31]

Thomas Jefferson felt the same painful tensions between his revolutionary activism and responsibility for his young family. After getting stuck in Philadelphia in 1776 while Martha suffered in Virginia, Thomas was cautious about his time away from family. When his infant son died in 1777, he temporarily abandoned public life, much to the dismay of his peers prosecuting the Revolutionary War. Writing from the Continental Congress in Philadelphia, Richard Henry Lee could not disguise his disdain at Jefferson's choices. "It will not perhaps be disagreeable to you, in your retirement," Lee chided Jefferson, "sometimes to hear the events of war; and how in other respects we proceed in the arduous business we are engaged in."[32] Though he held a seat in the state legislature in 1778, Thomas Jefferson repeatedly let his political responsibilities slide in order to remain with Martha and their young family. For example, despite his position in the legislature he avoided returning to Williamsburg when his daughter Polly was born that August. Reluctantly, he eventually made his way there, so late that he had to pay a fine for non-attendance—a modest price, he apparently decided, for ensuring the safety of his sickly wife and infant child.[33]

Despite the personal costs of public service, Jefferson agreed to succeed Henry as governor. As he feared, the decision brought grim consequences for his reputation, home, and family. In January 1781, during Governor Jefferson's second term, British forces under the command of the American traitor Benedict Arnold pressed toward the capital, which had been moved to Richmond. Martha Jefferson was forced to flee with her three young children, including two-month-old Lucy, as were many state leaders and their families. Governor Jefferson stayed another night, trying frantically (if belatedly) to rally a defense before escaping on horseback. That haphazard effort at defending the capital proved no challenge to Arnold's troops. "In ten minutes," slave Isaac Jefferson later recalled, "not a white man was to be seen in Richmond; they ran hard as they could."[34] Jefferson was hammered by critics after the invasion for his failed defense of Virginia's capital.

The costs kept accruing. In mid-April 1781, baby Lucy Jefferson died. Despite the ever-present mortal threat before Virginia, Governor Jefferson refused to attend a meeting of his own council. As he explained to the likely stunned council members, "there being nothing that I know of very pressing, and Mrs. Jefferson in a situation in which I would not wish to leave her, I shall not attend." The next week British forces undertook a major offensive. General Cornwallis ordered the governor captured, and he dispatched troops to Monticello. Martha again gathered her children and fled, this time to Poplar Forest, their plantation in Bedford County. The Jeffersons escaped being captured but not the British seizure of their mountaintop retreat as well as their Elk Hill plantation.[35] For inexplicable reasons, the British cavalry officer Banastre Tarleton let Monticello stand, though not without plundering the wine cellar, the corncrib, and the meat house. Cornwallis occupied Elk Hill for ten days, during which time his troops destroyed all the crops, feasted on the livestock, took the strongest horses and cut the throats of the rest, and burned the barns and fences. They left Elk Hill, in Jefferson's bitter words, "an absolute waste."[36]

It was another humiliating episode that marked the end of Jefferson's willingness to sacrifice his family responsibilities for the war effort. State leaders reconstituted the Assembly in exile in Staunton, but the siege of Monticello coincided with the end of Jefferson's term as governor. He refused to participate in the meetings, even though the choice briefly left Virginia without a governor. Instead, he withdrew entirely from public life. For three months after he returned to Monticello, Thomas wrote no one, not even his best friend, James Madison.[37]

In retreating home Jefferson put his reputation in jeopardy. The ensuing controversy over his actions was overshadowed in October when the British surrendered at Yorktown, though Patrick Henry tried to keep the issue alive by getting his friends in the legislature to open an inquiry into Jefferson's conduct. Later that winter, Jefferson allies within the Virginia legislature hoped to counter Henry and blunt the lingering criticisms of Jefferson's character by passing a resolution thanking him for his "impartial, upright, and attentive administration" and praising his "ability, rectitude, and integrity as a Chief Magistrate of this Commonwealth." When the resulting resolution came to a vote, Henry apparently abstained.[38]

Jefferson never forgave Henry for what he took to be malicious exploitation of his political difficulties and his family's misery. Jefferson could rebuild the barns at Elk Hill and replace the supplies at Monticello. But he could not so easily repair his reputation. (It is revealing of the values of eighteenth-century gentlemen that Thomas Jefferson held his grudge against Patrick Henry longer than he did against the troops that invaded Monticello.) In the summer of 1782, Jefferson confided to his friend James Monroe how futile all his service seemed: "By a constant sacrifice of time, labour, loss, parental & family duties, I had been so far from gaining the affection of my countrymen . . . even lost the small estimation I before possessed."[39]

After the summer of 1781, Jefferson focused on his family, rejecting civic duties. Once combat ceased he was again elected to the Virginia legislature, but Martha had just delivered another baby—the second daughter named Lucy and her last child. Thomas refused to leave her side, despite his contemporaries' varyingly coaxing and criticizing him. James Monroe warned him that if he did not show up at the legislative session he risked, in addition to the contempt of his friends, formal censure and even arrest. Thomas replied that he did not see how Virginia could rightfully assert a "*perpetual* right to the services of all it's members." And he maintained that he now saw "public service and private misery inseparably linked together."[40] Part of Jefferson's reluctance to serve in public office in 1781–1782 derived from his resentment over how his fellow Virginians, particularly Patrick Henry, judged his wartime governorship. But Jefferson's love for Martha and their home life mattered just as much. A French official who visited Monticello during that time praised the idyllic domestic life that so captivated Jefferson: "A gentle and amiable wife, charming children whose education is his special care, a house to embellish, extensive estates to improve." The visitor understood, even as he lamented, Jefferson's consequent decision to decline serving as American peace ambassador in Europe.[41]

The ambitious and single James Madison was taken aback by Jefferson's choices. He told Edmund Randolph that Jefferson's refusal to serve "does not appear to me to be dictated either by philosophy or patriotism." In letters to Jefferson himself, Madison hedged those criticisms and tried to encourage his return to politics. Other Virginians were less forgiving. Edmund Randolph condemned Jefferson's decision to "persist in his unpardonable rage for retirement."[42] But persist he did. Neither his friends' pleas nor his critics' censure changed his mind, which was set on Martha and their children and his happy life at Monticello.

The death of Martha Jefferson and the end of the family life Thomas Jefferson idealized recast his priorities. Before her death in September 1782 he shared more in common with George Mason than George Washington. Both Jefferson and Mason were deeply involved in the political radicalism of the 1770s, and together they became the principal architects of the foundational texts of the republican revolution. But both fathers left their families reluctantly and as briefly as possible. Jefferson retreated from political life in 1781 convinced that "all prospects of future happiness" rested "on domestic and literary objects." Then Martha died. "A single event wiped away all my plans," Jefferson mournfully explained.[43]

Where Jefferson felt anguish, Madison saw opportunity. Though deeply sympathetic to his friend's "irreparable loss," Madison also wondered if "perhaps this domestic catastrophe may prove in its operation beneficial to his country by weaning him from those attachments which deprived it of his services." Madison's speculation, though perhaps cruel in its emotional detachment, was accurate. Before too long, Jefferson was bound for France, and a career at the pinnacle of national politics.[44]

For Thomas Jefferson and Patrick Henry, the sacrifices they made during the Revolutionary War felt, on a personal level, enormous and, at times, unbearable. They risked their reputations, estates, and families, forsaking the foundational duties of a patriarch for the patriot cause. In Jefferson's case, he put his wife and children directly in harm's way.

Instead of sacrificing *for* families, they found themselves sacrificing *of* families. Then, to their dismay, others found their best efforts inadequate. In the face of such steep costs met with public scorn, it is understandable why some men retreated home.

Men choosing family life over political service had to answer to their peers. The Revolution made clear that leadership could not be spurned without consequences. One of the "fundamental maxims of a republican government," James Monroe reminded Thomas Jefferson, was that "you should not decline the service of your country." When Patrick Henry left politics behind, Edmund Randolph cautioned that "his sighs for home expose him to a daily loss of his popularity." Retreats from service and sacrifice required justification.[45]

Even the ever candid and always resolute George Mason knew that a man of his means should be serving his country. So he was careful about which governmental positions he accepted and always found a way to remind his peers of two mitigating factors when he declined: his single fatherhood and poor health. Mason repeatedly turned to these matters to explain his conspicuous absence from national office. He was less successful at dodging service to his state. Mason often complained about being "against my Inclination drag'd out of my Retirement, by the People of my County." And he was quick to point out that he served in the Virginia legislature "to the no small Neglect & Injury of my private Fortune." But serve Virginia he did, while carefully weighing his political principles against his children's needs: "If I can only live to see the American Union firmly fixed, and free Governments well established in our western world, and can leave to my children but a Crust of Bread, & Liberty," he concluded, "I shall die satisfied."[46]

James Madison likewise felt compelled to explain his conspicuous absence from combat. Madison was precisely the right age to join the Continental Army. He might well have become a military protégé of General Washington, a wartime companion to his friends Alexander Hamilton and James Monroe. But he did not take up arms, Madison insisted, because of poor health. He led instead in government, serving in the Virginia General Assembly in 1776 and in the state's constitutional convention that same year. By 1780 he was in the Continental Congress, commencing a nearly thirty-five-year record of service. Yet Madison never got over the perceived need to defend his absence from the battlefields of the Revolutionary War. In his 1831 autobiographical sketch, he still wanted to clarify his record: he was, he explained, "restrained from entering into the military service by the unsettled state of his health." Madison had long since escaped any risk that his service in the Revolution posed to his life or fortune. But at the close of his life he was still worried that it might cost him his "sacred honor."[47]

Meanwhile, the Revolutionary War came home in immediate and visceral ways. Governor Jefferson was the highest-ranking Virginian to endure a military assault on his home, but he was hardly alone. For many Virginians, home was no longer a *refuge* from political and military duties but now a *site* of conflict. Among the greatest sacrifices leaders made was their ability to protect their families, to retain control of homes and of loved ones—which had long been an elemental patriarchal duty.

Patrick Henry was appalled at the predations on private homes and the insidious effects of the war on Virginia families. "In common wars," he explained, "children are not obliged to fight against their fathers, nor brothers against brothers, nor kindred against kindred. Our men were compelled, contrary to the most sacred ties of humanity, to shed the blood of their dearest connections."[48] The war divided several high-profile Virginia families. John Randolph split with his brother Peyton and his son Edmund over the question of loyalty during the Revolutionary War. He moved to London and remained there throughout his life. Sally and George Fairfax, neighbors and friends of the Washingtons, also fled to England in 1773.[49] But mostly the presence of British troops besieged Virginia families.

As British soldiers moved into the Northern Neck of Virginia, George Mason worried that they would attack Gunston Hall. He wrote his son George that "we are in daily expectation of sharing the same Fate with our Neighbours upon this, & the other Rivers; where many Familys have been suddenly reduced from Opulence to Indigence . . . the Enemy taking all the Slaves, Horses, Cattle, Furniture, & other Property, they can lay their Hands on; and what they can't carry away they wantonly destroy." Responding to repeated rumors about troop movements, Mason moved his furniture back and forth across the river so many times that he damaged it nearly as much as an actual raid on Gunston Hall might have done.[50]

Though Gunston Hall was spared, Britain brought the war to many Virginians' front doors. In addition to routing their state capital and wrecking their economy, British military forces destroyed Virginians' crops, slaughtered their livestock, and threatened their families. This most intimate assault pushed to the breaking point leading Virginians' resolve to sacrifice. James Madison, who was known for his judicious and dispassionate judgment, wrote a friend a blistering appraisal of the war: "No description can give you an adequate idea of the barbarity with which the Enemy have conducted the war in the Southern States. Every outrage which humanity could suffer has been committed by them. Desolation rather than conquest seems to have been their object. They have acted more like desperate bands of Robbers or Buccaneers than like a nation making war for dominion."[51]

As the war came to their homes, patriots likewise sent their kinsmen and sons to the front lines. Henry's sons and Washington's nephews served, and all of Mason's sons fought in the Revolutionary War after they finished their education.

Women did not escape sacrifice, either, for patriarchs could not shield them from the ordeals of war. George Washington worried from the first hours after he received his commission about being forced to live apart from Martha. And he understood that his absence from home put her in harm's way. He was desperate enough to seek the aid of Jack Custis, telling him, "My great concern upon this occasion, is the thoughts of leaving your Mother under the uneasiness which I know this affair will throw her into." He futilely hoped that Jack would do "every thing in your power to promote her quiet." George also asked a relative, Lund Washington, to help Martha escape if British troops threatened Mount Vernon. Lund's plan could not have inspired much confidence. He calculated that even if British forces attacked at night, "10 minutes notice would be Sufficient for her to get out of the way." Luckily, Martha Washington never had to test that shaky proposition.[52]

For her part, Martha Washington seemed to worry more about her husband than herself. His frustrations "distressed me exceedingly," she confessed to her brother-in-law.[53] Though it was not the proper role of a respectable eighteenth-century woman—or at least it would not have been in normal times—she became a quick study of military matters and kept abreast of troop movements. Despite her husband's fears, she ably managed their long separations and her added responsibilities without complaint.

For eight years, Martha Washington divided her time between Mount Vernon and wherever George was stationed. Since she had no minor children, she could, like him, be gone from home for long periods. Every winter, she was with him, including at New York, Valley Forge, Morristown, and Newburgh. The trips were never easy: they required her to be apart from her favorite sister, Anna Bassett, who was often ill and died in 1777; her daughter-in-law, Eleanor Custis, who was proving quite fecund; and the Custis grandchildren Martha adored. Winter was hardly an ideal time to travel, but Martha Washington always tried to see the best in a situation. And she could take comfort in knowing she was providing vital support for her husband and the patriot cause. Martha organized sewing circles of the camp wives, tended the sick, boosted morale. One camp follower observed, "I never in my life knew a woman so busy from early morning until late at night as was Lady Washington, providing comforts for the sick soldiers. . . . giving all the comforts to them in her power."[54] Because fighting mostly ceased in the winter months, she could do a great deal of good and not be in grave danger.

When Martha Washington died in 1802, an Alexandria newspaper pronounced her "the worthy partner of the worthiest of men."[55] It was a title she earned over decades, beginning in the Revolutionary War, when, mirroring her husband, she willingly sacrificed for the patriot cause at home and on the front lines.

Martha Jefferson was not as fortunate as Martha Washington. The war proved devastating to her family. She delivered three children during the war years and buried two of them. She had miscarried in 1776, the same month that her husband drafted the Declaration of Independence, and she was pregnant again—for a last and fatal time—when Cornwallis surrendered in October 1781. In the last year of the war, Britain laid siege to three of Martha and Thomas's residences: the capital, Monticello, and Elk Hill. In two of those cases, at Richmond and Monticello, Thomas turned to a most unlikely group of protectors: his slaves. The young boy Isaac Jefferson recalled staying behind in Richmond in January 1781 as British forces besieged the city and whites, including the governor and legislators, fled. Other slaves remained at Monticello that summer, with Martin Hemings in charge, when the white members of the household ran. The only witnesses to the raid on Monticello were members of the slave community: they risked the brunt of Tarleton's wrath, and they saved the Jefferson family silver. In the family stories told by both black and white residents of Monticello, Martin Hemings refused to disclose Thomas Jefferson's location even when British soldiers threatened to shoot him.[56]

As these episodes suggest, the intersections between the front lines and the home front ran deeper than plundered houses and scorched fields. The chaos of war coupled with the unintended social implications of embracing republican principles set off a revolution in family values that reshaped domestic life in the newly independent United States. "We live in an age of wonders," observed Yale president Ezra Stiles at the close of the Revolutionary War. "We have seen more wonders accomplished in *eight* years, than are usually unfolded in a century."[57] Victory in the War for Independence not only transformed governance and social order, it also encouraged a shift in Americans' understanding of family duties and their definition of family membership.

The exigencies of war unavoidably recast long-standing relationships in Virginia households. It simply was not possible, while in leading
military and government positions, to maintain the close family oversight that patriarchs had long idealized. Service compromised dominion
over others: men could not control their relatives, sometimes to their
great embarrassment. Washington, for example, was distressed—
though he could not have been surprised—to learn that his ne'er-do-well
stepson Jack Custis was absent from sessions of the Virginia legislature.
He futilely prodded him to "be punctual in your attendance."[58] As usual,
the advice fell on deaf ears, and Washington could do no more than
write letters. Washington faltered not only as a father but also as a son.
His mother applied to the state government for public support in 1781,
to his mortification. More galling still was the fact that she had plenty
of money and devoted relatives more than happy to come to her aid.
Plus, Washington had left directions with his friends to answer all appeals from his accounts. He learned of this family embarrassment, as he
did those arising from Jack Custis, through letters, from too far away
and too late to fix things.[59]

Men's sacrifices for the patriot cause required them to rely on people they had long thought of as dependents: wives, children, even slaves.
Governor Jefferson in particular exposed the fiction of white men's assertions that they needed to protect their slave "families," when he turned
twice to slaves to face British troops that he fled.

The sacrifices of service also meant missing important milestones:
births, deaths, weddings, and the day-to-day events and face-to-face en-
counters that make relatives a family. It was impossible for fathers to exercise the same influence during war—especially a war besieging their
hometowns and personal estates—as they could in times of peace. Of
course the fears and atrocities of war could also strengthen bonds, forming an "us vs. them" solidarity among relatives and neighbors. But if
leaders sometimes benefited from such emotions, they often did so from
afar, since a good deal of service in the Continental Congress and Continental Army required protracted absences from home. Fathers preoccupied with the vicissitudes of war usually could not remain the emotional
center of their families any more than they could control the conduct of
their relatives and ensure hierarchical order in their households.

Virginia patriarchs had long welcomed visiting relatives, orphaned children and widows, and protégés to live on their estates; their households became even more fluid during the war. Martha Jefferson spent much of her time with her half-sister Elizabeth Eppes while Thomas was in Philadelphia for the Continental Congress and later, from time to time, when he was governor. When the widowed Patrick Henry served as governor, his sisters Anne and Elizabeth moved with him to Williamsburg to act as hostesses. Soon thereafter his twenty-one-year-old daughter, Martha, moved there as well, taking care of her younger siblings, along with her own children.[60] And while General Washington was at camp—"banished from home" as he put it—Lund Washington ran Mount Vernon. George reminded Lund that he placed "my entire dependence upon your Fidelity and Industry."[61]

In sum, families changed to match the exigencies of war. Dependents sometimes became protectors, subordinates equals. Out of necessity, families became more fluid and more flexible. These wartime adjustments both anticipated and fueled larger changes in family life that far transcended the great houses of patriot leaders, particularly the shift away from authoritarianism and toward self-determination and mutuality, and from perceiving family as innate to contractual. Nowhere was this more evident than in General Washington's quarters.[62]

D isillusioned to see the (often hollow) rhetoric of sacrifice laid bare—including among men he admired—George Washington turned to a new family of his own making on the battlefield. The family that George Washington forged among his wartime peers and protégés was, like the military itself, voluntary. Merit determined status, both in the army and in Washington's heart. He loved the men who most deserved his favor, who earned it by their sacrifice, talents, and virtue. The connections they shared were not biological. Rather, their ties of loyalty and affection were born of individual worth and choice. In both its composition and values, his military family fulfilled the revolutionary ideals he was ostensibly fighting for. The emotional network Washington built helped him endure the boundless disappointments of the Revolutionary War. And it predicted the tenor of family life writ large that emerged in the late eighteenth century. In the fictive family that George Washington fashioned in the extremis of war, we can see the beginnings of a major shift in family values.

The language Washington used to define the bonds forged between men in war was clear and consistent. In his farewell address to the army, he praised all the men who "from different parts of the Continent, strongly disposed . . . to despise and quarrel with each other" put aside those parochial biases and instead fought as "one patriotic band of Brothers." But his particular military family was selective. He bonded with faithful allies among the senior officers such as Massachusetts native Henry Knox, who like Washington lost his father at a young age and who became President Washington's secretary of war, and Nathanael Greene, a Rhode Island private who, by sheer talent and achievement, rose through the ranks to become one of Washington's most esteemed commanders. Washington surrounded himself as well with a close-knit cohort of young protégés, notably John Laurens, Alexander Hamilton, and the Marquis de Lafayette. Washington mentored and molded these young men. He looked out for them and their children for the rest of his life. And he was emotionally expressive about them, referring to them as his "boys" and "sons." In fact, blood ties were the only missing element in Washington's military family.[63]

Some of these young men chose to unite themselves with General Washington against their own biological family's wishes and best interests. John Laurens, known as Jack, was the oldest son of one of the richest men in North America. Henry Laurens made a fortune in the rice market and was a partner in Austin and Laurens, one of the largest slave trading businesses in colonial America. He played a leading role in South Carolina revolutionary politics and served in the Continental Congress. He was even imprisoned in the Tower of London in 1779 while on diplomatic assignment for the United States. Despite his enthusiasm for the patriot cause, Henry Laurens much preferred that his firstborn son continue his legal studies, an education he was funding in Europe (at great expense). At first, Henry Laurens refused even to let Jack return to America. When Jack complained, "I feel like a Man avoiding the Service of his Country because his Father tenderly commands him to be out of Danger," Henry relented—but only to Jack coming home. He envisioned his son far from the front lines, serving in some political office, perhaps similar to James Madison, another well-educated first son of a rich man.[64]

Jack Laurens, however, had other ideas. Against his father's objections, he joined the military in 1777. It was not Henry Laurens's first disappointment. The prior summer Jack confessed that he had impregnated the daughter of a London merchant and been obliged to marry her. But she, their child, and his father's plans posed no rival to Jack Laurens's zeal for battle. In August General Washington asked him to become an aide-de-camp. The position was not, Washington made clear, solely a military one: "If you will do me the honour to become a member of my Family, you will make me very happy." Laurens reported to Washington's headquarters the next month. He fought valiantly and was wounded at Brandywine and had his horse shot from underneath him at Monmouth.[65]

All the while, Jack Laurens's young bride and the daughter he had never seen remained in England. "If I may judge from his conduct," regretted Henry Laurens, "he has forsaken Father & Wife & Child." Jack also had younger siblings and a complicated South Carolina estate that he was supposed to be responsible for. But those obligations also were swept away by Laurens's commitment to the patriot cause and to General Washington's "band of Brothers." His battlefield bravery may have impressed the men in Washington's camp, but it did not convince his father that he had made the right choice. Henry Laurens worried endlessly about Jack, while also rebuking him for, as he characterized it, "Robberies he has committed" in stealing "a husband & Father from his young family, a Guardian from his Brother & Sister, a Son & friend from a dependent Father."[66]

Jack Laurens became fast friends with another audacious and ambitious "son" in Washington's camp, Alexander Hamilton. He came recommended by Henry Knox and, like both Knox and Washington, had been essentially orphaned in his youth. Hamilton's father abandoned his mother, who died when he was just a boy. By the force of his personality and valor, young Hamilton rose from humble origins ("a bastard brat of a Scotch Pedler," hissed John Adams) to the highest echelons of power and into the heart of George Washington. Washington was impressed by Hamilton's intellect, courage, and skill in battle and from their first meeting "marked him for his own." Hamilton and Laurens became "kindred spirits, brothers alike in arms, in affection, and in accomplishments."[67]

So deep were these men's connections that Washington's own grandson, the son of Jack Custis, praised their well-deserved bond with his grandfather. In his *Recollections*, George Washington Parke Custis included several chapters on Washington's military protégés. Doubtless echoing his beloved grandfather, Custis lauded "the illustrious Alexander Hamilton . . . the patriot, the soldier, the statesman, the jurist, the orator, and philosopher, and he was great in them all." Hamilton "had employed his pen and drawn his sword in the cause of liberty before a beard had grown upon his chin."[68]

Washington also mentored Virginians John Marshall and James Monroe, both of whom served in the war. Marshall was a particularly faithful ally of Washington for the remainder of his life. The most influential Chief Justice in the history of the United States recalled that because of Washington's example during the Revolution, "I was confirmed in the habit of considering America as my country and Congress as my government."[69]

Washington's favorite "son" was the Marquis de Lafayette, another fatherless young man. In Washington's eyes, Lafayette was brave, selfless, forceful, and inspiring. At age nineteen, he left his French estate— and, like his friend Jack Laurens, a pregnant wife—to fight for the patriot cause. When Lafayette was wounded at Brandywine, Washington rushed to his side and ordered the doctor to tend to Lafayette as if he were his son. The letters Washington sent to Lafayette were among the most expressive he ever wrote, clearly conveying how much he loved him. In the middle of the war, Washington told Lafayette that he had earned his "perfect love and gratitude that neither time nor absence can impair."[70]

Washington cultivated within this inner circle the qualities he prized most: dutifulness, bravery, self-sacrifice, and loyalty. He also encouraged a sense of fraternity among the men under his command, particularly his closest protégés. Hamilton, Lafayette, and Laurens were close with one another and they all emulated Washington.

Ever the Virginian, Washington was camp patriarch in the fullest sense: his slave William Lee was his constant companion. Along with Martha Washington, William Lee rounded out the idealized family George Washington created during the war. The general was first among equals within the command, a father figure to young soldiers, revered husband of his devoted wife, and a slave master.

The one person conspicuously absent from General Washington's military family was Jack Custis. Despite brilliantly molding his own life to fit Virginia's highest ideals of manhood, Washington failed to inspire his stepson toward a noble character. Jack's early tutor, Jonathan Boucher, pronounced the boy spoiled and lazy, consumed with "Love of Ease & Love of Pleasure." Custis did not like books; he cared mostly for expensive clothing, fox hunts, and races. He was, his schoolmaster complained, "perpetually doing something or other displeasing to Me." Though nervous about offending Washington, Boucher nonetheless confessed, "I never did in my Life know a Youth so exceedingly indolent, or so surprizingly voluptuous."[71] Throughout his adolescence Jack Custis refused to apply himself to anything other than his own gratification. After reaching majority, he sold for a song several of his late father's properties to cover an increasingly toxic gambling addiction. He seemed to care little for the mother who doted on him, failing even to confirm her safety during the height of the war. And after he married Eleanor Calvert in 1774, they had children he could not support—four in seven years.

The contrast between the valiant, self-sacrificing young men Washington mentored in camp and the self-indulgent stepson he left at home could not have been sharper—or more hurtful to the commanding general. When Washington wrote in 1779 that he saw such an epidemic of "idleness & dissipation" that "I shall not be at all surprized if there should be a general wreck of every thing," he might just as well have been talking about Jack Custis as about Virginia politics.[72]

With his stepfather consumed by the war effort, Jack had been warned to take charge of his own life. The letters he wrote George Washington about his efforts on that score would seem touching were they not utterly lacking in follow-through. "I am extremely desireous . . . to return you Thanks for your parental Care which on all Occasions you have shewn for Me," Jack wrote George in the summer of 1776. "It pleased the Almighty to deprive me at a very early Period of Life of my Father, but I can not sufficiently adore His Goodness in sending Me so good a Guardian as you."[73]

Despite his assurances, Jack squandered money on a number of poorly conceived financial deals during the war, mostly related to selling land for depreciating paper money rather than—as George Washington repeatedly advised in stern terms—holding onto his property or at least trading land for land. While nominally serving in the state government, Custis continued ignoring Washington's advice and accruing debts at a prodigious rate. When, in 1779, he (again) proposed to sell even more of his land, Washington (again) explained that land "retains in itself an intrinsic and real value" and so avoided the wild fluctuations of paper money. If Custis sold his land for money that depreciated, "where are you then? Bereft of your land, and in possession of a large sum of money that will neither buy victuals nor clothes." George, clearly frustrated, noted, "This was my advice to you before, and I now repeat it."[74]

Jack Custis proved no better steward of his family obligations than of his inheritance, failing to fulfill that part of his duty as a Virginia patriarch as well. George expected Jack to do all in his power to alleviate the stress Martha faced during the war, but he was, again, let down. Jack and Eleanor had to be upbraided for failing even to write Martha. The obligation for maintaining contact fell to Martha, who, though exceedingly indulgent of the young couple, nevertheless was reduced to threatening, "If you do not write to me I will not write to you again."[75]

As Jack Custis continued to squander his inheritance and shirk his domestic responsibilities, Washington grew increasingly exasperated with this stepson who seemed to exemplify all that Washington spurned and nothing that he prized. Such disregard for manly duties would have been bad enough in ordinary times; that Jack would remain so self-centered when his family and his country needed him most only made his behavior more contemptible. The Revolutionary War called on responsible men to sacrifice for the common good. And here was the stepson of the commander-in-chief of the Continental Army, wallowing in irresponsibility and self-indulgence.

The young officers Washington mentored, meanwhile, embodied

the qualities he cherished, and they, unlike Custis, deserved his love. Laurens, Hamilton, and especially Lafayette became for George Washington the sons that Jack Custis never would be. At the same time that his correspondence to Custis grew increasingly terse and distant, Washington wrote Lafayette with warm admiration. In September 1778 he praised "the ardent Zeal which you have displayed during the whole course of the Campaign," and told him, "Your love of liberty—The just sense you entertain of this valuable blessing—and yr noble, & disinterested exertions in the cause of it, added to the innate goodness of your heart, conspire to render you dear to me."[76] Not even a casual reader of Washington's papers could mistake that letter for one to Jack Custis. Washington never wrote of Custis's "innate goodness," and he did not tell Jack that he was "dear to me" because of "noble" service to the patriot cause.

When the war ended, Washington continued to write loving letters to Lafayette, who had returned to France, praising "the excellence of your heart" and conceding he lacked the words "which could express my affection for you." Lafayette visited America in 1784, and when he left, Washington feared he might never see his beloved surrogate son again: "In the moment of our separation . . . & every hour since—I felt all that love, respect & attachment for you, with which length of years, close connexion & your merits have inspired me."[77] Lafayette loved Washington in return, calling him "My Adoptive father" and "My father, My Best friend." When he came back to the United States in 1824–1825—a quarter century after Washington's death—Lafayette visited his tomb at Mount Vernon and grieved, one contemporary observed, as if "a father dearly loved" had just been buried.[78]

Lafayette and his wife named their first son George Washington, and George and Martha were the boy's godparents. Young George was sent to America in the 1790s to study at Harvard and escape the fate of his parents, who were arrested during the French Revolution. He lived for a time at the president's residence in Philadelphia and then at Mount Vernon. A visitor to Washington's estate was struck by the close ties between the president and his young namesake, "whom he treats more as his Child than a Guest."[79]

Although Washington's bond with his favorite wartime protégé continued long after peace, just as the Revolutionary War ended he lost both a disappointing stepson and a beloved military one. Jack Laurens was cut down in a mostly meaningless skirmish in the South Carolina Lowcountry in August 1782, not long before the British finally evacuated the state. His friends were devastated, though not shocked: Laurens had cheated death many times before in his daring military escapades. His battlefield death after such illustrious service could not have been more different from the end that Jack Custis met. In the closing days of the war Custis determined to participate in the glory. But he never saw action, soon caught camp fever, and died shortly after Cornwallis surrendered. His was a pointless death that left four fatherless children, the oldest just past five and the youngest still a babe in arms.

Jack Custis's disapproving stepfather became the star of his death scene, even in the family's romanticized retelling of events. As Custis lay dying, those keeping vigil suddenly heard "a trampling of horse, and, looking out, discovered the commander-in-chief." After talking with the attending doctor, who offered no hope, "The general retired to a room to indulge his grief, requesting to be left alone. In a little while the poor sufferer expired." Washington "tenderly embracing the bereaved wife and mother" and though "absorbed in grief, he then waived with his hand a melancholy adieu, and, fresh horses being ready, without rest or refreshment, he remounted and returned to camp."[80]

Washington's actions after Custis's death were revealing. He took in two of Jack's children, George Washington Parke (Washy) Custis and Eleanor Parke (Nelly) Custis, and he and Martha raised them. He watched out for Jack's widow and the Custis holdings; like his father, Daniel Custis, Jack died intestate. George felt sorry for Martha's loss of her only child and responsible for the fatherless young family Jack left behind, but he did not seem to personally mourn the stepson he had raised since the boy was four years old. In contrast, when Jack's sister, Patsy, lay dying of an epileptic seizure in 1773, Washington held her in his arms and wept openly with Martha. He shared his heartbreak with friends and canceled his professional plans to mourn her at home. After Jack's death, he did not, in word or deed, convey a sense of genuine loss. The immediate "return to camp" was, in the family story, meant to convey Washington's self-sacrifice. But it matched his emotional detachment from his dissipated stepson.

At the outset of the Revolutionary War, in a letter filled with hollow promises of rectitude, Jack Custis had professed his filial attachment to Washington because, as he put it, "He best deserves the Name of Father who acts the Part of one."[81] Washington's attitude toward Jack during his brief adult life and in his death indicates that he felt the same about sons. Custis had not acted the part of a worthy son, and so he did not warrant paternal love as one. Lafayette, Laurens, and Hamilton, by contrast, became all that a man would want in a son. They deserved the love and loyalty of their surrogate, military father.

I t had seemed from the day that George Washington accepted his commission to head the Continental Army through the terrible summer of 1781 that Americans could not realistically hope to triumph over Great Britain's splendid army and formidable navy. Everything appeared in Britain's favor—at least on paper. But Britons were fighting in the communities and countryside of the patriots. The Americans, English commanders complained contemptuously, refused to fight according to the "civilized" rules of war; whenever possible, Washington avoided direct confrontation, choosing instead to lead the pursuing British forces into the interior of North America where their movements and then their supply lines, communications, and effectiveness ground to a near halt. There was, as well, the deceptively simple matter of defining victory. What would conquering rebellious countrymen mean? What city needed to fall for Britain to prevail? At one time or another British forces occupied every major town in North America, but the Continental Army never surrendered. After 1777, the alliance with France turned a seemingly minor if frustratingly intractable rebellion in some far-flung provinces into an international and then an unwinnable war.

When Cornwallis's men surrendered at Yorktown on 19 October 1781, so the story goes, the British played the tune "The World Turned

Upside Down." If true, it was a fitting choice. The most unlikely of heroes had stumbled toward the most improbable of victories.

What would be next? Thomas Paine had told Americans in 1776 that they could "begin the world over again." Having won independence in the Revolutionary War, they had the opportunity to see if Paine was right, and whether all the sacrifice had been worth it, after all.

To General Washington, it was not clear for a long time after October 1781 that the war was really over. Fighting continued in the South; Jack Laurens was killed ten months after Yorktown. Washington did not resign his commission until late 1783, and he did not make it home until Christmas Eve. At last resettled at Mount Vernon, he wrote Lafayette about the pleasures of leaving behind his military burdens and returning to domestic peace: "At length my Dear Marquis I am become a private citizen on the banks of the Potomac, & under the shadow of my own Vine & my own Fig tree, free from the bustle of a camp & the busy scenes of public life." Washington was profoundly grateful to be "retired from all public employments" and at last able to "tread the paths of private life with heartfelt satisfaction." He assumed that his sacrifices were all behind him and that "I will move gently down the stream of life, until I sleep with my Fathers."[82]

As Jefferson, Mason, and Henry had done during the war, at its end Washington turned homeward at last. Martha was elated to be at home for good. "My little family are all with me," she proudly told a friend, and her biggest worry was that some in the household had contracted a mild case of the measles. The most pressing matter before George: "the deranged situation of my private concerns, occasioned by an absence of almost nine years, and an entire disregard of all private business during that period." Mount Vernon needed too-long-delayed repairs and his account books desperate attention. A hodgepodge of orphaned children required surrogate parents. The winter of 1783–1784 was especially severe, which suited the Washingtons just fine. Fewer guests meant uninterrupted time to focus on all those overdue matters. The family, "fast locked up in frost & snow," included Washy and Nelly Custis, Martha's motherless niece Fanny Bassett, and George's nephew and namesake George Augustine Washington.[83]

But what George Washington and other Virginia fathers found

when they returned from the war was not what they had left behind. Parts of the Revolution had come home to stay. In addition to pulling Virginia fathers away from their families and rendering some children orphans, the war years also saw the beginning of the unraveling of colonial-style patriarchal authority. The physical disruption of households, combined with the unanticipated implications of revolutionary principles, eroded the ability and the will of Virginia fathers to control their children. Families increasingly idealized youthful self-determination. Sons, of both the biological and adoptive varieties, imbibed the revolutionary call for independence and liberty far more enthusiastically than the commensurate responsibility for sacrifice—all of which proved as messy a set of principles to practice in the parlor as in the public square.

CHAPTER 4

Liberty and Power

Though he fathered no offspring of his own and buried both of his stepchildren in their youth, George Washington raised quite a large family. After the Revolutionary War, he and Martha welcomed into their home Martha's two youngest grandchildren, various nephews and nieces, and several protégés whom they considered family. But of all those relatives, he turned to his nephew Bushrod Washington as he lay dying in December 1799. According to Washington's will, Martha would remain at Mount Vernon as long as she lived, but on her death George's cherished home would pass to Bushrod. Washington also entrusted this nephew with an even more precious legacy: his papers.

The bequest was carefully thought out and highly discerning. In leaving to Bushrod his most treasured possessions—his home and the sources for his historical reputation—Washington passed over his grandson and several nephews he helped to raise. He turned not to his closest kinsmen but rather to the one who best embodied the republican values he revered: virtue, civic leadership, and respectability. Bushrod Washington seemed the most capable steward of his famous uncle's legacy; George trusted him to protect both his place in history and the Republic's future.[1]

When Bushrod Washington was a young man, his uncle wrote him, and a host of other adolescents he took under his wing, long advisory letters, explaining that each man, through personal initiative and talent,

would decide his own place in the new American meritocracy. Study
hard, cultivate friends in high places, avoid scandal, always act in a dignified manner, and seek excellence, he advised, and public renown and
family love will surely follow. Youth, Washington believed, was the only
time to set such a proper course. "Your future character and reputation,"
he explained in one typical letter, "will depend very much, if not entirely,
upon the habits and manners which you contract in the present period
of your life; they will make an impression upon you which can never be
effaced."[2]

George Washington thought exactly the same about the new nation.
Announcing his 1783 retirement, he echoed for his country the counsel
he often gave to young men. "There is an opinion still left to the United
States of America," Washington reasoned, "whether they will be respectable and prosperous, or contemptible and miserable as a nation:
This is the time of their political probation; this is the moment, when the
eyes of the whole world are turned upon them, this is the moment to
establish or ruin their national character forever." The postwar course
Americans charted would, Washington maintained, decide "whether the
revolution must ultimately be considered as a blessing or a curse."[3]

Young Bushrod Washington absorbed the wise counsel his uncle
gave to him personally and to the American Republic. He thrived at William and Mary, where he became a founding member of Phi Beta Kappa.
His impressed uncle later secured him a position reading law with James
Wilson, the famed Pennsylvania jurist and constitutional thinker. Bushrod worked hard to capitalize on his family name and conducted himself
in such a manner to earn the respect of his peers and deserve their confidence in public office. By age twenty-five he took a seat in the Virginia
General Assembly, and he served as a pro-Constitution delegate to the
Virginia Ratifying Convention in 1788. He built a distinguished and
lucrative law practice in Virginia, which he left in 1798 for the United
States Supreme Court. Bushrod Washington was appointed by President Adams and took the seat of his former mentor, James Wilson. He
became, in sum, the kind of man his renowned uncle sketched in his advisory letters.

Similar counsel sent to Bushrod's cousin, George Steptoe Washington, fell on deaf ears. George Washington threw good money after bad

trying to educate George Steptoe and his equally irresponsible brother Lawrence Augustine. They were dismissed from school after school for every conceivable offense including, in the summer of 1788, physically assaulting a teacher. "So often, and strenuously have I endeavoured to inculcate this advice, and to Shew you the advantages which are to be expected from close application to your studies, that it is unnecessary to repeat it," wrote an exasperated George Washington. Their teachers complained often and bitterly: the brothers stayed out late, flaunted their defiance of school rules, squandered money, and showed unmitigated contempt for authority. They were a "grievous Burthen," one teacher complained, and caused "more trouble than 10 other Boys."[4]

Washington was mortified that his nephews would behave so badly, and he repeatedly warned the teenaged George Steptoe (whom he held responsible for his younger brother Lawrence) that his unacceptable conduct was jeopardizing his future. He wrote letter after unambiguous letter beseeching the feckless teenager "to pay a diligent attention to your studies" while admitting that if George Steptoe remained determined to follow a path toward "vice & dissipation," then "nothing I could now say would prevent it."[5] Only the boy could decide which course to take in life; his uncle could merely offer advice.

In short, George Washington explained, it was past time for his nephew to "quit the trifling amusements of a boy, and assume the more dignified manners of a man."[6] But what did that mean in the new Republic? And what could the founding generation do to inspire more young men to be like Bushrod and fewer to repeat the mistakes of George Steptoe?

The households of Virginia's leading founders afford a rich opportunity to witness how this first generation of Americans carried home their most cherished civic ideals: men could govern themselves; leadership ought to be earned and not a birthright; individuals would determine through their character, as Washington put it, "whether they will be respectable and prosperous, or contemptible and miserable." Like citizens in a republic, sons in a family needed to be at once self-governing and dutiful, always independent but ever vigilant about the collective good. Raising boys centered on this odd, often untenable blending of autonomy and submission—a familial corollary to the political balance between liberty and power. It was, like establishing a republic, tricky business. And sometimes the outcomes bore no more than a passing resemblance to the founders' high-minded ideals.

E ven as they embraced the most radical implications of the "natural rights" philosophy and cast off all allegiance to King George III and the British Empire, the Virginia founders felt deeply apprehensive about democracy and individualism. If the people could legitimately reject imperial authority, might they not also justifiably overthrow their representatives at home? Building on the ideas of the Enlightenment philosopher John Locke, Virginia's intellectual elite, most notably Mason, Jefferson, and Madison, believed that independence from Great Britain left the North Americans in a state of nature. Governments, this time, as the Declaration of Independence announced, "instituted among men," had to be created to return man to a state of society. So they quickly set about planning constitutional structures to restore civil order, to create systems of *power* to channel individuals' *liberty.*

The Second Continental Congress had not even formally proclaimed the country's independence before the Virginians clashed over the most fundamental elements in republican government: representation and citizenship. George Mason, who designed Virginia's (which was also America's) first constitution, wanted to expand the electorate and regularize representation—both of which would have curbed planter dominance by enlarging the influence of new citizens. Jefferson agreed. But the majority of the delegates to the Virginia Convention, including Patrick Henry, wanted to conserve electoral regulations and thereby retain more of the old hierarchy—and their authority over it. After an intense debate and close vote, Henry's position held sway.[7]

The contradictory desires to advance individual rights and promote social order became the central struggle in American political life. Even before independence, politically astute English Americans understood the adversarial relationship between liberty and power. Power, they knew, was aggressive and would, if not vigilantly monitored, destroy liberty. Power was not by its nature evil but could be easily corrupted and, in turn, corrupted men who wielded it. Individual liberty rested on checking governmental power which depended on an engaged and active citizenry.[8]

The problem facing the architects of a republic was how to find structures for the legitimate exercise of necessary governmental power that would also allow citizens' liberty to flourish. This was debated in the abstract during the 1763–1775 crises. But as these men drafted state constitutions, led by the Virginia example, theoretical abstraction became a concrete—and contentious—reality. The Virginia Convention was only the start of an intractable struggle to promote individual rights without imperiling the collective good. It would expand to other states, to the Constitutional Convention of 1787, and to the practical operations of the new federal government after 1790.

The conflict between liberty and power in governance reverberated in Virginia's plantation homes, as founders tried to raise a new generation of independent yet self-sacrificing republican leaders. In the late eighteenth century, southerners made a shift in child rearing, in both the goals of parents and the methods of raising children. These changes were bound up in the reconsideration of the imperial family and new republican values. But whereas the political *revolution* was led by a small cohort of colonial gentlemen, the familial *evolution* was more broad based. Men like George Washington and Thomas Jefferson experienced and expressed these shifting family dynamics rather than intentionally designing them. Still, this cohort's voluminous writings provide the fullest picture of the transformations occurring in American family life.

How did family dynamics change in the revolutionary age? Authoritarianism gave way to affection as the basis of family attachment; self-determination rather than deference became the most highly prized trait in boys. Instead of requiring children to submit to patriarchal authority, adults sought to instill in each individual child a self-regulating drive to behave respectably. Only then could they, in the common trope of the age, shine as "ornaments" to their families.

The catch was that young people had to *choose* dutifulness, to decide to conduct themselves in ways advantageous to their families, society, and selves. Ideally, children behaved well because they loved their parents and wished to make them happy, not because they feared them. Gender did not much matter to those core family values. Sisters and brothers alike understood that as they grew up, their doting relatives' favor would depend on how they acted: good boys and girls secured love, support, and respect.

For boys, though, such childhood lessons bore a distinctly political imprint after the 1770s. Good sons would choose to personify revolutionary values, including sacrifice, independence, and virtue. If they did, they would earn the respect of fellow citizens while collectively ensuring the success of the young nation. Over and over and over again adolescents heard that their conduct would decide not only their personal reputations, and with that the standing of their families, but also the very survival of the Republic. These convictions formed the foundation of George Washington's advisory letters to his young nephews Bushrod and George Steptoe Washington and ran through the family correspondences of all Virginia elites. Indeed, parents throughout the United States set about grooming young men to take responsibility for their own success and to become citizens worthy of the Republic.[9]

The Virginia planter St. George Tucker captured this mindset perfectly in a 1787 letter to his teenage stepsons:

> The world is a circle about every man, exactly of such a size as his Abilities make it.—It is very well known five miles about Petersburg that Mr. Booker is a good Chair-maker—that Alexander Taylor is a very tolerable Cabinet-maker. . . . but it is known all over the civilized World that General Washington is a great General—that Doctor Franklin is a great Philosopher & Politician, and that Mr. Rittenhouse is a great mathematical Genius. It is in your election at present whether you will have a world like Mr. Booker's & Alexander Taylor's worlds, or a world like General Washington's, Doctor Franklin's and Mr. Rittenhouse's.[10]

As Tucker's counsel indicated, in the wake of the Revolution, Virginia elites' definitions of success ran particularly, perhaps insuperably, high. It was not enough to be a skillful craftsman or well-regarded merchant. For the rising generation, achievements should be displayed on the national, even international, stage—a far cry from the comparatively humble "vine and fig tree" of their planter-patriarch fathers.

As St. George Tucker's evocative imagery intimated, Virginians also aspired to set aside the organic, hereditary values of the colonial world. They imagined that in the new American nation a man would not be born to a place but would determine—by ambition and actions—what kind of world he would have. But there were clear limits to that vision. Self-determination, just like the civic rights the founders idealized, extended only to white male property owners. Despite proclaiming a commitment to egalitarianism, universal manhood suffrage and legal equality remained controversial throughout the eighteenth century. The Virginians did debate but ultimately declined efforts to broaden rights in their constitution, as did leaders in several other states. In the republican government imagined by the founding generation, the "better sort" would still lead and only stakeholders—landowning white males—would participate in electoral politics. Farther-reaching innovations lay in the future. Looking back from the twenty-first century, these seem like modest steps at best, particularly in light of the continued enslavement of African American men and women and denial of an independent legal identity to white women.

But the idea that men could and should govern themselves—either collectively in their political institutions or individually in their careers and character—was quite new in the eighteenth-century Atlantic world, and frightening at that. In this as-yet-unproven experiment, men would theoretically chart their common fate, rejecting hereditary power exercised by a few in favor of republican virtue—citizens reasoning together to put the greater good above their individual interests. Individuals (again, only white men) would, likewise, decide the scope of their own lives.

Thomas Jefferson succinctly captured the sentiment of his age when he explained to his much-loved and often-errant nephew Peter Carr, "Your fortune and fame are in your own hands." St. George Tucker heartily agreed, and he expressly located that turn toward self-reliance in the American Revolution. In 1809 he observed that the years after the Revolution stood out in the sweep of history for having "demonstrated the necessity of a Man's being able to place his reliance on *Himself*."[11] Virginia patriarchs had prized initiative and talent in the colonial era, but the Revolution pushed them further toward self-determination while it also led them to imbue youthful behavior with tremendous political weight.

Of course, leading Virginia families did all they could not only to encourage but also subsidize their young relatives' quest for "fortune and fame." Family remained a key resource for young men to draw on—if they chose to do so and proved themselves deserving of their relatives' aid. Prominent families still set sons up with land, slaves, and connections. Peter Carr's future may have been in his own hands, but he was not, in fact, on his own. The young man had a devoted uncle coaching him, connections through his Uncle Jefferson to leading men including James Madison and George Wythe, an expensive education paid for by his family, and a promising inheritance awaiting him in Louisa County.

However much these Virginians idealized self-determination, they also could not give license to individual freedom of action. They understood that the choices young men made regarding the circle about their lives still echoed far beyond the individual. Families' futures continued to be tethered to the conduct of men. In fact, the Revolution politicized the long-standing colonial tradition of paternal leadership: the traditional influence of men over estates, reputations, and relatives also became infused with new political meanings.

It became the duty of fathers, uncles, and father figures to cultivate responsible republican sons: young men able to excel, to exercise virtue, to lead their communities and country. Women certainly shared in this politicized family agenda; good daughters imbibed republican values and reputable mothers raised patriotic children. The main political role women were supposed to play in the American Republic was to guide their sons toward virtuous citizenship, and they took that charge very seriously.[12] But only men were citizens, so fathers played the central role in readying sons for civic life. When death or political obligations took fathers from sons, male relatives and friends stepped in, as George Washington and Thomas Jefferson did for their fatherless young kinsmen.

The *founding fathers* believed with unshakable conviction that the fate of their republican experiment depended on how *republican sons* conducted themselves. Each generation of American citizens, they insisted, had to prove their worthiness. At Fourth of July events and other patriotic occasions, the rising generation was called upon to live up to the example set by the first patriots. And they were warned that they would be judged by history accordingly: "Generations past, and generations to come, hold us responsible for this sacred trust."[13] Whatever doubts revolutionary leaders had about themselves and their peers—and there was plenty cause for concern in the 1770s and 1780s—those worries paled in comparison to their anxieties about the future.

Properly educating sons became the means to assuage those fears. In the minds of revolutionary leaders, youth was the time for boys to prove their ability to answer the call to service, to get ready to lead the Republic into a glorious future. Education was the means. Adults from the gentry class typically sent boys away to boarding school as early as age ten or twelve and usually not later than fifteen or sixteen, and they returned home from college in their late teens or early twenties. While female kin wrote to and counseled adolescent students, fathers, uncles, and surrogate fathers nearly always took the lead. They filled their advisory letters with appeals to cultivate virtue, disinterestedness, and service, on top of—often paramount to—academic lessons. And they repeatedly cautioned adolescent boys that the future of the American Republic, the fate of their families, and their personal reputations were all wrapped up in their conduct while at school.

George Washington left the Revolutionary War convinced "that the best means of forming a manly, virtuous and happy people, will be found in the right education of youth." It was vital, he believed, that leaders dedicate themselves to "qualifying the rising generation for patrons of good government, virtue & happiness."[14] Washington impressed this conviction on every one of the many young men who fell under his influence in the 1780s and 1790s. In his many letters to George Steptoe and Lawrence, George Washington tried to persuade them of the necessity of their taking advantage of his assistance and responsibility for their futures. "Time is limited," he cautioned, and "every hour misspent is lost forever." Expressing the convictions of his generation, he warned the boys that "future *years* cannot compensate for lost *days* at this period of your life."[15]

What was true for individual boys held for the Republic. In the founders' minds, the education of youth and the preservation of liberty were inextricably linked. "What spectacle can be more edifying or more seasonable," reasoned James Madison, "than that of Liberty & Learning, each leaning on the other for their mutual & surest support?"[16] Madison expressed the widespread understanding that the only way for the Republic to endure was for subsequent generations to educate themselves, to prepare for the tremendous challenge of self-government. To that end, he and the other Virginia founders paid for the educations of relatives and protégés, mentored the young sons of friends and political allies, and helped found schools and universities.

"A popular Government, without popular information, or the means of acquiring it," Madison insisted, "is but a Prologue to a Farce or a Tragedy; or, perhaps both. . . . And a people who mean to be their own Governors, must arm themselves with the power which knowledge gives." As president, Madison encouraged the creation of educational institutions, including a national university to complement the universities founded in the various states. In an 1810 address to Congress, he reminded the legislators that "it is universally admitted that a well instructed people alone, can be permanently a free people."[17]

Thomas Jefferson's private writings and civic activities mirrored Madison's and Washington's. In retirement, he built his beloved University of Virginia, an edifice to educational excellence, self-determination, and Virginia's sons. Like Washington, Jefferson impressed upon all the boys he helped raise the enormous weight of youth. "Every moment you lose," Jefferson cautioned his grandson Thomas Jefferson (Jeff) Randolph, "is irrecoverably lost." To his other grandson, Francis Eppes, he patiently though relentlessly explained that success would depend on the choices he made in his youth about his time and talents: "time is now the most pressing and precious thing in the world to you, and the greatest injury which can possibly be done you is to waste what remains."[18] Jefferson sent Peter Carr elaborate advice, down to specific reading lists and hourly schedules of how best to spend his time. His many copious letters to Carr all articulated the same foundational hope: that his sister's fatherless son would work hard to prepare for "your entrance on that public stage." Only diligent attention to education, Peter's concerned uncle counseled him, could "render you dear to your friends, and give you fame and promotion in your own country."[19]

It was not only the intensely cerebral Madison or his capaciously minded friend Jefferson who shared these convictions. Fathers throughout the South, really all of the Republic, instructed sons on the necessity of education and achievement. Founding schools and state universities further testified to the founders' faith in education to preserve their experiment in self-government. In American universities the generational sons of the founders could cultivate their talents and acquire skills to merit the respect of other men. Young men coming of age in the early national period needed to be, one typical father reasoned, "educated in America upon patriotic principles." "The wide "diffusion of education," proclaimed another, "gives the hope that we shall have able & worthy men for every department of government."[20]

Revolutionary era leaders celebrated the radical idea that, in their republic, ability and achievement should be the only factors separating white men. "In our new forms of government, no one," insisted eighteenth-century historian David Ramsay, "can command the suffrages of the people, unless by his superior merit and capacity." It mattered not whether a young man sought political office, a legal career, or a future in business. "Every thing," George Mason warned his son John, as he commenced a partnership in a commercial house, "depends upon Diligence, Frugality, and Prudence; for without these, the fairest Prospects will quickly dwindle into Nothing." Heirs of the founding generation so often heard this refrain that they learned to repeat it to one another. In 1826, for example, one of Thomas Jefferson's grandsons-in-law, Joseph Coolidge, wrote another, Nicholas Trist, echoing Jefferson's highest aspirations. "In this country," Coolidge declared, "far more than in another, education makes the man; almost all of our fine fellows—the bones and sinews of the commonwealth—are the founders of their own fortunes: and in a republican form of government it ever must be so."[21]

So, precisely what kind of sons did founding fathers imagine might preserve the Republic? First and foremost, young men needed to safeguard the principles of the Revolution for future generations. Nothing mattered more. As George Mason explained, "I have endeavour'd to impress upon the Minds of my Boys, from their earliest Years" a reverence for "the Cause of Liberty" and an unwavering dedication to "Republican & independent Principles." He was particularly proud that his favorite son, John, had imbibed "a Spirit of Enthusiasm" for exactly these values. The educational institutions the founding generation created mirrored those family values. The 1783 charter of Hampden-Sydney, which Patrick Henry helped write, set as a top priority to "preserve in the minds of students, that sacred love and attachment which they should ever bear to the principles of the present glorious revolution." The school's founders, intent on cultivating patriotism, went so far as to forbid the hiring of any professor "unless the uniform tenor of his conduct manifests to the world his sincere affection for the liberty and independence of the United States of America."[22]

Succeeding at cultivating a virtuous character worthy of republican leadership would have been hard enough for boys, but patriotism only ranked first on a long list of essential traits. The Revolution created new politicized obligations for young men without changing some of the old.

As had generations of gentry men, republican sons lived in a highly performative culture that required respectable men to conduct themselves according to codes of genteel behavior. Boys still needed to learn to "act the part" of gentlemen. Familial advice covered every topic from dress to table manners to physical comportment. Clothing mattered so much that when Thomas Jefferson's grandson, Jeff Randolph, visited him in Washington on his way to college, the president inspected the contents of the teenager's suitcase and took him shopping the very next day. Boys also needed to learn how to ride horses, go hunting, and entertain guests. The outward appearance of an ordered life was essential. "System in all things should be aimed at," George Washington urged Washy Custis. He recommended the boy rise early, eat all meals on an exact schedule, and always prioritize work over leisure: "The practice will produce a rich harvest forever thereafter; whether in public, or private Walks of Life." Any excessive emotion had to be curbed. "Whenever you feel a warmth of temper rising," Jefferson coached his grandson, "check it at once, and suppress it. . . . Nothing gives one person so great advantage over another, as to remain always cool and unruffled under all circumstances."[23]

If that weren't enough, the performance of a gentleman had to appear effortless. Adults offered nearly ceaseless advice about *acting naturally* confident. Boys were told the proper way to sit, stand, talk, eat, dance, smile, drink, and walk—and none of it should seem affected. Then, relatives and mentors added that all this gracious socializing should not bleed into pretentious showiness. Talking too much was as bad as shyness, overdressing as bad as sloppiness. Financial responsibility mattered not only for practical reasons, such as practicing judiciously running plantations and businesses, but also for social motivations. Profligate boys merited the same contempt as tightfisted ones.

So, young men needed to socialize confidently but not excessively, to spend generously but not lavishly, to dress genteelly but not foppishly, to be gregarious but restrained. And it needed to appear completely natural. And they needed to do it all very quickly.

Young men coming of age in the new nation, like their fathers and grandfathers before them, also needed to dedicate themselves to traditional planter-patriarch roles. Wealth and land still traveled through family lines and still shaped social status. Political transformations of the late eighteenth century did not change the demand that patriarchs ably manage their family estates and preserve assets to pass to the next generation. Elite sons knew that running plantations would occupy much of their adult lives, and success required a capacity for crop cultivation and, despite the egalitarian rhetoric of the Revolution, mastering slaves. Ensuring harmony in their households and their family's respectability within the broader community also fell to men of the rising generation. Capably heading a well-run, highly regarded, self-sufficient household remained crucial.

Taking in orphaned relatives or other kin in need was a long-standing custom among the southern gentry, and revolutionary rhetoric about individualism and independence did not weaken that tradition of fluid households. Young men were still expected to take responsibility for their relatives, sometimes even before they had children of their own. For example, after Thomas Jefferson's daughter Maria Jefferson Eppes died, leaving only one son, Francis, her husband remarried and started a second family. John Eppes told Francis that it would be his duty to supervise his young half-siblings. "To you," John wrote Francis, "I look as the friend protector and guardian" of the children he himself might not live long enough to launch. Should those younger children be "deprived of the advantages of my assistance long before they can arrive at an age to take care of themselves," John expected Francis to parent them in his stead. When George Washington's brother Charles died in 1799, George wrote his nephew Samuel, expressing the same expectations. "By this event," Washington explained, "you have become the Guardian of your mother; and as it were, the father, of your fathers family."[24] And, relatives made clear, men who failed to meet such obligations should expect to lose respectability.

Last, and most important, young men needed to become, both as patriarchs and as patriots, independent. Independence had long been the foundation of Virginia planter culture, it became the cornerstone of the Revolution, and it remained the most desired masculine trait. Planter families fairly obsessed over manly autonomy in the colonial era, and it had long shaped their child rearing.

Domination of slaves remained inseparable from white Virginians' independence, both before and after the break with Great Britain. "The whole commerce between master and slave," remarked Jefferson, "is . . . the most unremitting despotism on the one part, and degrading submissions on the other." And that part of independence was learned early: "Our children see this," Jefferson continued, "and learn to imitate it."[25] Because even as their disdain for the institution of slavery grew, Virginians' reliance on it for wealth and power persisted, that command experience remained a vital lesson for boys to learn.

This long-standing gentry emphasis on masculine independence was intensified by the rhetoric of the Revolution and by economic downturns in early national Virginia. The tobacco culture that had long brought wealth and leisure to colonial patriarchs eroded in the Revolutionary War and never fully rebounded. The Virginia economy, no less so than the political ideals of the revolutionary age, taught boys that it would take hard work and personal initiative to succeed in the American Republic—even for boys enjoying substantial inheritances. As one Virginia law student succinctly put it, "My happiness depends on my own exertions."[26] For some young men independence would manifest itself principally in running a plantation and slave mastery. Others undertook careers in the law or medicine. Some families defined success in economic terms, others by political power, and they coached sons accordingly. But whatever primary career a man pursued (from the short list of respectable vocations), he needed to exercise political virtue whether as a representative or simply as a voter. And he absolutely had to be self-sufficient and self-governed.

The result of this veneration of independence in Virginia, long tethered to racial slavery and thrown into high relief by the Revolution and postwar economy, meant that white men could not be compelled to act—or else they were not really men at all. Despite the overwhelmingly high stakes attached to young Virginians learning to exercise virtue, merit respect, and lead a life of distinction and service, men had to *choose to submit* to societal expectations of republican manhood. Each boy had to decide on his own whether, as George Washington had told his nephew, to "quit the trifling amusements of a boy, and assume the more dignified manners of a man."[27]

It was a difficult needle to thread. Autonomy and submission proved every bit as challenging a balancing act at home as liberty and power did in the civic square. And the specific methods the founding generation relied on to train their heirs, which centered on their zeal for independence, did not make things any easier.

The Revolution both dovetailed with and deepened child rearing changes already unfolding over the course of the eighteenth century. Just as they had borrowed from John Locke's political theories, early Americans embraced his ideas about childhood. Leading Virginia families adopted Locke's premise that children represented a "tabula rasa." Character, he argued and they believed, was not inherent but formed by experiences in childhood, and therefore malleable. If they were purposeful in their parenting, adults could imprint upon children the values they prized. By mid-century, British Americans increasingly sought to inculcate from early childhood the character they wanted sons to exhibit. In the plantation South, that meant being self-willed and self-reliant. These values fit perfectly with Virginia's planter culture.[28]

Parents wanted vigorous, vivacious children. Both Patrick Henry and Thomas Jefferson delighted in leading childhood games aimed at instilling competition and hardiness. Jefferson often challenged his Randolph grandchildren to race one another around the property at Monticello. Blending competition with affection, he awarded each child who crossed the finish line with hugs and kisses. Henry's children were "as wild as young colts," and visitors to his home sometimes found him "lying on the floor with a group of these little ones climbing over him in every direction, or dancing around him with obstreperous mirth to the tune of his violin."[29] Such playful scenes were part of the very serious business of raising children.

Environments were carefully tended to plant the right seeds for elite children's futures. Graceful, learned conversation required early lessons in reading; parental writings were filled with suggestions of books and essays. Penmanship would reveal a person's character to strangers, so practice, practice, practice was the order of the age. Adults bought horses and saddles and musical instruments and they paid for dancing lessons and the latest fashions to set their youngsters on the right path toward refinement. They watched to see what individual interests children showcased and then nurtured their particular talents. Fathers mustered resources—money and contacts—to help sons reach their fullest potential. In sum, a tremendous amount of energy and money went into filling out the "tabula rasa."

The Revolution intensified those patterns in child rearing, especially for the sons of the founding generation. Locke had urged parents to balance indulgence (to win the favor of children and inspire their fidelity) and discipline (mostly effected by shame and emotional distancing). But republican fathers eager to raise worthy heirs of the Revolution grew increasingly loath to compel filial obedience through traditional means, such as public shame and threats of disinheritance. Physical discipline was certainly spurned; slaves, not future masters, got whipped. Virginia's founders did not want passive children, and certainly not docile, quailing sons. Boys needed to practice the autonomy essential to the life of a successful planter and republican leader.

Money management provides an especially revealing look at the ethics and tactics of raising sons in the new nation. It was vital that men manage finances judiciously and respectably, and not simply because of the bottom line. Excessive frugality scarred reputations as much as extravagance. Unwise investments not only undercut family assets but also imperiled social standing. Political power and social reputation, to say nothing of the day-to-day well-being of relatives, thus rested on a foundation of financial proficiency. Finally, the viability of the American Republic required economic independence of citizens and fiscal integrity in government. (Among the most compelling of arguments in favor of revising the Articles of Confederation were the myriad fiscal failures confronting the Republic. Unable to cover its debts, the Confederation Congress risked internal insurrections and foreign invasion.) Men, then, needed to teach boys to exercise financial autonomy without compromising the greater good. But how could adults train teenagers to submit to stewardship without compromising their independence?

On first blush, the approach adults took in teaching boys about money seems indulgent if not downright misguided. "If you want any thing let me know," wrote Francis Eppes's father, "nothing will give me so much pleasure as to furnish all your wants." In return he asked only that Francis, who was at boarding school, attend to his studies and remain "good humoured and cheerful." Although he was typically scrupulous about his finances, George Mason evidenced a similar attitude toward his son when he was studying abroad: "As to the Money you have spent in Europe, provided . . . it has not been spent in Extravagance, Dissipation, or idle Parade, I don't regard it." When he elaborated on his motivations, Mason captured the family values of Virginia's planter elite: "All my views are center'd in the Happiness & well-fare of my children; you will therefore find from me every Indulgence which you have a right to expect from an affectionate Parent."[30]

It was not at all uncommon for families to send teenagers off to boarding school or college with sole management of their finances, including the money allotted for the entire term or even year. Some men supervising adolescent kin required accountings of expenditures, but others simply offered the general counsel to refrain from "extravagance"— which did *not* preclude hiring servants, buying fashionable clothes, treating friends at social gatherings, and enjoying vacations. Usually adults did send stern warnings against gambling, but that approach did not appear to work very well. Gambling was a rampant addiction among college-age boys with ready money and slim oversight.

What in retrospect seems like a recipe for recklessness was, in the minds of adults, a chance to test a boy's ability to balance financial freedom against fiscal restraint or, to adopt the language of that age, liberty and power. Too much oversight would have crippled the ability of boys to practice their financial skills and compromised their autonomy. Better to watch and see what individual choices young men made about this small part of their family assets. Errant behavior could be criticized and, it was hoped, contained. The greater fear was not that students would spend too much money but that they would fail to learn the larger lesson: worthy men *chose* to act responsibly. Strict oversight compromised more than a few hundred misspent dollars.

The same attitude prevailed in academic matters. Thomas Jefferson helped his son-in-law Thomas Mann Randolph manage Jeff Randolph's education, in hopes of enabling the boy "to be happier and more useful to yourself, to be beloved by your friends, and respected and honored by your country." When Jeff asked about changing his studies, his grandfather replied that he and Jeff's father decided "to leave the matter to yourself rather than hazard a decision on our imperfect information."[31] That duplicated Jefferson's copious letters to Peter Carr: he always pitched his elaborate plans as "advice" that he hoped, but did not demand, Carr would use.

This mindset lay behind the student culture that Thomas Jefferson imagined for the University of Virginia. "We studiously avoid too much government," Jefferson proudly explained about his university. "We treat them as men and gentlemen, under the guidance mainly of their own discretion."[32] He expected the students, knowing the stakes of youth and the weight of their duty to the future of the Republic, to set themselves on a path toward academic excellence and personal integrity. Some were studying law, others planning a future in medicine or running family plantations. It mattered not what specific career a young man chose, the basic requirement remained unchanged: each would need to—and given the right environment would resolve to—prove his capacity. Or at least that was the design.

Generous allowances with little oversight given to students far from home and raised to be self-willed worked out in the late eighteenth century just as we would imagine in the twenty-first. Three months after Jefferson boasted about leaving college students to "their own discretion," the Charlottesville campus erupted in a riot.[33] It was sometimes no better in the founders' families, where, unfortunately, the initiative several boys took undermined rather than advanced their fathers' grand plans. Washy Custis offers a notable case in point. David Stuart, a prominent physician, married Washy's widowed mother, Eleanor Calvert Custis, in 1783. Though Washy did not live with his mother and stepfather, remaining instead at Mount Vernon, David and Eleanor Stuart often talked with George and Martha Washington about the boy, particularly his education and character. Washy's chronic inattention to study during his teen years greatly distressed his relatives. In response to their unease, Washy flaunted his academic laziness. "In conversation with his mother," Stuart explained to Washington, "respecting his seriousness, he declared, he had no cause for it, and that his mind was perfectly easy." After numerous failed attempts to coax Washy to act better, Stuart let his exasperation show: "His habits and inclinations are so averse to all labour and patient investigation, that I must freely declare it as my opinion that not much is to be expected from any plan."[34]

In retrospect, often absentee, always permissive fathers hoping that headstrong boys would choose dutifulness over self-indulgence seems improbable if not downright foolish—but no more so than imagining that citizens would set aside their own interests and reason together to achieve the common good. The founders' family values, like their political philosophy, were certainly idealistic. But they also served an important, practical purpose: revolutionary leaders saw the choices that young men made as important tests for discerning character.

Even youthful failures, though certainly never welcome, could be instructive of the larger aims of Virginia gentlemen. As Patrick Henry explained, "Adversity toughens manhood, and the characteristic of the good or the great man, is not that he has been exempted from the evils of life, but that he has surmounted them."[35]

T he main leverage that Virginians in this era used to prompt boys to choose to be good and great men was fear of loss: of liberty, of power, and, above all, of love. Men tried to teach their young relatives that families, mirroring a republic, had become centers of reciprocal duties and conditional ties: in the public square only citizens who advanced the greater good deserved to hold power, and in families affection had to be earned through proper conduct. Adults raised boys to understand that they needed to prove themselves worthy of sustained love, just as they would be required to demonstrate their capability for political leadership. Families sacrificed to provide for young children, and relatives did all they could to guide boys toward a character that made them worthy of love as a father and respect as a patriot. They expected children to honor those sacrifices and reciprocate by leading a dutiful and distinguished life.

Training in conditional love commenced during childhood. Though he was extremely affectionate with his grandchildren, Thomas Jefferson told them, beginning when they were very young, that his devotion depended on their conduct: "The more I perceive that you are all advancing in your learning and improving in good dispositions the more I shall love you." In the same vein, James Madison praised his eleven-year-old nephew, Richard D. Cutts, as a "good boy" for attending to his studies, and he urged Richard to "go on . . . as you have begun," so that he could "add to the happiness of your parents, and of all who love you and are anxious to see you deserving to be loved."[36]

Elite boys who took advantage of family-created opportunities, who followed advice about earning love and respect, could, they were promised, secure a place of prominence in the Republic. On the other hand, fathers and mentors warned, harsh consequences awaited young men who disappointed their relatives' and their country's expectations. Those who failed to prove their merit would "sink into obscurity & even wretchedness from squandering the precious period between sixteen and twenty one."[37]

George Washington told his nephew George Steptoe that if he persisted in his bad behavior, "You may depend upon losing that place which you now have in my affections—and any future hopes you may have from me." And he was equally firm with Washy Custis. Washington admitted that "from his infancy, I have discovered an almost unconquerable disposition to indolence in every thing that did not tend to his amusements." Throughout Washy's childhood, George had "exhorted him in the most parental and friendly manner, often, to devote his time to more useful pursuits." He had begged the boy to do better, but nothing he said seemed to move Washy. His patience with the teenager nearly exhausted, Washington decided it was time to "let him understand what will be the consequences of his opposition to the will of his friends."[38]

But when sharp words failed to motivate boys, families not yet ready to wash their hands of wayward sons found themselves fairly impotent. David Stuart could do little more than commiserate with George Washington about their shared failure to inspire the teenaged Washy Custis to drop his lackadaisical attitude. When Stuart attempted, yet again, to remind Custis about the importance of attending to his studies, he was met with derision: "He observed with much coldness, that it would be all useless, as he should forget it immediately." Stuart's reaction was telling: "Being much hurt at it, I dropped the conversation."[39]

Even as they insisted on judging each boy's worthiness based on his conduct, members of elite families still did whatever they could to advantage their sons. Independence did not require abandonment, after all. Adults had a duty to smooth the way for responsible children, and leading Virginians undertook this with great diligence and dedication. "Altho we cannot expect that none of our posterity are to become the victims of imprudence or misfortune," Thomas Jefferson explained to his daughter Martha Jefferson Randolph, "yet we cannot but be particularly anxious to ward off the evil from those . . . who have been brought up in our bosoms."[40] Meticulously managed childhoods and endless advices to collegians was only the start. Powerful men held out to young relatives who heeded their counsel promises of loans, jobs, social ties, introductions to influential politicians, appointments in government, and business partnerships. But such connections were increasingly predicated on their judgment about individual merit: the proven ability of particular young men to balance liberty and power in their own lives.

Neddy Henry affords a good example of how parents and mentors balanced independence and responsibility, pressing young men on the necessity of self-determination while using all their wealth and connections to promote boys' status. Patrick Henry wanted to see his son "independent by his own industry," and he knew that "I must turn him loose to shift for himself." But, Henry quickly added, he would do so only "after giving him a plantation and some negroes at Leatherwood this fall." And he asked friends to watch out for the young man. So, Neddy Henry was to become a self-made man, but with bequests of land and slaves and the aid of his father's well-connected friends.[41]

Neddy Henry was hardly alone. Virginians used their extended family and political networks to promote promising young kinsmen after the Revolution as they had done before. When Thomas Jefferson left Virginia for Paris, he committed Peter Carr to James Madison's care. Because of the death of his boyhood friend and brother-in-law Dabney Carr, Jefferson saw himself as the father figure for Peter. Jefferson trusted Madison to help him with this "tender legacy." Madison dutifully kept Jefferson abreast of Carr's progress and placed him under the guidance of another of their friends, George Wythe, at William and Mary. As George Mason prepared to send his son George to Europe, he also drew on a wide and illustrious network of friends to watch out for him. Mason asked George Washington to write the Marquis de Lafayette and Benjamin Franklin, which he did. And Richard Henry Lee contacted Arthur Lee and John Adams on young George's behalf.[42]

The difference after the 1770s was that merit rather than lineage became the deciding factor in who got to remain in such circles. Not even the heirs of George Washington or Thomas Jefferson could depend on their lineage to secure their place in the American Republic. In fact, while they worked to advance worthy protégés, members of the founding generation balked at the idea of reflexive nepotism. When Washington's nephews George Steptoe and Lawrence Augustine Washington boarded with Samuel Hanson while ostensibly studying at an Alexandria academy, it was not long before Hanson complained to Washington that "your Kinsmen arrogate to themselves no Small degree of Self-Estimation from those high & distinguished Offices to which you have been appointed." Hanson assured Washington that he tried mightily "to discourage any pretensions arising in them" from anything other than their own achievements, "but not," he wryly conceded, "with entire effect."[43] Hanson and Washington agreed: being descended from a Virginia founder was supposed to provide republican sons with *inspiration* to, not a *substitution* for, personal achievement. The Washington brothers needed to make their own names rather than dropping their uncle's.

Leading men also sought to give more young men—their generational rather than biological heirs—a chance to compete. To that end Virginia's founders undertook innovations in family law and educational institutions. For instance, they abolished primogeniture and entail—vestiges of the old organic, patriarchal colonial order. Jefferson, Madison, and Mason were all firstborn sons. Their rejection of primogeniture stemmed not from personal advantage but rather from principle.[44] The founders also set about creating schools specifically designed to train the next generation of republican leaders, not just their kin. Hampden-Sydney College and the University of Virginia are only the most renowned of such efforts. Boarding schools, public primary schools, and even women's academies proliferated in the wake of the Revolution as Americans sought to have children properly educated for the good of the Republic. Imagined as crucibles of republican values, educational institutions offered up-and-coming young men the chance to cultivate their talents and to decide, according to their abilities and efforts, what kind of world they would make for themselves. If Washy Custis, George Steptoe Washington, and the stepsons of St. George Tucker did not intend to follow the examples of Benjamin Franklin and George Washington, perhaps the talented son of a farmer or carpenter would.

George Washington continued to embrace in peacetime the ethics behind the voluntary, selected "family" he had begun in the Revolutionary War. When Washington's ne'er-do-well nephew Fielding Lewis Jr. asked him for money, Washington tersely refused. He informed Fielding, whose father had condemned him for squandering his wife's estate, that if he would behave in an industrious and responsible way he could secure credit on his own. Conversely, Washington effusively praised George Washington Lafayette, the son of his military "son," for being a model young man: "His conduct, since he first set his feet on American ground, has been exemplary in every point of view—such as has gained him the esteem, affection & confidence of all who have had the pleasure of his acquaintance."[45] And Washington was not unique in this regard. Throughout the great houses of Virginia and, more generally, the early United States, favored relatives and protégés were chosen, not simply born.

The conditionality of love and respect in early national families cut both ways. Accomplished, grateful boys repaid their benevolent relatives with love that they, too, earned. "You have been to me ever, an affectionate and tender Father," Francis Eppes told his Grandfather Jefferson, "and you shall find me ever, a loving, and devoted son."[46]

But not every father or father figure held up his end of the bargain. The high-minded, sometimes contradictory child rearing ideals of the late eighteenth-century South would have been hard enough to live up to had men devoted themselves wholeheartedly to the enterprise. But the most accomplished patriot leaders did not always prioritize family life. Ambition and duty kept calling them back to civic service and away from their family responsibilities.

For founders who were fathers, time was often a zero-sum game: the greater the national glory, the less time for domestic matters. For example, James Madison wanted to do right by his stepson Payne Todd. He took the thirteen-year-old with him to Washington, DC, in the fall of 1805 and promised Dolley he would "endeavor to keep him . . . in the path of the Student." But James's many duties as secretary of state took precedence. He admitted "the close employment on my time, at this juncture leaves much to his own disposition." Washy Custis's own daughter, Mary Anna Randolph Custis Lee, freely admitted that her father never reached his full potential. His grandparents were held to account in an otherwise celebratory book that Lee published in the Civil War era. Martha Washington had "always spoiled" Washy Custis, and George Washington's "public duties . . . prevented the exercise of his influence in forming the character of the boy."[47] But then again, even diligent fathers did not want to control their sons; doing so ran counter to the qualities they most wanted to cultivate in boys. And even the most attentive of adults sometimes found their high hopes and idealistic plans no match for the bruising reality of adolescent boyhood.

Virginia's founders discovered in the Continental Congress and the state legislature, during the brief Confederation era, in the tumultuous ratification debates, and under the early federal government that putting theory into practice made for a grueling ordeal. And the exact same problems were born out in their efforts to raise republican sons.

What the Virginians knew about the fragile nature of republics and what they witnessed within the rising generation left them deeply fearful about the future of the Revolution. As they left the stage of public service and contemplated who might take their place, anxiety ran high. Near the end of his life Patrick Henry saw plummeting virtue and morality among the country's youth, a perception he shared with Archibald Blair, who wrote him in January 1799: "Unhappily for America, our youths have imbibed the poison [of self-interest], and having been born to liberty without knowing how they came by it, they are as prodigal in their politics as those young men generally are of their property, who were born to fortunes." Thomas Jefferson was usually more sanguine than most men of his generation, but even he held those doubts. "Our post-revolutionary youth," he sarcastically told John Adams in 1814, "are born under happier stars than you and I were. They acquire all learning in their mother's womb, and bring it into the world ready-made." He derisively continued: "Information of books is no longer necessary; and all knowledge which is not innate is in contempt, or neglect at least."[48]

This cohort had just cause to worry. To see examples of self-determination devolving into self-indulgence, of the destructive end to unchecked liberty or unbridled power, they needed to look only around their households.

Seldom does a name so aptly fit a person's character as Payne Todd. Payne was Dolley Payne Todd Madison's only child. She lost her first husband, John Todd, and their other son, William Temple Todd, on the same day, both victims of yellow fever raging through Philadelphia in 1793. Devastated with grief over the loss of the family she had just started to build, Dolley clung to Payne. Once when Payne fell ill, she confided to her sister that "my prospects rise & fall to sadness as this precious Child recovers or declines!"[49] When it came to Payne, Dolley was always hoping and always disappointed. A willful, spoiled child, he became a manipulative youth and a drunken, gambling-addicted, narcissistic man—the exact antithesis of his stepfather, James Madison. Todd ran through money at a staggering rate: Madison paid over $40,000 of his stepson's gambling debts, and even that was not enough to keep Payne out of debtor's prison. In his youth he was either expelled from or summarily quit every school he attended. Madison, who was named secretary of state in 1801 when Todd was nine years old, had neither the inclination nor the time to make him behave. Madison spent the next sixteen years, while his stepson came of age, at the seat of national power, first as secretary of state and then as president. During Madison's two administrations, Payne was supposed to be assuming responsibility for honing his talents. Often left to his own devices, he took the low road every time. As he aged, Payne Todd chased pipe dreams of fast wealth despite his anguished mother's endless appeals and his supremely reasonable stepfather's ever-steady counsel. And he disappeared for long periods, resurfacing to play on Dolley Madison's emotions just long enough to finagle more money. After she learned that he had landed in debtor's prison, Dolley confessed to one of her favorite nieces, "Every feeling of my soul is wounded." When James Madison paid Payne Todd's later debts, he did so more to save Dolley from further heartache than from any hope that Payne would change his ways. In time, James quit telling Dolley about the expenditures; if Payne wouldn't think of his mother's feelings, James could.[50]

Todd was so incorrigible that Madison appears to have lost all hope for and interest in him. He quit even mentioning him in letters. Certainly James and Dolley might have culled upsetting letters about the young man; the Madisons spent much of James's retirement compiling his papers for publication, and Dolley continued the project in earnest after his death. But editing embarrassing family incidents from their papers—which was not uncommon—can explain only so much. Casual greetings from correspondents routinely mentioned the nieces, nephews, and protégés who resided with the Madisons. Friends often passed along well wishes to those young folks in their letters to James and Dolley. But there was scarcely a word about Payne, who had become, by his twenties, a notorious disgrace. Dolley never fully reconciled herself to that fact. At the close of her life, she was still paying his debts, still begging him to visit her, still being humiliated by his escapades. Though she never cut ties with Payne, both she and James turned their attention to the worthy young men who sought out James's mentorship. It was those young men Dolley cultivated and James appointed to important offices, not Payne Todd.

Thomas (Tom) Mason hardly matched Payne Todd's dissipation, but he too disappointed his famous father. Although Tom told George Mason that he wanted to pursue a career as a merchant like his brother John, his actions in the early 1790s revealed little inclination toward the work necessary to learn about business and a great deal of self-indulgence. George saw in this son "a Fickleness of Disposition, & want of Steadiness" that, if Tom failed to correct, would "prove highly injurious to him." Tom, in stark contrast to his older brother John, spent too much money on all the wrong things, ignored advice, and refused to write regularly—all of which were grievous to a father eager to see the young man improve himself. Faced with this disappointing son, George Mason turned to a favored one for advice. "Your Knowledge & Experience in mercantile Affairs," he explained to John, "enables you to judge better than I can, what will be the most advantageous Prospects" for his younger brother. Tom had an ideal model in his brother John and his father's complete support. But nothing they tried would work, George knew, without Tom's commitment to self-improvement: he would have to *choose* to take the right course. George Mason did not live long enough to see how Tom turned out. In his last correspondence with John he remained troubled: Tom was still ignoring his advice and refusing even to respond to his letters.[51]

The difference between Tom Mason and his brother John came down to choices. Both received the same kind of education and guidance as children, each inherited large tracts of land from their father and had similar access to family and political connections, and both knew what was expected of them. But one brother learned to beautifully balance the expression of autonomy with respect for authority. In his judicious blending of personal liberty and societal duty, John Mason became all that his father's generation had hoped for. He started a successful mercantile firm and honed his skills until he became a respected international businessman. He was president of the Bank of Columbia between 1798 and 1816. Mindful of the need for public service, he became a justice of the peace in Washington, DC. He befriended and advised Presidents Jefferson, Madison, and Monroe.[52]

Bushrod Washington was equally distinguished, admirably carrying the Washington name into the early nineteenth century. Even Washy Custis, who as a teenager was disparaged by his frustrated grandfather as "moped & Stupid," eventually found his way to respectability. As a man he was called Washington Custis, or sometimes G. W. P. Custis, and he became a well-regarded writer, particularly of plays, served in the War of 1812, and ably managed his Custis and Washington inheritances.[53]

Francis Eppes and Jeff Randolph, Thomas Jefferson's two oldest grandsons, proved themselves thoroughly dedicated to perpetuating his values. Francis Eppes founded Florida State University on the model of the University of Virginia. Jeff Randolph became rector of the University of Virginia. Several of Jeff's younger brothers rather coincidentally grew into the specific names given them to honor their famous grandfather's friends. Benjamin Franklin Randolph became a doctor, George Wythe Randolph studied law and ran a thriving practice, and Meriwether Lewis Randolph found success on the western frontier.[54]

These men's lives bore out the advice of their fathers (and father figures), the founders. Each benefited enormously, of course, from family wealth and connections. And the accident of birth, as affluent white men, made it possible for them even to contemplate competing in the American meritocracy. But the most important difference between Bushrod Washington and Tom Mason, between Jeff Randolph and Payne Todd, was the choice each made regarding the circle about his world. Well-circumstanced young men who aspired to excellence and worked tirelessly to prove themselves worthy of respect and power earned it. Those who ignored their relatives' guidance, who never learned to balance their own ambitions against the needs of society, who refused to choose virtue over self-indulgence, did not, and, in the worst cases, fell into ignominy.

For descendants of the revolutionaries, growing up in the new nation was a relentless struggle for a perilous balance between clashing principles. It was an ordeal as well for fathers (both biological and fictive) trying to inspire dutifulness without compromising independence. Raising young men to reconcile liberty and power taxed the founding generation's talents and resolve, to say nothing of their pocketbooks. And the commonplace understanding of the precariousness of republican government upped the ante: both adults and young men knew that the future of the Republic rested on the character of the rising generation. But for all the angst, at least there seemed to be some logic and fairness to the matter: if liberty and power, personal ambition and the collective good, could somehow be balanced, then talented boys could prove themselves worthy men and the American Republic would endure.

That reasoning was predicated on the first self-evident truth in the Declaration of Independence: that all *men* were created equal. But what about the patriotic, talented, ambitious women in these families? What place could they take in what Thomas Jefferson called America's "natural aristocracy"?

CHAPTER 5

A "Natural Aristocracy"

Virginia's founders prided themselves on ushering in what they imagined was a fairer, more enlightened age. In their new American Republic a "natural aristocracy among men," based on talent and achievement, would supersede the old hereditary power structure that defined the colonial age.[1] Much of what made the Revolution radical was, in fact, this shift from lineage to merit as the ideal determinant of political power. Among men.

But American women, Thomas Jefferson proudly proclaimed, were "too wise to wrinkle their foreheads with politics." Happily for both their families and the Republic, "They are contented to soothe and calm the minds of their husbands returning ruffled from political debate. They have the good sense to value domestic happiness above all other."[2]

In the revolutionary age, family values transformed alongside political culture. Turning away from the organic worldview of the colonial age, adults in the early national era nurtured egalitarianism and individualism in their households no less than in government. They increasingly focused their attentions on developing the talents of individual children and training them to compete for rank and respect. Reciprocity became the centerpiece of relationships in families as it did in the public square. Love, like power, was conditional, and individually earned by the worthy rather than inherited.

But one thing remained the same: men outranked women by *nature*. It was simply a given that men alone would govern the American Republic. Full civic participation by females was largely unthinkable in the revolutionary era.[3] What, then, would be the proper place of women in the Republic? What would be expected and allowed of the girls raised by Virginia's leading families?

The life of Ellen Randolph, Thomas Jefferson's granddaughter, offers some answers. Ellen was born in 1796 and spent much of her youth at Monticello, where she grew up knowing that her behavior would determine her place in her family and Virginia society. When she was only five, the president of the United States explained to her, along with her eleven-year-old sister and nine-year-old brother, how to earn love: "The more I perceive that you are all advancing in your learning and improving in good dispositions the more I shall love you, and the more every body will love you." The way to obtain love, Jefferson explained, was "never to quarrel or be angry with any body and to tell a story. Do all the kind things you can to your companions, give them every thing rather than to yourself. Pity and help any thing you see in distress and learn your books and improve your minds."[4]

As the Randolph siblings cultivated those character traits and their individual talents, Ellen seemed of all the grandchildren the most naturally inclined to improve her mind. Martha Jefferson Randolph praised her as "wonderfully apt"—and this was not simply a mother's pride, for Martha also conceded that Ellen's two older siblings, Anne Cary and Jeff, "excite serious anxiety with regard to their intellect."[5] When Ellen visited Washington in the winter of 1805–1806, Margaret Bayard Smith, a leading society figure, pronounced the nine-year-old "without exception one of the finest and most intelligent children I have ever met with." At ten Ellen was studying Greek history, Latin, French, and mathematics and corresponding with her grandfather about topics as varied as the fine arts and natural history.[6]

Ellen clearly shared her grandfather's boundless intellectual curiosity. "I have often thought that the life of a student must be the most innocent and happy in the world," she said. To be highly educated, Ellen believed, was to be free and fulfilled: "The pursuit of knowledge unlike other pursuits is subject to no disappointments. It is a road where every step counts, where every advancement is secure, what you have acquired is beyond the risk of loss."[7] She learned this from her grandfather's example. He was endlessly curious about subjects as wide-ranging as botany, architecture, philosophy, and music. Eager to promote intellectual pursuits, he devoted a great deal of time during his retirement to planning the University of Virginia. Its founding ranked, alongside the Declaration of Independence and the disestablishment of religion in Virginia, as the source of Jefferson's greatest pride: those were the achievements he wanted commemorated on his tombstone.

But it was Jeff Randolph and Ellen's cousin Francis Eppes who received the education she craved. Ellen would have been a better steward of the academic opportunities given her brother and cousin, but the talents she shared in common with her grandfather were undercut by another, far more powerful legacy: the subordination of women. It was not possible for Ellen to study at her grandfather's university and there to make the most of her intellectual capacity. Ellen both accepted and resented this limitation. If she had been a man, Ellen said, she would have become a student of the larger world like her grandfather. "But being a woman," she recognized, "I must be content with peeping every now and then into a region too blissfull for my inhabitance."[8]

How women and men of the founding generation raised girls like Ellen Randolph reveals the powerful imprint of revolutionary principles on family life. The values idealized in civic life—egalitarianism, individualism, the conditionality of allegiances—shaped the coming-of-age experiences of girls no less than boys. Both sons and daughters learned the importance of sacrifice, the nuance of balancing individual desires against the greater good, and the imperative of self-motivated achievement. They understood that they would be judged and should judge others by accomplishments more than lineage.

But raising girls also demonstrated the limits of the Revolution—its egalitarian impulses proved no match for deep convictions about the proper place of females. Families raising children to cultivate their talents, exercise virtue, and earn esteem—in essence to model republican values—also made certain that girls, including the gifted and curious Ellen Randolph, understood that their *achievements* could never transcend their *nature*.

Patrick Henry

Thomas Sully, *Patrick Henry*, oil on canvas, 1851. Courtesy of
Virginia Historical Society (1851.1)

George Mason IV

Louis Mathieu Didier Guillaume, *George Mason*, oil on canvas, 19th c.

Courtesy of Virginia Historical Society (1858.2)

George Mason's Gunston Hall, formal dining room
Photograph by Hal Conroy (C. Harrison Conroy Co., Inc.)

James Madison's Montpelier
Photograph by Maggie Wilson, Courtesy of The Montpelier Foundation

The Washington family

Edward Savage, *The Washington Family*, oil on canvas, 1789–1796.
Andrew W. Mellon Collection (1940.1.2). Courtesy of the National Gallery of Art,
Washington, DC

The Declaration of Independence

John Trumbull, *Declaration of Independence*, oil on canvas, 1818.

Courtesy of Architect of the Capitol

Martha Jefferson, daughter of Thomas Jefferson

Joseph Boze, *Martha Jefferson Portrait Miniature*, watercolor on ivory, gilded copper case, 1789.
Photograph by Will Brown, Courtesy of the Diplomatic Reception Rooms, US Department of
State, Washington, DC

John Payne Todd, son of Dolley Madison

Attributed to Joseph Wood, *John Payne Todd*, watercolor on ivory, c. 1817. Courtesy of
The Metropolitan Museum of Art, Gift of Miss Mary Madison McGuire, 1936 (36.73)

Thomas Jefferson (Jeff) Randolph
Charles Willson Peale, *Thomas Jefferson Randolph*, oil on paper, 1808.
Courtesy of Thomas Jefferson Foundation, Inc.

Monticello in disrepair, c. 1870
Photograph of Monticello, no date, acc. no. 15428, Special Collections,
University of Virginia, Charlottesville

The foundational values that Virginia's founders and the women in their families tried to instill in daughters differed little from what they wanted in their sons. In part, the shared world of men and women derived from long-standing Virginia planter traditions. The men and women who occupied Virginia's great houses created in the colonial era a common gentry culture built on racial and class power. Their zeal for refinement led elites to work hard to comport themselves in a dignified manner, appear well-read, make sparkling conversation, play musical instruments, dress fashionably, and inhabit graciously appointed homes.[9] Much of that genteel lifestyle bore no gendered dimensions but rather fostered close connections among siblings, spouses, and kin. Thomas Jefferson grew up playing music with his favorite sister, Jane, for example. George Washington became a gentleman under the tutelage of his half-brother Lawrence and Lawrence's wife, Anne Fairfax. James Madison was only drawn out of his shell by the vivacious and enchanting Dolley. As each married, members of this cohort became partners with their wives in building genteel households: they dressed, entertained, and decorated to reflect their rank.

Girls and boys growing up on these refined estates in the early Republic learned to perform the same precise social rituals: dancing gracefully, meticulously grooming themselves, avoiding excessive displays of emotion, and especially socializing effortlessly. Parents wrote endlessly about social conduct, covering every topic from proper gestures to body weight. It hardly mattered whether they were raising boys or girls, as the counsel was usually indistinguishable. Letter writing affords an excellent case in point. An inviolable gentry family duty, correspondence gave absent parents a way to check youthful conduct. Parents scrutinized every part of a son's or daughter's letters starting with the contents. Did the young person write convincingly about books studied, music practiced, friends made? Did the child employ proper grammar? There were other, equally telling bits of evidence that attentive parents looked for in letters. Was the penmanship uniform and attractive? Did the writer choose a fine quality of paper and fill the page neatly?[10]

The shared world of boys and girls was not just about appearances, though; they learned to prize as well many of the same basic character traits. Though women usually took the lead in raising adolescent daughters, women and men worked as partners in teaching these foundational lessons. (More evidence remains for men, even in the guidance of young women, because more of their writings have been preserved.) As a nearly lifelong single father to his daughters (in the white family he acknowledged), Thomas Jefferson's vast correspondence offers especially revealing evidence of a founder's vision for worthy daughters. Much of his advice to Martha and her younger sister Polly (later known as Maria) could have easily been written to a boy—or, for that matter, by a mother for a son or a daughter. In fact, in many instances Jefferson repeated the counsel he offered his daughters to his grandsons and nephew Peter Carr.

It was essential, for example, that daughters no less than sons be industrious and exercise integrity. In the spring of 1787 Thomas explained to his older daughter Martha, "It is your future happiness which interests me, and nothing can contribute more to it (moral rectitude always excepted) than the contracting habits of industry and activity. Of all the cankers of human happiness none corrodes with so silent, yet so baneful an influence, as indolence." A few years before that he had told Peter Carr, "You are now old enough to know how very important to your future life will be the manner in which you employ your present time. I hope therefore you will never waste a moment of it."[11]

Jefferson, who avoided overt conflict whenever possible, also counseled both boys and girls in his family to follow his example: to be accommodating and coolheaded. He repeatedly urged Martha and Polly to be generous in spirit. This was precisely the advice he gave Jeff Randolph: "I have mentioned good humor as one of the preservatives of our peace and tranquility. It is among the most effectual," he believed, and "of first rate value."[12]

Martha Washington held up those standards to her granddaughters and nieces, and Dolley Madison expected the same from her young kinswomen. Madison was proud that her niece Madisonia was "dutiful & attentive" but worried that she seemed "unfortunately nervous" in company. Washington fretted that young Nelly Custis was easily distracted from studies—"a little wild creature"—not unlike her brother Washy.[13] The lessons Madison and Washington tried to teach girls differed little from what they expected from boys, though, as these examples indicate, children in these extended families could be awkward and defiant.

Adults also raised all children to be stalwart advocates of the American Republic. Patriotism was cherished among women as well as men, and both boys and girls learned that their conduct would be crucial to the future of the Republic.

As they did with boys, founding fathers and mothers taught daughters that youth was the only time to cultivate a proper character. President Washington warned his niece Harriot Washington about the "folly of misspending time" in her youth precisely as he had her erratic brothers George Steptoe and Lawrence. He pressed Harriot to develop a steady character, "industry and frugality . . . gentleness of manners," and "a well cultivated mind." Unfortunately, Harriot shared her brothers' careless disposition, which grieved her benefactor uncle. He cautioned her, as he did her brothers, about the "delicacy and danger of that period, to which you are now arrived . . . you are at this moment about to be stamped with that character which will adhere to you through life."[14]

As the Washington correspondence suggests, children of the Republic needed to be self-motivated, to focus on personal achievement, for hard work and conscientiousness would decide who rose and who fell. At the same time, they needed to dedicate themselves to service to the greater good. Using one's personal talents, polished to a high sheen by commitment to excellence, for the benefit of others would mark young people as deserving of esteem. The conditionality of status in the larger community and of love at home meant that young people could lose both if they made poor choices about how to conduct themselves. That was as true for girls as for boys.

Nor did parents discriminate based on gender when weighing whether adolescents measured up to their expectations. The founding generation continued to practice conditional love as they raised children. That long-standing family value got recast in the late eighteenth century, however, as the Revolution infused into households an increasing enthusiasm for youthful independence. As a result, whereas previous generations had compelled appropriate behavior with physical force, shame, and threats of disinheritance, now parents modeled, advised, negotiated, and beseeched. As George Washington did with his niece and nephews and Thomas Jefferson with his daughters, adults wanted children to *choose* the right path rather than be forced down it. If young people failed to heed their parents' counsel they could expect consequences. Still, the choice was theirs to make.

His conditional love for his daughters was a recurrent theme in Thomas Jefferson's many advisory letters to Martha and Polly. When their mother died in 1782, Martha was three weeks shy of her tenth birthday and Polly was just four. Thomas never remarried, but he nevertheless pursued an extraordinary political career after 1784 that took him from Monticello for months and years at a time. During those long separations, Jefferson wrote the sisters regularly, and he repeatedly reminded them that his favor depended on their behavior. In a typical letter—both for Jefferson and that generation of parents—he told Polly to focus on excelling in her studies and her character formation so that she might "grow daily more and more worthy of love." That counsel echoed the clear-cut letter he wrote eleven-year-old Martha, who attended boarding school while her father served in Congress in 1783: "The acquirements which I hope you will make under the tutors I have provided for you will render you more worthy of my love." In subsequent letters he was even more frank: "The more you learn the more I love you." He linked the conditionality of his love even to following mundane directions. For example, he told seven-year-old Polly "not to go out without your bonnet, because it will make you very ugly, and then we shall not love you so much." If, on the other hand, she chose to follow all his guidance, "we shall continue to love you as we do now."[15]

The Jefferson sisters learned that lesson well and lived it with their father. Martha and Thomas's exceptionally close relationship can be traced to events following her mother's death. For the rest of her life she proudly recalled that she seldom left his side that sad summer, even as he inconsolably wandered the estate. After she married and had children, she remained deeply attached to him. Martha attributed that bond to the time they spent together: "Separated in my infancy from every other friend, and accustomed to look up to you alone, every sentiment of tenderness my nature was susceptible of was for many years centered in you, and no connexion formed since" could ever match the one to him. It was, she avowed, "interwoven with my very existence."[16]

Polly, meanwhile, was separated from her father from the time of her mother's death until she was nine years old. Jefferson believed her too young to travel abroad and in need of a woman's guidance, so Polly moved in with her Aunt Elizabeth Eppes, and she came to think of Elizabeth as her mother. Then, in the summer of 1787, a father she did not know ripped her from that home. When she arrived in London en route to Paris, Abigail Adams greeted the child, whereupon she discovered that Polly did not recognize her father's face when shown a portrait. Not long after the family returned to Virginia from Paris, politics again called Thomas away, and his younger daughter moved back into the Eppes home. Jefferson told Polly, now called Maria, to be loving and dutiful to her Aunt and Uncle Eppes because, as he put it, "What would you do without them, and with such a vagrant for a father?"[17]

As an adolescent, Maria Jefferson was less eager to please her self-described "vagrant" father than her older sister, who received more of his time and attention. Reprimands and invidious comparisons appeared routinely in Thomas's letters to Maria but were conspicuously absent from most everything he wrote Martha. Eventually Maria's lackadaisical attitude toward correspondence became a running joke between Martha and Thomas, a further sign of Maria's outsider status. "Maria's brain is hard at work to squeeze out a letter," Thomas sarcastically told Martha in 1793. "She has been scribbling and rubbing out these three hours, and this moment exclaimed, 'I do not think I shall get a letter made out to-day.' We shall see how her labours will end."[18] So Maria did not always honor her father and he did not always prioritize her. The ever-faithful Martha only threw Maria's disappointment into bold relief, leaving her with a lifelong perception that she was less favored than her sister. Decades later, her niece Ellen Randolph Coolidge remembered that "my aunt sometimes mourned over the fear that her father *must* prefer her sister's society, and *could* not take the same pleasure in hers." Ellen also recalled that while her aunt was an especially attractive woman, far more so than Martha Jefferson Randolph, she discounted her beauty and wanted to be esteemed for her achievements. Ellen speculated that "the extraordinary value she attached to talent was mainly founded in her idea that by the possession of it she would become a more suitable companion for her father."[19]

The emphasis that Maria Jefferson placed on talent and on deserving her father's approval—and judging him, too—reflected the coming-of-age experiences of young men and women raised in Virginia's great houses after the Revolution. Gentry culture required them to become refined, good humored, and gracious. Relatives expected children to be both dutiful and self-determined, to prove they deserved love, and to judge others' worthiness by their conduct. Revolutionary values put a premium on cultivating virtuous character, individual talents, and an ambition to serve the common good. And none of it much varied according to gender.

What did differ, wildly, were the practical *outcomes* of these shared coming-of-age lessons. Whereas boys behaved respectably and responsibly in order to claim a place in the Republic, girls focused on readying themselves for domestic duties. The celebrated achievements of a Virginia daughter centered on family: marrying well, rearing virtuous sons and dutiful daughters, managing a complex household with aplomb, graciously entertaining guests, and tending to the needs of the kin group. This was, in their worldview, the natural order of things: the sons of founders grew up to be citizens, while their sisters became wives and mothers. And so it was that while a contemporary of Patrick Henry found his sister Jane "in my judgment, as eloquent as her brother," she never got the chance to put her talents to the same use as her famous brother. Jane Henry Meredith was praised for displaying her eloquence at social gatherings. The acquaintance had never, he continued, "met with a lady who equalled her in powers of conversation." Whereas Patrick's voice fills legislative halls, Jane's remained in the parlor.[20]

In an elegiac tribute to his deceased wife, George Mason captured what Virginians prized in female character and conduct. Ann Mason was, he maintained, "blessed with a clear and sound judgment, a gentle and benevolent heart, a sincere and an humble mind, with an even, calm and cheerful temper." Those qualities could just as easily have been praised in a man. It was what Ann Mason did with those traits that made her a model woman: "Her modest virtues shunned the public eye . . . content with the blessings of a private station, she placed all her happiness here, where only it is to be found, in her own family." George Mason praised his wife for fulfilling every desirable role of a woman: "An easy and agreeable companion, a kind neighbor, a steadfast friend, a humane mistress, a prudent and tender mother, a faithful, affectionate, and most obliging wife."[21]

This was not simply a set of expectations imposed on gentry women; it was, as well, how they imagined their best selves. In 1798 Martha Washington reconnected with her old friend Sally Fairfax, whose family had left Virginia in 1773. "The changes which have taken place in this country since you left it," Washington told Fairfax, "are, in one word, total." Between 1773 and 1798, Martha Washington witnessed the fitful move toward independence from Britain, the Revolutionary War from the front lines, and all the complex business of building republican governments. She was just home from eight years at the pinnacle of federal power. But that Revolution was not what Washington had in mind when she wrote Fairfax. In fact, she said nothing of politics past allowing as how, during her husband's presidency, she had tolerated living "at the seat of the general government, occupied in scenes more busied, tho not more happy than in the tranquil employment" of life at Mount Vernon. The entire letter recounted deaths of kin and neighbors, the children born to the children the women had known in their youth, and happy reports on Martha's grandchildren and great-grandchildren. She was a woman at peace, at home at last, and proud of her most important achievement: the "promising youth" of her family.[22]

Respectable girls raised in the homes of Virginia's founders, though taught many of the same foundational values as their brothers and cousins, learned to follow the examples set by honored women like Ann Mason and Martha Washington. Returning to Thomas Jefferson's desire that all of his grandchildren spurn conflict offers a powerful example of how gender-neutral character traits were put to strictly gendered purposes. In his grandson Jeff Randolph's case, Jefferson linked the young man's ability to get along with others to Jeff's anticipated future in government: "In stating prudential rules for our government in society, I must not omit the important one of never entering into dispute or argument with another. I never saw an instance of one of two disputants convincing the other by argument." For his daughters and granddaughters, however, amiability would be employed only at home or social functions.[23]

Self-motivation and diligence, taught equally to girls and boys, likewise produced very different results. Whereas Peter Carr, Francis Eppes, and Jeff Randolph needed to master *Euclid*, cultivate an aptitude for debating, and adopt an abiding devotion to civic service, Martha and Maria Jefferson had to learn a different skill set. "I shall insist on eating a pudding of your own making, as well as on trying other specimens of your skill," Thomas Jefferson wrote his younger daughter in the summer of 1790. The following month, he expanded his list of expectations. In addition to the pudding, he hoped "to see that you are improved in Spanish, in writing, in needle work, in good humor, and kind and generous dispositions." The next year he continued to encourage her to master a long list of female talents: "Go on then my dear Maria in your reading, in attention to your music, in learning to manage the kitchen, the dairy, the garden, and other appendages of the household, in suffering nothing to ruffle your temper or interrupt that good humor which it is so easy and so important to render habitual."[24]

Men's education was directly linked to the future of the American Republic, whereas women's intellectual development was imagined as an extension of their familial duties. The revolutionary generation wanted women to be educated enough to converse confidently and to raise young children for the betterment of the nation. Training the rising generation of children was, in fact, a central component of "republican motherhood"—a concept that was both rhetorical and cultural, that defined women's responsibility to the state and explained their exclusion from civic life. Good mothers in the new nation raised virtuous sons and dutiful daughters, and this included supervising their formal education during childhood. Thus there was a clear limit to how educated a woman needed to be—and in what subjects.[25]

When asked about his opinion on women's education, Thomas Jefferson explained that when it came to his daughters, "I thought it essential to give them a solid education, which might enable them—when become mothers—to educate their own daughters, and even to direct the course for sons, should their fathers be lost, or incapable, or inattentive." But, remarkably for a man who dedicated so much of his life in retirement to fostering a strong educational system for Virginia's (and America's) sons, Jefferson said that "a plan of female education has never been a subject of systematic contemplation with me. It has occupied my attention so far as only the education of my own daughters occasionally required."[26] The reasoning, in Jefferson's mind, was unassailable. The purpose of higher education, as he saw it, was "to form the statesmen, legislators, and judges, on whom public prosperity and individual happiness so much depend." Since females could not be leaders or even citizens in a republic, they had no place in a university. Enough education to be a good mother was enough education for a woman.[27]

The ultimate focus of Thomas Jefferson's plans for and advice to his daughters was domestic, as had been the case for his sisters and for prior generations of Virginia women. Reflecting the general attitudes of his era, he believed that by cultivating genteel qualities and mastering the skills of a homemaker Martha and Maria could reach their highest potential: as wives, mothers, and plantation mistresses. Since he could not teach these precise lessons directly, he turned to his sister-in-law Elizabeth Eppes—herself a model Virginia woman. She became the surrogate mother for Maria in particular, but also the trusted adviser to an anxious father struggling to guide two girls toward womanhood.

The ambition of turning his daughters into proper women helped pull Thomas Jefferson from his ambassadorship in Paris back to Virginia. The nuns at the Abbaye Royale de Panthemont did a stellar job of inculcating upright, ethical behavior. But the Jefferson girls needed to learn proper female skills that only their Virginia kinswomen could teach. In 1787 Thomas confided to Elizabeth Eppes his growing fear that France was exerting a dilatory effect on his daughters. Martha, being the older, concerned him more. "She will need," he wrote Eppes, "your instruction to render her useful in her own country." Usefulness had only a familial payoff: "Of domestic economy she can learn nothing here, yet she must learn it somewhere, as being of more solid value than any thing else."[28] Time was not on his side, either. Martha Jefferson was fast approaching the age to enter Virginia's marriage market and make the most important decision of her life, the end toward which all her training had been building.

Marrying wisely represented the pinnacle of womanhood in the early national era, just as it had in the colonial period. Preparing young women to attract a good marital prospect and, once courted, to possess the wisdom to choose the right kind of mate, lay at the heart of raising girls. George Washington's advice to his niece Harriot echoed what he wrote to her brothers in that it centered on her "progress thro' life." However, he imagined a profoundly different result of that "progress" for Harriot: she would acquire all the qualities necessary to "form a matrimonial connexion." Only by nurturing her mind and character while privileging "the domestic concerns of the family" could she ever hope for "a happy establishment for life"—by which he meant attract a desirable husband.[29]

Whereas they worried about their sons' future leadership of the Republic, adults dreaded a daughter's wrong move in marriage. "I have always considered Marriage," George Washington proclaimed, "as the most interesting event of ones life. The foundation of happiness or misery."[30] His was a most fortunate match: because of Martha he rose to the upper echelons of colonial Virginia society, and he consistently relied on her throughout his long career. But, as was so often the case, in the eyes of the founders the future seemed shaky. Thomas Jefferson knew it was essential that Martha pick a mate judiciously. But he saw little in the younger generation to inspire confidence, ruefully concluding, "The chance that in marriage she will draw a blockhead I calculate at fifteen to one."[31] On the other hand, an accomplished woman could bring out the best in a promising young man, which had political payoffs. Raising daughters to be conscientious republican wives would, indirectly, make men of the rising generation better stewards of the founders' political experiment.

For a host of reasons, then, there was a consensus in gentry circles about the significance of marriage: no decision in life mattered more, and all the more for women. Women did not have an independent legal identity in the early national era; the laws of coverture remained essentially intact in the wake of American independence, so that land, slaves, houses, personal property, and even children legally belonged to husbands. It was extraordinarily difficult to secure a divorce in the southern states, even after the disestablishment of the Anglican Church. In short, a wife was nearly wholly legally dependent on her husband for their entire marriage. As George Washington put it, "Once formed, agreeable or not, the die being cast, your fate is fixed."[32]

Because marriage fixed a bride's fate, young women needed to accept only those suitors who fit a very long and particular bill. A successful woman attracted a husband with enough wealth and refinement to claim gentry status, who was a virtuous, respected citizen, who would advance the interests of the larger family, and whose conduct predicted that he would be a devoted father. All the better if he was a relative and the marriage could merge family inheritances. And, if that weren't enough, love and happiness were also crucial.

To make the right choice required a woman to skillfully balance personal desire—the pursuit of happiness—against the collective good. To that end and reflecting the ethics of the age, they could be coached and cajoled, but not compelled. Parents resolved—within reason—to let daughters decide for themselves whom to marry, just as they expected sons to choose their own careers. Martha Washington, for example, told her beloved niece Fanny Bassett Washington that in selecting a husband, "You must be governed by your own judgment. . . . It is a matter more interesting to yourself than any other." Her husband agreed. "It has," he explained to a young kinsman, "ever been a maxim with me, through life, neither to promote, nor to prevent a matrimonial connection." But he immediately added an important qualifier: "unless there should be something, indispensably requiring interference in the latter"— meaning the prevention of an unwise match, for example, one that disrupted family harmony or finances.[33]

Elites never dictated whom a woman could marry, but they also did not leave courtship to the whim of youthful passion. If women wished to retain their relatives' favor, they needed to square their own preferences with the interests, including the financial aims, of the larger family. Just as the list of respectable professions gentlemen might pursue was short, so too were women's spousal choices limited. Money remained high on the list of gentry courting concerns. Martha Washington was quite happy with the matches her two eldest granddaughters made: Elizabeth married "a man of fortune," and Martha chose a husband "who is also very wealthy." Patrick Henry was pleased with the men his daughters Anne and Betsy married for the same reason: "The matches are agreeable to me, the gentlemen having good fortunes, and good characters."[34] As Washington and Henry indicated, the best matches continued the long-standing southern tradition of marrying for love *and* money.

Responsible daughters entering into courtships understood that love should not subvert family interests. As his granddaughter Nelly attended her first ball, George Washington gave her some advice about affairs of the heart. Love, he warned, was often depicted as "an involuntary passion." But this was not true, he assured her. "Love," he argued, "may and therefore ought to be under the guidance of reason." He urged Nelly to decide for herself to "love with moderation." Whenever she felt attracted to a suitor, Washington cautioned the teenager to consider the man's character, his fortune, his reputation, and how her relatives would view him.[35]

This balancing of personal desire and family duty ran through all the marital advice that Martha and George Washington offered to their young relatives. When, for example, Martha's niece Fanny Bassett Washington considered accepting the widower Tobias Lear's proposal, she sought her aunt and uncle's advice. Martha first urged her to rely on her own judgment—to be independent and self-determining. But she also listed Lear's many promising qualities, which perfectly matched what wise women sought in a mate. Lear was "esteemed by every one that is acquainted with him," industrious and accomplished, and "a man of strict honor and probity." And, Martha added, though George did not wish to "influence your judgment," he "has a very high opinion of and friendship for Mr. Lear." George was likewise skittish about advising his late stepson's young widow, Eleanor Calvert Custis, on a potential second marriage to David Stuart. But when pressed he listed the "many considerations" that made for "a prudent choice": the man's family connections, his wealth and character, his attentiveness to his prospective wife, and the perceptions of her relatives. The Washingtons clearly taught the same lessons about marriage to Nelly Custis, for her descriptions of her fiancé Lawrence Lewis fit this bill exactly: he was her grandfather's nephew, friends with her brother, highly regarded, able to care for Nelly's needs, and in love with her—in sum, "in every respect calculated to ensure my happiness."[36]

Like Nelly Custis, Martha and Maria Jefferson succeeded beautifully in following the script for a great marriage: they picked men who matched all that gentry society expected in a husband and perfectly balanced personal fulfillment against familial needs. Typical of the southern gentry, the sisters even chose their mates from a close circle. The link between Martha Jefferson and Thomas Mann Randolph Jr. derived from a long, distinctly Virginia history. William Randolph, grandfather of Thomas Mann Randolph Jr., was a founder of Albemarle County, along with Peter Jefferson, Martha Jefferson's grandfather. Peter and William were friends as well as relatives: Peter Jefferson married William's cousin Jane Randolph. When William Randolph died in 1745, his will named Peter Jefferson as a guardian for his son, Thomas Mann Randolph. Further in accordance with William's last wishes, the Jefferson family, including four-year-old Thomas, moved from their home to Tuckahoe, the Randolph estate, to look after William's land and his son. The blended family lived there for seven years, and young Thomas Jefferson began his education in the Tuckahoe schoolhouse, alongside Thomas Mann Randolph. More than half a century later, the two Thomases looked back with pride on the "knot of friendship between us, as old as ourselves." The occasion for their fond memories? The wedding of their eldest children, Martha Jefferson and Thomas Mann Randolph, Jr.[37]

Maria Jefferson's marriage was no less a family affair. She would have been hard pressed, in fact, to find a closer relative to wed without violating Virginia's conveniently narrow incest taboo. Maria Jefferson's maternal grandmother, Martha, had been an Eppes before she married John Wayles. Martha Eppes Wayles died shortly after delivering her daughter and namesake Martha (Maria's mother). When the widowed John Wayles remarried, he fathered three other daughters, one of whom, Elizabeth, grew up to marry Francis Eppes. Francis was Martha Wayles Jefferson's first cousin (but no blood relation to her half-sister Elizabeth). As Martha lay dying, her beloved half-sister (and cousin by marriage)

Elizabeth Eppes never left her side. And when Thomas Jefferson left Virginia shortly thereafter, it was Elizabeth and Francis Eppes who welcomed Maria (then called Polly) and her infant sister Lucy into their home. The Eppeses raised Polly alongside her cousins, including their son John. After her time in Paris, Maria Jefferson returned to live with the Eppeses. So close was the bond that she often referred to Elizabeth as her mother. What was felt became fact in 1797 when Maria married her first cousin, John Eppes, with whom she had grown up, making her surrogate mother her mother-in-law.

In both Martha and Maria's choices, at least three generations of family ties preceded the match. Thomas was thrilled that Maria had followed her sister's example. Capturing the family values of his generation, he praised John Eppes for possessing "every quality necessary to make you [Maria] happy and to make us all happy." Thomas delighted in his conviction that Maria's marriage to her cousin "has composed for us such a group of good sense, good humor, liberality, and prudent care of our affairs. . . . It promises us long years of domestic concord and love." He echoed this vision of family harmony in a letter to Martha: "I now see our fireside formed into a group, no one member of which has a fibre in their composition which can ever produce any jarring or jealousies among us. No irregular passions, no dangerous bias, which may render problematical the future fortunes and happiness of our descendants."[38]

Soon enough, the brothers-in-law John Eppes and Thomas Mann Randolph Jr. would be quarreling, the so-promising Randolph marriage would falter, Maria would be dead, and a newspaper would disclose Thomas Jefferson's second family. But for a brief moment, Jefferson could be treasure his "domestic concord and love," thanks to his daughters' matches.

Once married, respectable wives were expected to sacrifice for the happiness of their families, just as worthy men were obliged to forego their self-interest for the Republic. Both men and women shared their accomplishments and exercised virtue for the benefit of a larger community. Only the outcomes were different: men employed those traits for the success of government and women for their households.

Young wives needed to learn to subordinate their opinions and desires to those of their husbands. In one of the first letters Thomas Jefferson wrote Martha Jefferson Randolph after her wedding, he explained that "your new condition will call for abundance of little sacrifices. . . . The happiness of your life depends now on the continuing to please a single person. To this all other objects must be secondary." He repeated the warning in a letter to Maria. "Harmony in the married state is the very first object to be aimed at," he explained. "Nothing can preserve affections uninterrupted but a firm resolution never to differ in will."[39] The implicit message was that Maria, and not her husband, was responsible for ensuring their love by never disagreeing.

"You must learn to bear things with patience," Patrick Henry similarly counseled his daughter Betsy. "Experience will teach you that this world is not made for complete happiness." Bishop James Madison, cousin to James Madison of Montpelier, laid out the same strategy for his newlywed daughter. She should, he cautioned, studiously avoid ever opposing her husband. A disagreeable wife would not only lose an argument with her husband, "she loses every thing; she loses her husband's respect for her virtues, she loses his love and with that, all prospect of future happiness."[40]

Women's responsibility for ensuring domestic happiness started with their marriages and extended to in-laws, children, and kin—the larger family they served. The promise was that by subordinating their individual desires to the best interest of their relatives, starting with the head of household, women could ensure family happiness and their own, too. It was, in fact, their elders promised, the one key to personal fulfillment. As Thomas Jefferson counseled Martha Jefferson Randolph: "Be you, my dear, the link of love, union, and peace for the whole family. The world will give you the more credit for it, in proportion to the difficulty of the task, and your own happiness will be the greater as you perceive that you promote that of others."[41]

Martha Jefferson Randolph adopted that advice as the principal maxim of her life. And she turned out to be a particularly precocious student of the lessons of womanhood. After she and Thomas Mann

Randolph Jr. wed in 1790, she lived much of the time at Monticello; both her husband and her father were only intermittently residing there over the next twenty years as their careers carried them from home. Martha had prepared well for her job as an independent plantation mistress, and she excelled at managing the myriad of duties that fell to her. Ably running Monticello signaled to Martha Jefferson Randolph that she was a woman in her own right, a milestone she proudly shared with her father. Writing in 1791, the eighteen-year-old confidently informed him: "I have wrought an entire reformation of the rest of my household, nothing comes in or goes out without my knowledge and I believe there is as little wasted as possible." She supervised the kitchen, smokehouse, and gardens and kept a close accounting of household supplies. She also oversaw her younger sister's studies whenever Maria came to Monticello, which was no easy feat since Maria needed to "surmount her Laziness of which she has an astonishing degree." A self-assured woman, Martha proudly reported besting her sister's lackadaisical tendencies: Maria was working on grammar and would soon start playing the harpsichord.[42] Martha was doing all this while pregnant with her first child.

In the context of Virginia's plantation culture, Martha Jefferson Randolph was, at the tender age of eighteen, an extraordinarily accomplished woman: refined, married, pregnant, and smoothly supervising a complicated household at Monticello. She "kept the keys" in the vernacular of that age, which meant she held ultimate authority over household goods, including the supplies for the white residents and the slaves on the plantation. She was understandably proud of those achievements and of meriting her father's affection and trust. Her success had, as her father promised her, made Martha "more and more worthy of love." But happiness was another matter.

Ideally, wives and husbands carried out reciprocal responsibilities within a marriage. When men fulfilled their duties of leading their families, women repaid them with well-run households and respectable children. In exchange for domestic dutifulness and promoting family happiness, wives expected husbands to provide for the family financially and represent the family with integrity. By accommodating to their roles, wives earned their husband's love and husbands earned their wives' deference. *Ideally.*

In reality, women (and men) learned to endure the inevitable frustrations of married life, when mates failed to live up to expectations. But chronic and egregious violations of paternal duties could be another matter. Wives had the right to resist tyranny and corruption at home, just as their fathers and husbands could in the civic realm, though women often found it difficult to hold men to account because of the economic, social, and legal power husbands held over wives.

The two revolutionary daughters about whom we can know the most, Martha Jefferson Randolph and Nelly Custis Lewis, show what happened when founders' daughters confronted the difficulty of submitting to husbands who seemed undeserving of their sacrifices.

Nelly Custis carried down the aisle all the high hopes of any bride. She had followed her grandparents' advice about carefully choosing the right kind of husband. She met the widower Lawrence Lewis, nephew of her Grandfather Washington, when he came to live at Mount Vernon in 1797. They wed within a year, on George Washington's birthday. Nelly was well-educated, sophisticated, and sociable. Lawrence was twelve years older, serious-minded and responsible, a seemingly good balance to and provider for Nelly. She was certain that he would, she assured her best friend, faithfully "watch over my future happiness." She believed she would joyfully devote her whole life to him, which would guarantee happiness for both of them. The only source of happiness Nelly could contemplate beyond being Lawrence's wife was becoming a mother, which she imagined as "a source of delight" without parallel.[43]

It did not take long after her wedding for Nelly Custis Lewis to realize that meeting all the expectations of a good wife did not ensure a fulfilling marriage. On their honeymoon her new husband got sick—the first of countless such illnesses—and took to his bed for several weeks. His poor health did not affect his fertility. Over the next fourteen years, Nelly delivered eight children and buried four as infants. She had to give up horseback riding, music, and painting, she complained, for "pickling, preserving, & puddings." Nelly Custis Lewis also felt frustrated with Lawrence's modest ambitions and his retiring demeanor. In her writings he appears ordinary, even dull. Six years into her marriage, she confessed to her best friend that "I look back with sorrow, & to the future without hope." Motherhood, like marriage, hardly turned out to be the idyllic state she had imagined: "The anxiety and fears of a Mother, are beyond anything you can conceive." Nelly could neither cure her sick children nor avoid crippling dread that the recovered would relapse. "Happiness," she forlornly concluded, "is out of the question." After her last child, Angela, was born in 1813, Nelly moved out of her husband's bedroom. He remained a disappointment to her throughout their marriage.[44]

It was quite a comedown for the granddaughter of the "father of his country" to be mistress of her unambitious husband's moderately profitable plantation. Still, Nelly and Lawrence's troubles were hardly unusual or scandalous. Lawrence might have been a disappointing mate, but he was hardly a failed man. So they kept their problems to themselves, avoiding public embarrassment and putting on a facade of domestic success. The Lewises quietly lived apart for long periods, including the last four years of Lawrence's life.[45]

The expectation that women would put the needs of their families ahead of their own inclinations explains why Nelly Custis Lewis stood by her mate, even when her youthful dreams of happiness eluded her. She eventually moved in with her daughters under the pretense of caring for them and their young children—a respectable action for a devoted grandmother—but she remained Lawrence Lewis's wife until the day he died.

Martha Jefferson Randolph found married life to be no more rapturous than Nelly Custis Lewis. Both she and her husband, Thomas Mann Randolph Jr., held responsibility for their rocky relationship. Throughout her life, Martha routinely privileged her father's interests over all others, including her husband's—a fact she proudly proclaimed. Two months after her wedding, she parroted Thomas's advice about being a dutiful wife but with one catch: "I have made it my study to please him in every *thing* and do consider all other objects as secondary to that *except* my love for you." Motherhood did not weaken Martha's loyalty to her father, either. The mother of two young children in early 1793, she was devastated to learn of a delay in Thomas's trip to Monticello: she had hoped that with this return they were "never to separate again." The news of his staying away longer than they had planned was heartbreaking: "Having never in my life been more intent upon any thing I never bore a disappointment with so little patience."[46] Sometimes Randolph felt pulled between honoring her father's desires and submitting to her husband's will, a divided loyalty she first gave voice to when Thomas Mann Randolph Jr. decided where the newlyweds should live. He carried her to Richmond, a move that did not comport with Jefferson's plans. Martha clearly felt caught between her husband and father, bound to defer to both and loath to disappoint either. And she gave a hint that all was not blissful in her new marriage: "I am afraid you will be displeased in knowing where I am," she wrote Jefferson, "but I hope you will not, as Mr. Randolph certainly had some good reason, though I do not know it." The subtle reproach was a sign of things to come.[47]

For his part, Thomas Mann Randolph Jr. was never an easy man. Entitled and irascible from his youth, his mercurial temperament worsened as he aged. By midlife he was often erratic and sometimes irrational. The surviving sources do not clarify the exact nature of his problem, but he suffered from emotional or mental breakdowns in his later life, episodes exacerbated by heavy drinking. By the 1820s Randolph was ranting in the streets of Richmond. His instability coupled with a host of sketchy financial decisions made him an unreliable patriarch.

Martha Jefferson Randolph learned from her father and from the Revolution he helped lead that power was conditional. In the civic realm, this meant that only virtuous leaders should enjoy citizens' respect. What was true in the Republic was, theoretically, true at home. In reality, many disappointed wives lacked the power to hold their failing husbands to account. But Martha could and did. When she applied the standards of conditional love that she learned from her father to her husband, he came up short.

Martha, though raised to respect patriarchal authority, did not feel bound to defer to her irresponsible husband's poor choices. When Thomas's behavior grew increasingly volatile in the early nineteenth century, she stepped outside her prescribed role. Randolph revealed her rejection of her husband's authority in word and deed. For most of her marriage, including the nearly two decades of Jefferson's retirement, she chose to live with her father at Monticello. This certainly did little to bridge the widening rift between the couple. It is easy to empathize with Thomas Mann Randolph Jr., always in the shadow of his famous father-in-law, an outsider at Monticello and even in his family circle. His children, like their mother, idolized their grandfather; Jefferson doted on them, took charge of their education when their father squandered his estate, and showered them with affection and presents. During one of Thomas's breakdowns, Martha confided her exasperation to her father, while at the same time underscoring her capacity to manage their family in his stead: "The agonies of Mr. Randolph's mind seemed to call forth every energy of mine. I had to act in the double capacity of nurse to my children and comforter to their Father."[48] Later she proudly proclaimed her capabilities as both mother and father to her children.

The children took Martha Jefferson Randolph's side, and, as they witnessed their father's failures, they adopted the same disregard toward him. He did not act the part of a father, and they did not respect him as one. The Randolph children openly voiced their disappointment and even disdain for their father and with him the larger Randolph family. Traveling with one of her paternal aunts to Washington in late 1821, Ellen Randolph reported to her mother that her aunt "was out of spirits & of course a little out of humour, for you know that in the Randolph family there is no separating these states of mind." While in Washington, Ellen also criticized her father's financial mismanagement and paternal irresponsibility when he failed to follow through on a promise to send her money: "I very much wish Papa could be prevailed on to make some little exertion to relieve me." She considered writing directly to him but confessed to her mother, "I am so much afraid of his strange temper."[49]

The courtship of Virginia Randolph offers a telling commentary on the family dynamics. When Nicholas Trist wanted to marry Virginia, he wrote to Martha at Monticello to get her—and only secondarily her husband's—permission: "You may possibly have perceived that an attachment has existed, for some time, in my bosom, to your daughter Virginia. . . . Hoping that my sentiments may be agreeable to yourself and Mr. Randolph, I address you these lines to request the permission of making them known to miss Virginia." Martha responded without giving any indication that she had consulted her husband. She gently but firmly declined the offer because, she said, "You are both too young to be entangled by an engagement which will decide the happiness, or wretchedness of your lives." Revealingly, Virginia was the same age that Martha had been when she married. Apparently two decades as a wife had taught her a great deal about her own choices. She did not want the same for her daughter.[50]

After Thomas Jefferson's retirement, Thomas Mann Randolph Jr. came and went from Monticello, quarreling with nearly everyone there before moving away. He clashed bitterly, and at least once violently, with his son, Jeff Randolph; they became so estranged that they refused even to enter the same room. Randolph lost his family estate through a series of bad financial decisions and with it his right to vote in Virginia—a state he had once served as governor.

The paragon of female virtues, Martha Jefferson Randolph, prevailed over her husband in the hearts of her children and the eyes of her community. She, not he, earned their children's devotion and guided them toward respectability and self-determination. But for all her capacity, Martha remained wholly constrained from exercising those abilities in her father's republic.

The shared belief within the founding generation that women were fundamentally different from men and necessarily excluded from certain realms of authority was so deep-seated as to seem reflexive. All the experts of that age—theological, medical, and legal—agreed about the differentness of the sexes. The wives and sisters of the founders voiced no serious critique of their status, even when their own lives contradicted assumptions about what women could do. And that included such talented and experienced women as Martha Jefferson Randolph, Dolley Madison, and Martha Washington.

Sometimes, of course, female engagement in legal matters and family businesses could not be helped. Martha Custis, for example, ably managed Daniel Custis's accounts when he died. Martha Jefferson Randolph was her father's proxy at Monticello during his presidency. The Revolutionary War pushed many white women into traditionally male roles: running farms and family businesses as men left home to join the military. But in such cases those duties were temporary, perceived by both men and women as exceptions forced by family needs.

For the wives and daughters and sisters who provisionally managed plantations and businesses, family security was their paramount concern. They were "deputy husbands"—acting temporarily as surrogates to kinsmen in order to protect their families. Ideally, men and women fulfilled their familial duties in complementary roles: women at home and with kin and community, men in politics and business. Sometimes, though, women had to cross the lines into male roles, but not permanently. Martha Jefferson Randolph, despite all her talents and experience, could not become Thomas Jefferson's business manager when his health began to falter. Instead, he turned to his most trustworthy male relative: Martha's son, Jeff Randolph. And when Martha Custis married George Washington, without a pause she turned over Daniel Custis's accounts to him.[51]

The flexibility in family duties necessitated by death, political office holding, and military service never extended into the governmental realm, either. Widows and wives of soldiers did not vote or hold office in their husbands' stead. Rather, women's supposed nature, as less reasoned, less able than men, made female subordination particularly important when it came to government—the most public and masculine of realms.

While the Revolution inspired men to reconsider so much of their social order, none of the founders seriously contemplated the actual inclusion of women in republican government because their very *nature* precluded independence and civic virtue. Thomas Jefferson shared that perception although he was surrounded by extraordinarily capable women: his favorite sister Jane, his talented granddaughters, his unfailingly reliable sister-in-law Elizabeth Eppes, his illustrious friends Dolley Madison and Abigail Adams, and his ever-faithful daughter Martha. In fact, Jefferson ranked among the most contemptuous of women's political participation; neither his dependence on women nor his immersion in revolutionary activism changed his views about the immutable differences between men and women. For all his fondness of France, Jefferson left Paris with deep contempt for what he perceived to be the most disturbing misstep in the French Revolution: women "meddling" in politics. He invidiously compared the political engagement of women in revolutionary France with the auxiliary roles women played in America. French women, he groused, were constantly "hunting pleasure in the streets . . . and assemblies, and forgetting that they have left it behind them in their nurseries." "Compare them," he continued, "with our own countrywomen occupied in the tender and tranquil amusements of domestic life, and confess that it is a comparison of Amazons and Angels." In a 1788 letter to George Washington, he expressed his relief that the unseemly politicization of French women remained "an influence which, fortunately . . . does not endeavor to extend itself, in our country, beyond the domestic line."[52]

Martha Jefferson Randolph followed her father's lead. Though she "kept the keys" at Monticello and even took over leadership of her own family from her unreliable husband, she never challenged in any way her father's view on the proper "domestic line." The Monticello family was typical. Virginia elites—both women and men—routinely dismissed the very idea of women's political participation—that was, if they thought about it at all. Nelly Custis wrote her best friend a blistering critique of the French government in 1797 but prefaced her comments with an apology "for troubling you with a political opinion." In other letters the two women joked about becoming politicians or soldiers, clearly thinking the idea ludicrous. Once when Patrick Henry wrote his daughter Betsy about politics, he offered both an apology and an explanation: "Thus, my dear daughter, have I pestered you with a long letter on politics, which is a subject little interesting to you, except as it may involve my reputation." Since his reputation influenced hers, he made an exception in this particular case. Generally, though, he assumed that Betsy would play no part in government affairs and that politics held no interest for her. And while George Mason kept his son John abreast of all the latest political news during the ratification debates in Richmond, he relied on his daughters to share family events: "For domestic Occurrences, I refer you to your Sisters."[53]

It would be a mistake, however, to take this widespread attitude toward women in government as the last word on women's political roles in the early Republic. None of the architects of the American Revolution wanted their wives or sisters directly participating in representative government. But there was a great deal of civic life beyond electoral politics in that decidedly politicized age. As historian Catherine Allgor skillfully demonstrated, First Lady Dolley Madison presided over "a third sphere" between public and private, between domestic and governmental. Her involvement in informal politics is simply the best chronicled. Less well known were the important roles that Martha Washington and Abigail Adams filled during their husbands' administrations.[54]

Dolley Madison was, unlike her shy husband, ideally suited for social-political networking. She was outgoing, a great conversationalist, and able to put nearly everyone she met at ease. Her special skill at forging connections, including upwards of a dozen politically advantageous marriages, and her elegant yet easy social functions helped build in the capital a working political culture, which proved immensely beneficial to the introverted president. Or, as one friend put it, Madison "softened the asperity of party feelings, disarmed prejudice, consolidated general good will, and won a popularity for her husband which his cold and reserved manners never could have done."[55]

The centerpiece of Madison's networking took place on Wednesday nights. Her "drawing rooms" at the White House brought together Republicans and Federalists, up-and-coming congressmen and cabinet officers, men and women. Madison served drinks, ice cream, and cake but, most important, access to power. Guests made political alliances and personal friendships and forged mutual trust, an essential element of working government.

Madison also gave Americans a powerful symbol of their new country when she redesigned the White House interior. Her Wednesday gatherings took place in the elegant Drawing Room, decorated with red velvet curtains, blue-accented woodwork, and cream-colored wallpaper. Thirty-six chairs, bearing the insignia of the United States, struck the same patriotic note. A portrait of George Washington by Gilbert Stuart loomed large in the new State Dining Room, which Madison created. Under her direction the White House was transformed from a shabby hodgepodge of leftover furniture and vacant rooms into a gorgeous and gracious seat of power.

Importantly, Dolley Madison undertook her work with family as her paramount concern. She helped craft that political society in Washington as an outgrowth of her duties as a refined woman, at the center of a deep and wide kin network, guiding the young relatives and protégés that she and the president mentored. Her and James's success derived from her exceptional talents as an ideal woman: helpmate to her husband, devoted maternal figure, gracious hostess, and vigilant kin guardian.[56]

Martha Washington had followed a similar course. She was always the loving and beloved partner to her very accomplished husband. She accompanied George to winter encampments during the war and then to the federal city to launch the new national government. Relatives turned to her to mentor politically ambitious kinsmen "as a relation as well as . . . advisor." Martha was service-minded and patriotic, and she felt proud of the life she and George led on the national stage. But it is clear from her words and deeds that she always prioritized family. "I am greved at parting," she told her relatives when George accepted the presidency. And once he was in office she felt "more like a state prisoner than anything else."[57] She found no fault in George "obeying the voice of his country," but confided to her friend Mercy Otis Warren that she "placed all the prospects of my future worldly happiness in the still enjoyments of the fireside at Mount Vernon." The advantages to her husband's power, as Martha saw it, centered on family. For example, during his presidency it especially pleased her that their grandchildren had "good opportunities for acquiring a useful and accomplished education."[58] Like Dolley Madison, Martha Washington was an important figure in the early federal scene: she hosted balls and salons, made marital matches, and helped launch the careers of aspiring young politicians. For both women, that work often had important political payoffs, but Washington like Madison undertook it as part of her domestic responsibilities. Whenever she secured governmental and military appointments, she did so to help members of her complex, extended family.

Their significant achievements and renown on the national scene did not lead Martha Washington or Dolley Madison to fundamentally rethink their "proper" place. Indeed their successes confirmed their status as honorable women, looking out for the best interests of their families. Even when they were away from their homes for years at a time—a pattern afforded by their not having a houseful of young children—they identified as mothers and as mistresses of households. They performed their service to a nation, not just a community, but their actions represented an outgrowth of their gendered duties.

Nor did their female kin's accomplishments reshape the founders' views on gender. Like George Washington and James Madison, all of the members of this cohort had supremely capable women around them, and none could have achieved what they did without women's support. Their marriages brought them wealth and connections; as politics consumed more of their time, female deputy husbands managed estates in their absence; wives and daughters and sisters oversaw gracious households and thus class identity and respectability; leading women negotiated politically-advantageous marriages for younger kin and protégés. Whether it was Elizabeth Eppes raising Maria Jefferson while Thomas pursued his career or Dolley Madison shaping a political culture in Washington, DC, the founding fathers relied on women as they built the American Republic and for their status as Virginia patriarchs. But none of them saw in their experiences cause to challenge assumptions about women's proper place.

Even the personal political culture that Dolley Madison successfully shaped in Washington and that so many women participated in there and in the states did not alter the early national consensus that direct participation in elections, policy making, and governance lay beyond the capacity of women. Formal politics was a man's world, regardless of how accomplished a woman was and no matter how definitively she proved her abilities and virtue.

Among Virginia's founders, their long-standing conviction that women were naturally suited for domestic concerns held sway over the radical implications of their revolutionary ideals and even their own experiences with women they loved and respected. In the early nineteenth century the implications of their political ideals moved the culture and governance of United States in directions these founders had not anticipated and did not welcome, including toward women's rights. But within their own homes the line between men and women remained as sharp as ever—and they taught the same to their children and their children's children.

In 1809, Thomas Jefferson headed up his mountain to the life he always said he preferred. Throughout his long career of public service he maintained that "domestic life and literary pursuits, were my first . . . inclinations." Only the exigencies of the Revolution and his dedication to the Republic drew him from his family and into the public square. Home at last, he was greeted by his adoring grandchildren, eight from Martha along with Maria's only son, Francis Eppes. Over the next seventeen years he welcomed three more grandchildren, followed by grandsons-in-law and great-grandchildren, and proclaimed, "Among these I live like a patriarch of old."[59]

Jefferson's relationship with his grandchildren reveals the rising emotionalism of the nineteenth century and the full flowering of affective family values. Often absent from Monticello during their early childhood, he tenderly cultivated close connections with them through letters. He began corresponding with each child as soon as he or she learned to write. Several of the literary conversations commenced while he was president, and in every case he nurtured a shared interest. Cornelia Randolph loved architecture and poetry, so Thomas praised her drawings and sent her poems. Anne Cary Randolph shared his zeal for gardening, and he mailed her seeds and advice for improving the grounds at Monticello. Jefferson also involved himself in their education, including helping to supervise the collegiate studies of Jeff Randolph and Francis Eppes. He expressed his love for them far more candidly than he had when raising Martha and Maria. Secretary of State Jefferson even described his eagerness to return to Monticello and gallop on a stick horse with the toddler Anne Cary. In part, Jefferson's transformation can be attributed to the difference between a widower father raising two girls from a distance and a grandfather supremely confident in the parenting skills of his daughter. But the early nineteenth century was also marked by more expressiveness and emotionalism; the culture had changed as much as Jefferson's circumstances.[60]

Shifts in values altered the *tone* of Jefferson's family life. He filled his letters to and about his grandchildren with effusive professions of love, from the moment the first was born. He told Martha that the news of Anne Cary's birth (at the parents' request, Jefferson named her) afforded him "the greatest pleasure of any I ever received from you." And he bragged to his sister-in-law Elizabeth Eppes about "my advancement to the venerable corps of grandfathers" and declared, "I expect from it more felicity than any other advancement ever gave me."[61] Jefferson often referred to Martha Jefferson Randolph's sons and daughters as "our children." On temperate evenings, the siblings raced around the grounds at Monticello, in games Thomas planned. Visitors saw how much he "delighted in delighting them." The last hours of the day the family usually spent reading together. In those quite moments, Virginia Randolph Trist could recall decades later, "I have seen him raise his eyes from his own book, and look round on the little circle of readers and smile, and make some remark to mamma about it."[62]

These much-loved children repaid their grandfather in kind. "I can not describe the feelings of veneration, admiration, and love that existed in my heart towards him," insisted Virginia. Ellen Randolph Coolidge was no less rhapsodic than her sister Virginia when she recalled their childhood: "I loved and honored him above all earthly beings."[63]

But greater affection and expressiveness—tonal shifts in domestic life—did not translate into meaningful transformations in gender dynamics. Families became more effusive over time, but not more egalitarian when it came to women. As Ellen Randolph found out, their vaunted position at Monticello did not allow her and her sisters to rise above the larger cultural convictions about the differences between men and women. Jefferson enforced boundaries between what was acceptable for boys and girls, even with his cherished granddaughters.

It was not to the gardener Anne, the cerebral Ellen, or even the supremely capable Martha that Thomas Jefferson turned when he could no longer manage his estate. In a complete "natural aristocracy" he would likely have chosen one of them to oversee his mountaintop retreat when his health and abilities failed him. Martha had, in his long absences, succeeded admirably at running the household, even serving as a deputy son of sorts. But independently supervising a vast estate, like leading in government, required competence *and* the proper gender. So Jeff Randolph, not his sisters, took over his grandfather's holdings in the 1820s. The two men developed a close partnership as Jeff struggled mightily to sort out the impossibly tangled mess of Thomas's accounts. The granddaughters' husbands contributed as well, particularly Virginia's husband, Nicholas Trist. But tackling such matters lay beyond the legitimate purview of women, even such extraordinarily devoted and accomplished women as the Randolph sisters.

At Monticello and across revolutionary America, gender was a central, inviolable divide, and it remained so well into the nineteenth century. No matter how talented and capable a woman might be, she could not claim a place in the meritocracy imagined by the founding fathers.

Ellen Randolph understood this all too well. Though she had inherited her grandfather's inquisitiveness and love of books, she saw that there was no place for female intellectualism in the great houses of Virginia, not even in her venerable grandfather's study—and certainly not at his university. He had written her when she was just five years old to compliment her for her precocious reading. He sent along two books and told Ellen that "if you continue to learn as fast you will become a learned lady and publish books yourself."[64] She spent much of her youth perusing the library at Monticello and relishing the seclusion of Poplar Forest, where she could pass hours on end in quiet study. But she never got to make the most of her abilities. In time, feminist-minded Americans would insist that the rhetoric of the Revolution be reconciled with the reality of women's abilities, but not soon enough for Ellen Randolph. In the early 1820s she both complained about her situation and resigned herself to it. "Was I a man," she told her brother-in-law Nicholas Trist, and "could my studies have any object of sufficient importance to stimulate my exertions, I would now, even now [at age twenty-seven], commence my education." But, she sorrowfully concluded, "[I] could promise myself no competent reward for so much trouble." The reason was self-evident: "I am nothing but a woman."[65]

CHAPTER 6

"All Other Persons"

When Ellen Randolph married Joseph Coolidge in the summer of 1825, her grandfather chose as his wedding gift a writing desk. It was a fitting present for the intellectually minded Ellen, and, no doubt, an intentional reminder of the importance of keeping in touch with her Virginia relatives as she headed off for her new life in Boston. Jefferson adored Ellen: "Ten thousand kisses," he wrote, would "still fall short of the measure of my love to you."[1] But the desk—his slave John Hemings's finest handiwork—never made it to Massachusetts. Along with Ellen's books, it was lost at sea. Though Ellen, John, and Thomas were all devastated at the loss of the precious cargo, the desk was, in the scheme of things, a small matter. Except that it wasn't, or at least it isn't in retrospect. In the story of Ellen Randolph Coolidge's lost wedding present it is possible to glimpse the inner workings of the Monticello family, black and white, and the politics of racial power in the new nation.

John Hemings was born at Monticello in 1776, the year his owner asserted the equality of all men. And he remained a slave there forty-nine years later. John Hemings and his kin were both *a part* of the Jefferson family and *apart* from it. Sally Hemings was his half-sister, and two of her and Thomas's sons, James Madison Hemings and Thomas Eston Hemings, worked in John's carpentry shop. John Hemings and his wife, Priscilla, helped raise the Randolph grandchildren, who called him "Daddy" and her "Mammy." Ellen Randolph and her siblings had been born in stair-step with the Hemings children, who were their aunts and uncles. The two families shared a home, a lineage, and even their names. James Madison Hemings was born a year before his nephew James Madison Randolph. But it was never forgotten that the Jeffersons owned the Hemingses.[2]

Thomas Jefferson both respected and appropriated John Hemings's carpentry skills. Hemings was the most accomplished and highly regarded artisan at Monticello, and he labored over Ellen's present as his slave status required. But the writing desk was clearly a gift from Hemings as well. Jefferson backhandedly acknowledged as much when he told Coolidge that Hemings was distraught over "that beautiful writing desk he had taken so much pains to make for you!"[3] At the same time, Jefferson erased the role his (enslaved) sons likely played in helping to make his (free) granddaughter's present. And, seemingly indifferent to Hemings's feelings, he casually asked him to build a replacement. Resisting his owner's exploitation in the best way he knew how, John told Thomas he could not do so, for his eyesight was failing and he had forgotten the design.

Typical of Virginia slaveholders, Jefferson simply expected the black members of his household to sacrifice for his white relatives. In this particular instance John Hemings rather cleverly thwarted him. So Thomas found a substitute gift: the desk he had used to write the Declaration of Independence. Though not nearly so beautiful as the first one, the replacement was far more important, he explained, "from the part it has borne in our history." He apparently decided that it was not proper for Ellen, a woman, to own so meaningful a piece of American history. Instead, Jefferson sent the desk to Joseph Coolidge, with speculation that the couple might one day see it carried in processions at Fourth of July events "as the relics of the saints are in those of the Church."[4]

Thomas Jefferson got to control that part of his legacy. The desk is now a prized possession of the National Museum of American History at the Smithsonian Institution, and the Thomas Jefferson Foundation at Monticello, echoing his language, calls it "one of the most precious historical relics of the United States." But the "other persons" in Jefferson's family and the centrality of slavery to the nation he helped build—that would be another matter. Justice did not, as he had fearfully predicted, "sleep for ever."[5]

During the Revolutionary War, Virginia's founders saw the long-standing symmetry between politics and family break down. Political duties increasingly threatened rather than dovetailed with family values. Men who had long perceived public service as an outgrowth of their lineage had to make hard choices between honoring paternal obligations and fulfilling civic responsibilities. Revolutionary principles also pushed changes—unintended and disruptive—in families, and fathers sometimes pushed back. Emerging divisions between politics and family, and in particular the limits of revolutionary principles on family values, were laid bare in the treatment of founders' daughters. But nothing more graphically revealed the gulf between political ideals and domestic actions in the revolutionary age than the persistence of what was fast becoming a distinctly southern institution: slavery.

Racial slavery thrived in nearly all the mainland colonies and made the English Atlantic profitable. Rarely was its legitimacy or morality even questioned in the colonial period. The principal architects of America's independent Republic were owners of large plantations and scores if not hundreds of slaves, and they were both personally practiced in the denial of freedom and financially dependent on the institution. Not surprisingly, then, racial slavery also lay at the heart of the American Revolution, even as that revolution raised new, existential questions about slaveholding.[6]

Calls to resist "enslavement" provided patriots a compelling rallying cry and the ultimate moral arch to the revolutionary narrative they crafted. Between the Stamp Act Crisis and the outbreak of the Revolutionary War, Virginians depicted their contest with Britain over tax measures as a mortal struggle between liberty and slavery. By 1775, Patrick Henry proclaimed, Americans had exhausted every conceivable means "to avert the storm which is now coming on." After the Coercive Acts, the last resort against "the tyrannical hands of the ministry and parliament" lay in fighting the tools of that oppression: the British army and navy. "There is no retreat," his voice rang out, "but in submission and slavery!" Only by willingly wagering their lives could men prove themselves worthy of liberty and avoid "chains and slavery."[7]

But the connections were not just rhetorical. In the foundational designs of the American Republic—the Virginia Declaration of Rights, Declaration of Independence, and Constitution—slaveholders made certain to preserve their mastery. Even the peace treaty with England protected slavery. Congress directed the negotiators to secure the return of "slaves & other property" taken during the war.[8]

Yet even as slavery was being safeguarded in Americans' creed and governments, it seemed self-evidently a betrayal of their treasured civic values. As early as 1765, in the midst of the Stamp Act Crisis, George Mason condemned slavery as "an Evil" destructive of good government, a thriving economy, and community viability. But, in a pattern to be replicated again and again, he changed course, afraid to "expose our Weakness by examining this Subject too freely."[9]

Mason and his contemporaries simultaneously condemned and defended slavery throughout the 1770s and 1780s. Mason's opening phrasing of the Declaration of Rights provoked conflict among Virginia slaveholders: leading men wanted to make a strong statement about the philosophical underpinnings of their actions without jeopardizing their racial dominance and with it their political and economic power. Mason's originally unqualified statement that "all men are born equally free and independent, and have certain inherent natural rights" therefore needed to be checked lest it spark, one delegate warned, "civil convulsion." The commitment to slavery won out, and the text was edited to include a key restriction: "when they enter into a state of society."[10] Mason himself embodied those contradictory impulses during the 1788 debates over Virginia ratifying the Constitution. On one hand, he denounced the Constitution for allowing "this detestable trade" of international slave trafficking to continue for at least twenty years. On the other hand, he complained that nothing "will prevent the Northern and Eastern states from meddling with our whole property of that kind."[11] Certainly Mason and his contemporaries drew a line between the international slave trade (which they generally held in contempt and sometimes tried to end) and the ownership of slaves (which they varyingly defended, regretted, and reviled but never personally rejected). And founders' perceptions of the ethics of slaveholding varied, not only from man to man, but over time and depending on the audience. Yet if their ideas were complicated, their actions were not. Whatever aversion or ambivalence they felt, Mason, Henry, Jefferson, Washington, and Madison owned slaves until the day they died—which in Jefferson's and Madison's cases ran half a century after Independence. When asked in 1823 if there was in Virginia any plan for general emancipation, James Madison answered, uncharacteristically, with a single syllable: "None."[12]

Each of Virginia's leading founders knew that slavery was antithetical to his political principles. Though some were more publicly vocal than others, their own writings provide a litany of blistering rebukes of their hypocrisy of perpetuating racial slavery in an ostensibly free republic. Patrick Henry was appalled that Virginians—himself included—would embrace "a principle as repugnant to humanity, as it is inconsistent with the bible and destructive to liberty." He was shocked that such an "abominable practice" would continue in an otherwise enlightened age. James Madison similarly lamented the protection of slavery under the Constitution and condemned it as an evil surpassed only by the potential destruction of the union. Although usually circumspect on the subject, Madison criticized making "the mere distinction of colour" the basis for "the most oppressive dominion ever exercised by man over man" during the Constitutional Convention. The passage of time did not change his opinion that "in proportion as slavery prevails in a State, the Government, however democratic in name, must be aristocratic in fact." George Washington seldom publicly discussed slavery, doubtless out of concern for his future reputation. But in 1794 he admitted his desire to be free of "a certain species of property which I possess, very repugnantly to my own feelings."[13]

The betrayal of their political ideals was not even the Virginians' only objection. Slavery "discourages arts & manufactures," George Mason complained, and by undermining white immigration imperiled stability and prosperity. He blamed slaveholding for the fact that "one half of our best lands . . . remain unsettled and the other cultivated with slaves." Patrick Henry agreed, invidiously comparing Virginia's farms with Pennsylvania's, which seemed "five times the value of ours." Henry also pointed out that in the most prosperous parts of Virginia, in the west beyond the mountains, "Europeans, instead of Africans, till the lands, and manufacture." Surely, he concluded, no man was "so degenerate as to wish to see his country the gloomy retreat of slaves."[14]

Especially concerning to this cohort was the effect of slaveholding on white families: it made them entitled, violent, callous, and cruel. "Every master of slaves," Mason saw, "is born a petty tyrant." Jefferson agreed: "The whole commerce between master and slave is a perpetual exercise of the most boisterous passions, the most unremitting despotism on the one part, and degrading submissions on the other."[15]

"Unremitting despotism" meant inevitable resistance. Throughout the entire slaveholding era, whites feared violent retribution at the hands of slaves. And some of these founders' kin experienced it. James Madison's grandfather was poisoned by three of his slaves. Martha Wayles Jefferson's cousin Richard Henry Eppes was beaten and left for dead by two of his slaves in 1766.[16] Such violent acts were rare in the colonial era because slaveholders went to great lengths to protect themselves, but even a few cases could leave a lasting impression on white communities. Usually, resistance was less lethal. The enslaved men Dick and Watt ran away from Gunston Hall in 1786; Washington's cook fled in 1797. Such "elopements" were commonplace during the entire slavery era but became more frequent and caused greater problems in the wake of the Revolution, since even if runaways were recaptured, explained George Washington, "they are sure to contaminate and discontent others."[17]

When the revolutionary age inspired African American men and women to seek liberty, their actions only heightened white anxiety. James Madison worried in 1774 about the racial implications of American radicalism: "If America & Britain should come to an hostile rupture I am afraid an Insurrection among the slaves may & will be promoted." And worried he should have been. The next year royally appointed Governor Dunmore offered freedom to Virginia slaves willing to join the British forces. Several hundred black men immediately answered the call, despite a warning from the *Virginia Gazette* that they should not be "tempted by this proclamation to ruin yourselves."[18] When the British military raided Richmond in 1781, ten of Governor Jefferson's slaves self-emancipated, including the two most intimately connected to the Jefferson family: Ursula Granger, who had nursed young Martha, and Jupiter Evans, Jefferson's personal attendant, or "body servant," as they were called in that age. Though they were returned after Cornwallis's surrender, Jefferson's fear—and that of his generation—that justice for slavery might come in his lifetime persisted. In the summer of 1787, he shared with St. George Tucker his suspicion that "if something is not done & done soon, we shall be the murderers of our own children."[19]

These founders believed that, in time and one way or another, white Americans would pay for their unjust enslavement of black Americans. "As nations can not be rewarded or punished in the next world they must be in this," George Mason reasoned. "By an inevitable chain of causes & effects providence punishes national sins, by national calamities." Jefferson reached the same grim conclusion: "I tremble for my country when I reflect that God is just."[20]

Aware that history, as well as their creator, would judge them harshly, James Madison and the Philadelphia delegates representing the southern states were careful to keep the words "slave" and "slavery" out of their crowning achievement, the US Constitution, even as they made absolutely certain that the federal government would protect slaveholding. Twenty-five of the fifty-five men gathered in Philadelphia owned slaves, and three-fourths of those were dependent on slave labor for their economic well-being. Most delegates were determined to protect slavery in the new government, and most of those were ashamed of themselves for it. They certainly went to great lengths to ensure that those words never appeared in their document. For men dedicated to precision of language and eloquence, the handling of slavery in the Constitution represented an unusually—and tellingly—infelicitous move. The Constitution expressly sanctioned slaveholding: with the "3/5 Compromise" (Article 1, section 2, clause 3), the fugitive slave law (Article 4, section 2, clause 3), and the protection of the international slave trade (Article 1, section 9, clause 1). But one must read closely between the lines in order to see *who* exactly the framers meant when they allowed the "Migration or Importation of such Persons" until 1808 and counted "three-fifths of all other Persons" in apportioning representation in the House. To be sure, the delegates were grappling with a range of complex issues when they settled on that language. Political expedience, particularly the desire to count slaves toward apportioning representation, required their designation as persons. Delegates who hoped to set the institution on a path toward extinction might have preferred to emphasize legal obligations and duties of one group of people (slaves) to another (citizens). And certainly members of this generation understood a distinction between owning slaves' labor, time, even their bodies and children, and denying their humanity. Still, delegates knew they were gambling with their future reputations in history, and they chose their words accordingly. One delegate explained that the linguistic choices were "an endeavor to conceal a principle of which we are ashamed." And another added that they "anxiously sought to avoid the admission of expressions which might be odious in the ears of Americans."[21]

Adding to leading Virginians' embarrassment was that their peers, men they admired, pointed out their hypocrisy for allowing slavery to thrive not only in their state and nation but in their homes. In 1783 Lafayette proposed that he and Washington partner in buying land so that Washington could free his slaves and make them tenant farmers. If Washington took that bold stand, Lafayette hoped, it "Might Render it a General Practice." Even if they did not inspire others, Lafayette said he preferred failure to the dishonor of appearing to tolerate slavery. Robert Pleasants, a Quaker merchant from Henrico County well known to all these men, freed his slaves in the wake of the Revolutionary War, and he warned both Washington and Madison that they jeopardized their legacy by perpetuating slavery. In 1791, Robert Carter, one of Virginia's richest planters, likewise followed his convictions and emancipated more than five hundred slaves—perhaps the largest private manumission in America before the Civil War. John Randolph numbered among those who committed to manumission: he freed hundreds of slaves in his will and bequeathed them money to purchase land. And Edward Coles, President James Madison's personal secretary (and brother to Isaac Coles, Jefferson's secretary), left Virginia for Illinois and freed his slaves after fairly begging, unsuccessfully, both Jefferson and Madison to set an example of manumission. Coles frankly informed Madison that it appeared to him "repugnant to the distinctive & characteristic traits of your character . . . not to restore to your slaves that liberty & those rights which you have been through life so zealous and able a champion."[22]

So, these founders were not without models for a way out. They clearly saw examples from individual Virginians, and mid-Atlantic and northern states commenced gradual emancipation programs starting in the 1770s. Pennsylvania, where these men so often gathered and even lived for months and years at a time, took the lead; the first antislavery society was founded in Philadelphia in 1775.[23]

Residing in Pennsylvania occasionally frustrated these founders' ability to control their slaves but not their will to do so. James Madison complained that the enslaved man William Gardner had become "too thoroughly tainted" by Philadelphia values "to be a fit companion for fellow slaves in Virginia." Although Madison insisted that he did not blame Gardner "for coveting that liberty for which we have paid the price of so much blood, and have proclaimed so often to be the right . . . of every human being," he was not prepared to liberate him either. Madison's solution was to sell Gardner into servitude for seven years, the longest period of time Pennsylvania state law would allow (and so the highest price he could set). He tolerated the loss because he saw that it was simply not prudent to send Gardner and his new ideas to Virginia. President George Washington similarly found his domestic interests at odds with a Pennsylvania law that allowed slaves residing in the state for longer than six months to seek their freedom. His solution: rotate his slaves back to Virginia. He asked Tobias Lear to coordinate with Martha Washington; Martha would devise a pretense for going home and Tobias would send with her the slaves nearing the deadline. To avoid damaging his reputation in Philadelphia, Washington added a catch: "I wish to have it accomplished under pretext that may deceive both them [his slaves] and the Public."[24]

To be certain, from time to time Virginia's leading founders made efforts to curb slavery. President Jefferson, for example, proposed that Congress close the international slave trade at the earliest possible date and signed the bill immediately upon passage. After his retirement from the presidency, James Madison became president of the American Colonization Society and contemplated a number of (implausible) schemes to rid the nation of slaves. To work, he believed, a general emancipation would have to be gradual, compensate white owners, and segregate if not wholly remove African Americans. The federal government would need to bear the expense of compensating whites and relocating blacks. Madison estimated the total cost at around $600 million, which he imagined might be raised by selling lands in the West—for example, two hundred million acres could be sold for $3.00 per acre. It was transparently a hopelessly fanciful plan, from a man renowned as the most meticulously logical thinker of his age.[25]

For twenty-four of the first twenty-eight years of the nation's existence under the Constitution, with the single-term exception of the John Adams administration, three Virginians led the country they created. From that perch, none made a significant effort to right what they themselves uniformly believed a moral, and perhaps mortal, failing in their republic.

Perhaps a national or even a statewide plan of emancipation was politically impossible. But even when it came to their own households, there was always some qualification, some cause for delay. James Madison passively hoped he might someday "depend as little as possible on the labour of slaves." Patrick Henry felt embarrassed that he was "master of slaves of my own purchase!" but admitted, impotently, "I am drawn along by the general inconvenience of living here without them. I will not, I cannot justify it." Jefferson said, "There is nothing I would not sacrifice to a practicable plan of abolishing every vestige of this moral and political depravity." And he vowed that there was "not a man on earth who would sacrifice more than I would to relieve us from this heavy reproach, in any practicable way." But apparently no *practicable* solution ever presented itself.[26] Instead, Jefferson and his contemporaries debated one improbable scheme after another—diffusion, recolonization—all the while perceiving that they were standing on the wrong side of history.

So, Virginia's founders knew that slavery could not be reconciled with the values of the Revolution, that it was morally bankrupt, that it weakened economic innovations and imperiled social stability, that it warped the character of masters and their children, and that it jeopardized their historical legacy. Where then was the audacity of 1776? The bold vision of 1787? In response to Edward Coles's far-sighted plan to exercise moral courage, Thomas Jefferson urged him to resign himself to the "unfortunate condition." James Madison refused Robert Pleasants's repeated calls to introduce legislation in Congress countering slavery because he said he feared it was "likely to do harm rather than good." Despite his fierce condemnation of slavery, Patrick Henry did nothing but hope that his generation might "transmit to our descendants . . . an abhorrence for slavery."[27]

Something clearly mattered more to Virginia's leading founders than practicing their political principles. What greater harm did they fear? What led them to perpetuate a "moral and political depravity"?

During the 1788 Virginia ratification debates George Mason offered an uninspiring commentary on why these daring visionaries failed to act. "It is far from being a desirable property," he allowed. "But it will involve us in great difficulties and infelicity to be now deprived of them." That was the same reason that Dolley Madison gave when contending with her decidedly undeferential "maid," Sukey. She "made so many depredations on every thing, in every part of the house," including refusing to work and breaking and taking household goods, that Dolley could hardly keep track of it all. But, an exasperated Dolley conceded, it was "terribly inconvenient to do without her." Had letting go of slavery been simply a matter of convenience, these founders would surely have followed their consciences. They sacrificed so much for the revolutionary cause that it seems highly improbable that a mere "infelicity" would have made them cling to what James Madison called "the most oppressive dominion ever exercised by man over man."[28]

When it came to the controversy over slavery, Virginians knew two contradictory truths. First, slaveholding violated their republican principles. And second, their family status and economic security depended on slavery. So the patriot leaders faced an unwelcome choice: to be either principled founders or dutiful fathers. They were not about to sacrifice what Jefferson called his indoors family for his outdoors family. So, fatefully, they chose family values over political principles.[29]

Slave mastery was the foundation of Virginia gentry identity. White slaveholding families before the Revolution had been genteel, leisured, wealthy, and powerful because of racial slavery, and they remained so afterward. George Washington could spend his retirement riding across Mount Vernon—to say nothing of years in public service—because he commanded scores of slaves. Jefferson could open Monticello and James Madison Montpelier to droves of visitors, who marveled at their dinner parties and beautifully appointed homes, because slave labor bought those lifestyles. George Mason and Patrick Henry could educate their sons and endow them with thriving estates because their slaves turned handsome profits on their plantations. Slave mastery was also an elemental part of their identity as family men. "With respect to the domestic character of Mr. Henry," one of his sons-in-law proclaimed, "nothing could be more amiable. In every relation, as a husband, father, master, and neighbor, he was entirely exemplary." Another kinsman agreed: "He was uniformly an affectionate husband and parent, and a kind master to his servants."[30]

The independence of planters, and therefore their civic identity, depended on mastering slaves. John Mason's recollections of his father's supposed self-sufficiency captures both the ideal of southern plantation life and the centrality of slavery to that illusion. There was a slave for every job: "Carpenters, Coopers, Sawyers, Blacksmiths, Tanners, Curriers, Shoemakers, Spinners, Weavers & Knitters, even a Distiller." Mason's forests were harvested by slaves into lumber that other slaves made into barrels that other slaves packed with tobacco that other slaves had cut from the fields. His slaves cultivated cotton for their own clothes and raised sheep and cattle for their food. And, as John Mason recalled, his father's "carpenters & sawyers built and kept in repair all the dwelling houses, barns, stables, ploughs, harrows, gates, &c." And so on and so on, from corn to nails, from shoes to cider. Scores of slaves worked Mason's fields, and the "Mansion slaves" lived within earshot of Gunston Hall, called at any time, day or night, to manage any matter. No wonder that Mason, fierce advocate for liberty though he was, freed not one slave in his entire life.[31]

Mason was hardly alone. It took no fewer than thirty-seven house slaves to maintain Monticello after Jefferson's retirement. At Mount

Vernon, the cook knew just when to signal the fisherman to bring in his catch so that family and guests could sit down to the freshest possible dinner at a table immaculately tended by slaves. And at the presidential home in Philadelphia, the dishes, recalled one dazzled guest, were presented by Washington's slaves "with a silence and speed that seemed like enchantment."[32]

The reliance of supposed independent masters on slaves was so thoroughgoing that George Mason took it as a point of pride that while his body servant, James, attended to all his personal needs and traveled with him, he, George, always shaved himself. George Washington even bought teeth from his slaves, which he used as dentures.[33]

The connection ran from the cradle to the grave. When he was a very young boy James Madison's father gave him his first slave, William Gardner, who was his near constant companion during his childhood. When James went off to study at Princeton, he took another slave, Sawney, as a body servant. Sawney was still living at Montpelier, taking care of James's mother, fifty years later. Gardner took care of Madison's needs in Philadelphia for nearly four years in the 1780s, while Madison served in the Continental Congress. Paul Jennings was the last of the line. He grew up in the Madison White House and became James's body servant after he retired in 1816. As Madison's health deteriorated, Jennings's responsibilities grew ever more intimate. He shaved James every day for the last sixteen years of the former president's life, and during Madison's last months, after he could no longer walk because of crippling arthritis, Paul dressed and bathed him. Jennings was at Madison's bedside when he died and wrote the only first-person account of his passing.[34]

Thomas Jefferson's earliest memory was as a three-year-old being lifted up by a slave onto a pillow so that he could take a comfortable horseback ride. His whole life he was shadowed by a series of body servants, starting with Jupiter Evans, born the same year as Thomas and his boyhood companion, and ending with Burwell Colbert. Jupiter even accompanied Thomas when he courted Martha Wayles Skelton. And as Thomas lay dying, only Burwell Colbert—not any member of his white family—knew how he needed to be raised higher in his bed. And so, eighty years after that first memory, another slave adjusted another pillow for another passage.[35]

This cohort handed down this legacy to their white children. Martha Jefferson's mother, Martha, could not breast-feed her enough, so she was wet-nursed by the enslaved woman Ursula Granger. As Maria Jefferson Eppes neared death, slaves carried her four miles up the mountain from Edgehill to Monticello, so that she could die in her father's house. Jupiter Evans's son, Philip, became the long-term companion to Jeff Randolph. When Jeff passed out after a knife fight, he awoke in Philip's arms. And after Maria Jefferson Eppes died, her widowed husband, John, fathered children with Betsy Hemings, a niece of Sally Hemings. Betsy was buried next to John in the Eppes family cemetery.[36]

At every critical stage of the American Revolution, Virginia's founders depended on slaves, though they usually mentioned this only in passing, if at all. Robert Hemings lived with Thomas Jefferson in Philadelphia in 1776. William Lee was nearly always at General Washington's side during the Revolutionary War, and he accompanied him to the Constitutional Convention, as did two other slaves, assigned to handle Washington's horses and drive his coach. George Mason also brought two slaves to Philadelphia, one for himself and another for his horses. Christopher Sheels lived in the first presidential households, in New York and then in Philadelphia. He became President Washington's body servant after William Lee grew too feeble for the job.[37]

Each of the Virginia presidents kept slaves as attendants and laborers, using them for state dinners, construction projects, childcare, personal grooming, and anything else that arose. Paul Jennings was among the last people to leave the White House in 1814 as British forces advanced on the nation's capital. He was setting the table when a frantic rider called out the warning to "clear out, clear out!" Later he learned that invading British soldiers ate the very meal he set out. Jennings also held the ladder that several men, including other slaves, climbed to cut down George Washington's portrait (though Dolley is usually given credit for saving it). And he watched the federal city go up in flames.[38]

Given the centrality of slaves to every part of rich slaveholders' lives, it was not surprising that men like Jefferson and Washington thought about their bondsmen and women as being part of their families. This was not simply rhetoric. Family in the perceptions of early southern elites was never confined to the conjugal unit. Plantation households were fluid and extended, populated by cousins, in-laws, orphaned young kin, widowed sisters and mothers, half-siblings and step-families. The domestic ideal of planters also required mastery of slaves, both field laborers, who turned the profits, and house "servants," who ensured the beauty and comfort of homes. Though certainly never on a par with any white relatives, slaves constituted an important part of the domestic scene over which patriarchs and patriots presided. For example, in 1776 Thomas Jefferson counted the "number of souls in my family" at 117. This included his wife and children, sixteen overseers and hired workers and their wives and children, and eighty-three slaves.[39] Washington likewise considered his slaves as members of his family. In the fall of 1792 illnesses at Mount Vernon distressed him, and he told Tobias Lear that many among "my family" had suffered but added, "All the whites of it however have kept up" except one person. At other times, Washington and Jefferson referred to their slaves as "my black people," "my laboring people," or just "my people"—consistently using the possessive form.[40]

It was not uncommon for the African American "souls in my family" to be biological kin. Martha Washington's first husband, Daniel Parke Custis, had a young half-brother, Jack, born of his father and a slave woman named Alice. Martha Washington was herself rumored to have an interracial half-sister. Though there is no evidence to verify that specific claim, interracial relationships certainly occurred in the extended Dandridge-Custis-Washington family. George Calvert, brother-in-law of Martha's son, Jack Custis, had two families: one with his white wife, Rosalie Stier, and another with Eleanor Beckett, a slave.[41] Thomas Jefferson's father-in-law, John Wayles, and Jefferson's son-in-law, John Eppes (the grandson and namesake of John Wayles), both had long-term relationships with women of the Hemings family. And now, despite generations of historians essentially repeating Ellen Randolph Coolidge's insistence that "there are such things, after all, as moral impossibilities," we know Jefferson did, too. Historians have reached a near consensus on the existence—though certainly not the tenor—of the

Jefferson-Hemings relationship. The evidence of his fathering several of her children has been meticulously laid out by historian Annette Gordon-Reed, among others. It is, therefore, unnecessary to repeat that here, but it is relevant to linger over what the Jefferson-Hemings relationship says about family values in the revolutionary age.[42]

Thomas and Sally's relationship had been going on, apparently as an open secret in Charlottesville, for a dozen years when a former and now disgruntled Jefferson political operative, journalist James Thomson Callender, broke the story in a Richmond newspaper in September 1802. It quickly went national. Callender condemned President Jefferson for carrying on with his "concubine" in his own home and "before the eyes of two young ladies!" (meaning Martha and Maria).[43] Though his friends rose to defend his character, Jefferson's public response was silence, indicating that the story was simply beneath him.

Though he said nothing, what Jefferson did in the wake of the Callender story revealed the importance of white women in white men's respectability. Jefferson did not have a model wife, like Martha Washington and Dolley Madison, to project a counternarrative of domestic rectitude and harmony. So, he called Martha and Maria to Washington, DC. With his accomplished white daughters in the executive mansion, joined by their congressmen husbands, Jefferson could portray an image of respectability, public service, and family happiness. And the Hemings half of the family could be erased from public view. The following summer a drunken Callender fell in the James River and drowned, and the story (temporarily) died with him. Jefferson and his heirs continued silently erasing the Hemingses as long as he lived.

The Hemings story also revealed the fixed connection between race and power, even in the most intimate corners of life and for the most powerful members of society. It was perfectly fine for white Virginians to exploit their slaves—even for men to do so sexually. But discretion and inequality were mandatory. A white man did not have the liberty to pursue his happiness by publicly cohabiting with an African American woman or parenting African American children. Those norms applied even for the president of the United States. Indeed, African Americans could only be seen as subordinate members of plantation households, not as beloved or blood kin—even if they were.

Thomas Jefferson, for all his power, could not acknowledge, let alone emancipate, his black children without jeopardizing his white heirs. Even if he wrestled with the idea, which we do not know, in the end it was a price he was unwilling to pay. So he hid them: in his writings, including in his will, and throughout his life. Harriet and Beverley Hemings were quietly sent away in 1822, to live free and white, away from Virginia in ways they could never do while remaining at Monticello. Madison and Eston's continued service was given in their father's will to their Uncle John Hemings, who was freed, Thomas said, for his faithful service. Jefferson could emancipate them in this way without naming them as freedmen and raising questions about why in death he singled them out. The woman he had lived with for thirty-eight years also could not be named in his will without the threat of scandal, and so she was not freed. When a discrete interval passed, Martha Jefferson Randolph sent Sally Hemings to live with her sons in Charlottesville. Hemings carried their secret to her grave in 1835.

The image that Jefferson tried to convey of his family, black and white, was replicated in a rare portrait capturing a Virginia founder with his slave. Usually artists painted revolutionary leaders alone, in public spaces and to convey their power, or with other politicians or soldiers. George Washington, for example, was often shown heroically commanding his troops. But Washington was also depicted in a rare domestic scene that became one of the most popular images of a political leader in the nineteenth century. *The Washington Family* by Edward Savage (1796) was reproduced as woodcuts, lithographs, even embroidery patterns. In it, George sits at once casually and stately, with Martha and the Custis grandchildren beautifully attired. To the back of Martha, a slave enters the scene to wait on the whites. He is *a part* of his owner's family life but *apart* from it as well.[44]

The perceived inclusion of slaves in plantation families (always as subservient members and never as acknowledged blood kin) did not slow patriarchs' use of slaves to their best economic advantage. As James Madison put it, he wanted "to treat the Negroes with all the humanity & kindness consistent with their necessary subordination and work." Such labor began as early in life as was practical. Washington expected African American children to earn back his investment: "Soon as they are able to work out, I expect to reap the benefit of their labour myself." Jefferson moved boys of age ten or twelve from their parents at his other estates to work long hours at the Monticello nailery.[45] Owners certainly cared about the health of their slaves, but usually that derived from economic ambition more than empathy. Planters directed overseers to provide adequate housing and food for their slaves and to shield pregnant women from dangerous labor because they knew that healthy slaves produced higher profits. Often they wrote about slave families as simply another part of their plantations. Secretary of State Jefferson, for example, quizzed Martha Jefferson Randolph, who managed Monticello in his absence, about the repayment of his debts, the wheat crops, and his slaves' clothes. President Washington directed his overseers about how to sow grass seeds, reap buckwheat, and balance the corn crop to best feed his slaves and horses.[46] And so the bottom line was usually the bottom line: Mason advertised for runaways; Washington applied for and received a tax credit when one of his slaves was executed for a crime; Jefferson published a book in which he pronounced he had never met an African American who "uttered a thought above the level of plain narration" nor seen in a black person "even an elementary trait of painting or sculpture."[47]

In the slave quarters on these founders' plantations, African American women and men created their own families, likewise apart from and a part of whites. Linked spatially with the great houses of their owners, slave quarters on the outside seemed a part of the overall landscape design: often ordered and uniform in construction, particularly for the household slaves, who were kept closer by. Inside slaves' homes, the stark differentness of the worlds of white and black plantation residents was staggering. In sharp contrast to the spacious, elegantly appointed, light-filled residences families like the Masons and Washingtons inhabited, their slaves lived in cramped spaces with little privacy and few personal possessions.

Slaveholders fully understood the familial relationships of the people they held in bondage, and they often spoke of their desire to honor their family ties. Recognizing slave families helped planters, too, though, by militating against runaways and giving them added emotional leverage over bondsmen and women. Mothers were loath to flee without their children; fathers' love could be used to undercut flights to freedom. The importance of black families meant that patriarchs sometimes had to negotiate with individual slaves. For example, George Washington wanted to take the cook Hercules to Philadelphia, but he found he needed to bring along Hercules's son, too. He ruefully accepted the boy "not from his appearance or merits I fear,—but because he was the son of Hercules and his desire to have him as his assistant."[48] But such instances were rare. More common by far was the sale and separation of black family members because of the needs of white planters.

These founders, like generations of Virginia planter-patriarchs before them, expected black families to sacrifice and be sacrificed for white families. Though sometimes insisting it violated their ethics, plantation owners sold slaves away from their families whenever it suited their economic needs. Even more often slaveowners divided husbands and wives, parents and children between their various estates. Sometimes they broke up slave families casually, sometimes regretfully. But the deep emotional bonds of enslaved men and women never seemed to rival the immediate needs of planters. Generally, owners honored or ignored "abroad marriages" (that is, between couples living on different plantations) as it profited them. At Mount Vernon, married slave couples lived apart more often than together. In 1799, for example, eighteen women lived with their husbands, and thirty-two lived apart. Since another twelve were unmarried or widowed mothers, forty-four families had no resident father—nearly two and a half times the number living together. Jefferson, meanwhile, preferred that slaves intermarry and "stay at home." He calculated that slaves "are worth a great deal more in that case than when they have husbands and wives abroad." Madison agreed with Jefferson about the desirability of "home" marriages. He complained that slave men, however, preferred wives on different plantations "as affording occasions & pretexts for going abroad, and exempting them on holidays from a share of the little calls to which those at home are liable." Of course, it seemed to Madison entirely reasonable that slaves should remain ever at the ready to answer the "little calls" of whites.[49]

Sales of black members of plantation households sometimes sparked pity, but usually of a misplaced sort. When, for example, George Washington learned about the forced sale of slaves to satisfy claims against his late brother Samuel's estate, he found the matter so "exceedingly distressing" that he interceded to "see if this evil can not be averted." He hoped the main creditor could be encouraged to "have mercy," and insisted that the sale was "inconsistent with that benevolence which should be characteristic of every man." At first blush, it might seem that Washington was worried about the slave children who, should a sale occur, would be torn from their parents. Instead, his concerns lay only with Samuel Washington's children and their inheritance: "If the negroes are sold for ready money they will go for a song."[50]

It was this same mindset that led Dolley Madison to insist, upon the sale of Montpelier and many of the plantation slaves, that no one understood her "feeling of grief and dismay at the necessity of transferring to another a beloved home." But just the month before Dolley had received a heartbreaking reminder of the cost of her financial problems to slave families. Sarah Steward was among several Montpelier slaves held in the Orange County jail, seized as part of a judgment against Madison. From her cell Sarah asked Dolley to imagine "what our sorrow must be." The men and women were all "afraid we shall be bought by what are called negro buyers and sent away from our husbands and wives." She begged Dolley to try and "get neighbours to buy us that have husbands and wives, so as to save us some misery."[51]

That same attitude allowed Jefferson's granddaughter Mary Randolph to "thank heaven" after the sale of Monticello and nearly all the slaves who had worked there their entire lives. The auction, she told her sister Ellen, "has been attended with as few distressing occurrences as the case would admit." One hundred thirty people had been advertised by Mary and Ellen's brother, Jeff Randolph. Among those sold were the wife and four minor children of Joseph Fossett. Though Fossett had been freed in Jefferson's will, his family was not. His wife and children, including two infant sons, went to three different bidders, a chilling rebuttal to Mary Randolph's sanguine account.[52]

The naming of slaves, which owners arrogated to themselves, was also revealing. Enslaved men and women became, with names like Billy,

Jimmy, Sally, and Polly, perpetual children. At other times, owners assigned names that mocked the realities of enslavement: Queen, Samson, and Pompey were common. Washington owned Hercules, Jefferson owned Jupiter. But in either case, surnames and thus family ties got erased. The estate inventories of Daniel Parke Custis—listing the men and women who became Washington's "dower" slaves—were typical. Men, women, girls, and boys were listed like household goods or personal effects: quantified and calculated. The only things that mattered to the appraisers were the gender and age—stand-ins for market value—of each slave. It was a myth, of course, that slaves did not have surnames. Owners just deliberately chose to ignore that fact. For example, James Madison allowed as how the man he always identified as "my man servant Paul," was "sometimes called Paul Jennings." Using only given names—and caricaturing forms at that—linguistically tethered slaves to their owners and infantilized them.[53]

Owners' reactions to slaves' deaths offer another instructive take on their attitudes. When a slave child belonging to her niece Fanny Bassett Washington died, Martha Washington offered condolences—to Fanny. She was "sorry that any thing should happen in your family to give you pain." She added, quite cavalierly, that such things were to be expected: "Black children are liable to so many accidents and complaints that one is hardly sure of keeping them." Without any condolences, James Madison told his father to pass along to "Old Anthony & Betty" the news that "their son Billey is no more." He had fallen ill during a voyage to New Orleans. When the medicine he took on the ship weakened him even further, "he tumbled in a fainty fit overboard & never rose."[54]

Such coldness extended even to the closest of companions. Thomas Jefferson had not simply known Jupiter Evans his entire life but Jupiter had been Thomas's near-constant companion during his youth. In January 1800, Evans fell gravely ill, and he convulsed so badly, Martha Jefferson Randolph reported, that "it took 3 stout men to hold him." He suffered for nine days before death finally came. In response to Martha's graphic descriptions of Jupiter's anguished passing, Thomas replied, "The death of Jupiter obliges me to ask of Mr. Randolph or yourself to give orders at the proper time in March for the bottling of my cyder." And, when telling Maria Jefferson Eppes about the death of the man she called Uncle Jupiter, he explained: "You have perhaps heard of the loss of Jupiter. With all his defects, he leaves a void in my domestic arrangements which can not be filled."[55]

But perhaps the most telling commentary on the place of African Americans in planter households is to be found in the sounds of silence. Enslaved men and women were consistently erased from the historical record of this cohort's day-to-day lives. In their writings the founders sometimes depicted slaves' labor as an extension of their own: they said they "planted" or "harvested" crops, as if they did it themselves. Or, they fell into the passive voice when describing the work of slaves: carriages "were brought" and meals "were presented." Visitors to Monticello and Montpelier marveled during tours of immaculately maintained residences and beautifully cultivated gardens, but the people who created this refined image were secreted away, physically and in prose.

Architectural features in these men's homes helped erase their slaves from visitors' sights. Jefferson's was the cleverest. Hidden staircases, a rotating dining room door, and dumbwaiters concealed his slaves, leaving the illusion of effortless refinement and "self-serve" meals. In fact, enslaved women worked all day long in dangerous kitchens and then carried heavy trays up narrow winding staircases to be carefully loaded onto devices (built most likely by slaves at the joinery) so that white guests could be delighted. Someone waited in the damp cellar to send up wine. Someone washed the dishes between meal services. Someone caught the fish and starched the linens and slaughtered the hogs and churned the butter.

The layout of their plantations further elided these founders' dependence on slaves. Though some slave quarters at Montpelier were unusually close to the main house and therefore visible from the second floor terrace, visitors would not see where the household slaves lived on approach. At Gunston Hall, the household slaves' quarters were, according to John Mason, "skirted by a wood, just far enough within which, to be out of sight."[56]

White women were celebrated for the picturesque, welcoming homes that African American women actually maintained. After the Madisons left the capital, Montpelier buzzed with activity. Dinners with twenty people at the table were not unusual, and travelers often stopped by for the day and stayed overnight. "We have had," Dolley reported to her niece Mary Cutts, "more company this summer than I can describe." The same held true at Monticello. Edmund Bacon, a Monticello overseer, recalled that two dozen stalls in the main barn often could not accommodate guests' horses and that Martha Jefferson Randolph routinely borrowed six beds from his wife to lodge the visitors who overflowed the house. Of course it was not Martha who actually gathered the beds or set them up or cooked meals or mended linens or washed laundry or cleaned floors. Whites simply appropriated the work of slaves to make these mansions welcoming to the throngs of admirers longing to spend time in the homes of America's founders. Bacon complained that "I got tired of seeing them come, and waiting on them." One can only imagine the fatigue of African Americans who did the lion's share of the "waiting on."[57]

The erasure of slave labor from white domestic scenes was another legacy passed from the founding generation to their children. When Maria Jefferson became engaged to John Eppes, her father hoped the couple would spend most of their time living with him, though he allowed as how they should have their own estate as well. He recommended nearby Pantops plantation, which would "furnish to Mr. E. useful and profitable occupation as a farmer, and to you occasional rides to superintend the spinning house, dairy &c."[58] Left unsaid, but abundantly clear, was that the work at Pantops would be done by slaves, with John reaping the profits and Maria managing the household economy.

Though they hardly ever discussed their physical dependence on slaves, a close reading of these founders' writings reveal slaves' presence in every part of their daily lives. For example, George Mason and George Washington, longtime friends and close neighbors, often corresponded by courier, sometimes replying to each other's letters the same day. If a relative or protégé carried the letter, the opening lines said so. At other times, no such note appears; these letters most likely were carried the twelve-mile trek by slaves, who merited no mention by their owners. In their vast correspondence covering a boundless range of topics, Thomas Jefferson and James Madison rarely brought up slavery. But their mastery of slaves ran just below the surface of much of what they discussed, from high-minded political theories to the day's weather. During a July 1793 heat wave, for instance, Madison wrote Jefferson that the corn crop was burning up, the dire situation made worse by the fact that heavy spring rains had preceded the blistering summer sun, baking the soil "into Brick."[59] And who would plow the rock-hard earth, work outdoors in the relentless heat, and suffer from the lost crops?

The Jefferson family liked to tell the romantic story of newlyweds Thomas and Martha making their way up the snow-covered mountain when Monticello was a single inhabitable room. Arriving late at night, the couple found that "part of a bottle of wine, found on a shelf behind some books," would have to suffice "both for fire and supper." But Martha's fifteen-year-old slave, Betty Brown, almost certainly traveled with the couple, as did Jupiter Evans—though their presence was ignored in the story. And there were other slaves living there as well: the fires had gone out, relatives later explained, because "the servants retired to their own houses."[60]

An often repeated and poignant story from Mount Vernon echoes the same themes. In 1797 the former president was writing to a friend when he realized that, dinner hour approaching, he and Martha were about to "do what I believe has not been done within the last twenty Years by us,—that is to set down to dinner by ourselves." In fact, his and Martha's meal was prepared and served by slaves that night, as it was every night of Washington's life at Mount Vernon.[61]

Perhaps some of this erasure was simply the reflex of men attended in every way and for their whole lives by slaves. But the reluctance to mention particular slaves in their service—as opposed to extensive discussions of the institution as an abstraction—had a striking parallel to the Constitution. And the consistent effort to obscure slave quarters on estates like Mount Vernon, Gunston Hall, and Monticello, which these patriarchs personally designed, was no coincidence. It was, rather, all of a piece with their determination to protect a domestic institution of racial power that ran counter to their political ideals about liberty and equality. In the end, these founders' convictions about the irreconcilability of slavery and republicanism gave way to their determination to protect their white relatives and preserve their estates and social standing for the next generation.

Thehe winter after Ellen Randolph Coolidge left Monticello was hard on her eighty-two-year-old grandfather. In March, as his birthday neared, Thomas Jefferson prepared his will. By late June he was mostly bedridden. He died at Monticello on the fiftieth anniversary of the passage of the Declaration of Independence, surrounded by his grandchildren and lovingly attended by his treasured daughter Martha Jefferson Randolph. After Maria Jefferson Eppes died in 1804, Jefferson told his friend John Page that he felt he had "lost even the half of all I had." In July 1826, as he lay dying, Thomas penned one last message for Martha: "Then farewell my dear, my lov'd daughter, adieu. The last pang of life is in parting from you!" In the final months of his life Jefferson worried that he would not leave behind an estate large enough to take care of Martha, "the cherished companion of my early life, and nurse of my age," and her children, who were, he said, "as dear to me as if my own." He felt heartsick that he might be leaving them in "a comfortless situation."[62]

He knew as well that in the fifty years since he drafted the Declaration he had done nearly nothing to end the "moral and political depravity" of slavery. By the 1820s, the matter was dividing the nation: the Missouri Crisis of 1819 set the stage for a generation of bitter political clashes between northern and southern politicians over slavery in the West. Slaveholding was also, as Mason and Henry had predicted in the 1760s, crippling their beloved Virginia. Ellen Randolph Coolidge was correct when she speculated in one of the last letters she wrote her grandfather that the southern states could never keep pace with the rest of the country "whilst the canker of slavery eats into their hearts, and diseases the whole body."[63]

Because of that "canker," Jefferson's other daughter, Harriet Hemings, never felt the paternal tenderness showered on Martha Jefferson Randolph, and her father said nothing of her "comfortless situation." Harriet and her brothers belonged to a second family that Thomas Jefferson denied even to the grave. Race precluded Harriet enjoying the love of a devoted father just as it excluded her brothers Madison, Beverley, and Eston Hemings from citizenship in the republic their father helped build. Instead, the Hemings' labor bought the lifestyle and material comfort of their Randolph nieces and nephews. The exploitation of Jefferson's black family ensured the happiness of his white one.

The divisions between Jefferson's two families replicated the nature of the early United States. Jefferson believed that the two races could never "live in the same government" because "nature, habit, opinion has drawn indelible lines of distinction between them."[64] That was precisely how he dealt with his two families. Even the architecture of his living quarters policed that line; separate entrances divided the worlds of Martha Jefferson Randolph and her children and Sally Hemings and hers.

Jefferson may have been the only prominent Virginia founder known to have fathered offspring he held in bondage, but all of Virginia's revolutionary leaders owned large numbers of slaves their whole lives. And each viewed those men and women as part of their families—both subordinate and indispensable to their domestic happiness. Mount Vernon, Gunston Hall, Red Hill, and Montpelier, no less than Monticello, depended on slavery. Slaves attended the gardens, prepared the meals, cared for the white children, maintained the buildings, raised the livestock, and worked in the fields to secure the wealth of these Virginia patriots.

James Madison died a slaveholder in June 1836, the last of Virginia's great founders. Although he had no children to provide for and many friends urging him to take a stand against perpetuating racial slavery, he made no emancipatory plans in his will. Dolley Madison inherited his slaves, some of whom she sold, some she lost to creditors, and some she kept. She sold Paul Jennings, who had faithfully cared for James for decades, for two hundred dollars. Shortly after James Madison died, the abolitionist Lewis Tappan apparently anonymously penned an essay about Madison's will in the *Emancipator*. Explaining how Madison had bequeathed all his slaves to his wife and $2,000 to the American Colonization Society, the author wondered, "Why did not Madison, who was President of the Colonization Society, when he made his will, manumit his slaves that they might go to Liberia?"[65] It was a good and devastating question.

Thomas Jefferson had passed away ten years before, having owned by his own accounting some six hundred people over the course of his life (around two hundred in any given year) while freeing fewer than a dozen. George Mason and Patrick Henry died in the 1790s. Neither man apparently ever emancipated a single person. Their wills apportioned their slaves among their heirs. It is unclear whether Henry's descendants inherited his "pity" for slaves' "unhappy lot" or his "abhorrence" of slavery, but they certainly took ownership of the men and women he bequeathed them.[66]

The Washingtons did take a stand, of sorts. In his will, George freed William Lee immediately and granted him a lifetime annuity. The other 123 slaves that he owned outright, however, would have to continue to labor throughout Martha Washington's life. It did not take long for Martha to realize that those slaves saw their freedom in her death. It became "necessary, (for *prudential* reasons)," her grandson explained, for her to free them all. John Adams, not one for circumspection, was far blunter about her motivation: "She did not feel as tho her Life was safe in their Hands." Martha Washington, then, not George, freed the Mount Vernon slaves. And her decision was not motivated by ethics or principles.[67] Those facts do not diminish the significance of George and Martha Washington's actions, either to the lives of the men and women who otherwise would have remained in bondage or in the context of their generation or for subsequent generations of Americans. But they also don't negate the other fact: only in death did the "father of his country" begin to bring freedom home.

Unlike other elements of their changing familial values, Virginia patriots' attitudes toward the black members of their plantation households—the men and women they constitutionally designated "other persons"—remained impervious to revolutionary principles. The architects of the American Republic accepted their whole lives what they themselves saw as a contradiction to their most deeply held civic values. Slavery would remain central to their domestic lives, their self-identity, their household economies, and the structure of their republic: at once a part and apart. However intellectually exercised they became, not one of the five most influential Virginia political leaders chose to act during his lifetime—a glaring reversal of their courageous and principled conduct during the Revolution. Instead, they codified this institution in their new governments and upheld it in their homes. In time, each man retired from public life to a splendid family estate of white leisure and black labor, unable to see the Revolution through to fruition because they were unwilling to sacrifice the status of their white families and violate their duties as fathers.

CHAPTER 7

"Ourselves and Our Posterity"

The stakes of the meeting in Philadelphia in the summer of 1787 could scarcely have been higher. As George Mason saw it, "The Revolt from Great Britain, & the Formations of our new Governments at that time, were nothing compared with the great Business now before us." The delegates believed their convention was momentous especially because of what the outcome would mean for future generations of Americans. "The Influence which the Establishments now proposed may have upon the Happiness or Misery of Millions yet unborn," Mason understood, "is an Object of such Magnitude, as absorbs, & in a Manner suspends the Operations of the human Understanding."[1] Even as they quarreled endlessly about every nuanced detail of their enterprise, the men at the Philadelphia Convention looked to the future, to how their actions would echo across time. *Posterity* preoccupied their minds and was embedded in the preamble to the US Constitution.

While the design of the new government that would decide the fate of "millions yet unborn" was hammered out in Philadelphia, the existential struggle over ratification ultimately turned, as did so much in the revolutionary era, on Virginia. Technically any nine states could have ratified the Constitution, but in 1787–1788 everyone understood that without Virginia the proposition would almost certainly fail. The state held one-fifth of the land in the United States, and one in six Americans lived there. And there was the not insignificant weight of recent history.

More of the men who conceived the American Republic hailed from Virginia than any other state, arguably more than all the other states combined. If the home of George Washington and Patrick Henry was not to be in the United States, could there be a United States at all? But there was a problem in the Old Dominion: though they agreed that justly governing the *country* centered on promoting the well-being of *posterity*, Virginia's founders disagreed vehemently over whether the Constitution could fill that bill.

During the ratification debates, proponents of the Constitution lauded it as the fulfillment of the Revolution. The proposal, its supporters proudly announced, satisfied a sweeping range of needs: it would secure the "common defense" and "general Welfare" of the states and defend the "Blessings of Liberty" for Americans and "our Posterity." It created, the framers declared, "a more perfect Union," advancing the greater interests of the citizens of all the states, now bound together in an unprecedented federal government.[2]

Others balked at this sanguine salesmanship of a radical restructuring of the union of the states. The Constitution, they saw, created a country bigger than most men had previously imagined possible for a republic, one larger than any state in Europe. Patrick Henry was incensed from the opening phrase. "What right had they to say, *We, the people?*" he demanded to know in the Virginia Ratifying Convention in June 1788. "Who authorised them to speak the language of, *We, the people*, instead of, *We the states?* States are the characteristics, and the soul of a confederation. If the States be not the agents of this compact, it must be one great consolidated National Government." While avowing his respect for delegates who attended the Philadelphia Convention, Henry insisted they explain their actions since "that they exceeded their power is perfectly clear." Even George Washington was called to account. Americans at a distance from the former commander-in-chief of the Continental Army might have deified him in their minds, but Henry's familiarity with Washington was long and personal, and he was not impressed with the deliberations over which his old friend had presided: "I wish to hear the real actual existing danger," Henry railed, "which should lead us to take those steps so dangerous in my conception." As ever, his concerns centered on Virginia. "Disorders have arisen in other parts of America," he conceded, "but here, Sir, no dangers, no insurrection or tumult, have happened—every thing has been calm and tranquil." It seemed preposterous to Henry that patriotic Virginians would even consider "wandering on the great ocean of human affairs." "I see no landmark to guide us," he warned. "We are running we know not whither."[3]

Nothing less than sovereignty itself—one of the most important concepts in eighteenth-century political theory—was at stake.[4] Americans redefined sovereignty in 1776 by denying imperial authority. But even as they declared independence from their mother country, patriots had not clearly decided where or how sovereignty would operate in the union of sister states. Once independence was won, Americans had to confront that troublesome question. Debates came to a head over the proposed Constitution, but its shared powers and sometimes ambiguous language certainly did not decide the issue.

The summer of 1788 was, in fact, only the start. Thereafter high-minded ideals about seeking the common good and reasoning together to reach consensus gave way to near constant turmoil. From the debates in Richmond through the hit-and-miss efforts of the 1790s and 1800s to forge a working federal government, leaders found themselves beset by conflicts and controversies, and they must have often felt as if they were, as Henry warned, running blind.[5]

To fully understand this cohort's cacophonous debates over building a new United States we must, as they did, look homeward. The connection between fatherhood and political perspective was not lost on Virginia's most prominent nineteenth-century historian, Hugh Blair Grigsby. When the Virginia Historical Society president studied the state's ratifying convention, he was struck by the fact that the leading advocates, including Washington and Madison, were "men of wealth, or held office by a life tenure, and that, though married, neither of them ever had a child." Less concerned with what Grigsby termed "the destinies of posterity," Madison and Washington were willing to sacrifice Virginia's sovereignty to build a stronger, national country. "In the same spirit," Grigsby continued, "Mason and Henry were men of large families. . . . In the case of Henry, the cradle began to rock in his house in his eighteenth year, and was rocking at his death in his sixty-third."[6] With sons to launch, these men could not afford to subordinate state interests, particularly land claims, to a federal union. Washington and Madison might think of their duties to posterity in general terms, puzzling through the best interests of future generations of citizens, but Mason and Henry saw the faces of posterity at their dinner tables. To be sure, Grigsby oversimplified a complex set of circumstances. Household composition did not correlate with constitutional opinions. But the two were not unrelated.

The family circumstances of some Virginia founders turned them more inward, to their households, local communities, and an allegiance to their country defined as Virginia. Other men, less tethered to domestic concerns, strayed farther from home, physically and conceptually, and their perception of country moved beyond the boundaries of the Old Dominion. While Grigsby might not have been completely accurate, there is in his reflection a larger truth about the connections between family values and revolutionary politics.

Divergent attitudes toward fatherhood played a foundational role in the contentious formation of the federal government and, then, in the quarrelsome politics of the early national era, though not in the uncomplicated way Hugh Blair Grigsby suggested. For some of Virginia's most prominent leaders, fatherhood remained mostly personal and experiential, which led them in the 1780s and 1790s to privilege a more traditional conception of posterity centering on ensuring that sons would enjoy lucrative inheritances. For others, fatherhood became more abstracted—a political concept rather than a paramount familial role. Imagining themselves as fathers of a nation rather than just a household led some powerful men to embrace a new generational perception of posterity. Their legacy was more ideological than financial.

In this fractious early federal age, just as had been the case during the tumult of 1765–1775, family gave Virginia's founders a context for perceiving politics. In the constitutional era, however, they were not a band of brothers facing down a cruel father-king. Rather, they turned on themselves. The fierce conflicts over the best government for a country committed to securing a republican future for posterity turned on hotly contested meanings of *country* and *posterity*. Where did the allegiance of good fathers and virtuous founders lie? What country did they serve? What posterity did they privilege?

W hen James Madison took the lead in defending the Constitution at the fateful Virginia Ratifying Convention in June 1788, he was thirty-seven years old, still single and living with his parents, and free of any substantive familial responsibilities. Patrick Henry's son-in-law Spencer Roane, in a direct comparison between Henry and Madison, pointed out that James Madison Sr. gave his son a lucrative estate and managed it for him. James Jr. could pursue his political career "unencumbered," as Roane put it, "with the cares of a family."[7]

Madison's experiences, particularly his freedom from familial duties, shaped his political attitudes. He spent the lion's share of his nearly forty-year-long career in government on the national level. Madison came of age during his collegiate years in Princeton, when British Americans saw themselves as most united against imperial aggressions, and he always tended toward a perspective that transcended Virginia. As early as 1774, young Madison expressed his confidence in the Continental Congress to formulate the right response to imperial crises; it should be the governmental body "to whose wisdom and Judgment all private opinions must give place." That view hardened during the war. While serving in Congress Madison witnessed the dire consequences of state sovereignty, particularly when it came to funding the military. He complained in 1781 of the "shameful deficiency of some of the States" to sacrifice for the common good.[8]

Madison did not marry until 1794, when he was forty-three years old, having made politics the center of his life down to that point. In his thirties and early forties he was gone from Virginia far more than he was at home. He resided at Montpelier in 1797–1798, between the time he left the House of Representatives and rejoined the Virginia Assembly. Not since 1769 had he spent an entire year in Virginia. He returned to federal service in 1801, first as secretary of state and then president. When Madison retired to Virginia after his presidency, he had been absent from Montpelier for the better part of sixteen years.

Madison's immersion in politics outside of Virginia and near absence of family responsibilities likewise shaped his intellectual pursuits, notably in the spring of 1786, when he began an intensive study of politics and history to understand the problems facing the Confederation

Congress. It was a pivotal period in Madison's life and, in turn, for the future of the United States. His long exploration resulted in "Vices of the Political System of the United States," in which, in quintessential Madison style, he systematically laid out the governmental problems that, he concluded, derived principally from insufficient checks on local biases. The inability to collect requisitions, defend treaties, regulate commerce, and avoid civil unrest all crippled the general welfare at the expense of local interests. In cleaving to narrow agendas, Madison reasoned, states failed to promote justice and ensure the rights of citizens.[9]

It was both necessary and possible, Madison concluded, for Americans to transcend their local prejudices and broaden their allegiance to include the whole of the union of states, to look beyond their provincial needs, to become, in effect, a *national family*. "Hearken not," he cautioned in Federalist No. 14, "to the unnatural voice, which tells you that the people of America, knit together as they are by so many chords of affection, can no longer live together as members of the same family. . . . The kindred blood which flows in the veins of American citizens, the mingled blood which they have shed in defence of their sacred rights, consecrate their union." He continued to promote his ideal of a national family in the Virginia Ratifying Convention, where he took on both the greatest orator of the age, Patrick Henry, and the most revered intellectual in the state, his old mentor George Mason. In Richmond and beyond, it remained Madison's firm belief that a "spirit of locality" was undermining "the aggregate interests of the Community."[10]

Without children at Montpelier to supervise, Madison could devote himself wholly to the young Republic. He did not often have to weigh that service against the duties of a Virginia patriarch. No sick wife suffered in his absence, no adolescent heirs called his attention home. He could leave Orange County emotionally when he left physically. In 1794, James married Dolley Payne Todd, a woman deeply in love with him and possessing talents that perfectly matched his ambitions. They had no children together, and Dolley relished the national political scene. Not coincidentally, throughout his political career Madison concerned himself with one overriding question: "Will the aggregate strength, security, tranquility, and harmony of the whole nation be advanced or impaired"? That particular language concerned policy regarding the future of slavery in the nation. But it applied just as well to his attitude during his tenure in Congress and while serving as president. A just republic, Madison understood, required "sacrificing private opinions and partial interests to the public good."[11]

Patrick Henry agreed about the importance of sacrifice, but because of his family circumstances his perception of what constituted the "public good" became more circumscribed. Whereas Madison made his name on the national stage, Henry spent his entire career, except for a brief stint in the Continental Congress, serving Virginia, near his family and where he was better able to guide his relatives and expand his landholdings. When he went to the Virginia Ratifying Convention, Henry said, "I consider myself as the servant of the people of this Commonwealth, as a centinel over their rights, liberty, and happiness."[12] He was guardian, too, of a large and growing family. By 1788, Dorothea and Patrick Henry had six young children, along with six from his first marriage. It was not that either Henry or Madison self-consciously or self-servingly privileged the political power they themselves exercised. Rather, their political views emerged out of their very different experiences—experiences shaped by the weight or absence of family responsibilities.[13]

The demands of fatherhood often kept Patrick Henry at home, and he focused on family and community in more traditional ways. His duty to posterity, as he imagined it, consisted first in launching his sons and daughters in Virginia, where, he believed, sovereignty justly belonged. Henry's patriot zeal always reflected his steadfast allegiance to his country, which he defined as Virginia. Henry was not a particularly rigorous thinker, and he was the least philosophically consistent of Virginia's leading politicians. The one constant in his career was his abiding attachment to local interests, which was on abundant display in the summer of 1788. Henry fought ratification with a ferocity that surprised even those who knew him well. Holding forth for hours at a time with blistering rebukes of the federal plan and its advocates, Henry insisted that the Constitution represented "a revolution as radical as that which separated us from Great Britain."[14]

"This Government is not a Virginian but an American government," Henry warned.[15] And he wanted no part of it. Some of Henry's contemporaries thought him petty for refusing to participate in that "American government" after his failed effort to block the Constitution. But his choices can better be understood as deriving from his commitment to the duties of a traditional Virginia patriarch. Like most of his influential gentry friends and neighbors—including many who supported the Constitution—Patrick Henry focused on Virginia interests, which drew him to the local rather than the national scene. Aware of Henry's talents and hoping for a powerful symbol of reconciliation between Federalists and Antifederalists, President Washington made several attempts to recruit him to a federal office. But Henry always said no: to becoming secretary of state, an ambassador, a senator. Each time he emphasized his determination to remain close to home. The "great Distance to Philadelphia" precluded him taking a seat in the Senate in 1794. And he declined to serve as an envoy to Spain that same year because it would have required him to move too far away from the country (Virginia) and the posterity (children) he prized.[16]

When Washington pressed him to become secretary of state in 1795, Henry offered a full-throated defense of his values, which prioritized family-based localism and paternal duty: "My domestic situation pleads strongly against a removal to Philadelphia, having no less than eight children by my present marriage." Besides his children with Dorothea, Patrick was providing for his widowed daughter Martha Fontaine and her children. When his sister Anne Christian died, caring for her children and supervising their educations fell to Henry. "What a weight of worldly concerns," noted one neighbor, "rest upon this old man's shoulders." Faced with so many family duties, Henry was still willing to serve Virginia, but he would not leave the state for national office.[17]

Like Patrick Henry, George Mason thought of Virginia as his country, and he too saw his duty to posterity in familial terms. His priorities remained consistent throughout the revolutionary era. While George Washington complained about inadequate support for the Continental Army, Mason saw failures to sacrifice as state-centered issues. The House of Delegates, he protested in a letter to Richard Henry Lee in the summer of 1779, spent precious time on "Trifles & Whims" when they should have been "restoring our Finances & defending our Country." By "Country" he meant Virginia.[18]

While Madison and Washington bemoaned self-interested parochialism during the war years, Mason charged the Continental Congress with pursuing "illegal, & dangerous Schemes" aimed at "dismembering the Commonwealth of Virginia." Mason saw that such plans derived from a belief on the part of some delegates in the Continental Congress that sovereignty lay with the Congress itself—which he emphatically rejected. Nor did he truck with similar notions during the Confederation era. Mason maintained that Virginians accepted the Articles of Confederation only because it recognized the sovereignty of every state. The idea of the Confederation Congress controlling western lands represented to him a flat deal-breaker: "There is not a single Word in the Articles of Confederation giving Congress a Power of limiting, dividing, or parceling out any of the thirteen States, or of erecting new ones."[19]

George Mason was no less strident than Patrick Henry in his opposition to the Constitution's centralization of power. Late in the Philadelphia debates he declared, as Madison wryly recorded in his copious notes, that "he would sooner chop off his right hand than put it to the Constitution."[20] Mason carried the fight home to Virginia, where he and Patrick Henry very nearly prevailed. After weeks of passionate debate the final vote was stunningly close: 89–79. Five votes swung the other way would have altered the course of the nation.

Mason's perceptions of country and posterity put him at odds with his longtime friend George Washington. The two men's lives had been so similar and connected in the 1760s. But the Revolution pulled one friend further from that world, and for far longer, than the other. By 1787, they found themselves on opposite sides of a great political divide and personally estranged.

Washington's willingness to sacrifice his domestic happiness for the patriot cause and Mason's faithfulness to his family despite opportunities to achieve great renown changed the arc of their lives, their views on country, and their perceived obligations to posterity. When Mason fought against the Constitution and refused after ratification to take part in the national government, he lost his friendship with Washington. Mason was disappointed at the outcome but unapologetic as to the cause. "I am truly conscious of having acted from the purest motives of honesty, and love to my country," he wrote his son John. Whatever his opposition to the Constitution cost him, Mason was convinced that his conduct "will administer comfort to me in those moments when I shall most want it, and smooth the bed of death."[21]

In stark contrast to George Mason and Patrick Henry, George Washington operated on a national field from the early stages of the Revolution and never left it. His support for the Constitution, including its centralizing definition of country, was consistent with the views he first adopted during the Revolutionary War. From the outset of the military contest, George Washington prioritized the country—the United States—that chose him as its father. His military campaigns convinced him that the citizens of the American Republic shared a common future. As the contest dragged on, he repeatedly complained about trifling local concerns undermining vital national service. After he resigned his military commission, Washington continued to deride the disorder that devolved from thirteen states acting autonomously under the Article of Confederation. In late 1786 he commiserated with David Stuart about the necessity of revising that government. "The present constitution is inadequate," he bluntly stated. "The superstructure totters to its foundations, and without helps, will bury us in its ruins."[22]

Without sons of his own to launch, George Washington focused on building a national family of citizens bound together by earned mutual respect and service. (Washy Custis had a Custis inheritance awaiting his majority and so was not financially dependent on his grandfather.) Washington's perception of posterity and definition of country remained broad—generational and continental, in turn, rather than centered primarily on Mount Vernon. To be certain, Washington relished his peaceful life with Martha at Mount Vernon. But he was convinced in 1787 that the happiness of future generations of Americans depended on a stronger union and fully persuaded "that the primary cause of all our disorders lies in the different State Governments." So long as "local views" refused to "yield to a more enlarged scale of politicks," he warned, America would remain "weak at home and disregarded abroad."[23]

In leading the effort to build the federal union, Washington left behind the allegiance to Virginia that consumed—and, he thought, misled—many of his peers. His identification with America as his country was so strong that he dismissed as "Demagogues" men, including many Virginians, who stubbornly refused "to lose any of their state consequence." In the fall of 1787 he warned Bushrod Washington, who would participate in the Virginia Ratifying Convention, to ready himself. "Virginians," he concluded, "entertain *too* high an opinion of the importance" of their state. He conceded that Virginia was the largest and most populous state, "but in point of *strength*, it is, comparatively, weak." Washington declined attending the Virginia Ratifying Convention because he was widely imagined to be the first president should the Constitution pass muster; lobbying for its adoption seemed inappropriate. But he was a committed advocate and exerted tremendous influence from Mount Vernon. Washington insisted that the Constitution's critics—including his now estranged neighbor George Mason—sought "to rouse the apprehensions of the ignorant, & unthinking." They clung to their narrow "local views," he protested, and refused to see that "the Union of the whole is a desirable object."[24]

Family circumstances, then, made a huge difference for the two most outspoken rivals in the Richmond debates, Henry and Madison, and their respective seconds, Mason and Washington, who, though absent from the proceedings, kept in close contact with Madison.[25] Other factors, of course, including perspectives on the economy and political philosophy, were at play. But it remains striking that Henry's and Mason's duties as fathers of large families had so often directed their attentions to the domestic and the local and that predisposition shaded their views of the federal union. Madison, meanwhile, had no paternal obligations, which was itself a new situation for a respected leader. And though Washington fulfilled traditional paternal roles for the young people he and Martha welcomed into their household, he prioritized civic life. Both men were wholeheartedly committed to continental service during the war years—and they acted accordingly in 1787–1788.

As the first president, Washington continued to prioritize the good of the nation and to invidiously compare the localistic outlook of many Virginians with what he saw as the farsighted perspective of federal leaders. Through all the tumult that plagued his administration, Washington never lost his faith in the federal government as the best hope for the promotion of the general welfare. During his second term in office, his specific policies in pursuit of that goal undermined his relationship with Thomas Jefferson and James Madison, who launched an opposition faction against Washington and his most influential ally, Alexander Hamilton. But he remained resolute. In his will, Washington bequeathed stock to help fund a national university where, he hoped, students might "free themselves" from "local attachments and State prejudices." A national university, instilling national allegiances could, he imagined, help cement a national family.[26]

Thomas Jefferson shared George Washington's and James Madison's commitment to defining country as the United States and predisposition to think about posterity in the abstract, even though he did have children of his own. Jefferson's entry into national politics was spurred by the loss of his wife, Martha. After she died in September 1782 he seemed to want to be anywhere but home. Two months after her death, he accepted an appointment that would have carried him to Europe to negotiate a peace treaty with Great Britain. He moved to Philadelphia in December 1782 to ready for his crossing. When that appointment was delayed, he accepted a seat in the Confederation Congress. By the spring of 1784 Jefferson had again agreed to serve his country abroad. From August 1784 through September 1789 he remained in France. He arrived back in Virginia in November 1789, but within three months he accepted the appointment as secretary of state and, with it, more years away from home.

In these years, Jefferson had two motherless children to raise, but they were daughters, generally more in need, he believed, of a maternal presence than even his own. Martha and Polly could therefore be left in Virginia with Elizabeth Eppes or in France with the nuns at the abbey, and if they married well they would, he presumed, become the responsibility of their husbands. None of Jefferson's peers looked askance at a single father turning young daughters over to the care of experienced kinswomen. To do otherwise, in fact, could be a disservice: girls needed women to teach them how to be useful and respectable. Those assumptions freed Thomas to answer calls to national service.

During his many years in the federal government, though he loved Virginia, Jefferson imagined America as his country. Even though he became bitterly estranged from President Washington over governmental policies, Jefferson still shared Washington's desire to build a national family—just not in the way that Washington and Alexander

Hamilton imagined. In his second inaugural address, President Jefferson defended the Louisiana Purchase by echoing Madison's Federalist No. 10. "The larger our association," he reasoned, "the less will it be shaken by local passions." "And in any view," he continued, "is it not better that the opposite bank of the Mississippi should be settled by our own brethren and children, than by strangers of another family?" Late in life, Jefferson's world narrowed. Once he returned home in 1809, he never again left Virginia and seldom traveled beyond the Charlottesville area, and his views grew increasingly parochial. But while he was on the national stage, even when he birthed a political faction committed to reining in federal powers, Jefferson saw the United States as his country. Along with Washington and Madison, he stood apart from the localistic perspective prioritized by Mason and Henry.[27]

Jefferson's, Washington's, and Madison's families were all different, to be certain. One man was a single father to only daughters (and a secret second family of slave children), another head of a household of assorted kin but no financially dependent sons, and the third a middle-aged bachelor. But they shared an important common denominator: the absence of sons and inheritance anxieties, which influenced their perceptions of posterity and country. As they achieved great things in the civic realm, they adopted different outlooks on politics and family than men running households filled with children. The further Madison, Jefferson, and Washington involved themselves in continental and even international affairs, the less their devotion to Virginia-based matters held sway. Virginia might be their home, but it alone was not their country. Their individual families, then, encouraged them to think of posterity in historic rather than personal terms and to define their country as the United States.

When Patrick Henry and George Mason wrote about their country, they meant Virginia. And as Virginia patriarchs had long done, they devoted themselves to taking care of households and meeting community obligations. Their focus remained on Virginia: acquiring land, launching sons, and exercising power there. Their political priorities ran accordingly.

Neither Mason nor Henry held any significant national offices to substantively challenge that viewpoint, not because they were not able or asked, but because they wanted to remain in Virginia, where their families lived and their interests lay. Mason raised nine children, for many years as a single father, and Henry eventually had fifteen (one died in infancy). While state politics often distracted them, both laid down clear limits to how far from home they would go. Neither felt willing to trade their domestic obligations for the national political stage— certainly not when there were strategically advantageous political offices to fill in the Old Dominion. They spent their energy amassing land and wealth for their posterity and in their country, Virginia, which they believed in 1787–1788 was sacrificed to a tyrannical federal government—bound, as Henry evocatively put it, by the "ropes and chains of consolidation."[28]

Political principle and family interest merged, then, in Mason and Henry's resolve to spurn any national office under the Constitution. Having lost on the central political question of their age, they saw that family offered a noble justification for refusing to serve in the federal government they had feared and fought. They could claim the moral high ground by determining to spend more time with their children, to focus on their personal posterity, at home in Virginia.

Although Washington, Jefferson, and Madison earned the greater share of national renown, Mason and Henry reflected the dominant political culture in Virginia, where long-standing traditions persisted well after Independence. Western newcomers joined the state legislature in the early national era, and nonelites began to fill more offices, especially on the local level, but gentlemen still mostly governed the Old Dominion. This fact became a source of frequent derision among travelers. An 1804 visitor thought the state oddly out of step with republican values: "Their *public affairs* are in an absolute monopoly by the rich." Local and state interests preoccupied those leaders—even many of the men who agreed to represent Virginia in the federal government. Regardless of the faction they identified with after the 1780s, many of Virginia's leaders held different priorities from the state's first three presidents when they, in terms of loyalties as well as quite literally, left Virginia for the new nation.[29]

A s he pondered what he might say in his inaugural address, President-Elect George Washington realized that having no sons to provide for concentrated his attention on the well-being of future generations of Americans. His name would not, Washington explained, be "perpetuated by the endearing, though sometimes seducing channel of immediate offspring." Therefore, he reasoned, "I have no child for whom I could wish to make a provision—no family to build in greatness upon my Country's ruins."[30] During the Revolutionary War, Washington's childlessness had freed him to focus on the military service essential to the creation of the American Republic. Washington's wartime accomplishments changed perceptions of legitimate power, moving idealized fatherhood from the biological to the generational, from the personal to the national. He presented a vision of fatherhood of his country, absent actual parenthood, which, in the colonial era, had been a key marker of manhood and purpose of leadership. Then, as he prepared to assume the presidency, Washington expressly framed his childlessness as important for posterity writ large and for his country, the United States.

That President Washington could imagine his family's success as detrimental to the best interest of his country reveals how much the connection between politics and family had changed by the 1790s. In colonial Virginia, family and politics had fit together seamlessly: men served in elected and appointed offices as a consequence of their kin ties, and political power advantaged family networks. But in the new nation, merit was supposed to supplant lineage, calling those deep traditions into question.

Virginia's presidents confronted a new issue, one unfamiliar to men of their fathers' generation: Should family matter in politics? Their individual actions merit close consideration, for they were at the pinnacle of the precarious new federal government, inaugurating practices that future generations would scrutinize. They believed (and it was not hyperbolic) the very survival of the federal government hung in the balance. The wrong move, they imagined, and the whole enterprise could fail. They needed to be above reproach: model leaders, whose conduct would determine the viability of republican government and be judged by history.

Presidents Washington, Jefferson, and Madison—and John Adams, during his single term—needed to figure out how to make traditional connections between family and politics conform to republican ideals. They were, as Henry had warned, "wandering on the great ocean of human affairs." And each new day brought them, in Jefferson's words, "storms of a new character."[31] The struggle was not abstract. Even though the three Virginians had no sons of their own to raise, they certainly had large families to watch over. Their relatives' needs could not be ignored. Neither could a president's concern for his family members appear to override his duties to the country.

Their households provide the first clue as to how these men tried to work this all out. Continuing a practice he had commenced during the Revolutionary War, President Washington brought into his household and his heart a number of young political protégés deeply loyal to him and with whom he shared a fierce commitment to the new nation. "His domestic family," as Washington's grandson called it, was quite large and highly selective. Of course there were Martha and the Custis grandchildren. But, according to Washington Custis, President Washington also counted David Humphreys, a Connecticut native, as a member of his family. Humphreys had been a Revolutionary War officer and aide-de-camp to Washington. After the war he stayed from time to time at Mount Vernon, and he moved with the Washingtons to New York in 1789. In a letter to Benjamin Franklin, Washington praised Humphreys's "zeal in the cause of his Country" and said that "his good sense, prudence, and attachment to me, rendered him dear to me." William Jackson, another member of the president's self-selected family, had been orphaned as a boy and raised by a family friend in South Carolina. He too fought in the Revolutionary War and in 1787, with the help of Washington, became secretary to the Constitutional Convention. Also included in Washington Custis's list of family members was Tobias Lear, a New Hampshire native, who started out as a secretary in 1786. In 1795 he married Fanny Bassett Washington, Martha's niece, who was the widow of one of George's nephews. After Fanny Bassett died in 1796, Lear married another of Martha Washington's nieces, Fanny Dandridge Henley. So, rather than the colonial tradition, in which marital ties begat political power, it worked the other way for Lear. In all three men's cases, they joined Washington's family, and he advanced their careers because of individual talents and personal loyalty.[32]

The Washingtons continued as well to take in young kin who might benefit from their guidance. In 1792, Washington's sister, Betty Lewis, sent her son Howell to work as a secretary to the president and become "one of your family." Howell's father had died when the boy was only ten, leaving him, Washington knew, "very slenderly provided for," and he wanted to "give him a turn to some pursuit or other that might be serviceable to him hereafter."[33] Other nephews who seemed less deserving of his time received no such welcome.

George Washington's "domestic family" remained highly selective, populated by accomplished young men, some of whom also happened to be kin. But genealogy was by no means a prerequisite or guarantee of inclusion. Thomas Jefferson had a similar perception of family, which included not only his sons-in-law and Carr nephews but also protégés such as William Short, whom Jefferson considered a son. Washington and Jefferson cultivated political families of both relatives and protégés they expected to ably lead the Republic in the future. This personal, elective understanding of family—usually absent any financial responsibilities—at once reflected and advanced their political values.[34]

James Madison's household offers the richest example of the new dynamic between family and politics. To begin with, he achieved national prominence without a wife or children and while financially dependent on his father. Respectable colonial patriarchs traditionally married and headed households on their way to office holding. But Madison, born in 1751 and reaching maturity in the height of the Revolution, was able to make national politics his full-time career and become a celebrated leader without a wife or an independent estate. When he reached his mid-thirties and remained single, James Madison's friends sometimes teased him. They longed to see him, William Grayson said, "in the character of a married man." Another friend jokingly cautioned James that even "the best services to the public" would not always protect him from "the Taunts to which Old Bachelors are justly exposed."[35] But bachelorhood did not, in fact, slow Madison's rise to power. He was in his early forties when he began to court Dolley Payne Todd. They met years after he drafted the design for the Constitution, ensured its ratification in Virginia, and pushed a Bill of Rights through the US Congress.

James Madison's fatherhood was strictly metaphorical—of the Constitution. The paramount expectation of fatherhood did not change: a man would ably guide and protect the interests of posterity. Yet Madison fulfilled those expectations not for his children but rather for those generations of Americans yet unborn.

James was forty-three when he and Dolley, seventeen years his junior, married. It was a great match, both personally and politically. They called one another "my beloved" in their affectionate letters and seldom spent a night apart. When he went to Charlottesville in 1826—better than thirty years into their marriage—she told him that "four days passed without my beloved, seem so many weeks." He felt exactly the same and replied, "I hope never again to be so long from you, being with devoted affection ever yours." The couple formed a great political partnership, too. He was the intellectual force behind the federal government, and she the progenitor of Washington society.[36]

Their family values mirrored James's political philosophy, focusing on the collective interests of virtuous citizens and the future well-being of the United States. In addition to being the site of Washington, DC, political culture, the Madison household teemed with nephews and nieces, cousins, and siblings as well as unrelated charges. Death and need pushed some young people into their home. After Dolley's brother-in-law George Steptoe Washington died, Dolley's sister Lucy and her children lived in the White House. After James's brothers Francis and Ambrose Madison died, their children also turned to James for guidance. Madison paid for his nephew Robert Madison (son of another brother, William) to attend Dickinson College. Ambrose's daughter Nelly Willis was widowed in 1812, and she often stayed with the Madisons, becoming a favorite of her uncle. Affection drew other kin into their homes. Dolley's sister Anna Payne lived so long with the Madisons that Dolley referred to her as a "daughter-sister." After Anna married Richard Cutts, the couple resided in the District of Columbia in property Madison owned. After Madison retired, Anna's children spent their summers at Montpelier and thought of the estate as their second home.

Annie Payne lived most of the time with her Aunt Dolley, eventually moving permanently to Montpelier. James's nieces and nephews visited frequently as well, and Rebecca Chapman, daughter of William Madison, joined her cousin Nelly Willis as especially beloved. An 1826 visitor to Montpelier calculated that a dozen young relatives were staying with the Madisons.[37]

Even as they looked after a fluid household of kin, James and Dolley included in their domestic circle a political family that transcended these ties of blood and marriage. As was the case with George Washington and Thomas Jefferson, young members of Madison's self-determined family were drawn in by friendship and political allegiance. James also forged connections with men of his own generation. For example, when President Jefferson appointed Charles Pinckney to be minister to Spain in 1801, Pinckney wrote Secretary of State Madison to proclaim proudly, "I am now to become one of your political family & am to rely on your goodness & friendship."[38]

Madison's faithful political partnership and brotherly bond with Jefferson constituted the most successful part of his political family. Paul Jennings saw the connection up close and over decades: Madison and Jefferson were, he recalled, "extremely intimate," and though they shared no kin ties, "in fact, two brothers could not have been more so."[39] The friendship commenced in the darkest days of the Revolutionary War. The two grew close in 1779, when Madison served on the executive council, providing political advice to Governor Jefferson. They met sometimes daily as they struggled to protect Virginia from encroachments by the vastly superior British forces. That was when Jefferson came to appreciate, as he put it, what a "luminous and discriminating mind" Madison possessed. Through all the turmoil and backbiting of the early national era, they never had a serious disagreement. Their bond endured until Jefferson's death nearly fifty years after they first became friends.[40]

James Monroe also belonged to their tight circle. Even when Madison and Monroe clashed over ratification of the Constitution and ran against each other during the congressional election of 1789, they remained close, traveling together and sharing rooms on the campaign trail. Jefferson told Monroe, "I have ever viewed Mr. Madison and yourself, as two principal pillars of my happiness. Were either to be withdrawn, I should consider it as among the greatest calamities which could assail my future peace of mind." It was a sentiment that could have been expressed by any of the three and the basis of a decades-long shared commitment to service and fraternity.[41]

Generally, though, Madison focused his political family-making on the next generation. As president, he surrounded himself with loyal and talented young men. He encouraged their ambitions, rewarded their achievements, and safeguarded their interests. They were not simply political apprentices but, in his mind and by his actions, members of his family. Some were related, of course. Edward Coles, for example, was Dolley's cousin. Many other members of the Madison family shared personal connections but no blood ties. Nicholas Trist was Thomas Jefferson's grandson-in-law. Richard Rush was the son of the famous Philadelphia physician Benjamin Rush. None, importantly, were financially dependent on him or counting on a future inheritance.

The protégés President Madison mentored pursued distinguished careers in government and diplomacy long after Madison's retirement, and owing much of their start in life to him, they remained committed to his legacy. Rush was a nearly lifelong public servant, working both domestically and in the diplomatic corps, including as minister to both Britain and France and serving as the youngest attorney general in US history (an appointment from Madison). Trist helped administer the University of Virginia and worked in the State Department under Henry Clay during Andrew Jackson's presidency.

Madison wanted to give his meritorious young kin a helping hand, but he certainly did not want unqualified men in government service. He therefore insisted that the young men he aided, whether kin or not, understand they would have to prove themselves worthy of his efforts and ultimately make their own way in the world. His nephew Madison Macon offers a good case in point. At the request of his brother-in-law, Thomas Macon, President Madison helped launch his nineteen-year-old namesake into a career as a merchant. Madison enjoyed a rich reservoir of contacts from which to draw, and he started at the top: with Secretary of the Treasury Albert Gallatin. Gallatin assured Madison, "It would be easy to place *your* nephew in many mercantile houses."

Madison and Gallatin agreed, though, with Thomas Macon that, even with this wonderful assistance, Madison Macon's future would ultimately rest "on the manner in which the two or three next years of his life is spent." Similarly, in 1828 Nicholas Trist got his appointment with the State Department by making excellent use of family ties while knowing he had to prove himself worthy of the job. Trist's mother-in-law, Martha Jefferson Randolph, asked a friend to approach Secretary of State Henry Clay, who told James Madison that hiring Trist would require him to pass over several current employees. Clay was willing to do the favor for "the family of Mr. Jefferson," but only if former President Madison assured him that Trist "possesses the requisite qualifications. This," Clay added, "is an indispensable condition."[42]

James Madison met a difficult challenge: blending family traditions and republican values. Eager to advance the greater good of the Republic, he and Dolley nurtured promising young men from the rising generation, seeking always to perpetuate cherished civic ideals. Even as he understood that a strong national family could not be built on nepotism, Madison wanted to be responsive to his relatives' needs, to assist the young men in his family circle. Under his leadership, then, family ties still helped ambitious young men secure political appointments, and men continued to cement political allegiances through strategic marriages, thanks especially to Dolley Madison. But those family connections became more selective and less often lineal. Political advancements became dependent on merit more than—though not instead of—kinship. It was a nuanced balancing of innovative political ideals and traditional family roles, required even of the men who reached the highest echelons of power.

Even as Virginia's presidents tried to build a national family, some of their closest kin became their biggest disappointments. Washy Custis mostly squandered his youth and frustrated his grandfather's hopes for making him into a leader worthy of his family's name, or at least avoiding embarrassing the president of the United States. President Jefferson invited his two sons-in-law to reside with him at the executive mansion, imagining they would all live happily together. But Thomas Mann Randolph Jr. grew so jealous of John Eppes that he moved out, and he soon thereafter left national politics and descended into an embarrassing decline.[43]

Again the Madison household is especially revealing, this time of how the most successful founders struggled as fathers. President Madison found his extended family beset by conflicts, scandal, and heartbreak. Three months into his job, Isaac Coles assaulted a congressional representative while on official White House business and had to quit. John Jackson, Dolley Madison's brother-in-law, got shot dueling with a North Carolina representative and had to resign from Congress to recover. James's promising nephew Alfred died despite the president's sending him to the nation's most renowned doctor, his friend Benjamin Rush. And there were appeals from Orange County regarding his aged mother. In the middle of the War of 1812, James's sister Frances Rose complained, "We have not learnt whether you expect to visit Orange this spring," adding that "no circumstance could afford our Mother more satisfaction than your doing so."[44]

Particularly hurtful to the Madisons were Dolley's erratic brothers. Walter Payne was expelled from the Quaker community in Philadelphia for "dishonest proceedings" in his businesses. He "absconded" without paying his creditors and left men who trusted him "in danger of suffering great loss." Isaac Payne was an alcoholic who died in the 1790s after also being expelled from the Quakers for gambling. John Payne struggled for years with alcoholism as well as mental problems, despite numerous efforts by James and Dolley to help. They even tried getting him out of the country, but appointing him to the diplomatic corps did not solve his drinking and money problems. He was forced to return to America in disgrace in 1811.[45]

More devastating still was the unremittingly dreadful conduct of Dolley's only son, Payne Todd, who resisted at every turn the Madisons' efforts to coach him toward respectability. James Madison could never see in his stepson what he wanted for his country: posterity worthy of inheriting the Republic. James regretted Payne's choices, but there was little he could actually do to right Payne's life. He forced no estrangement with Payne—Dolley would never have tolerated it—but shifted his interests elsewhere, to young men like Richard Rush and Nicholas Trist, who were worthy of his time and who knew how to put opportunities to good use. In his vast correspondence with Thomas Jefferson, James Madison never once asked for help with Payne. Dolley both indulged Payne and felt mortified by his behavior. But she could not give up hoping he would change, despite decades of disappointment. Dolley told Payne in 1824, in one of many beseeching and unanswered pleas, that she was "ashamed to tell, when asked, how long my only child has been absent." She begged him to at least "have the appearance of consulting your parents, on subjects of deep acct. to you." But at the close of the same letter she told him she had paid for him $200 of an outstanding loan, and she sent him $30. Even at the end of her life as she faced penury at his hands, Dolley continued to beg Payne to be responsible. He never changed. "We are without funds," she told him, "and those we owe are impatient."[46]

In addition to enduring these familial heartaches, Dolley and James Madison suffered during the War of 1812 the humiliating destruction of the presidential mansion that she had so meticulously turned into the nation's house. When President Madison left the White House on the morning of 22 August 1814, he knew British troops were dangerously close to Washington. He asked Dolley whether she had "the courage, or firmness to remain" in his absence, and when she assured him she "had no fear but for him and the success of our army," he rode out to survey the American troops. Working alongside her slaves on 23 August, Madison shoved as many governmental papers as she could into trunks and those onto waiting wagons. "Our private property," she concluded, "must be sacrificed," so that the words and ideas of the Republic could endure. She was up on 24 August at sunrise, "turning my spy glass in every direction and watching with unwearied anxiety." At three o'clock in the afternoon, she heard the cannon fire. By nightfall the White House was engulfed in flames: the velvet curtains, engraved chairs, carefully chosen china, all lost. The Stuart painting of George Washington survived, though. Dolley Madison could not allow it to fall into the hands of invading British forces.[47]

British troops not only destroyed the White House that late August; they laid waste to nearly every government building in the capital. But they left citizens' residences alone, intentionally distinguishing between public spaces, which were legitimate targets of war, and private spaces, which were not. The White House, though, was at once the seat of the executive branch and the home of the president's family: both public and private. When the British set fire to the Capitol building, the Library of Congress was destroyed. To begin to replace it, former president Thomas Jefferson offered his personal library to Congress: his private collection of books became the nation's public repository.

The divide between "public" and "private" was often invoked in the revolutionary era, but it was, as the burning of Washington hints, never precise. George Mason wrote political treatises in his family room at Gunston Hall. Martha Washington made war camps her home. James Madison's political opponents derided his and Dolley's supposedly mismatched sex life—she, rumor held, was wantonly aggressive—as symptomatic of his impotence as a leader.

In this cohort's writings, the public-private divide seems most stark in Thomas Jefferson's often-quoted invidious comparisons between the political realm into which he found himself inescapably drawn and the domestic realm for which he said he endlessly pined. He often wrote his daughters of his desire to leave national politics and return to the bliss he imagined awaiting him at Monticello. While secretary of state, for example, he insisted that the "toils and inquietudes of my present situation" could never match the joys of "domestic love and society." He wanted to be home, "exchanging labor, envy, and malice for ease, domestic occupation, and domestic love."[48] But, in fact, when Jefferson did go home, he usually did not stay long. Despite his repeated condemnations of early federal politics, Jefferson agreed two years after leaving his cabinet position to become vice president. Not a year into that position he was complaining again to Martha: "When I look to the ineffable pleasures of my family society, I become more and more disgusted with the jealousies, the hatred, and the rancorous and malignant passions of this scene." In the spring of 1798 he longed "to leave this place, and every thing which can be disgusting, for Monticello and my dear family, comprising every thing which is pleasurable to me in this world."[49] But he did not; two terms as president still lay in his future.

Jefferson's closest peers did not see things the same way. Washington complained that the Continental Army command required "the loss of all my domestick happiness." And he was delighted when he was finally freed "from the bustle of a camp & the busy scenes of public life." "The first wish of my Soul," he insisted in 1789, was "to spend the evening of my days on the bar of a private citizen." But whenever duty called he returned to office, and never with the rhetorical condemnations that Jefferson leveled. He admitted while president that he found politics "too interesting to be neglected."[50] Madison, meanwhile, seldom pined for Orange County and rarely declined an office. The varied views held by just these three men underscore the difficulty of overgeneralizing about perceptions of "public" and "private" in the early national era.

Close consideration of how this cohort defined family, how they blurred domestic and political connections, how often family values and political ideals changed in tandem in the revolutionary age, and how profoundly family influenced politics and vice versa—it all argues for seeing public and private as relative rather than as fixed terms, as interrelated rather than oppositional.

At the same time, a tension is clearly discernible between being a founder and being a father—and widening for men who sought the greatest national influence. Virginia's first three presidents understood that political service on the national level required sacrifices of time and attention to their kinfolk. Domestic lives had to be of secondary concern to political duties. Jefferson repeatedly insisted the exact opposite was true—always in letters from some distant city. Jefferson's juxtaposition between the bliss of home and the drudgery of politics predicted the nineteenth-century rhetoric of family representing a soothing retreat from the ordeal of work.[51] He was also idealizing what he did not know experientially. Jefferson praised the peace and pleasures of home *from afar*. His actions contradicted his rhetoric, as did his advice to his friends. In response to Washington's reluctance to serve as president, Jefferson lobbied for political service. "Nobody who has tried both public and private life can doubt but that you were much happier on the banks of the Potomac," he conceded. "But there was nobody so well qualified as yourself to put our new machine into a regular course of action." Madison had offered the same advice regarding Washington's participation in the Constitutional Convention. Martha and the Custis grandchildren, they believed, had to take a backseat to the country that so desperately needed its father.[52]

That was, more often than not, the choice made by the three Virginia founders who rank highest in our national imaginations, who are perceived to have achieved the most for the United States, and who, in fact, played the most meaningful roles in charting how the Republic would work under the Constitution. Madison, Jefferson, and Washington were exceedingly ambitious men, aware of the rare moment of history in which they were acting and eager to realize historical fame through their political, military, and intellectual triumphs. There is no doubt that they missed their relatives when serving their country. But there is equally no denying that they made their choices clear-eyed, weighing the cost to their kin against the benefits to their country and their place in history. For them, fatherhood became an abstraction more than an experience. In their own minds they were fathers—of the Declaration of Independence, the Constitution, and the United States. Their political service would be their legacy, the "millions yet unborn" their posterity.

At the opposite end of the spectrum stood Patrick Henry and George Mason, who decided that if family and politics could not dovetail, they would prefer to honor the former rather than be honored for the latter. It suited Henry just fine to know that, after he lost the ratification debates, "I have generally moved in a narrow circle." Mason cared less for the sacrifice that service on the national stage required than Henry. He had not been in Philadelphia for the Constitutional Convention more than two weeks before he longed for home. "I begin to grow heartily tired of the etiquette and nonsense so fashionable in this city," he told his son.[53] Mason wanted to be where things were familiar—and familial. So long as family and politics could be smoothly reconciled, Mason and Henry would lead. But they would not betray their duties as fathers to continue to work as founders, especially once they saw that the federal government did not reflect their vision of the Republic. Despite their leadership of the Revolution, they belonged to an earlier age and, in their perception, a different country than the one taking shape under the Constitution.

I n the end, Washington, Jefferson, and Madison didn't get the country they wanted either. On their watch, political turmoil roiled the
young United States. Factionalism became bitter and entrenched.
Partisan newspapers spread baseless rumors (and damaging truths)
about politicians' conduct and character. Principled disagreements between federal officials devolved into fistfights and duels. Such politics
destroyed decades-long relationships and reputations and seemed to
pose a mortal threat to the republican-style government the Virginians
had spent their lives trying to build.

To a one, as their time in office grew short, Virginia's presidents
longed to be retired and each left the national scene apprehensive about
the future. When he finished his second term, Washington likened himself to a "wearied traveller who sees a resting place, and is bending his
body to lean thereon." Jefferson could hardly wait for his last days as the
chief executive: "I look with infinite joy," he told his daughter, "to the
moment when I shall be ultimately moored in the midst of my affections,
and free to follow the pursuits of my choice." Even Madison felt as "playful as a child" on leaving behind the cares of the presidency.[54]

In the wake of the Constitutional Convention, Virginia's patriot
leaders found they could not agree about what constituted their country,
where sovereignty should lie in the Republic, the best course to pursue
for the good of posterity, or how to balance their domestic and political
duties. What they did share in common as they aged was fear: that all
their efforts had produced not virtuous progeny but rather a generation
of prodigals. Jefferson, usually the optimist in the cohort, suspected
"that I am now to die in the belief that the useless sacrifice of themselves
by the generation of 1776, to acquire self-government and happiness to
their country, is to be thrown away by the unwise and unworthy passions of their sons."[55] So, retirement did not bring an end to their struggle to craft the American Republic. As Virginia's founders headed home
from their last political offices, they continued their labors, this time to
find a way to build an enduring legacy that might somehow protect
themselves and their posterity after all.

CHAPTER 8

Reputation

As he drew up his last will and testament in late 1798, Patrick Henry was set to fulfill a goal he had worked toward his whole life: taking care of his posterity. His surviving children by Sarah Henry were grown, some with large families of their own. In their youth and early adulthood, their father made sure they got a strong financial start, with educations, land, money, slaves. "I have," he said in the will, "heretofore provided for the children of my first marriage." So, he decided to leave the bulk of his remaining estate to "my ever dear and beloved" second wife, Dorothea Dandridge Henry, and their children. Thousands of acres of land throughout Virginia and into Kentucky eventually would be divided among their six sons, the youngest of whom was just two years old. Dorothea Henry had proven herself responsible and knowledgeable in her husband's eyes: she would be guardian to their minor children, an executrix, and a principal beneficiary. But Patrick Henry did not want another man's family to share the estate he had built for his own. If Dorothea remarried, she lost all claim to his assets. To ensure that his wishes were met, Henry named trusted relatives as his executors: his son-in-law George Winston, the husband of his and Dorothea's oldest daughter; his cousin Edmund Winston, who was George Winston's father; Philip Payne, the husband of Dorothea's sister, Elizabeth; and Dorothea. Facing the end of one's life is never easy, but Patrick Henry could take comfort in knowing that he was leaving a self-made and secure fortune for his "dear family."[1]

Alongside that will Henry left a small envelope, sealed with wax and containing a single sheet of paper to be read only upon his death. The front was a handwritten copy of his 1765 resolutions against the Stamp Act, what he imagined to be his greatest gift to the patriot cause and to posterity beyond his own children. On the back Henry left a message for the future: a call for the rising generation. Whether the Revolution "will prove a blessing or a curse," he cautioned, "will depend upon the use our people make of the blessings which a gracious God hath bestowed on us. If they are wise, they will be great and happy. If they are of a contrary character, they will be miserable." The last words he had for the world were simple and transcendent, capturing the most important and difficult duty of citizens in a republic: "Reader! whoever thou art, remember this; and in thy sphere, practise virtue thyself, and encourage it in others."[2]

As they confronted their own mortality, the minds of Virginia's leading revolutionaries turned to the legacy they would leave behind. For Patrick Henry, that legacy began with his financial responsibility for his children, but it did not end there. He and his cohort felt a larger, political responsibility to the future of the American Republic. They worried, too, about whether their reputations and the Revolution would endure.

Retirement from office redirected rather than relieved these men's sense of duty to their republican experiment. Well-chosen members of their families became vital partners in creating what the founders decided was an essential reputational legacy for "ourselves and our Posterity." In some instances they turned to female kin; women excluded from their republic became the most trustworthy stewards of their reputations. At Monticello, Mount Vernon, and Montpelier, creating a history of the Revolution became a consuming family enterprise. And long after these founders were laid to rest, their heirs continued to craft a story about the past—and shape the future of a country—faithful to the vision of their fathers, the founders.

R eputation, what they sometimes called character, had been paramount in the minds of the founders from the earliest phases of the Revolution. The rising idealization of self-determination after 1776 only added to that concern. Untethered from the old colonial organic social structure, a man's actions would now determine his reputation. Character was performative, for outward consumption. A man was what others thought him to be; perceptions became reality.[3]

Their preoccupation with reputation, with weighing the potential gain of renown against the risk of disgrace, is evident in nearly all of these founders' political dealings. While George Washington feared commanding the ragtag Continental Army would harm his reputation, he was an ambitious man, eager for recognition. "To obtain the applause of deserving men is," he decided, "a heartfelt satisfaction." Washington was proud when his conduct "merited the approbation of this great country" and considered that respect "one of the most fortunate and happy events of my life." Before attending the Constitutional Convention, Washington contemplated the cost to his reputation, ultimately concluding that not attending would be the more damaging choice both for the prospects of his country and for perceptions of his character. When Washington considered becoming the first president of the yet unproven federal government, Thomas Jefferson urged him on. Acknowledging that Washington's "measure of fame" was "full to the brim" and that the future was unclear at best, Jefferson still thought it Washington's duty "to risk all against nothing."[4]

A misstep could dog a man for a lifetime. Patrick Henry's criticism of Thomas Jefferson's behavior during the Revolutionary War provided political ammunition for his rivals for years to come; the question of whether Governor Jefferson behaved honorably when fleeing Richmond in 1781 was even resurrected in the presidential elections of 1796 and 1800. Jefferson's consequent contempt for Henry never abated. It was abundantly clear when, in 1784, Jefferson corresponded with Madison about possibly revising Virginia's constitution. Henry, he concluded, posed an insuperable obstacle: "What we have to do I think is devoutly to pray for his death." Years after Henry died Jefferson continued to deride him, most significantly in letters he wrote to William Wirt as Wirt prepared a biography of Henry.[5]

No matter how much these men achieved, they never got over their reputational anxieties. The last visitor Jefferson ever received, in late June 1826, was the son of Henry "Light-Horse Harry" Lee. The younger

Lee was revising his father's memoirs and sought Jefferson's counsel, which a dying Jefferson insisted on giving, despite his relatives' concerns for his health. Jefferson hoped, among other things, to shape Lee's account of his actions while governor—forty-six years after the fact. A few months before, sensing that the end was drawing near, Jefferson had asked his closest friend, James Madison, for a final favor: "Take care of me when dead, and be assured that I shall leave with you my last affections."[6] Madison honored his friend: the last letter he ever penned, in 1836, focused on Jefferson's and his historical reputations. Just hours before he died Madison wrote about their "sincere and steadfast cooperation" in building a government that "would provide for the permanent liberty and happiness of the United States." Madison also nursed reputational concerns dating back to the Revolutionary War. Throughout his life he worried about how history would judge his absence from the battlefield. In his autobiography—drafted a half century after Independence—he carefully explained that his health had prohibited military service and that he contributed politically instead.[7]

Members of this cohort worried, too, about how the reputation of the American Republic—in the international community, among citizens, and in the future—would shape its destiny. "We are a young Nation," Washington observed in 1783, "and have a character to establish. It behooves us therefore to set out right for first impressions will be lasting."[8] They shared those apprehensions about perceptions, even when their definitions of "country" diverged. Mason and Henry tried to protect Virginia's status vis-à-vis other states; Jefferson, Madison, and Washington worked more to advance the standing of the United States in the eyes of European powers. They all understood that if others perceived their country as weak or corrupt, it could be imperiled. At the same time, they felt great pride in their experiment with representative government, envisioning it as unique in the world, to be both guarded and honored.

Much, then, was at stake as these men left the political stage. To borrow their language, lives, fortunes, and honor had been wagered on the Revolution. As they retired from politics, they saw the fate of the Republic leaving their hands, passing to a new generation. And they believed that what later generations remembered about the founders and what they made of their example would decide how long the "sacred fire of liberty" could burn.[9]

Patrick Henry thus captured in his will and accompanying note the sentiments of his peers at the close of their lives: a clear desire to shape historical reputation, a still-keen enthusiasm for self-determination, apprehension about the fragility and future of republican government, a strong sense of duty to posterity, and pride in their own achievements. In Patrick Henry's particular case, the impact of his oratorical gifts on the patriot cause quickly became the stuff of lore—even Jefferson granted him that—and it was celebrated among succeeding generations. As Henry's grandson put it, "The effects of his eloquence were not only immediate & irresistible; but they were permanent, & *immortal*."[10] Those "millions yet unborn" would long celebrate his name alongside Thomas Jefferson's and George Washington's.

The larger ambitions of the generation of 1776 remained in doubt, though. They worried: Would the Revolution and its leaders become just a story about some lost past?

As they grew old, Virginia's founding fathers wanted to offer an inspirational example to posterity. For meaningful reputational immortality, they needed their heirs, both personal and political, to carry their achievements forward, to extend the successes and defend the character of the Revolution. Whether the Revolution would falter or endure, Henry predicted, would turn on "the Use our people make" of the founders' example. So, while to the end Patrick Henry disagreed with many of his contemporaries about how to structure the US government, he shared their sense of urgency about training the next generation to be good stewards of their founding fathers' legacy.

Surveying the fruits of their labors inspired little confidence. The children of the early Republic seemed to have imbibed too much of the rights of the revolutionary era and too little of the responsibility. Talent was not filtering as fast or as reliably as the founders had imagined. In retirement they often wrote one another to grouse about members of the younger generation, who not only indulged in self-interest but outright celebrated it—all of which gave founders added incentive to focus on their legacy.

Disappointments ran from the federal city to their own families. The list of difficulties the young country faced was long and taxed the founders' hopes for a thriving republic. Civil unrest, sparked by tax revolts, roiled the country: in Shays's Rebellion, the Whiskey Rebellion, and Fries's Rebellion. International politics proved no less perilous. The nation found itself drawn into conflicts with France and England, the Barbary States in North Africa, and Indian nations in the interior of North America. Factional tensions during Washington's presidency gave way to full-blown party structures. Emerging political leaders embraced partisanship and, far from seeking the common good, extolled the competition of ideas. So, Americans failed to heed both of Washington's warnings in his farewell address and instead ran headlong toward political factions and foreign entanglements.

Leading members of the founding generation did not escape culpability. Supposed exemplars of republican character indulged in less than admirable conduct. The presidential election in 1800 might have subsequently been celebrated by the victor as a revolution as important as the one of 1776, but many observers were appalled at the depths to which Thomas Jefferson and John Adams descended in trying to assassinate each other's character. Alexander Hamilton disputed a charge of corruption by confessing to an extramarital affair. Jefferson and Madison challenged Washington's leadership by spreading gossip about his supposed senility, caricaturing him as a doddering, gullible old man. Watching Jefferson's machinations in 1792, one of President Washington's supporters warned him: "You have cherished in your Bosom a Serpent, and he is now endeavouring to sting you to death." Federal leaders sometimes turned to violence to settle scores; Aaron Burr killing Alexander Hamilton in 1804 was only the most high profile of the bloody duels waged over early federal politics.[11]

Far from improving over time, political divisions seemed to grow ever more self-consciously sectional and destructive. Jefferson was devastated by the Missouri Crisis, which, he famously said, "like a fire bell in the night, awakened and filled me with terror. I considered it at once as the knell of the Union." He viewed southerners' open threats of civil war over the future of slavery as an "act of suicide on themselves, and of treason against the hopes of the world." James Madison, the youngest of this cohort, lived long enough to feel not just misunderstood by but irrelevant to the new men leading the country—in his opinion, in the wrong direction. He worried in particular that proslavery politics was undermining the Constitution and with it his legacy. After he learned that he was the last surviving signer of the Constitution he reflected: "I ought not to forget that I may be thought to have outlived myself."[12]

On top of grievous political tumult, Virginians had to witness the ignominious decline of their beloved Old Dominion in the early nineteenth century: in agriculture, manufacturing, national political influence, and reputation. Decades of tobacco overproduction left once-thriving plantations like those in Jefferson's native Albemarle County a "scene of desolation that baffles description."[13] Visitors to the state were stunned at the poorly maintained roads, dilapidated houses, and abandoned farms. Population declines relative to other states cost Virginians seats (and power) in the US House of Representatives. Many ambitious sons of established gentlemen moved west of the Blue Ridge Mountains or even out of state. In 1833 Martha Jefferson Randolph lamented that "Virginia is no longer a home for the family of Thomas Jefferson."[14]

Many of the families occupying Virginia's great houses watched their fortunes decline alongside the prospects of their state. Thomas Jefferson and Dolley Madison were financially ruined at the end of their lives, but they were hardly alone. James Monroe kept Oak Hill afloat by selling land and slaves and borrowing money. He went badly into debt to the Bank of the United States, but, lucky for him, the bank was loath to bring suit against a former president. Edmund Randolph and Henry "Light-Horse Harry" Lee could never clear their accounts, either. Lee was jailed for his debts in 1809–1810.[15]

Education proved an illusory hope for correcting this slide. No one worked harder on that front than Thomas Jefferson, who in his retirement threw himself into designing every aspect of the University of Virginia. His vision was equal parts noble and grand: to "form the statesmen, legislators and judges, on whom public prosperity and individual happiness are so much to depend . . . develop the reasoning faculties of our youth, enlarge their minds, cultivate their morals, and instill into them the precepts of virtue and order . . . rendering them examples of virtue to others, and of happiness within themselves."[16] But the actions of the Charlottesville students left Jefferson dismayed and disillusioned. He estimated that a full third of students were "idle ramblers incapable of application." They routinely defied school rules and their professors' authority, and sometimes even rioted when they felt their rights— which, to their minds seemed boundless—were threatened. Though in poor health during a student uprising in 1825, he insisted on going to Charlottesville, where he, Madison, and President James Monroe convened the entire campus community to try and restore order. Jefferson told the audience that they were witnessing one of the most painful moments of his life; he was then overcome with emotion and had to sit down. Shortly before his death Jefferson bitterly conceded, "I have been long sensible that while I was endeavoring to render to our country the greatest of all services, that of regenerating the public education, and placing our rising generation on the level of our sister states . . . I was discharging the odious function of a Physician pouring medicine down the throat of a patient, insensible of needing it." Charlottesville was emblematic of the general character of southern boys in the early national era. Even Jefferson's own great-grandson saw it: Thomas Jefferson Coolidge, born and raised in Boston, said that his Harvard classmates from the South were dissipated, heavy-drinking, quarrelsome braggarts.[17]

As Jefferson's Charlottesville experiment floundered, scandals in Virginia's most prominent families piled up. Thomas Mann Randolph Jr. had a psychological breakdown. A relative murdered George Wythe. Edmund Randolph was forced to resign as secretary of state in disgrace. Meriwether Lewis committed suicide. Henry "Light-Horse Harry" Lee was incarcerated for unpaid debts. Richard Randolph was tried for incest and infanticide.[18]

Our cohort was certainly not immune. Two of Patrick Henry's sons apparently shared their late mother's mental frailties. Martha Washington's sister Elizabeth Henley married a drunk and, Martha regretted, lived in a "wretched situation." James Madison and his siblings squabbled over their father's estate in a lawsuit that dragged on two years. George Washington spent his retirement struggling with his mercurial grandson. Washy Custis's chronic insolence was, Washington complained, "disgraceful to himself & me."[19]

On top of these real troubles, newspapermen working in an aggressively activist press saw founders' families as vulnerable targets and spread hurtful, unfounded rumors. For example, reporters claimed that President Madison's manhood was sapped by his oversexed young wife, that Dolley and Thomas Jefferson were lovers, and that James prostituted his nieces for political gain.[20]

Family troubles sometimes erupted despite a devoted father's best efforts. Though Patrick Henry took tremendous care preparing his will, after he died his son-in-law Spencer Roane sued the estate for what he called "an act of injustice towards some of his first children." He laid the blame on Henry's greedy and fecund second wife, Dorothea, who, Roane claimed, made sure Sarah Henry's children got shortchanged. And soon enough Dorothea Henry got around the restrictions against her remarrying by taking as her second husband fellow executor Edmund Winston. The couple, aided by the other executors, who happened to be Dorothea's brother-in-law and Edmund's son, had no trouble holding Patrick's assets after their marriage. (It is noteworthy that in marrying her son-in-law's father, Dorothea Henry Winston became her daughter's stepmother-in-law.)[21]

The Jefferson descendants wrote more fully about their family sagas than most Virginians, but there is no reason to think they suffered from more frequent domestic heartbreaks than their neighbors. During her disastrous marriage to Charles Bankhead, Anne Cary Randolph, the firstborn grandchild of Thomas Jefferson, weathered humiliation, profligacy, and violence before meeting an early death. Soon after they married at Monticello in September 1808, Bankhead showed himself to be a violent drunk, and Anne had to endure, her mother grieved, "a hard fate." Bankhead's father and Thomas Jefferson stepped in and took over the young couple's finances so that Bankhead couldn't squander all their money. Jeff Randolph got into a violent confrontation with Bankhead over his abuse. At her wit's end, Martha Jefferson Randolph suggested hiring a caretaker to keep Charles at home and let him drink himself to death. This she found preferable to sending him to an asylum—which the family also debated—because, she reasoned, institutionalization would only allow him to "torment his family the longer." Anne ran from time to time, sometimes for her life. But she did not leave him. Charles did not beat Anne to death, which some of the family reasonably feared; she succumbed to complications of childbirth just a few months before her grandfather died, in February 1826.[22]

By the time Anne Cary Randolph Bankhead died, Monticello was sliding toward bankruptcy. Jefferson continually spent more than he had, and he trusted friends he should not. He was a meticulous record keeper; he could do the arithmetic, he just couldn't obey it. By the 1820s the Randolph siblings talked openly about "our fallen fortunes," and the sisters considered ways they might support themselves. But since family reputation precluded female independence, the sisters concluded that it simply would not do "for the grand daughters of Thomas Jefferson to take in work or keep a school." They could not respectably support themselves, and their grandfather could not provide for them. "I am overwhelmed," Jefferson confessed in February 1826, "at the prospect of the situation in which I may leave my family."[23]

Against this rather dismal backdrop arose a valiant effort on the part of the founders and their descendants to craft a story for history—a heroic depiction of the men who led the Revolution that would secure their own reputations and inspire posterity to idolize them and build a strong national heritage. Retirement proved an ideal time for historically minded leaders to groom their reputations. And their families became both a motivation for and a means to that end.

The founding fathers understood that later generations of Americans would know them (and celebrate or censure them) depending on what version of history they learned. Some had self-consciously planned for as much during their careers, and in their later years they counted on select kin and allies to help them appear to be both dutiful fathers and virtuous founders.

With the help of their kin, these men became in memory what their careers sometimes precluded in life: attentive and loving fathers to their families no less than their country. Children and protégés always depicted them as ideal fathers; family controversies evaporated in the stories they told about growing up with a founder as a father. Correspondence, newspaper interviews, virtually every piece of evidence that the founders' relatives produced painted an idyllic picture of paternal devotion. Consider, for example, the recollections of Thomas Jefferson's granddaughter, Ellen Randolph Coolidge, who proclaimed: "From him seemed to flow all the pleasures of my life." Her sister Virginia Randolph Trist likewise reverently recalled that Jefferson's "cheerfulness and affection were the warm sun in which his family all basked."[24]

The sacrifices revolutionary leaders made to family in order to serve their country were deliberately elided and replaced with narratives of exemplary paternal character. Washington Custis published personal accounts of his grandfather's life because "those who have only seen him as the leader of armies and the chief magistrate of the republic, can have but an imperfect idea of him." To really know the father of the country, his grandson insisted, one had to meet him "embosomed among his family and friends, cultivating the social and domestic virtues, and dispensing pleasure and happiness to all around him."[25]

Sanitizing the story of their political dealings was more challenging, however, because of the conflicts and estrangements that divided these Virginians at the end of their careers. Most notably, Thomas Jefferson sought not only to build up his own reputation but also to tear down Patrick Henry's. He insisted that President Washington offered Henry the position first of secretary of state and then as an envoy to Spain only because Washington believed Henry would decline. Jefferson archly added, "Washington knew that he was entirely unqualified for it." Though Henry was always more popular in Virginia than Jefferson, Jefferson also insisted that Henry's opposition to the federal government "sunk him to nothing, in the estimation of his country." Jefferson's greatest influence came from the stories he told William Wirt for his 1817 biography of Patrick Henry. Jefferson cast Henry as a gifted orator who was otherwise shallow and selfish. Henry's storied legal career, in Jefferson's version of history, derived not from any real mastery of the law but from manipulating juries. Most significantly, Jefferson said Henry's contributions to the patriot cause were superficial and fleeting—he had a talent for soaring rhetoric but made no substantive intellectual, political, or legislative contributions. Those letters, though less influential with Wirt than Jefferson wanted, found their way into other writers' hands and shaped Henry's posthumous reputation.[26]

Jefferson's political estrangement from Washington was the source of further reputational wrangling. Years after her grandfather died, Nelly Custis Lewis refused to forgive Jefferson's disloyalty. She refused even to enter the same room as President Jefferson. "Nor," she wrote a friend, "can one who knew so well the *first President*, ever wish to be noticed by the present chief magistrate." When John Marshall and Henry "Light-Horse Harry" Lee published books about the Revolution that defended the Federalists and criticized the Democratic Republicans, Jefferson did everything he could to rebut those works, complaining that in the hands of partisan writers like Marshall, "history becomes fable instead of fact."[27]

These men's long experiences with one another made them excellent critics, skilled at pointing out each other's weaknesses and flaws. In their harshest opponents' eyes, Washington was a thin-skinned, intellectual lightweight, Henry a mercurial poseur, Jefferson duplicitous, Madison withdrawn and pedantic, Mason impossibly rigid.

Even when they and their heirs weren't purposely fighting over the future of the past, differing priorities skewed stories about the revolutionary era. After they left politics, Henry and Mason focused more on their families—posterity narrowly defined—and the financial legacy they would leave their children. Those numbered among the successes their dutiful descendants commemorated. George Mason's grandson, also a George Mason, lauded his grandfather's accomplishments as statesman and intellectual, but he also celebrated "his still more admirable talents for acquisition and economy." Surveying the vast lands and wealth Mason amassed, his grandson concluded, "his enterprise and economy in private fully equaled his genius and ability in public life." Patrick Henry's heirs cultivated an image of Henry as everyman. He chose to live a plainer lifestyle without the conspicuous consumption favored by many of his generation, and "his attentions were not confined to the rich, the great, or wise, but he was familiar with every man of good character."[28] Washington, Jefferson, and Madison, meanwhile, assumed greater responsibilities in the federal government and focused more on a national legacy.

Despite their differences, they all shared a dedication to celebrating the Revolution and to positioning themselves as models of republican service. The year before he died, Thomas Jefferson reflected on the importance of his and James Madison's achievements. "It has also been a great solace to me," Thomas told James, "to believe that you are engaged in vindicating to posterity the course we have pursued for preserving to them . . . the blessings of self-government." Madison heartily agreed, congratulating himself and Jefferson on "the pure devotion to the public good with which we discharged the trusts committed to us." Madison also kept his eye on the future: he hoped "that sufficient evidence" of their contributions "will find its way to another generation."[29]

Children and protégés proved to be stellar partners in mustering "sufficient evidence" of the admirable character of Virginia's founding fathers and advancing their campaign for the future of the Republic. Part of their zealous devotion to their fathers, the founders, derived from genuine love and respect. John Mason's memoir reveals how much he idealized his father, both as a "kind & affectionate" father and as a "profound statesman and a pure patriot." Nelly Custis Lewis adored her grandfather and warmly recalled how, after her father died, he became "the most affectionate of Fathers." Jeff Randolph held up his grandfather as the noblest of men, a paragon of integrity: "He never uttered an untruth."[30]

There were other motivations as well: reputation blended with patriotism. The status of members of these families remained, in their own minds and perhaps in fact, tethered to their famous ancestors. And defending their prominent progenitors was simultaneously a defense of the country they founded. So, Nelly Custis Lewis, Jeff Randolph, and John Mason had several reasons to erase the disappointing and controversial parts of their family history and record only the best.

Heirs to the founders continued for decades to protect these men and to make revisions to their life stories to suit the founders' and their own reputational needs. In 1856, for example, Edward Coles defended James Madison's handling of the War of 1812. And he also backed up an

1831 defense Madison made of Jefferson's actions while he was president in 1801! Truth was no obstacle to a good story. Even after Thomas Jefferson died so deeply in debt that Martha Jefferson Randolph was rendered homeless, she still fought to defend his legacy, insisting that when she considered the whole of his life, "I can not call to mind one solitary action that I would censure."[31]

The narrative the Randolph women crafted to explain their family's decline emphasized Jefferson's—and by extension their own—sacrifices for the nation. They could not hide their financial straits, but they could and did justify them on patriotic grounds. Just a few months after Jefferson's death, Ellen and Joseph Coolidge found themselves quizzed by a potential biographer who "wished to know exactly the causes of the embarrassment of his pecuniary affairs." The author wondered "how it came that having received from his father a large property, marrying an heiress & receiving for many years a regular salary from the public Treasury, he should have in his latter years fallen into the distress which induced him to apply for permission to sell his estate by lottery." In response, Ellen and Martha laid out a story of personal sacrifice for political service. Jefferson had neglected his plantation because he was busy building a nation. To secure the Republic he lost Monticello.[32]

The Randolphs' sense of dutifulness extended to covering up their grandfather's relationship with Sally Hemings for generations. In 1858—more than *thirty years* after Jefferson's death—Ellen Randolph Coolidge wrote a long, blanket dismissal of the very idea that he fathered children with Hemings and insisted on the absolute impossibility of his "carrying on his intrigues in the midst of his daughter's family and insulting the sanctity of home." She said things that were transparently untrue: that, for example, "no female domestic ever entered his chambers except at hours when he was known not to be there and none could have entered without being exposed to the public gaze." Ellen pointed to the Irish carpenters working at Monticello and her Carr cousins as possible fathers to the Hemings children, and she suggested that slaves, supposedly out of affection for Jefferson, took his name. But mostly she insisted that the grandfather she idolized would never "rear a race of half-breeds under their eyes and carry on his low amours in the circle of his family."[33] Though Ellen struggled to physically describe Thomas, admitting that she found it "very difficult" to craft "an accurate description of the appearance of one whom I so tenderly loved and deeply venerated," she had no qualms about defining his character.[34]

The Jefferson heirs were not unique. Aggrieved for decades about the influence Jefferson tried to exert over Patrick Henry's historical reputation, two Henry descendants, Edward Fontaine, a grandson of Patrick's oldest daughter, and William Wirt Henry, the son of his youngest son, decided to set the record straight about Henry's role in the Revolution. Edward Fontaine, born in 1814, began keeping a journal of family stories when he was seventeen years old (a telling commentary in itself). A minister and Confederate veteran, Fontaine completed "Corrections of biographical mistakes" in 1872. He told a story both about his great-grandfather and for his own age. "This family," Fontaine bragged, "has produced many sons and daughters highly gifted as historians, musicians, poets, & orators." But, like their eminent ancestor, the nineteenth-century Henrys preferred the "varied charms of a frontier or country life" to political power. Fontaine celebrated not only the character of his family—an inheritance from his great-grandfather—but also the failed Confederate States of America, which he likewise connected to Patrick Henry. Linking the "lost cause" of the Confederacy with the Revolution, he proclaimed, "Only the revolutions which have agitated our Country" pulled Henry men into political offices "demanding the exercise of daring, courage, incorruptible integrity, & commanding eloquence." Being a minister, Fontaine also, understandably, emphasized Henry's Christian faith. According to Fontaine, Henry's last wish was for his children to be good Christians, and as he lay dying he told them, *"I will now give you my last argument by showing you how a Christian can die."*[35]

William Wirt Henry also served in the Confederacy but emerged considerably less unreconstructed than his kinsman Edward Fontaine. A lawyer and historian, he produced three volumes of Patrick Henry's writings in the late nineteenth century, aimed at recasting the historical record to celebrate his ancestor. Like Fontaine he reflected the values of his own era; he praised the ennobling effects of slavery, for example. He did, though, revise Fontaine's celebratory depiction of secession as a legacy of the Revolution. In 1891 William Wirt Henry was president of both the Virginia Historical Society and the American Historical Association, and in his AHA presidential address he praised his grandfather's generation of Virginians for their many contributions in a *national* context. Ignoring how Patrick Henry—to whom he had devoted much of his professional career—fought against the Constitution, he argued: "There is one thing . . . for which the continent can not be too grateful to her [Virginia]. It is her efficient services in forming and securing our Federal Union. Indeed, the Virginia leaders of the Revolutionary period were most conspicuous for their broad and national views."[36]

Although put to contradictory ideological ends, the Patrick Henry stories told by Edward Fontaine and William Wirt Henry started from the same assumption: the character of their ancestor and the Revolution he helped lead should be studied and emulated. Like Ellen Randolph Coolidge, they also inadvertently revealed how malleable these men's lives could become in the hands of later generations.

The most forward-minded of our cohort anticipated that stories about their conduct and the Revolution might become distorted over time. So they did not leave their legacy to chance or even to the most carefully rehearsed family stories. Rather, they made sure to compile and preserve a lasting record of their life stories.

M uch of the American Revolution turned on words and ideas, so it is fitting that the centerpiece of the founding fathers' campaign for their reputation in history centered on their writings. Jefferson, Madison, and Washington commenced elaborate papers projects, posthumously published in various incarnations running from the early nineteenth century through the twenty-first. The quantity and intricacy of their writings are staggering. Teams of scholars are working right now on multiple series of dozens of volumes of the Madison, Jefferson, and Washington papers—and they will continue to do so for years to come. Editors of the current Jefferson projects hope that they will be able to finish their work by 2026, which would be the 250th anniversary of the Declaration of Independence and *seventy-six years* after the first volume in the first series appeared.[37]

For George Washington, the enterprise of fashioning a full record for posterity began even before the Revolution was secured. He knew from the 1770s that subsequent generations of Americans would want to know about his life from his own pen, and by gathering together his writings he began to shape a narrative for them. George and Lund Washington worried during the war that if British forces attacked Mount Vernon, his letters might be destroyed. "Have my Papers in such a Situation," George directed Lund, "as to remove at a short notice in case an Enemy's Fleet should come up the River." Washington also convinced the strapped Continental Congress to fund a secretarial staff to compile all his wartime correspondence. Richard Varick, a young officer, headed the team, which worked for two years and produced twenty-eight volumes. When the war ended, Washington shipped several wagonloads of his papers overland to Mount Vernon, knowing that the easier water passage was more dangerous to this precious cargo. And he wrote Congress to ask them to return the military commission he resigned in 1783 to add to his collection.[38]

The Mount Vernon papers project continued for the rest of Washington's life, picking up in earnest after his 1783 retirement from military service and again when he left the presidency in 1797. After the war's end he was accompanied home by David Humphreys and William Smith, trustworthy protégés included in Washington's political family. They soon set to work on the task that brought them to Virginia: compiling Washington's papers. After his last retirement in 1797, one of Washington's top priorities was, Washington Custis explained, "to arrange certain letters and papers for posthumous publication."[39]

Washington was hardly alone in his literary campaign for history. The efforts transcended Virginia. John Adams devoted great parts of his retirement correspondence with Thomas Jefferson to mutually fretting over how they and the Revolution might be misremembered. They feared that because so much of the creation of the Republic took place behind closed doors and with only sporadic attention to taking notes that "the life and soul of history must forever be unknown."[40]

Jefferson was deeply concerned that by being, as he put it, "too careless of our future reputation," the founding generation would imperil their republican legacy. Telling the "true" story of the American Revolution was not simply a matter of ego, then, although it was surely that in some measure. Abiding concern about posterity was a primary motivating force for Jefferson no less than Washington. Like Washington, Jefferson worried about losing precious historical records during the war, and after the siege of Richmond he assured congressional delegates that he was procuring copies of as many government documents as possible.[41]

Throughout his long career and especially during his retirement, Jefferson systemically cataloged his letters for posterity. Ever curious about inventions, he employed first a copy press and later a machine of parallel pens to make duplicates of his writings. He also collected historically significant documents, encouraged writers and men working on editorial projects, and wrote his autobiography and his only published book, *Notes on the State of Virginia*. In total, Jeff Randolph, who was the sole recipient of his grandfather's papers, estimated that Jefferson left him forty thousand letters.[42]

James Madison also started his papers project early and with a sharp focus on "future reputation." In addition to carrying on correspondences with political allies and rivals, business associates, neighbors, friends, relatives, intellectuals, lawyers, diplomats, and statesmen, Madison kept inventories and account books, wrote essays and political treatises, oversaw legislative proposals and diplomatic negotiations. Madison began preserving his correspondence in the 1780s, and he also collected primary sources from the 1770s and 1760s. As a legislator, Madison was a copious note taker, which added to his cache of important writings. Though he felt strongly that he had to honor the pledge to refrain from publishing his notes of the Constitutional Convention until the deaths of the delegates, Madison made allowances in his will for the speedy publication of the Philadelphia debates.[43]

Madison, like Washington and Jefferson before him, began to use those documents to cultivate his historical image in earnest once he was freed from the obligations of the presidency. As was the case at Monticello and Mount Vernon, Madison's family worked alongside him at Montpelier as editorial assistants. Dolley Madison and John Payne meticulously compiled, edited, and proofread his collection. Dolley grew exasperated by James's preoccupation with his epistolary legacy. In February 1820 she confided to a friend that "this is the third winter in which he has been engaged in the arrangement of papers, and the business appears to accumulate as he proceeds." The enterprise was, she complained, "out-lasting my patience." Still, she felt she could not ask him "to forsake a duty so important, or find it in my heart to leave him during its fulfillment." Ten years later he was still at work. In 1830 Jared Sparks, preparing his twelve-volume *The Writings of George Washington*, visited Montpelier, where he found Madison "busy in arranging his papers." The project was growing because Madison had written to the descendants of some long-dead members of the Confederation Congress to procure copies of his earliest political correspondence.[44]

The "fulfillment" of Madison's papers project remains elusive. At present, teams of scholars collaborating on multiple series of the Papers of James Madison project have collected some twenty-nine thousand documents. Editors have proceeded on four tracks, covering Madison's congressional career, his eight years as secretary of state, his two terms as president, and his twenty-year retirement. The first volume of the first series appeared in 1962. Excluding the retirement series, editors anticipate publishing about forty-five volumes.

In sharp contrast, the writings of Patrick Henry number in the hundreds, not the tens of thousands, of pages. And the definitive edition of George Mason's papers runs a comparatively scant three volumes. The divergence derives from both politics and family considerations. George Mason and Patrick Henry curtailed their political careers after the constitutional debates of 1787–1788, so they amassed far fewer papers— and of less historical significance—than Virginia's first three presidents. They also focused less intensely on their reputations among future generations of Americans than did Washington, Jefferson, and Madison. That is not to say they were indifferent to how later generations would view them—only that their concerns centered more on posterity within their family circles. Henry certainly took pride in the part he played in the Revolution. He told one friend that he "ever prized at a high rate the superior privilege of being one in that chosen age to which Providence entrusted its favorite work."[45] But he spent his later years working on his legal practice and building up his landholdings rather than running a papers project out of his home.

George Mason certainly wanted recognition for his commitment to republican principles and his leadership in the Revolution, but, like Henry, his audience was narrower than the one sought by Washington, Jefferson, and Madison. Mason, for example, was most concerned that his children know that his conscience was clear regarding his Anti-federalist advocacy. Mason apparently made no concerted effort to compile or even preserve his papers. But he was not unconcerned about the future. More than concentrating on how "millions yet unborn" would judge him, George Mason devoted his last years to building an estate large enough to secure his own children's futures. When he died in 1792 he owed no outstanding major debts and owned fifteen thousand acres of land along the Potomac River, sixty thousand acres in Kentucky, and three hundred slaves, on top of personal property valued in excess of $50,000.[46]

When later generations of Masons tried to compile his papers, they faced an uphill battle. Mason's grandson, George Mason, began in the 1820s to correspond with prominent men who knew his grandfather, including James Madison, and gather testimonials about Mason's contributions to the Revolution. Deep into his own voluminous editorial work, Madison sympathized with the younger Mason's struggle to recover his ancestor's pride of place in Virginia history. "It is to be regretted," Madison concluded, "that highly distinguished as he was," accounts of Mason's achievements "are more scanty than of many of his contemporaries far inferior to him in intellectual powers and in public services."[47]

Occasionally, evidence was willfully destroyed. In the 1780s George Washington disposed of some personal letters and edited parts of his writings. Martha Washington burned nearly everything they ever wrote to each other. Thomas Jefferson also destroyed his correspondence with his wife. Since we don't know *what* was in these letters, it is difficult to know *why* they were destroyed. It was not uncommon, as a romantic gesture, to burn marital correspondence. It is therefore perhaps telling that only those letters merited wholesale destruction. Or perhaps Martha Washington and Thomas Jefferson had sacrificed so much that they wanted to keep something for themselves. Maybe the letters from their most intimate relationships revealed an ordinariness and vulnerability in these men they wished to hide from history. One thing is certain: we don't have those letters because they did not want us to see them.

Self-editing took place, too. Patrick Henry never wrote about his wife's mental illness. The white residents of Monticello rarely mentioned their African American relatives, even in passing. James Madison went silent on Payne Todd.

Most of the time, however, Washington, Jefferson, and Madison were conscientious and forward looking in their papers projects. They imagined their work as a last—and lasting—virtuous service to posterity and their country. Washington thought that "nothing should be left undone to give his country and the world a fair and just estimate of his life and actions." Jefferson believed it was "the duty of every good citizen to use all the opportunities which occur to him, for preserving documents relating to the history of our country." Madison planned in his will for the at-long-last publication of his notes from the 1787 Philadelphia Convention because he understood it would "be particularly gratifying to the people of the United States, and to all who take an interest in the progress of political science and the cause of true liberty."[48]

For Virginia's presidents, art complemented literature in this cultivation of memory. Jefferson, Madison, and Washington sat for portraits and sculptures to preserve their images for posterity, and they collected art celebrating the revolutionary past. The most enduring of these efforts include the iconic paintings by artist John Trumbull, displayed at the Capitol rotunda. Collectively the works tell the heroic story of the founding of the American Republic, with scenes including the presentation of the Declaration of Independence, the resignation of Washington, and the surrender of Cornwallis at Yorktown. Such pictures captured republican values—independence, virtue, sacrifice, service—adding timeless force to the memory of the Revolution and visual guides to the founders' exemplary character.

When all that was left of these men were their papers and portraits, descendants continued cataloging their records. For those heirs, the work of history-making could be as grueling as it was inspiring. Jeff Randolph and several of his sisters and their mother labored for years editing Thomas's papers for publication. Many of his copied letters were, Martha said, "so faded as to be almost entirely obliterated." When the sun was at its brightest, the Randolph sisters used magnifying glasses to study the backs of those letters, "where alone the impressions shews; a few lines will sometimes cost as many days." They worked sometimes eight hours a day readying transcriptions for Jeff, the lead editor.[49]

After James Madison died, Dolley Madison's devotion to his papers project seemed to know no bounds. Once when her house caught fire, "as soon as she became conscious of the danger, she said 'the papers, the papers first.'" She—and the manuscripts—were saved by a slave. Dolley was not motivated by loyalty to James's historic legacy alone: she also saw the papers as her most lucrative inheritance. James had given her exclusive executorship over his estate and his papers, "having entire confidence," he wrote in his will, "in her discreet and proper use of them."[50]

Unfortunately, Dolley made a fateful mistake by including Payne Todd in the negotiations for publication. One observer caustically remarked, "If you are acquainted with him, you need not be told that he is the last man in the world to compass such a business." Payne was Dolley's worst, but not her only, obstacle to turning James's writings into lasting wealth. An economic downturn also complicated her work. In the end, she earned far less than she had imagined; instead of the $100,000 Dolley and James had hoped for, Congress paid her $55,000 total, in two installments. The last of these was held in trust for her, to keep the money from Payne Todd's grasping hands.[51]

Jeff Randolph faced a similar disappointment with his stewardship of his grandfather's papers. He, like Dolley, imagined that selling so prominent a founder's writings would not only enrich the country but, importantly, help Randolph cover some of Jefferson's massive debts. But the price the US government offered him was disappointing. In 1829, he published with a Charlottesville company *Memoir, Correspondence and Miscellanies: From the Papers of Thomas Jefferson*, but that private effort did not sell well, producing more frustrations. Eventually, in 1848, Randolph agreed to accept $20,000 from Congress for a portion of Jefferson's letters.[52]

As their originators intended, the real benefit of distributing the founders' papers was reputational and historical and not, to the frustration of their executors, financial. While some imagined a lucrative payoff to their closest heirs, the true purpose of the papers projects was to leave a guide for future Americans, posterity in the larger rather than the familial sense. Washington, Jefferson, and Madison hoped that the carefully tended images they left behind would inspire subsequent generations of Americans to study and venerate the Revolution. And if those "millions yet unborn" remembered, they might emulate the founders long after each man had, as Washington eloquently put it, moved "gently down the stream of life, until I sleep with my Fathers."[53]

A s their lives ended, Virginia's founding fathers left their families with one last piece of evidence of their heroism: their physical deaths. Driven by reputational ambitions, their families made the most of it.

George Washington's death, on 14 December 1799, was the most grievous in America's history: it produced nationwide mourning on an unprecedented and still unmatched scale.[54] His heirs, both the familial and national varieties, needed his death to match his life. So, while Washington probably succumbed to acute epiglottitis, which doctors today understand as an excruciating and frightening way to die—the patient would have felt himself gradually strangled by his own throat tissue—the relatives keeping vigil told a different story. Tobias Lear, who was called to George Washington's bedside by Martha, witnessed his last, torturous days. George was repeatedly bled and blistered and administered purgatives, even after he asked the doctors to stop. In the first draft of his accounting, Lear acknowledged that Washington was in "great pain" while insisting that he faced his illness with dignity, strength, and reason. According to Lear, Washington understood that he was dying and—ever mindful of his legacy—told Lear to manage his papers. While anguished caregivers fretted, Washington calmly told them, "Don't be afraid." The symptoms of his condition and the ghoulish treatments of his doctors would have been agonizing. Still, Lear maintained, after Washington had been satisfied that all his affairs were in order, he said, "'Tis well," and minutes before he died had the presence of mind to check his own pulse.[55]

Lear later added to his first account, bolstering the image of Washington as courageous and strong: "His patience, fortitude, & resignation never forsook him for a moment. In all his distress he uttered not a sigh, nor a complaint." The story is simply incredible. Yet two of the doctors attending the former president said the same thing. "During the short period of his illness," they wrote in a newspaper essay, "he economized his time, in the arrangement of such few concerns as required his attention, with the utmost serenity; and anticipated his approaching dissolution with every demonstration of that equanimity for which his whole life has been so uniformly and singularly conspicuous."[56]

In contrast to these apocryphal tales, Martha Washington faced real sacrifices that she did not hide after her husband's death. She was devastated to be left without "the Partner of my life" and longed for "the moment when I shall be again united" with him.[57] She moved out of their bedroom and into a small room on the third floor of her home. She was so inundated with condolence letters that Congress passed a bill giving her free franking. (In that age, recipients, not senders, paid postage.) Mount Vernon continued to be flooded with visitors, too, and Washington felt it her duty to welcome citizens of a grieving nation, though friends saw she had lost her zeal for socializing. Out of fears about self-preservation, she decided to speed up the emancipatory program in George's will. Then there was the matter of his remains. George Washington had made clear that he wanted to be buried at Mount Vernon. But political leaders had other ideas, claiming him for the Republic even in death. Congress wanted his body moved to the District of Columbia, and President Adams appealed to the brokenhearted widow. Washington initially gave her consent because of "the great example which I have so long had before me never to oppose my private wishes to the public will." But, she added, "I cannot say what a sacrifice . . . I make to a sense of public duty." Meanwhile, Virginia leaders staked a claim; they wanted the former president's body removed to Richmond and even built a crypt on Capitol Square. Martha died in 1802, with federal and state leaders still wrangling over a possible disinterment. (The matter dragged on for decades before descendant John Washington finally decided to leave George Washington "undisturbed, to mingle with his kindred dust.")[58]

Eyewitnesses to Patrick Henry's demise reported the same courage and acceptance as had those attending to George Washington. His death came much slower than Washington's. Henry had, in the words of one relative, "a lingering disorder, which gave him great time to prepare for death." The character Henry's kin sought to project was the same as Washington's, though they also added a strong message about paternal and Christian duty. In his last weeks, Henry did not gather his papers or write a self-celebratory memoir. Instead, witnesses said, he spent his time reading the Bible and talking with his children.[59]

Henry's final passage came in the early summer of 1799. His grandson, Patrick Henry Fontaine, was at his bedside. Henry was attended by Dr. George Cabell, who, when all else failed, offered his patient liquid mercury. In Fontaine's account, Cabell explained to Patrick Henry that the mercury might relieve his suffering but also could prove fatal. Henry decided for himself what to do next, and he prayed before he drank the vial of mercury. "Meanwhile Dr. Cabell, who greatly loved him, went out upon the lawn, and in his grief threw himself down upon the earth under one of the trees weeping bitterly," recalled Fontaine. When Cabell returned to Henry's bedside, he found him "calmly watching the congealing of the blood under his finger-nails, and speaking words of love and peace to his family, who were weeping around his chair." As had been the case with Washington, the patient comforted the physician, who lacked Henry's strength. Henry did not fight death or suffer an anguished demise. Fontaine said that his grandfather "continued to breathe very softly for some moments; after which they who were looking upon him, saw that his life had departed." It was a lesson for posterity, as was the eulogy published in the *Virginia Gazette*, which closed, "As long as our rivers flow, or mountains stand—so long will your excellence and worth be the theme of homage and endearment, and Virginia, bearing in mind her loss, will say to rising generations, imitate my Henry."[60]

The relatives at Jefferson's deathbed told essentially the same story. He was, to the end, "calm and composed." Like Washington and Henry, though aware of his impending death, Jefferson comforted those around him. His final moments, relatives maintained, were exemplary and inspiring. "He suffered no pain," Jeff Randolph proclaimed. "His mind was always clear—it never wandered. He conversed freely, and gave directions as to his private affairs. His manner was that of a person going on a necessary journey—evincing neither satisfaction nor regret."[61]

Jefferson died on 4 July 1826—fifty years to the day after the signing of the Declaration of Independence. That he and John Adams both passed on this anniversary quickly became, and remains still, an incredibly moving story. The Randolph family understood the poetry (and potential of perceived providence) of Jefferson dying on the Fourth of July. They, along with Jefferson, wanted it to happen on that specific day. He had roused himself in his last hours to ask if it was yet the Fourth of July. And witnesses to his demise watched the clock, literally. "At fifteen minutes before twelve" on the night of 3 July, Jeff Randolph recalled, "we stood noting the minute-hand of the watch, hoping a few minutes of prolonged life."[62]

James Madison, amazingly, also died without suffering or sorrow. Paul Jennings, who for six months before Madison's death tended to his every need, wrote the sole eyewitness account of his passing. Like Jefferson, Madison's "mind was bright" to the end, Jennings insisted, and he met death with brave acceptance. Jennings and Madison's niece Nelly Willis were the only ones with him on the last morning of his life. When he was unable to eat his breakfast, Willis asked what was wrong. "Nothing," he replied, "more than a change of *mind*, my dear." And then, Jennings said, Madison was gone: "His head instantly dropped, and he ceased breathing as quietly as the snuff of a candle goes out."[63]

In the closing years of his life, Thomas Jefferson had worried that partisan writers would corrupt the story of the American Revolution and make history "fable instead of fact." In death, he and his counterparts became the beneficiaries of the very thing he feared. When told of the peaceful passage of Jefferson, Madison said "I never doubted that the last scene of our illustrious friend would be worthy of the life which it closed."[64] There was no cause for doubt. Men and women present at the death of each founder knew that it would not do for revolutionary heroes on their way to becoming historical monuments to cry out in anguish, wallow in self-pity, or fight fate. So, regardless of the realities of each man's death, the eyewitnesses made sure that the "last scene" completed a picture-perfect life story. Death narratives, purged of complexity and suffering and rendered models of republican values, thus became a last chance to teach posterity a lesson while proclaiming the enduring legacy of the founding fathers.

I f anything, the efforts of the children of the founders to advance the historical reputations of their fathers proved a bit too successful. Many found themselves tending to a past that they could not escape. They knew all the ways they might fail to live up to the expectations of the revolutionary age, but how could they ever succeed? How could even the most virtuous, accomplished, and dutiful children match the reputations of their fathers, the founders?

For all their forward-looking focus, Virginia's founders unintentionally left the rising generation with an unattainable duty to an unmatchable past. No matter how responsible and respectable and virtuous the sons and grandsons of the founders became, their achievements seemed always eclipsed by their fathers. Madison, Washington, Henry, Jefferson, and Mason were surely men of exceptional ability. But it was the events of the age—paired with their talents and resolve—that allowed them and their contemporaries throughout British America to become historically transcendent.

Without the constitutional crises that called him to practice his genius on so grand a stage, James Madison would likely have become a respected political leader and intellectual in Orange County. Absent the test of the Revolutionary War, George Washington would have still been an exceptionally successful agricultural innovator and a well-respected gentleman in Virginia's Northern Neck. But we would probably not know his name. John Adams saw it clearly: the revolutionary generation had, he wrote, "been sent into life at a time when the greatest lawgivers of antiquity would have wished to live," a moment of such grand proportion that "few of the human race have ever enjoyed" or would ever duplicate. But nineteenth-century Virginians often forgot that historical reality as they turned toward an idealized past that they increasingly (and to their detriment) tried to re-create.[65] We sometimes forget it still.

No matter how radiantly the descendants polished their talents, there would be no moment in their lifetimes (or arguably in American history since) for them to shine so brightly as the founders or even escape their long shadow. "The elevated station held by your Grand Father," John Eppes wrote his son Francis, "ought to stimulate you to great exertion." Francis did his very best. He studied hard and married shrewdly, back into the Randolph family. He ably managed his grandfather's estate at Poplar Forest before moving to Florida. For thirty-five years Eppes served in civic life, including as a justice of the peace and the mayor of Tallahassee. Inspired by his grandfather's Charlottesville project, Eppes dedicated himself to creating a university in his adopted home state. He gave land and money to found the institution that became Florida State University, and he served on the board of trustees, including as president, for many years. Yet the Florida State University webpage celebrating the 150th anniversary of the school's founding introduced Eppes first as a "grandson of Thomas Jefferson."[66]

Sixty-four years old at the time of his passing, Alexander Spotswood Henry's obituary began with the most important fact of his life: "He was the son of the illustrious Patrick Henry, whose eloquence will live as long as the world stands." The eulogist then declared that Alexander, who was eleven when his father died, had "inherited the principles of his father" and "was a patriot in the full sense of the term" who "bore not only the impress of his father's image, but had received as a rich legacy his chivalrous spirit." Each quality the author praised in the departed, he attributed to his father. Both were intelligent, virtuous, temperate, sociable, and dedicated to public service. The eulogist explicitly concluded, however, that the son could never match the father, adding that there was not "a man in this country or on the face of the earth, now living, that would not suffer by such comparison!"[67]

It was no different for the Masons. John Mason lived to the ripe old age of eighty-three and was a successful and respected businessman, president of the Bank of Columbia, a justice of peace, and a corporate leader appointed by President Jefferson to head the federal Indian trade. But his hometown newspaper obituary gave the barest of details about Mason's life: it reported only where he died, the time and location of his funeral, and that he was "the last surviving son of Colonel George Mason." The eulogist filled the remainder of his essay admiring John's father.[68]

Thomas Mann Randolph Jr. died two years after his father-in-law, having never escaped the perception that he was a "silly bird" among "swans" at Monticello. Even his obituary in the *Richmond Enquirer* observed that "had he possessed less irritability of temper . . . he would have stood foremost" among his generation. Although he was included in the family cemetery he was laid to rest for all eternity at the feet of Thomas Jefferson.[69]

William Wirt Henry devoted much of his illustrious career to defending Patrick Henry's legacy, but he could not elude it. In addition to serving as president of the American Historical Association, Henry rose to great prominence in the legal profession. He was named president of the Virginia Bar Association and vice president of the American Bar Association. Virginians elected him to the House of Delegates and then state Senate. But his most acclaimed achievement was his collection of Patrick Henry's writings. And, though he died a century after his grandfather, his obituary began by noting that he was a grandson of Patrick Henry.[70]

No one faced a more impossible task than George Washington Parke Custis. Despite eventually becoming a renowned orator and pursuing a host of interests far afield from George Washington's—painting, writing plays, composing music—Custis always lived in his grandfather's shadow. His paintings often depicted revolutionary battles featuring Washington. When he spoke at public events, he sometimes wore an epaulette given to him by Washington. His home, Arlington House, doubled as a memorial to Washington. He filled the mansion with relics which he displayed for guests and took to patriotic gatherings. Though he lived well into his seventies, Custis was always, even his only daughter said, "universally known, beloved, and honored, as the 'child of Mount Vernon.'"[71]

The children growing up in the homes of Virginia's leading revolutionaries paid a high price—some higher than others—for their fathers' greatness. In their writings, the sons and daughters of this cohort celebrated without qualification the noble civic achievements of the founding fathers. But considering how their own lives played out, a question lingers: Did they, in their heart of hearts, see the Revolution as more "a blessing or a curse"?

Epilogue: Going Home

I n the fall of 1901, more than 250 Saint Louis residents made a pilgrimage to Monticello. The group left Union Station on Thursday, 10 October, filling six coaches on a train and carrying a commemorative marker made of Missouri granite, news of plans for the World's Fair (honoring the one-hundredth anniversary of the Louisiana Purchase), and an abiding reverence for Thomas Jefferson. From Charlottesville, a parade escorted them up the mountain, and several days of speeches extolled the virtue of Jefferson and his fellow revolutionaries.

"We have come to Virginia," one speaker declared, "to breathe the air, to see the sky, to tread the soil, that begat such men." The travelers returned to Missouri on Monday, 14 October, having gained by their visit to Jefferson's home a deeper appreciation "of the life and deeds and doctrines of the Father of Democracy, who, being dead, yet lives in every heart that beats for liberty."[1]

For more than a century before these Saint Louisans made their journey east, Americans had been traveling to the homes of leading revolutionaries, for the same reasons and with the same perspective. By going to the residences of men like George Washington, James Madison, and Thomas Jefferson, Americans could show respect, seek inspiration, and find connections to the founding generation. The pilgrimages started in the revolutionary era, when these men and their families occupied their now famous houses. (The endless stream of guests perhaps explains why Jefferson never left Virginia after his retirement from the presidency; the world came to him.) And the journeys continue apace, now almost two centuries after the last of the founders was ushered to the grave.

In the wake of the Revolution, as they looked to the future of their reputations and the American Republic, Virginia's founding fathers saw their homes as a vital part of their civic experiment. Their plantation estates allowed them to pursue what George Washington called the "republican stile of living."[2] Away from the disappointments and vexations of government, these founders could create in pastoral settings along the Potomac River and in the foothills of the Blue Ridge Mountains models of all they valued.

The layout of their estates communicated their civic ideals. The founders imagined their plantations as paragons of a well-governed republic writ small: independent, community-focused, self-sustaining, and racially divided. The grounds were beautifully maintained, the operations rationally organized, the collective good achieved by the hard work of all parties, and the entire enterprise led by men of unparalleled capacity and virtue.[3]

The mere fact that powerful men willingly retired to such homes was itself a quintessential republican act. In voluntarily leaving a governmental or military position, a man fulfilled a service to his country, modeling republican citizenship. From time to time all of these Virginians retreated home, choosing, as George Washington explained in 1784, to leave "the busy scenes of public life" to "tread the paths of private life with heartfelt satisfaction." Monarchs did not cede power to live "under their own vine and fig tree." Citizen-leaders of a republic did.[4]

But it was not enough to achieve this republican lifestyle; others needed to witness it. So beginning in the 1780s, the estates of Virginia's leading revolutionaries became tourist destinations. Going to the homes of patriot heroes was, in fact, a design of some members of the founding generation, to secure their place in history and inspire future generations to follow their example. The founders' homes served as repositories of republican values: they displayed the artifacts of their heroics for sightseers and opened their libraries to discuss with travelers the future of the country. Visitors who came to their residences could admire these men, study them, emulate them. In the new Republic where citizens feared being one generation away from collapse, visiting a living legend and an idealized past could, just maybe, inspire a better future. Mount Vernon and Monticello attracted the most travelers, but all of Virginia's leading patriots hosted Americans seeking lessons about the past for the future of the young nation.

Night after night, year after year, Martha Jefferson Randolph accommodated men and women who, often unannounced, trekked up the mountain to admire her father. The opening of the University of Virginia sped the flow. "Our lives," Martha said, "are literally spent in the drawing room." Randolph delighted the guests, talking for hours, strolling through the grounds, and supervising the logistics of boarding as many as fifty people a night, while the Monticello slaves did the real work. Martha Washington and the Mount Vernon slaves likewise hosted endless (usually uninvited) visitors on pilgrimages to witness the glory of America's revolutionary past at the home of the father of the country. Visitors to Mount Vernon were fascinated by every detail of Washington's life, including what he ate for breakfast (cornmeal cakes with honey and tea) and the name of his favorite horse during the war (Nelson). Washington's home, like Jefferson's, seemed to epitomize the highest ideals of their country and confirm the impulse of Americans to idolize them.[5]

Turning their meticulously designed homes into popular patriotic tourist destinations promoted the founders' quest for fame and helped secure the immortality many craved. One traveler to Mount Vernon captured the pervasive sentiment shared by people who toured Virginia's patriot houses—a perception no doubt gratifying to the men who welcomed their adulation: "So long as one lover of liberty lives among men . . . he will desire to make a pilgrimage thither."[6]

Because these founders were also self-styled Virginia gentlemen, the magnificent settings of their houses revealed the blending of gentry culture and republican values. Not only paragons of republican independence, virtue, and leadership, they appeared in retirement as consummate Virginia planter-patriarchs, running well-ordered, refined estates. Awed guests could witness and proclaim that, too.

Whether entering or leaving, when the front doors opened at Gunston Hall and at Monticello, the view was stunning. The vista from the front porch of Montpelier and the backyard of Red Hill still prompts amazed silence, which was the intended reaction. George Mason ordered the trees bordering the road to Gunston Hall planted in perfect paired alignment, so that visitors could enjoy the optical illusion of seeing dozens of trees appear only as four. George Washington moved the main entrance at Mount Vernon from west to east to ensure a longer, more majestic approaching gaze. Inside the residences, formal dining rooms, imported furniture, and commissioned paintings and sculptures expressed wealth, education, and gentility. Books lined the founders' offices; musical instruments rested in their parlors; their families ate on imported china, in the case of the Madisons and Washingtons, exclusively designed for their homes. Stables, gardens, blacksmith shops, tanneries, and orchards confirmed their (slave-based) independence. Maintaining such estates was a lifelong, ever evolving project.

When an eighteenth-century gentleman chose a home, he paid close attention to the setting, preferring a lofty place to symbolize his status. After the 1770s, visitors linked the positioning of these estates to these men's political achievements, each influencing the other. A Frenchman visiting Monticello in 1782 perceived that Thomas Jefferson "had placed his mind, like his house, on a lofty height, whence he might contemplate the whole universe." When Margaret Bayard Smith visited Monticello in 1809 she drew the same connection: "I looked upon him as he walked, the top of the mountain, as being elevated about the mass of mankind, as much in character as he was in local situation." And the 1901 Saint Louisans concurred, concluding that men like Washington, Jefferson, and Henry "built their homes upon the mountain tops" and consequently "had a breadth of vision, a singleness of purpose, a loftiness of ideals, a love of humanity, a moral fibre, a grace of life, a chivalry of deeds."[7]

If we look closer, past the genteel gardens and parlors and the displays for lovers of liberty, we can see that this cohort hid in their houses the same thing they did in the Constitution: their commitment to slave labor. Slave quarters were intentionally, discreetly located out of sight from the main houses: close enough so that every need could be quickly attended to but behind a tree line or down a hill, so as not to mar the view of white visitors. Distant kitchens suggested the owners did not concern themselves with their cooks' inconvenience of carrying hot pots and heavy platters. Inside the founders' houses, slaves often used separate entrances and navigated cramped internal staircases, so that they could rush to fill the master's desires and then slip away. Such architectural elements disguised the presence of slaves, just as these men's writings often erased slavery from their lives. At the same time, the plantations practically announced slave mastery: none of the handsome houses and the vast and scenic estates existed without slave labor. Slaves ran the workshops, cleaned the parlors, raised the crops and the white children. Their labor paid for the china and the dining tables and the art—everything that made these men refined. Slaves toiled in these men's fields while they retreated to their studies to ponder a government built on the concept of liberty. When Virginia's founders retired to their plantations decades later, having done nearly nothing to eradicate the institution of slavery, which they understood to be a "moral and political depravity," their slaves tended to the needs of their admiring, patriotic guests. And when these men made the final exit, their slaves dug their graves and buried them, in the shadows of the plantation homes that symbolized everything these founders held dear.[8]

After the founders died, their estates, like their republican experiment, passed into new hands, subject to different priorities and prospects. Descendants fell on hard times or added onto the estates or developed other priorities or wanted their own homes and their own lives. Monticello was the quickest to go. In the closing years of his life, Thomas Jefferson's massive debts forced him to sell off some of his holdings. Within months of his death, despite Jeff Randolph's best efforts, the creditors could no longer be kept at bay. Martha Jefferson Randolph was basically rendered homeless—this in repayment of decades of selfless devotion.

Dolley Madison held onto Montpelier a bit longer, but her financial straits, deepened by Payne Todd's dissipation, soon caught up with her. By the summer of 1844 she saw no choice but to part with the estate: slaves, land, livestock, even many of her and James's personal possessions went with the main house. Dolley Madison did not get to go home again even when she died, five years later. Not until 1858, after being buried and moved twice, was she at last buried by James's side.[9]

While the next generation of Henrys, Masons, and Washingtons remained at their ancestor's estate, the spaces themselves changed—as they always had in the past—to fit the familial needs, aesthetic tastes, and, in some cases, the straitened finances of the residents. The results were often grievous to Americans who imagined the founders' homes as a crucial (and fixed) link to the revolutionary past.

A few short years after Jefferson's death, visitors to Monticello were appalled at what they saw. "The first thing that strikes you," one antebellum tourist proclaimed, "is the utter ruin and desolation of everything." After the Civil War, the home seemed "a total wreck, as many years had passed without the slightest efforts at repair."[10]

Things were hardly better at Mount Vernon. An 1834 visitor found it deplorable: "Everything except the garden & interior of the house appears to be going to ruin." Just five years later another complained, "I was never more disappointed in my life, than on the visit." It was especially mortifying to see Washington's tomb left to languish "in a dilapidated condition." By the late 1850s—in a coincidence almost too rich to be true—George Washington's once stately house, like his country, was falling apart.[11]

Late antebellum visitors to Mount Vernon hoped against hope that Washington's home might inspire allegiance to the national family and forestall war. "Ye men of the North, ye men of the South, come, oh! come to this hallowed spot," begged one pilgrim, "and, around this sacred sarcophagus, promise to live together like brothers, for he was the Father of you *all!*[12] But it was not to be. Neither US nor Confederate troops dared to occupy George Washington's final resting place, but it was not lost on Americans that battles threatening the nation's very existence were being waged, brother against brother, perilously close to the home of the father of the country. One US sailor traveling on the

Potomac past Mount Vernon regretted that the nation Washington helped create was "scarcely a life time old; yet the children of the second generation are ready to tear it to pieces." Troops camped at Montpelier and Gunston Hall, but Monticello bore the hardest blows. Edmund Bacon, a former overseer at Monticello, recounted the painful seizure of the house by Confederate forces. "There could be no more sad and striking illustration of the folly and madness of this rebellion," Bacon concluded, "than the fact that the home of Jefferson has been confiscated, because its owner is loyal to the Stars and Stripes. The banner of treason—the Confederate flag—now waves over the bones of the author of the Declaration of Independence."[13]

Jefferson's former home decaying in the wake of the Civil War seemed to many visitors to symbolize the profoundly, perhaps irreparably damaged country. David Culbreath, visiting in 1872, left depressed: "Everything observed," he lamented, "belonged to a passed generation, had apparently seen its day of usefulness, and was on the rapid road to extinction. No one, seemingly, was left with sufficient means, interest or patriotism to stay the inroad of decay." A generation later, Americans had still not saved Monticello from the ravages of time and neglect. Another visitor offered sage advice for his generation and for posterity. "In recent years decay has set in in some places," Fiske Kimball acknowledged, and he observed "a few incongruous additions." "But," he believed, "the main fabric stands unharmed . . . the place waits only to be reclaimed by the nation and restored with loving hands."[14]

As time took its toll and the houses passed from owner to owner, the pilgrims kept coming. Imagining the founders' homes as belonging to the nation, visitors felt entitled to access. And they could get belligerent when thwarted. For decades, owners of Mount Vernon felt besieged by tourists—upwards of ten thousand a year by the 1850s. The physician of one owner, John Augustine Washington Sr., was mortified when uninvited guests refused to abandon their demands for a tour, even when told that John lay dying. The doctor insisted that his patient was "driven nearly distracted, every day of his Life! His family has no privacy, and he no peace, for the people flock there all the time; pulling down his fences—leaving open his gates—trampling his crops, and garden . . .

peering through the windows—and begging, or forcing their way into every room in the house!" As late as the 1940s, Lucy Gray Henry Harrison, great-granddaughter of Patrick Henry and owner of Red Hill, politely conceded that "it is not an unmixed blessing to own a famous estate and live there. Tourists appear at all times and in all seasons from every side of the house." At all these estates, sightseers' appropriation of souvenirs sometimes crossed the line into larceny and vandalism. They pulled flowers from the gardens, gouged wood from the houses, even chipped away at grave markers.[15]

Some enthusiasts of the founding generation perceived the simple act of these homes being occupied as offensive. Jefferson Levy, whose family acquired Monticello in 1834 and owned it longer than Thomas Jefferson, was condemned before the US Congress as "a rank outsider" subjecting what should be a national memorial to "the desecration of being lived in." Among other violations, the Levy family had the audacity to hang their own portraits on the walls of Monticello.[16]

Only restoring the "original" form of the houses, held in public trust, seemed an acceptably fitting tribute to the founding fathers. So, eventually, all of these houses came under the oversight of foundations, mostly owing to the commitment of American women. Led by Louisa Bird Cunningham and her daughter Ann Pamela Cunningham, the Mount Vernon Ladies' Association of the Union raised the funds to buy Mount Vernon in 1858, managed the reconstruction, and oversees the site still. Maud Littleton led the successful campaign to place Monticello under public trust in the early twentieth century. Gunston Hall is owned by the Commonwealth of Virginia but administered by the Colonial Dames of America. Lucy Gray Henry Harrison lovingly attended to her great-grandfather's estate and secured Red Hill's passage into public hands. Another Henry descendant, Margaret Henry Penick Nuttle, funded a major twenty-first-century renewal project. And Marion duPont Scott bequeathed Montpelier to the National Trust for Historic Preservation and planned in her will for the mansion to be restored to represent Madison's residency.[17]

Through their efforts, teams of scholars were eventually hired to re-create for curious tourists the lost physical domestic world of the

founders. Additions were dismantled—a side porch was torn down at
Mount Vernon, an entire floor painstakingly removed from Montpelier.
Staff members spent countless days scouring antique dealerships to find
not just suitable period pieces but if at all possible the exact furniture
and appointments owned by these families. The point is to present to
modern visitors the same image these men projected in their own time:
refinement, order, dignity, and self-determination.

Their houses today stand as physical testimonies to the "republican
stile of living" pursued by slaveholding planter-patriarchs, fathers who
became founders and, then, founding fathers. An illusion of timeless-
ness is built on top of decades of disheartening deterioration and cre-
ative adaptation—an unintentionally fitting metaphor for the Virginians'
Revolution.

Today, visitors to Virginia can tour the restored plantation
homes of all the state's greatest revolutionary leaders: Gunston Hall, Red Hill, Mount Vernon, Monticello, and Montpelier are open to the paying public. The foundations that manage these
properties have taken astonishingly meticulous care to accurately re-
produce for tourists the domestic spaces once inhabited by these men.
In 2001, for example, when the Montpelier Foundation began studying
the feasibility of returning the former Madison residence to its early
nineteenth-century incarnation, experts spent eighteen months con-
ducting over three hundred painstaking substructure investigations.
They drilled holes, stripped floors, and chipped away paint and plaster,
as well as scrutinized period drawings and scoured historical documents
to see if they could reasonably attempt to recover the lost world of James
and Dolley. A 2,300-page report concluded the work could be done, and
five and a half years and $24,000,000 later, on Constitution Day 2008,
the remarkable project was complete. It entailed the removal of nearly
24,000 square feet of living space, mostly added by the duPont family in
the twentieth century. Thirty thousand cypress shingles were cut by
hand, using period techniques. A carefully deconstructed rat's nest provided clues about wallpaper and upholstery; the evidence was verified

when it was discovered that a small shred of a letter in the nest contained James Madison's handwriting.[18]

Thanks to the dedication and imagination of the respective foundations overseeing the collaboration of chemists, botanists, artists, architects, historians, and archaeologists, these restored homes transport twenty-first-century visitors into the material culture of the revolutionary age. The houses appear frozen in time, as if their owners walked out sometime in the late eighteenth century and docents have been dutifully guarding them ever since. We, today, can enjoy the illusion of entering the world the founders "originally" inhabited.

The sites are, justifiably, very popular. Americans still visit the homes out of respect, patriotism, intellectual curiosity, and duty. Many want to know, and perhaps even feel they need to know, these men, and so try and go home with them. As they have since the eighteenth century, pilgrimages to these estates serve at once two purposes: the revolutionary leaders' hopes for immortality and their posterity's desire to heed their example. By going to their homes and celebrating their achievements, contemporary Americans, the posterity for which the founding generation sacrificed and worried, keep alive their legacy—or, more accurately, the idealized story these men sought to tell about their lives and the American Revolution.

Inadvertently, the exquisitely tended properties make it hard to imagine, even in the intimate act of entering their homes, the tumultuous past that unfolded inside those walls. Everything appears pristine and placid. Little is left to remind us of how demanding and dysfunctional these men's families could be. Men and women struggled in these idyllic homes with financial crises, alcoholism, gambling addictions, mental illness, domestic violence, bankruptcy, and estrangements. Loved ones suffered and died, children disappointed, relationships faltered. The houses cannot recapture that ordeal of being fathers in a transforming age. Nor is there much to remind visitors of the controversial political actions this cohort undertook, how many false starts and doubts beset them, or how bitterly they contested the creation of the American Republic. If you take a tour at any of these homes, you will hear the docents and guides work extraordinarily hard to convey the rich complexity of the past. But, as the revolutionary era owners intended, the beauty of their homes usually overawes visitors. Captivated by these grand, genteel homes, we, just like eighteenth-century guests, can lose sight of the complicated lives these fathers and founders led.

Virginia's house museums rightly commemorate the lives of Patrick Henry, George Mason, Thomas Jefferson, James Madison, and George Washington and celebrate how this cohort, living in an extraordinary age, dared to seize the opportunity to "begin the world over again." But they were only men, after all, not fundamentally different from us today—a fact easy to forget when gazing at the boxwood gardens at Gunston Hall or making the grand approach to Montpelier.

As in their portraits and sculptures, the image cast of these men in their now—for the first time—immaculate homes is that they are distant and awe-inspiring archetypes of an essential and yet unattainable American character, unsullied by doubt or turmoil or failings. From behind the velvet ropes, tourists can see (but never touch!) these men's personal possessions and peer even into their bedrooms, which their closest relatives entered only upon knocking and, as the Mason children and Jefferson grandchildren all reported, with great reverence. But more often than achieving real familiarity, visitors unknowingly experience a performance, choreographed in the eighteenth century for posterity's benefit and, even now, for ours.

I f they could somehow return to Virginia, Mason, Henry, Washington, Jefferson, and Madison would surely recognize their houses. The table is set at Mount Vernon with Martha Washington's best china. The long porch that James and Dolley Madison playfully raced down is fully restored. Sounds from the blacksmith's shop echo across Red Hill. The gardens are beautifully tended at Gunston Hall. Thomas Jefferson's copier rests on his desk.

The living parts of these founders' legacy, however, would seem foreign to them. The seduction of "originalism" and habitual queries about "what would the founders do?" never quite go away. But the truth is that Americans have so reinvented the government the founders fitfully designed as to make it nearly unrecognizable to them.

At least one thing remains the same, though. We still seem to fear that we—or, more accurately, the next generation—will let down the founders and ruin their great republican experiment. Are we today, as the patriots said they were then, "firmly determined, at the hazard of our Lives, to transmit to our Children & Posterity those sacred Rights to which ourselves were born"? Or, will the sacrifices of "the generation of 1776, to acquire self-government and happiness to their country" at last be "thrown away by the unwise and unworthy passions" of our sons and daughters?[19] For all the changes we have wrought in the American Republic since the late eighteenth century, these questions endure. So perhaps we have not strayed so far after all from our founding fathers.

Abbreviations

DUL   Duke University, David M. Rubenstein Rare Book and Manuscript Library

FLDA   Family Letters Digital Archive, Thomas Jefferson Foundation, Inc., accessed 2012 http://www.monticello.org/familyletters

JM Writings   Gaillard Hunt, ed., *The Writings of James Madison*, 9 vols. (New York: G. P. Putnam's Sons, 1900–1910)

LC   Library of Congress

PGM   Robert A. Rutland, ed., *The Papers of George Mason, 1725–1792*, 3 vols. (Chapel Hill: University of North Carolina Press, 1970)

PGW (Colonial)   W. W. Abbot et al., eds., *The Papers of George Washington*, Colonial Series, 10 vols. (Charlottesville: University Press of Virginia, 1983–1995)

PGW (Confederation)   W. W. Abbot, ed., *The Papers of George Washington*, Confederation Series, 6 vols. (Charlottesville: University Press of Virginia, 1992–1997)

PGW (Presidential)   Dorothy Twohig et al., eds., *The Papers of George Washington*, Presidential Series, 16 vols. (Charlottesville: University Press of Virginia/University of Virginia Press, 1987–present)

PGW (Retirement)   W. W. Abbot et al., eds., *The Papers of George Washington*, Retirement Series, 4 vols. (Charlottesville: University Press of Virginia, 1998–1999)

PGW (War)   Philander D. Chase et al., eds., *The Papers of George Washington*, Revolutionary War Series, 20 vols. (Charlottesville: University Press of Virginia/University of Virginia Press, 1985–present)

PHC   William Wirt Henry, *Patrick Henry: Life, Correspondence and Speeches,*
3 vols. (New York: Charles Scribner's Sons, 1891)

PJM (Congressional)   William T. Hutchinson et al., eds., *The Papers of James Madison,* [Congressional Series], 17 vols. (Chicago: University of Chicago Press, 1962–1977), vols. 1–10; (Charlottesville: University Press of Virginia, 1977–1991), vols. 11–17

PJM (Presidential)   Robert A. Rutland et al., eds., *The Papers of James Madison,* Presidential Series, 6 vols. (Charlottesville: University Press of Virginia/University of Virginia Press, 1984–present)

PJM (Retirement)   David B. Mattern et al., eds., *The Papers of James Madison,* Retirement Series, 1 vol. (Charlottesville: University of Virginia Press, 2009–present)

PJM (State)   Robert J. Brugger et al., eds., *The Papers of James Madison,* Secretary of State Series, 8 vols. (Charlottesville: University Press of Virginia/University of Virginia Press, 1986–present)

PTJ   Julian P. Boyd et al., eds., *The Papers of Thomas Jefferson,* 36 vols. (Princeton, NJ: Princeton University Press, 1950–present)

PTJ (Retirement)   J. Jefferson Looney, ed., *The Papers of Thomas Jefferson,* Retirement Series, 7 vols. (Princeton, NJ: Princeton University Press, 2004–present)

PMHB   *Pennsylvania Magazine of History and Biography*

VMHB   *Virginia Magazine of History and Biography*

WMQ   *William and Mary Quarterly*

Notes

Introduction

1. Henry Lee, *Funeral Oration on the Death of General Washington* (London, 1800). For reactions to Washington's death, see Gerald Kahler, *The Long Farewell: Americans Mourn the Death of George Washington* (Charlottesville: University of Virginia Press, 2008); Paul K. Longmore, *The Invention of George Washington* (Berkeley: University of California Press, 1988), ch. 17; Andrew Burstein, "Immortalizing the Founding Fathers: The Excesses of Public Eulogy," in *Mortal Remains: Death in Early America*, ed. Nancy Isenberg and Andrew Burstein (Philadelphia: University of Pennsylvania Press, 2003), 91–107; and "A Concert of Mourning," http://gwpapers.virginia.edu/project/exhibit/mourning/index.html.

2. Foundational works on Virginia in this era include Edmund S. Morgan, *American Slavery, American Freedom: The Ordeal of Colonial Virginia* (New York: W. W. Norton, 1975); Rhys Isaac, *The Transformation of Virginia, 1740–1790* (Chapel Hill: University of North Carolina Press, 1982); T. H. Breen, *Tobacco Culture: The Mentality of the Great Tidewater Planters on the Eve of Revolution* (Princeton, NJ: Princeton University Press, 1985); and Charles Sydnor, *Gentlemen Freeholders: Political Practices in Washington's Virginia* (Chapel Hill: University of North Carolina Press, 1952). More recent explorations include Emory G. Evans, *A "Topping People": The Rise and Decline of Virginia's Old Political Elite, 1680–1790* (Charlottesville: University of Virginia Press, 2009); and Brent Tarter, *The Grandees of Government: The Origins and Persistence of Undemocratic Politics in Virginia* (Charlottesville: University of Virginia Press, 2013). For limits of elite control, see Woody Holton, *Forced Founders: Indians, Debtors, Slaves, and the Making of the American Revolution in Virginia* (Chapel Hill: University of North Carolina Press, 1999); and Michael A. McDonnell, *The Politics of War: Race, Class, and Conflict in Revolutionary Virginia* (Chapel Hill: University of North Carolina Press, 2007).

3. John Adams to Patrick Henry, 3 June 1776, in *The Works of John Adams*, ed. Charles Frances Adams, 10 vols. (Boston: Little, Brown, 1854), 9:387; William G. Morgan, "The Congressional Nominating Caucus of 1816: The Struggle Against the Vir-

ginia Dynasty," *VMHB* 80 (1972): 461–475 (quotation on 461). See also Linda Kerber, *Federalists in Dissent: Imagery and Ideology in Jeffersonian America* (Ithaca, NY: Cornell University Press, 1970), ch. 2; and Susan Dunn, *Dominion of Memories: Jefferson, Madison, and the Decline of Virginia* (New York: Basic Books, 2007).

    4. Recent biographies include Kevin J. Hayes, *The Mind of a Patriot: Patrick Henry and the World of Ideas* (Charlottesville: University of Virginia Press, 2008); Jeff Broadwater, *George Mason, Forgotten Founder* (Chapel Hill: University of North Carolina Press, 2006); Richard Brookhiser, *James Madison* (New York: Basic Books, 2011); and Ron Chernow, *Washington, a Life* (New York: Penguin, 2010). Examples of the excellent, wide-ranging scholarship on politics include Joanne B. Freeman, *Affairs of Honor: National Politics in the New Republic* (New Haven: Yale University Press, 2001); Stanley Elkins and Eric McKitrick, *The Age of Federalism* (New York: Oxford University Press, 1993); Jeffrey L. Pasley, *"The Tyranny of Printers": Newspaper Politics in the Early American Republic* (Charlottesville: University Press of Virginia, 2001); Jack Rakove, *Revolutionaries: A New History of the Invention of America* (Boston: Houghton Mifflin Harcourt, 2010); and David Waldstreicher, *"In the Midst of Perpetual Fetes": The Making of American Nationalism, 1776–1820* (Chapel Hill: University of North Carolina Press, 1997). A few works explore the founders' families separate from political leadership, including Thomas Fleming, *The Intimate Lives of the Founding Fathers* (New York: Smithsonian/HarperCollins, 2009); and Harlow Giles Unger, *The Unexpected George Washington: His Private Life* (Hoboken, NJ: John Wiley and Sons, 2006). Two powerful exceptions to this pattern are Catherine Allgor, *Parlor Politics: In Which the Ladies of Washington Help Build a City and a Government* (Charlottesville: University Press of Virginia, 2000); and Jon Kukla, *Mr. Jefferson's Women* (New York: Knopf, 2007). For model analyses of these issues, see esp. Kathleen M. Brown, *Good Wives, Nasty Wenches, and Anxious Patriarchs: Gender, Race, and Power in Colonial Virginia* (Chapel Hill: University of North Carolina Press, 1996); Jay Fliegelman, *Prodigals and Pilgrims: The American Revolution Against Patriarchal Authority, 1750–1800* (Cambridge: Cambridge University Press, 1982); Thomas A. Foster, *Sex and the Eighteenth-Century Man: Massachusetts and the History of Sexuality in America* (Boston: Beacon, 2006); Richard Godbeer, *The Overflowing of Friendship: Love Between Men and the Creation of the American Republic* (Baltimore: Johns Hopkins University Press, 2009); Cynthia A. Kierner, *Beyond the Household: Women's Place in the Early South, 1700–1835* (Ithaca, NY: Cornell University Press, 1998); and Lisa Wilson, *Ye Heart of a Man: The Domestic Life of Men in Colonial New England* (New Haven: Yale University Press, 1999).

    5. See esp. Gordon S. Wood, *The Radicalism of the American Revolution* (New York: Knopf, 1992); and Rhys Isaac, *Landon Carter's Uneasy Kingdom: Revolution and Rebellion on a Virginia Plantation* (New York: Oxford University Press, 2005).

CHAPTER 1. THE LAST COLONIAL PATRIARCHS

    1. For Virginia planter culture, see T. H. Breen, *Tobacco Culture: The Mentality of the Great Tidewater Planters on the Eve of Revolution* (Princeton, NJ: Princeton University Press, 1985); Richard Beeman, *The Old Dominion and the New Nation, 1788–1801* (Lexington: University Press of Kentucky, 1972); Charles Sydnor, *Gentlemen Freeholders: Po-*

litical Practices in Washington's Virginia (Chapel Hill: University of North Carolina Press, 1952); John E. Selby, *The Revolution in Virginia, 1775–1783* (Williamsburg, VA: Colonial Williamsburg Foundation, 1988); and Allan Kulikoff, *Tobacco and Slaves: The Development of Southern Cultures in the Chesapeake, 1680–1800* (Chapel Hill: University of North Carolina Press, 1986), pt. 2.

2. George Mason to Martin Cockburn, 26 May 1774, *PGM*, 1:190.

3. George Mason to John Mason, 13 March 1789, ibid., 3:1142. For Mason, see Jeff Broadwater, *George Mason, Forgotten Founder* (Chapel Hill: University of North Carolina Press, 2006). For Madison, see Jack Rakove, *James Madison and the Creation of the American Republic*, 3rd ed. (New York: Pearson, 2007); Drew R. McCoy, *The Last of the Fathers: James Madison and the Republican Legacy* (Cambridge: Cambridge University Press, 1989); Lance Banning, *The Sacred Fire of Liberty: James Madison and the Founding of the Federal Republic* (Ithaca, NY: Cornell University Press, 1995); and Stanley Elkins and Eric McKitrick, *The Age of Federalism* (New York: Oxford University Press, 1993), 79–92.

4. Thomas Jefferson to William Fleming, October 1763, *PTJ*, 1:13. For this phase of Jefferson's life, see Jon Kukla's outstanding book *Mr. Jefferson's Women* (New York: Knopf, 2007), ch. 2.

5. Henry S. Randall, *The Life of Thomas Jefferson*, 3 vols. (New York: Derby and Jackson, 1858), 1:11.

6. George Mason to George Washington, 2 April 1776, *PGM*, 1:267. For Mason's political reluctance, see Broadwater, *George Mason*, ch. 1; Helen Hill Miller, *George Mason, Gentleman Revolutionary* (Chapel Hill: University of North Carolina Press, 1975); and Jack Rakove, *Revolutionaries: A New History of the Invention of America* (Boston: Houghton Mifflin Harcourt, 2010), 166–167.

7. This discussion of the Mason family comes principally from Pamela C. Copeland and Richard K. MacMaster, *The Five George Masons: Patriots and Planters of Virginia and Maryland* (Charlottesville: University Press of Virginia, 1975), 1–88. For women's property rights, see Marylynn Salmon, *Women and the Law of Property in Early America* (Chapel Hill: University of North Carolina Press, 1986).

8. Miller, *George Mason*, 26; Copeland and MacMaster, *Five George Masons*, 56, 73.

9. Quoted in Copeland and MacMaster, *Five George Masons*, 77–78.

10. Miller, *George Mason*, 44. See also Rakove, *Revolutionaries*, 157–169; Broadwater, *George Mason*, ch. 1; Peter Wallenstein, "Flawed Keepers of the Flame: The Interpreters of George Mason," *VMHB* 102 (1994): 229–260.

11. John Mason Recollection, transcribed by Terry Dunn, Papers of John Mason (1766–1849), Gunston Hall Library and Archives. The text is also available in Terry K. Dunn, ed., *The Recollections of John Mason: George Mason's Son Remembers His Father and Life at Gunston Hall* (Marshall, VA: EPM, 2004).

12. Harlow Giles Unger, *The Unexpected George Washington: His Private Life* (Hoboken, NJ: John Wiley and Sons, 2006), 9–11.

13. Ron Chernow, *Washington, a Life* (New York: Penguin, 2010), ch. 2; Rakove, *Revolutionaries*, 10; Joseph J. Ellis, *His Excellency: George Washington* (New York: Knopf, 2004), 9–10; Unger, *Unexpected Washington*, 13–15.

14. George Washington, "Rules of Civility and Decent Behaviour in Company and Conversation," is widely available, including at gwpapers.virginia.edu. For conduct lit-

erature, see C. Dallett Hemphill, *Bowing to Necessities: A History of Manners in America, 1620–1860* (New York: Oxford University Press, 1999); Sarah E. Newton, *Learning to Behave: A Guide to American Conduct Books Before 1900* (Westport, CT: Greenwood, 1994); and Richard Bushman, *The Refinement of America: Persons, Houses, Cities* (New York: Knopf, 1992).

15. Martha Custis to John Hanbury and Company, 20 August 1757, in *"Worthy Partner": The Papers of Martha Washington*, ed. Joseph E. Fields (Westport, CT: Greenwood, 1994), 6 (quotation); Unger, *Unexpected Washington*, 34, 40; Thomas Fleming, *The Intimate Lives of the Founding Fathers* (New York: Smithsonian/HarperCollins, 2009), 15–19. See also Patricia Brady, *Martha Washington: An American Life* (New York: Penguin, 2005), esp. 54–64.

16. George Washington to John Alton, 5 April 1759, *PGW (Colonial)*, 6:200.

17. Capel and Osgood Hanbury to George Washington, 1 October 1759, in Fields, *"Worthy Partner,"* 93.

18. Shipping List, 20 September 1759, ibid., 86–91.

19. For planter indebtedness, see also Breen, *Tobacco Culture*; and Herbert Sloan, *Principle and Interest: Thomas Jefferson and the Problem of Debt* (New York: Oxford University Press, 1995). For Washington's finances, see Bruce A. Ragsdale, "George Washington, the British Tobacco Trade, and Economic Opportunity in Pre-Revolutionary Virginia," in *George Washington Reconsidered*, ed. Don Higginbotham (Charlottesville: University of Virginia Press, 2001), 67–93.

20. Rakove, *Revolutionaries*, 118; Sydnor, *Gentlemen Freeholders*, 92, 114.

21. George Mason to George Washington, 9 April 1768, Gunston Hall Library and Archives; Miller, *George Mason*, 74–75, 84; Broadwater, *George Mason*, 57–58; Rakove, *Revolutionaries*, 157.

22. Thomas A. Foster makes this salient point in "On Sex and the Founding Fathers: America's Fascination with the Intimate Lives of the Political Leaders of the American Revolution," ch. 1, unpublished ms in author's possession.

23. George Washington to Richard Washington, 20 September 1759, *PGW (Colonial)*, 6:359.

24. Quoted in John P. Kaminski, *The Great Virginia Triumvirate: George Washington, Thomas Jefferson, and James Madison in the Eyes of Their Contemporaries* (Charlottesville: University of Virginia Press, 2010), 208. For Dolley Madison, see Catherine Allgor's excellent book *A Perfect Union: Dolley Madison and the Creation of the American Nation* (New York: Henry Holt, 2006).

25. Paul Jennings, *A Colored Man's Reminiscences of James Madison, by Paul Jennings* (Brooklyn, NY: George C. Beadle, 1865), 17. For Madison's character, see Gordon S. Wood, *Revolutionary Characters: What Made the Founders Different* (New York: Penguin, 2006), ch. 5; Elkins and McKitrick, *Age of Federalism*, 79–92; and Stuart Leibiger, *Founding Friendship: George Washington, James Madison, and the Creation of the American Republic* (Charlottesville: University Press of Virginia, 1999), 6–7.

26. For Madison's early education, see Douglass Adair, ed., "James Madison's Autobiography," *WMQ*, 3rd ser., 2 (1945): 191–209.

27. James Madison Jr. to James Madison Sr., 23 July 1770, *PJM (Congressional)*,

1:49–50; James Madison Jr. to William Bradford, 9 November 1772, ibid., 1:74–75. Madison said his politicization emerged during Virginians' debates over religious freedom. Adair, "James Madison's Autobiography," 194, 198–204. See also correspondence with William Bradford, *PJM (Congressional)*, 1.

28. William Byrd, *The Westover Manuscripts: Containing the History of the Dividing Line Betwixt Virginia and North Carolina* (Petersburg, VA: Edmund and Julian Ruffin, 1841), 142.

29. Richard R. Beeman, *Patrick Henry: A Biography* (New York: McGraw-Hill, 1974), 2–6; Mark Couvillon, *Patrick Henry's Virginia: A Guide to the Homes and Sites in the Life of an American Patriot* (Brookneal, VA: Patrick Henry Memorial Foundation, 2001), 11.

30. Thomas Jefferson to William Wirt, 4 August 1805, in Stan V. Henkels, ed., "Jefferson's Recollections of Patrick Henry," *PMHB* 34 (1910): 387–388.

31. Beeman, *Patrick Henry*, 12, 29.

32. Couvillon, *Patrick Henry's Virginia*, 47–50; Samuel Meredith Statement, in George Morgan, *The True Patrick Henry* (Philadelphia: J. B. Lippincott, 1907), app. A, 433 (quotation).

33. Samuel Meredith Statement, 431; Spencer Roane Memorandum, in Morgan, *True Patrick Henry*, app. B, 437. See also Kevin J. Hayes, *The Mind of a Patriot: Patrick Henry and the World of Ideas* (Charlottesville: University of Virginia Press, 2008).

34. William Wirt, *Sketches of the Life and Character of Patrick Henry* (Philadelphia: James Webster, 1819), 28 (first quotation); Thomas Jefferson to William Wirt, 4 August 1804, in Henkels, "Jefferson's Recollections of Patrick Henry," 389 (second quotation). For the Parson's Cause, see Henry Mayer, *A Son of Thunder: Patrick Henry and the American Republic* (New York: Franklin Watts, 1986), 58–70; Rhys Isaac, *The Transformation of Virginia, 1740–1790* (Chapel Hill: University of North Carolina Press, 1982), 144–146.

35. Thomas Paine, *Common Sense*, in *Common Sense and Other Writings*, ed. J. M. Opal (New York: W. W. Norton, 2012), 14.

36. For gender hierarchy in colonial Virginia, see Kathleen M. Brown, *Good Wives, Nasty Wenches, and Anxious Patriarchs: Gender, Race, and Power in Colonial Virginia* (Chapel Hill: University of North Carolina Press, 1996); and Terri L. Snyder, *Brabbling Women: Disorderly Speech and the Law in Early Virginia* (Ithaca, NY: Cornell University Press, 2003).

37. Among the most popular was the letters of Philip Dormer Stanhope, fourth Earl of Chesterfield. R. K. Root, ed., *Lord Chesterfield's Letters to His Son* (London: J. M. Dent and Sons, 1929). Though Chesterfield was published too late to influence Washington's "Rules of Civility" directly, the two works capture the same cultural ambitions.

38. Thomas Jefferson to William Wirt, 5 August 1815, in Henkels, "Jefferson's Recollections of Patrick Henry," 405.

39. Bernard Bailyn, "Politics and the Social Structure in Virginia," in *Seventeenth-Century America*, ed. James M. Smith (Chapel Hill: University of North Carolina Press, 1959), 111 (quotation); Brown, *Good Wives, Nasty Wenches*, ch. 8.

40. George Mason to unknown, 2 October 1778, *PGM*, 1:433.

41. For death patterns, see Kulikoff, *Tobacco and Slaves;* and Darrett B. Rutman and Anita H. Rutman, *A Place in Time: Middlesex County, Virginia, 1650–1750* (New York: W. W. Norton, 1984).

42. For the Hemings family, see Annette Gordon-Reed, *The Hemingses of Monticello: An American Family* (New York: W. W. Norton, 2008).

43. For Martha Jefferson's inheritance, see Virginia Scharff, *The Women Jefferson Loved* (New York: HarperCollins, 2010), 98–99. This inheritance irreparably damaged Jefferson's finances. Wayles died owing creditors, and by mixing Wayles's debts with his own estate, Jefferson became liable. He died half a century later without having settled Wayles's debts.

44. For elite control over Virginia politics, see Beeman, *Old Dominion and the New Nation;* Sydnor, *Gentlemen Freeholders;* and Brent Tarter, *The Grandees of Government: The Origins and Persistence of Undemocratic Politics in Virginia* (Charlottesville: University of Virginia Press, 2013).

45. For the centrality of tobacco to planter life, see Breen, *Tobacco Culture.* See also Jean B. Lee, "Mount Vernon Plantation: A Model for the Republic," in *Slavery at the Home of George Washington,* ed. Philip J. Schwarz (Mount Vernon, VA: Mount Vernon Ladies Association, 2001); Paul K. Longmore, *The Invention of George Washington* (Berkeley: University of California Press, 1988), ch. 7; and Ragsdale, "George Washington, British Tobacco Trade." Washington basically quit tobacco cultivation by 1766. Philip D. Morgan, "'To Get Quit of Negroes': George Washington and Slavery," *Journal of American Studies* 39 (2005): 413.

46. For childrearing values, see Daniel Blake Smith, *Inside the Great House: Planter Family Life in Eighteenth-Century Chesapeake Society* (Ithaca, NY: Cornell University Press, 1980); Jay Fliegelman, *Prodigals and Pilgrims: The American Revolution Against Patriarchal Authority, 1750–1800* (Cambridge: Cambridge University Press, 1982); and Jan Ellen Lewis, *The Pursuit of Happiness: Family and Values in Jefferson's Virginia* (Cambridge: Cambridge University Press, 1983). For reciprocity and order, see Jan Lewis, "Domestic Tranquillity and the Management of Emotions Among the Gentry of Pre-Revolutionary Virginia," *WMQ,* 3rd ser., 39 (1982): 135–149; and Brown, *Good Wives, Nasty Wenches,* 319–321.

47. George Mason to Alexander Henderson, 18 July 1763, *PGM,* 1:56.

48. George Washington to Jonathan Boucher, 30 May 1768, *PGW (Colonial),* 8:90.

49. John Parke Custis to Martha Washington, 5 July 1773, in Fields, *"Worthy Partner,"* 152.

50. George Washington to Benedict Calvert, 3 April 1773, *PGW (Colonial),* 9:209.

51. George Washington to Dr. Cooper, 15 December 1773, ibid., 406–407.

52. George Washington to Burwell Bassett, 20 June 1773, ibid., 243–244.

53. Mason Family Bible, in Kate Mason Rowland, *The Life of George Mason, 1725–1792, Including His Speeches, Public Papers, and Correspondence,* 2 vols. (New York: G. P. Putnam's Sons, 1892), 1:162–163.

54. George Mason to unknown, 2 October 1778, *PGM,* 1:433–434.

55. Mayer, *Son of Thunder,* 125–126; Couvillon, *Patrick Henry's Virginia,* 47–48.

56. Beeman, *Patrick Henry,* 64; Robert Douthat Meade, *Patrick Henry: Practical Revolutionary* (Philadelphia: J. B. Lippincott, 1969), 15–16.

57. George Mason to unknown, 6 December 1770, *PGM*, 1:129.

58. For the different figures, see Gordon S. Wood, *The American Revolution: A History* (New York: Random House, 2002), 17; and Edmund S. Morgan and Helen M. Morgan, *The Stamp Act Crisis: Prologue to Revolution* (Chapel Hill: University of North Carolina Press, 1952), 36.

Chapter 2. Independence

1. John Mason Recollection, transcribed by Terry Dunn, Papers of John Mason (1766–1849), Gunston Hall Library and Archives.

2. George Mason to unknown, 6 December 1770, *PGM*, 1:129.

3. Thomas Jefferson, *Notes on the State of Virginia*, ed. William Peden (New York: W. W. Norton, 1972), 117.

4. The most compelling explanation of the ideas behind the Revolution remains Bernard Bailyn, *The Ideological Origins of the American Revolution* (Cambridge, MA: Harvard University Press, 1967). For 1763–1776 events, see T. H. Breen, *The Marketplace of Revolution: How Consumer Politics Shaped American Independence* (New York: Oxford University Press, 2004); Pauline Maier, *From Resistance to Revolution: Colonial Radicals and the Development of American Opposition to Britain, 1765–1776* (New York: W. W. Norton, 1972); and Robert Middlekauff, *The Glorious Cause: The American Revolution, 1763–1789*, 2nd rev. ed. (New York: Oxford University Press, 2005).

5. John Adams to Thomas Jefferson, 24 August 1815, in *The Adams-Jefferson Letters: The Complete Correspondence Between Thomas Jefferson and Abigail and John Adams*, ed. Lester J. Cappon (New York: Simon and Schuster, 1971), 455.

6. For the importance of family imagery in the imperial-colonial crisis, see Gordon S. Wood, *The Radicalism of the American Revolution* (New York: Knopf, 1992), 165–166; Charles Royster, *A Revolutionary People at War: The Continental Army and American Character, 1775–1783* (Chapel Hill: University of North Carolina Press, 1979), 4–8; Richard Godbeer, *The Overflowing of Friendship: Love Between Men and the Creation of the American Republic* (Baltimore: Johns Hopkins University Press, 2009), 143–149; and Jay Fliegelman, *Prodigals and Pilgrims: The American Revolution Against Patriarchal Authority, 1750–1800* (Cambridge: Cambridge University Press, 1982). For European parallels, see Lynn Hunt, *The Family Romance of the French Revolution* (Berkeley: University of California Press, 1992).

7. American Colonies Act (Declaratory Act), 1766.

8. Patrick Henry, Conclusion of the "Caesar-Brutus" Speech, in David A. McCants, *Patrick Henry, the Orator* (Westport, CT: Greenwood, 1990), 121–122.

9. Loyalists responded by depicting Americans as ungrateful children rebelling against a caring parent. Fliegelman, *Prodigals and Pilgrims*, 93–99.

10. George Mason to Committee of Merchants in London, 6 June 1766, *PGM*, 1:65–71.

11. Joseph J. Ellis, *His Excellency: George Washington* (New York: Knopf, 2004), 59–62.

12. George Washington to George Mason, 5 April 1769, *PGM*, 1:96–97; George Mason to Richard Henry Lee, 7 June 1770, *PGM*, 1:119.

13. Maier, *Resistance to Revolution*, 116 (quotation). For elite male authority, see Kathleen M. Brown, *Good Wives, Nasty Wenches, and Anxious Patriarchs: Gender, Race, and Power in Colonial Virginia* (Chapel Hill: University of North Carolina Press, 1996), ch. 10. For the limits of gentry control, see Michael A. McDonnell, *The Politics of War: Race, Class, and Conflict in Revolutionary Virginia* (Chapel Hill: University of North Carolina Press, 2007); and Woody Holton, *Forced Founders: Indians, Debtors, Slaves, and the Making of the American Revolution in Virginia* (Chapel Hill: University of North Carolina Press, 1999). For the American invention of boycotting, see Breen, *Marketplace of Revolution*.

14. Letter of "Atticus," 11 May 1769, *PGM*, 1:108.

15. George Mason to Richard Henry Lee, 7 June 1770, ibid., 116–117.

16. George Mason to George Washington, 5 April 1769, ibid., 100.

17. Letter of "Atticus," 109.

18. Virginia Burgesses, 16–17 May 1769, *PHC*, 1:138–141.

19. See Gordon S. Wood, *The American Revolution: A History* (New York: Random House, 2002), 35; Breen, *Marketplace of Revolution;* and Benjamin L. Carp, *Defiance of the Patriots: The Boston Tea Party and the Making of America* (New Haven: Yale University Press, 2010).

20. *The Parliamentary History of England, from the Earliest Period to the Year 1803,* 36 vols. (London, 1813), 17:1315–1316.

21. Virginia Association, 27 May 1774, *PHC*, 1:177, 180 (quotation).

22. George Washington to George William Fairfax, 10–15 June 1774, *PGW (Colonial)*, 10:96.

23. Jeff Broadwater, *George Mason, Forgotten Founder* (Chapel Hill: University of North Carolina Press, 2006), 65–67.

24. Fairfax Resolves, 18 July 1774, *PGM*, 1:202–204.

25. Freeholders of Hanover County to Patrick Henry and John Syme, 20 July 1774, *PHC*, 1:191–192.

26. The following paragraphs derive from Thomas Jefferson, "Summary View of the Rights of British America," *PTJ*, 1:121–137.

27. Patrick Henry, c. 15 May 1776, *PHC*, 1:395.

28. Fairfax County Militia Plan, February 1775, *PGM*, 1:215–216; George Mason to George Washington, 2 April 1776, ibid., 267.

29. George Mason to unknown, 2 October 1778, *PGM*, 1:435; Patrick Henry, "Rough Resolution in favor of Independence," May 1776, *PHC*, 1:395 (second quotation); William Jameson, Charlotte County clerk, to Paul Carrington and Thomas Read, 23 April 1776, *PHC*, 1:374 (last quotation).

30. McDonnell, *Politics of War*, 132–144 (quotation on 134); Jan Lewis, "Domestic Tranquillity and the Management of Emotions Among the Gentry of Pre-Revolutionary Virginia," *WMQ*, 3rd ser., 39 (1982): 135–136; Brown, *Good Wives, Nasty Wenches*, 319–321. See also Rhys Isaac, *Landon Carter's Uneasy Kingdom: Revolution and Rebellion on a Virginia Plantation* (New York: Oxford University Press, 2005), ch. 2; and Alan Taylor, *The Internal Enemy: Slavery and War in Virginia, 1772–1832* (New York: W. W. Norton, 2013), 23–34.

31. Richard Henry Lee to Patrick Henry, April 1776, *PHC*, 1:378.

32. Thomas Paine, *Common Sense*, 3rd ed. (Philadelphia, 1776), in *The Complete Works of Thomas Paine*, ed. Philip S. Foner, 2 vols. (New York: Citadel, 1969), 1:45.

33. Pauline Maier, *American Scripture: Making the Declaration of Independence* (New York: Knopf, 1997).

34. Samuel Johnson, *Taxation, no Tyranny; An Answer to the Resolutions and Address of the American Congress* (London: T. Cadell, 1775), 89. The most compelling exploration of freedom and slavery in Virginia remains Edmund S. Morgan, *American Slavery, American Freedom: The Ordeal of Colonial Virginia* (New York: W. W. Norton, 1975).

35. Patrick Henry, "Liberty or Death" Speech, 23 March 1775, as later reported (no extant text of Henry's full address survives), in McCants, *Patrick Henry, the Orator*, 125.

36. Non-Importation Association, 23 April 1769, *PGM*, 1:103; Fairfax Resolves, 18 July 1774, ibid., 204.

37. George Washington to Bryan Fairfax, 24 August 1774, *PGW (Colonial)*, 10:155; George Washington to George William Fairfax, 31 May 1775, ibid., 368.

38. Henry, "Liberty or Death," 125. See also Francois Furstenberg, *In the Name of the Father: Washington's Legacy, Slavery, and the Making of a Nation* (New York: Penguin, 2006).

39. George Mason essay, 23 December 1765, *PGM*, 1:61; Patrick Henry, 18 January 1773, *PHC*, 1:152–153.

40. Jefferson, *Notes on the State of Virginia*, 162.

41. T. H. Breen, *Tobacco Culture: The Mentality of the Great Tidewater Planters on the Eve of Revolution* (Princeton, NJ: Princeton University Press, 1985), 158–159.

42. George Washington to Robert Cary and Company, 20 September 1765, *PGW (Colonial)*, 7:401.

43. George Washington to John Parke Custis, 1 February, 26 May 1778, *PGW (War)*, 13:435, 15:224–225.

44. George Mason Will, 20 March 1773, *PGM*, 1:159.

45. John Mason Recollection; George Mason to Martin Cockburn, 26 May 1774, *PGM*, 1:191.

46. Helen Hill Miller, *George Mason, Gentleman Revolutionary* (Chapel Hill: University of North Carolina Press, 1975), 108–109.

47. George Mason to William Ramsay, 11 July 1775, *PGM*, 1:239.

48. George Mason to Martin Cockburn, 22 August 1775, ibid., 250.

49. George Mason to George Wythe, 14 June 1777, ibid., 345–346.

50. Ibid.

51. George Mason, Remarks on Annual Elections for the Fairfax Independent Company, April 1775, *PGM*, 1:229.

52. John Mason Recollection.

53. Ibid.

54. George Mason to Martin Cockburn, 26 May 1774, *PGM*, 1:190; George Mason to Richard Henry Lee, 18 May 1776, ibid., 271.

55. For Madison's political awakening, see Douglass Adair, ed., "James Madison's Autobiography," *WMQ*, 3rd ser., 2 (1945): 194, 198–204; Madison correspondence with William Bradford, *PJM (Congressional)*, 1; and Jack Rakove, *Revolutionaries: A New History of the Invention of America* (Boston: Houghton Mifflin Harcourt, 2010), 345–347.

56. For Mason's contributions, see also Miller, *George Mason*, 153–155; and Broadwater, *George Mason*, 77–82.

57. Thomas Jefferson to Francis Eppes, 7 November 1775, *PTJ*, 1:252.

58. Thomas Jefferson to Edmund Pendleton, 30 June 1776, ibid., 408.

59. Thomas Jefferson to Richard Henry Lee, 29 July 1776, ibid., 477.

60. Thomas Jefferson to Richard Henry Lee, 8 July 1776, ibid., 456. For changes, see Maier, *American Scripture*, ch. 3.

61. Francis Eppes to Thomas Jefferson, 3 July 1776, *PTJ*, 15:576; Virginia Scharff, *The Women Jefferson Loved* (New York: HarperCollins, 2010), 122–123.

62. L. H. Butterfield, ed., *The Adams Papers: Diary and Autobiography of John Adams*, 4 vols. (New York: Atheneum, 1964), 3:323–325; George Washington, Address to the Continental Congress, 16 June 1775, *PGW (War)*, 1:1.

63. George Washington to Martha Washington, 18 June 1775, in *"Worthy Partner": The Papers of Martha Washington*, ed. Joseph E. Fields (Westport, CT: Greenwood, 1994), 159.

64. George Washington to Burwell Bassett, 19 June 1775, *PGW (War)*, 1:13; George Washington to John Parke Custis, 19 June 1775, in George Washington Parke Custis, *Recollections and Private Memoirs of Washington, by His Adopted Son, George Washington Parke Custis, with a Memoir of the Author, by His Daughter; and Illustrative and Explanatory Notes, by Benson J. Lossing* (New York: Derby and Jackson, 1860; reprint, 1999), 534.

65. Martha Washington to Elizabeth Ramsey, 30 December 1775, in Fields, *"Worthy Partner*," 164; Martha Washington to Mercy Otis Warren, 26 December 1789, ibid., 224.

66. George Washington to John Parke Custis, 19 June 1775, in Custis, *Recollections*, 534.

67. George Washington to Continental Army, 2 November 1783, LC.

68. Thomas Jefferson to Thomas Jefferson Randolph, 24 November 1808, in *The Family Letters of Thomas Jefferson*, ed. Edwin Morris Betts and James Adam Bear Jr. (Columbia: University of Missouri Press, 1966), 362–363.

69. Thomas Paine, "Crisis III," 17 May 1777, in Foner, *Complete Works of Paine*, 1:79.

70. George Mason, Remarks on Annual Elections for the Fairfax Independent Company, April 1775, *PGM*, 1:231; Thomas Paine, *Common Sense*, in Foner, *Complete Works of Paine*, 1:30–31.

71. Washington eulogy quoted in Furstenberg, *In the Name of the Father*, 75. For Washington as the father of his country, see ibid., 21, 36–37; Godbeer, *Overflowing of Friendship*, 151; Fliegelman, *Prodigals and Pilgrims*, ch. 7; and Edward G. Lengel, *Inventing George Washington: America's Founder, in Myth and Memory* (New York: HarperCollins, 2011).

Chapter 3. Sacrifice

1. The first town was probably Washington, Massachusetts, in 1779. Paul K. Longmore, *The Invention of George Washington* (Berkeley: University of California Press, 1988), 197.

2. Marquis de Lafayette to George Washington, 12 June 1779, in *Lafayette in the Age of the American Revolution: Selected Letters and Papers, 1776–1790*, ed. Stanley J. Idzerda

et al., 5 vols. (Ithaca, NY: Cornell University Press, 1977–1983), 2:277. For Washington's character, see Gordon S. Wood, *Revolutionary Characters: What Made the Founders Different* (New York: Penguin, 2006), ch. 1; Longmore, *Invention of Washington*, chs. 15–17; Edward G. Lengel, *Inventing George Washington: America's Founder, in Myth and Memory* (New York: HarperCollins, 2011); and Thomas A. Foster, "On Sex and the Founding Fathers: America's Fascination with the Intimate Lives of the Political Leaders of the American Revolution," ch. 1, unpublished ms in author's possession.

3. George Washington to Martha Washington, 18 June 1775, in *"Worthy Partner": The Papers of Martha Washington*, ed. Joseph E. Fields (Westport, CT: Greenwood, 1994), 159. For ambition, see Douglass Adair, "Fame and the Founding Fathers," in *Fame and the Founding Fathers: Essays by Douglass Adair*, ed. Trevor Colbourn (Indianapolis, IN: Liberty Fund, 1998), 3–36.

4. Abigail Adams to Thomas Jefferson, 26 June 1787, in *The Adams-Jefferson Letters: The Complete Correspondence Between Thomas Jefferson and Abigail and John Adams*, ed. Lester J. Cappon (New York: Simon and Schuster, 1971), 178. I have consistently referred to Jefferson's younger daughter as Polly until her return from Paris, when she changed her name to Maria. She married in 1797, and is thereafter Maria Jefferson Eppes. Martha Jefferson, the elder daughter, was sometimes called Patsy, but for consistency I only use Martha. She married in 1790 and is thereafter Martha Jefferson Randolph.

5. George Mason to Martin Cockburn, 18 April 1784, *PGM*, 2:800.

6. A lengthy exploration of the war lies beyond the scope of this project. For model overviews, see Edward Countryman, *The American Revolution*, rev. ed. (New York: Hill and Wang, 2003); John Ferling, *Almost a Miracle: The American Victory in the War of Independence* (New York: Oxford University Press, 2007); Robert Middlekauff, *The Glorious Cause: The American Revolution, 1763–1789*, 2nd rev. ed. (New York: Oxford University Press, 2005); and Charles Royster, *A Revolutionary People at War: The Continental Army and American Character, 1775–1783* (Chapel Hill: University of North Carolina Press, 1979). For class and racial tensions in Virginia, see Michael A. McDonnell, *The Politics of War: Race, Class, and Conflict in Revolutionary Virginia* (Chapel Hill: University of North Carolina Press, 2007); and Alan Taylor, *The Internal Enemy: Slavery and War in Virginia, 1772–1832* (New York: W. W. Norton, 2013).

7. George Washington, "Rules of Civility," no. 82; George Washington to John Augustine Washington, 20 June 1775, *PGW (War)*, 1:19.

8. George Washington to Fielding Lewis Jr., 27 February 1784, *PGW (Confederation)*, 1:161.

9. Samuel Cooper to his wife and children, 18 July 1775, in Charles H. McKee, "Letters of a Soldier of the American Revolution," *Connecticut Magazine* 10 (1906): 25.

10. For sacrifice, see Sarah J. Purcell, *Sealed with Blood: War, Sacrifice, and Memory in Revolutionary America* (Philadelphia: University of Pennsylvania Press, 2002); Royster, *Revolutionary People at War*; and Wood, *Revolutionary Characters*.

11. Richard Henry Lee to George Washington, 26 November 1775, *PGW (War)*, 2:430.

12. George Washington to Lund Washington, 30 September 1776, ibid., 6:441.

13. George Washington to John Parke Custis, 22 January 1777, ibid., 8:123.

14. James Madison to Philip Mazzei, 7 July 1781, *PJM (Congressional)*, 3:178.

15. George Washington to Patrick Henry, 19 February 1778, *PHC*, 3:148.

16. George Washington to John Parke Custis, 2 January 1779, *PGW (War)*, 18:554.

17. James Madison to Thomas Jefferson, 27–28 March 1780, in *The Republic of Letters: The Correspondence Between Thomas Jefferson and James Madison, 1776–1826*, ed. James Morton Smith, 3 vols. (New York: W. W. Norton, 1995), 1:136.

18. David Jameson to James Madison, 15 August 1781, *PJM (Congressional)*, 3:227–228.

19. George Washington to George Mason, 22 October 1780, *PGM*, 2:678.

20. James Madison to Margaret B. Smith, September 1830, *JM Writings*, 9:405. For the Jefferson-Madison connection, see Smith, *Republic of Letters*; Lance Banning, *Jefferson and Madison: Three Conversations from the Founding* (Madison, WI: Madison House, 1995); and Andrew Burstein and Nancy Isenberg, *Madison and Jefferson* (New York: Random House, 2010). For the cohort, see also Joseph J. Ellis, *Founding Brothers: The Revolutionary Generation* (New York: Knopf, 2000); Peter R. Henriques, "An Uneven Friendship: The Relationship Between George Washington and George Mason," *VMHB* 97 (1989): 185–204; John P. Kaminski, *The Great Virginia Triumvirate: George Washington, Thomas Jefferson, and James Madison in the Eyes of Their Contemporaries* (Charlottesville: University of Virginia Press, 2010); and Stuart Leibiger, *Founding Friendship: George Washington, James Madison, and the Creation of the American Republic* (Charlottesville: University Press of Virginia, 1999).

21. For Jefferson's correspondence with William Wirt, see Stan V. Henkels, ed., "Jefferson's Recollections of Patrick Henry," *PMHB* 34 (1910): 385–418 (quotation on 387). For Wirt's influence on Henry's reputation, see Andrew Burstein, *America's Jubilee* (New York: Knopf, 2001), ch. 2.

22. Jean Edward Smith, *John Marshall: Definer of a Nation* (New York: Henry Holt, 1996), 75–76.

23. George Washington to George Mason, 27 March 1779, *PGM*, 2:493.

24. Ibid.

25. George Mason to George Washington, 2 April 1776, *PGM*, 1:266–267.

26. George Mason to Henry Lee, 13 December 1780, ibid., 2:679–680; George Mason to unknown, 2 October 1778, ibid., 1:434.

27. Patrick Henry to Virginia Convention, 1 July 1776, in *Patrick Henry in His Speeches and Writings and in the Words of His Contemporaries*, ed. James M. Elson (Lynchburg, VA: Warwick House, 2007), 91.

28. Patrick Henry to Virginia General Assembly, c. 5 June 1777, *PHC*, 1:522.

29. Patrick Henry to George Washington, 29 March 1777, ibid., 516; Patrick Henry to Richard Henry Lee, 28 March 1777, ibid., 515.

30. Patrick Henry to Thomas Jefferson, 15 February 1780, in Elson, *Patrick Henry in His Speeches*, 100.

31. Mark Couvillon, *Patrick Henry's Virginia: A Guide to the Homes and Sites in the Life of an American Patriot* (Brookneal, VA: Patrick Henry Memorial Foundation, 2001), 58; Henry Mayer, *A Son of Thunder: Patrick Henry and the American Republic* (New York: Franklin Watts, 1986), 340–341.

32. Richard Henry Lee to Thomas Jefferson, 25 August 1777, in *Memoir of the Life*

of Richard Henry Lee and His Correspondence, ed. Richard H. Lee, 2 vols. (Philadelphia: Carey and Lea, 1825), 2:39.

33. Virginia Scharff, *The Women Jefferson Loved* (New York: HarperCollins, 2010), 127.

34. Isaac Jefferson Reminiscence, in *Jefferson at Monticello*, ed. James A. Bear Jr. (Charlottesville: University Press of Virginia, 1967), 7–8.

35. Thomas Jefferson to David Jameson, 16 April 1781, *PTJ*, 5:468; Smith, *Republic of Letters*, 1:177. For Martha's wartime experiences, see Scharff, *Women Jefferson Loved*, ch. 11; and Jon Kukla, *Mr. Jefferson's Women* (New York: Knopf, 2007), ch. 4. See also Michael Kranish, *Flight from Monticello: Thomas Jefferson at War* (New York: Oxford University Press, 2010).

36. Thomas Jefferson to William Gordon, 16 July 1788, *PTJ*, 13:363.

37. Smith, *Republic of Letters*, 1:204–205; John E. Selby, *The Revolution in Virginia, 1775–1783* (Williamsburg, VA: Colonial Williamsburg Foundation, 1988), 223.

38. Virginia House of Delegates, 12 December 1781, *Journal of the House of Delegates of the Commonwealth of Virginia* 1781 (Richmond, VA, 1828), 37; *PHC*, 2:150–151. See also Richard R. Beeman, *Patrick Henry: A Biography* (New York: McGraw-Hill, 1974), 132–133.

39. Thomas Jefferson to James Monroe, 20 May 1782, *PTJ*, 6:186.

40. Ibid. See also Jan Lewis, "'The Blessings of Domestic Society': Thomas Jefferson's Family and the Transformation of American Politics," in *Jeffersonian Legacies*, ed. Peter S. Onuf (Charlottesville: University Press of Virginia, 1993), 109–146.

41. François Jean Marquis de Chastellux, visit to Monticello, in *Travels in North America in the Years 1780, 1781 and 1782*, ed. Howard C. Rice, 2 vols. (Chapel Hill: University of North Carolina Press, 1963), 2:391.

42. James Madison to Edmund Randolph, 11 June 1782, *PJM (Congressional)*, 4:333–334; Edmund Randolph to James Madison, 10 May 1782, ibid., 225.

43. Thomas Jefferson to Marquis de Chastellux, 26 November 1782, in *The Domestic Life of Thomas Jefferson*, ed. Sarah N. Randolph (1871; Charlottesville: University Press of Virginia, 1994), 68.

44. James Madison to Edmund Randolph, 30 September 1782, *PJM (Congressional)*, 5:170. See also James Madison, Notes on Debates in Congress, 12 November 1782, ibid., 268–269.

45. James Monroe to Thomas Jefferson, 16 May 1782, *PTJ*, 6:183; Edmund Randolph to James Madison, 21 June 1783, *PJM (Congressional)*, 7:186.

46. George Mason to unknown, 2 October 1778, *PGM*, 1:434.

47. Douglass Adair, ed., "James Madison's Autobiography," *WMQ*, 3rd ser., 2 (1945): 199.

48. *PHC*, 3:622.

49. Helen Hill Miller, *George Mason, Gentleman Revolutionary* (Chapel Hill: University of North Carolina Press, 1975), 120; Fields, *"Worthy Partner,"* 315, n. 1. It is not possible, given the available sources, to conclusively assess the family values of Loyalist Virginians. For Loyalism, see Maya Jasanoff, *Liberty's Exiles: American Loyalists in the Revolutionary World* (New York: Knopf, 2011); and McDonnell, *Politics of War*, 151–160, 374–381.

50. George Mason to George Mason Jr., 3 June 1781, *PGM*, 2:690.

51. James Madison to Philip Mazzei, 7 July 1781, *PJM (Congressional)*, 3:180. For the war in Virginia, see esp. Selby, *Revolution in Virginia;* and McDonnell, *Politics of War.*

52. George Washington to John Parke Custis, 19 June 1775, *PGW (War)*, 1:15; Lund Washington to George Washington, 5 October 1775, ibid., 2:116.

53. Martha Washington to Burwell Bassett, 18 July 1780, in Fields, *"Worthy Partner,"* 183.

54. Harlow Giles Unger, *The Unexpected George Washington: His Private Life* (Hoboken, NJ: John Wiley and Sons, 2006), 122 (quotation). For women's wartime roles, see Holly A. Mayer, *Belonging to the Army: Camp Followers and Community During the American Revolution* (Columbia: University of South Carolina Press, 1996); and Linda Kerber, *Women of the Republic: Intellect and Ideology in Revolutionary America* (Chapel Hill: University of North Carolina Press, 1980), ch. 2.

55. *Alexandria Advertiser and Commercial Intelligencer*, 25 May 1802.

56. Isaac Jefferson Reminiscence.

57. Ezra Stiles, *The United States Elevated to Glory and Honor* (New Haven, CT: Thomas and Samuel Green, 1783), 36.

58. George Washington to John Parke Custis, 28 February 1781, in *George Washington: A Collection*, ed. W. B. Allen (Indianapolis, IN: Liberty Fund, 1988).

59. Thomas Fleming, *The Intimate Lives of the Founding Fathers* (New York: Smithsonian/HarperCollins, 2009), 40.

60. Scharff, *Women Jefferson Loved*, 113–116, 131; *PHC*, 1:248–249; Couvillon, *Patrick Henry's Virginia*, 58.

61. George Washington to Lund Washington, 28 February 1778, 26 November 1775, *PGW (War)*, 13:699, 2:431.

62. See also Wood, *Radicalism of the American Revolution;* Jay Fliegelman, *Prodigals and Pilgrims: The American Revolution Against Patriarchal Authority, 1750–1800* (Cambridge: Cambridge University Press, 1982); and Rhys Isaac, *Landon Carter's Uneasy Kingdom: Revolution and Rebellion on a Virginia Plantation* (New York: Oxford University Press, 2005).

63. George Washington to Continental Army, 2 November 1783, LC; Unger, *Unexpected Washington*, 119–120. See also Purcell, *Sealed with Blood;* and Richard Godbeer, *The Overflowing of Friendship: Love Between Men and the Creation of the American Republic* (Baltimore: Johns Hopkins University Press, 2009).

64. John Laurens to Henry Laurens, 24 November 1775, in *The Papers of Henry Laurens*, ed. David R. Chesnutt and C. James Taylor, 16 vols. (Columbia: University of South Carolina Press, 1968–2002), 10:512. For Laurens, see Gregory D. Massey, *John Laurens and the American Revolution* (Columbia: University of South Carolina Press, 2000); and Jack Rakove, *Revolutionaries: A New History of the Invention of America* (Boston: Houghton Mifflin Harcourt, 2010), ch. 5.

65. George Washington to John Laurens, 5 August 1777, *PGW (War)*, 10:509.

66. Henry Laurens to Isaac Motte, 26 January 1778, in Chesnutt and Taylor, *Papers of Henry Laurens*, 12:345; Henry Laurens to John Lewis Gervais, 8 October 1777, ibid., 11:547.

67. John Adams to Benjamin Rush, 25 January 1806, in *Old Family Letters: Copied from the Originals,* ed. Alexander Biddle, 2 vols. (Philadelphia: J. B. Lippincott, 1892), 1:92; George Washington Parke Custis, *Recollections and Private Memoirs of Washington, by His Adopted Son, George Washington Parke Custis, with a Memoir of the Author, by His Daughter; and Illustrative and Explanatory Notes, by Benson J. Lossing* (New York: Derby and Jackson, 1860; reprint, 1999), 345. For Hamilton, see esp. Ron Chernow, *Alexander Hamilton* (New York: Penguin, 2004).

68. Custis, *Recollections,* 353.

69. Don Higginbotham, *George Washington: Uniting a Nation* (Lanham, MD: Rowman and Littlefield, 2002), 33 (quotation). For Monroe, see Harlow Giles Unger, *The Last Founding Father: James Monroe and a Nation's Call to Greatness* (New York: Da Capo, 2009). For Marshall, see Smith, *John Marshall.*

70. Marquis de Lafayette to Adrienne de Lafayette, 1 October 1777, in Idzerda et al., *Lafayette in the Age of the American Revolution,* 1:116; George Washington to Marquis de Lafayette, 30 September 1779, in *The Writings of George Washington from the Original Manuscript Sources,* ed. John C. Fitzpatrick, 39 vols. (Washington, DC: Government Printing Office, 1931–1944), 16:369 (quotation). For Lafayette, see Harlow Giles Unger, *Lafayette* (Hoboken, NJ: John Wiley and Sons, 2002); and David A. Clary, *Adopted Son: Washington, Lafayette, and the Friendship That Saved the Revolution* (New York: Bantam, 2007).

71. Jonathan Boucher to George Washington, 18 December 1770, *PGW (Colonial),* 8:414–416.

72. George Washington to John Parke Custis, 2 January 1779, *PGW (War),* 18:554.

73. John Parke Custis to George Washington, 10 June 1776, ibid., 4:485.

74. George Washington to John Parke Custis, 24 August 1779, in Custis, *Recollections,* 559–560.

75. Martha Washington to John Parke Custis and Eleanor Custis, 19 March 1778, ibid., 548.

76. George Washington to Marquis de Lafayette, 25 September 1778, *PGW (War),* 17:129.

77. George Washington to Marquis de Lafayette, 1 February, 8 December 1784, *PGW (Confederation),* 1:89, 2:175.

78. Marquis de Lafayette to George Washington, 23 August 1790, *PGW (Presidential),* 6:315 ; Marquis de Lafayette to George Washington, 5 February 1783, in Idzerda et al., *Lafayette in the Age of the American Revolution,* 5:91; Auguste Levasseur, 1824, in *Experiencing Mount Vernon: Eyewitness Accounts, 1784–1865,* ed. Jean B. Lee (Charlottesville: University of Virginia Press, 2006), 125.

79. Benjamin Henry Latrobe, 1796, in Lee, *Experiencing Mount Vernon,* 62.

80. Custis, *Recollections,* 254–255.

81. John Parke Custis to George Washington, 10 June 1776, *PGW (War),* 4:485.

82. George Washington to Marquis de Lafayette, 1 February 1784, *PGW (Confederation),* 1:87–88.

83. Martha Washington to Hannah Stockton Boudinot, 14 January 1784, in Fields, *"Worthy Partner,"* 193; George Washington to Marquis de Lafayette, 1 February 1784, *PGW (Confederation),* 1:88–89.

CHAPTER 4. LIBERTY AND POWER

1. Bushrod Washington was less dutiful that George Washington hoped, even giving away some letters as souvenirs. Edward G. Lengel, *Inventing George Washington: America's Founder, in Myth and Memory* (New York: HarperCollins, 2011), 16.

2. George Washington to George Steptoe Washington, 5 May 1788, *PGW (Confederation)*, 6:263.

3. George Washington, Circular Letter to the State Executives, June 1783, in *A Great and Good Man: George Washington in the Eyes of His Contemporaries*, ed. John P. Kaminski and Jill Adair McCaughan (Madison, WI: Madison House, 1989), 6.

4. George Washington to George Steptoe Washington, 6 August 1788, *PGW (Confederation)*, 6:430; Samuel Hanson to George Washington, 19 February 1789, *PGW (Presidential)*, 1:322.

5. George Washington to George Steptoe Washington, 23 March 1789, *PGW (Presidential)*, 1:440.

6. Ibid., 438. For changing ideals of manhood, see Thomas A. Foster, *Sex and the Eighteenth-Century Man: Massachusetts and the History of Sexuality in America* (Boston: Beacon, 2006); Lorri Glover, *Southern Sons: Becoming Men in the New Nation* (Baltimore: Johns Hopkins University Press, 2007); Richard Godbeer, *The Overflowing of Friendship: Love Between Men and the Creation of the American Republic* (Baltimore: Johns Hopkins University Press, 2009); Mark E. Kann, *A Republic of Men: The American Founders, Gendered Language, and Patriarchal Politics* (New York: New York University Press, 1998); Janet Moore Lindman, "Acting the Manly Christian: White Evangelical Masculinity in Revolutionary Virginia," *WMQ*, 3rd ser., 57 (2000): 393–416; and E. Anthony Rotundo, *American Manhood: Transformations in Masculinity from the Revolution to the Modern Era* (New York: Basic Books, 1993).

7. For continuing elite control in Virginia, see Richard Beeman, *The Old Dominion and the New Nation, 1788–1801* (Lexington: University Press of Kentucky, 1972); and Charles Sydnor, *Gentlemen Freeholders: Political Practices in Washington's Virginia* (Chapel Hill: University of North Carolina Press, 1952).

8. Bernard Bailyn, *The Ideological Origins of the American Revolution* (Cambridge, MA: Harvard University Press, 1967), ch. 3. For a nuanced exploration of liberty, see Michal Jan Rozbicki, *Culture and Liberty in the Age of the American Revolution* (Charlottesville: University of Virginia Press, 2011).

9. For this generation, see Joyce Appleby, *Inheriting the Revolution: The First Generation of Americans* (Cambridge, MA: Harvard University Press, 2000); Andrew Burstein, *America's Jubilee* (New York: Knopf, 2001); Jay Fliegelman, *Prodigals and Pilgrims: The American Revolution Against Patriarchal Authority, 1750–1800* (Cambridge: Cambridge University Press, 1982); Glover, *Southern Sons;* and Steven Watts, *The Republic Reborn: War and the Making of Liberal America, 1790–1820* (Baltimore: Johns Hopkins University Press, 1987).

10. St. George Tucker to John and Richard Randolph, 12 June 1787, quoted in Daniel Blake Smith, *Inside the Great House: Planter Family Life in Eighteenth-Century Chesapeake Society* (Ithaca, NY: Cornell University Press, 1980), 96–97.

11. Thomas Jefferson to Peter Carr, 28 March 1790, *PTJ*, 16:277; St. George

Tucker to Alexander Campbell, 7 July 1809, quoted in Phillip Hamilton, *The Making and Unmaking of a Revolutionary Family: The Tuckers of Virginia, 1752–1830* (Charlottesville: University of Virginia Press, 2003), 3.

12. For women's roles, see Linda Kerber, *Women of the Republic: Intellect and Ideology in Revolutionary America* (Chapel Hill: University of North Carolina Press, 1980); Jan Ellen Lewis, "Motherhood and the Construction of the Male Citizen in the United States, 1750–1850," in *Constructions of the Self*, ed. George Levine (New Brunswick, NJ: Rutgers University Press, 1992), 143–163; Mary Beth Norton, *Liberty's Daughters: The Revolutionary Experience of American Women, 1750–1800* (Boston: Little, Brown, 1980); and Rosemarie Zagarri, *Revolutionary Backlash: Women and Politics in the Early American Republic* (Philadelphia: University of Pennsylvania Press, 2007).

13. Daniel Webster evoked this commonplace generational duty in a eulogy about the deaths of Thomas Jefferson and John Adams. Daniel Webster, "Eulogy, Pronounced in Boston, Massachusetts, August 2, 1826," in *A Selection of Eulogies, Pronounced in the Several States, in Honor of Those Illustrious Patriots and Statesmen, John Adams and Thomas Jefferson* (Hartford, CT: D. F. Robinson, 1826), 193–233 (quotation on 231).

14. George Washington to George Chapman, 15 December 1784, *PGW (Confederation)*, 2:183–184.

15. George Washington to George Steptoe Washington, 5 December 1790, *PGW (Presidential)*, 7:32.

16. James Madison to W. T. Barry, 4 August 1822, *JM Writings*, 9:108.

17. Ibid., 103; James Madison, Annual Message to Congress, 5 December 1810, *PJM (Presidential)*, 3:52.

18. Thomas Jefferson to Thomas Jefferson Randolph, 3 January 1809, in *The Family Letters of Thomas Jefferson*, ed. Edwin Morris Betts and James Adam Bear Jr. (Columbia: University of Missouri Press, 1966), 377; Thomas Jefferson to Francis Eppes, 13 December 1820, in *To the Girls and Boys: Being the Delightful, Little-Known Letters of Thomas Jefferson to and from His Children and Grandchildren*, ed. Edward Boykin (New York: Funk and Wagnalls, 1964), 201–202.

19. Thomas Jefferson to Peter Carr, 19 August 1785, *PTJ*, 8:405. See also Thomas Jefferson to Peter Carr, 28 March 1790, ibid., 16:276–277; and Peter Carr to Thomas Jefferson, 18 March 1788, ibid., 12:677.

20. Henry DeSaussure to Ezekiel Pickens, 27 October 1805, Henry William DeSaussure Papers, South Caroliniana Library (first quotation); John Ball Sr. to John Ball Jr., 9 May 1802, Ball Family Papers, South Carolina Historical Society (second quotation). For education and the future of the Republic, see Lawrence A. Cremin, *American Education: The National Experience, 1783–1876* (New York: Harper and Row, 1980), esp. ch. 4; Charles Crowe, "Bishop James Madison and the Republic of Virtue," *Journal of Southern History* 30 (1964): 58–70; Carl F. Kaestle, *Pillars of the Republic: Common Schools and American Society, 1780–1860* (New York: Hill and Wang, 1983); Gail S. Murray, "Rational Thought and Republican Virtues: Children's Literature, 1789–1820," *Journal of the Early Republic* 8 (1988): 159–177; Gilman Ostrander, *Republic of Letters: The American Intellectual Community, 1776–1865* (Madison, WI: Madison House, 1999); David W. Robson, *Educating Republicans: The College in the Era of the American Revolution, 1750–1800* (Westport, CT: Greenwood, 1985); and Bernard Wishy, *The Child and the Republic:*

The Dawn of Modern American Child Nurture (Philadelphia: University of Pennsylvania Press, 1967), chs. 1–2.

21. David Ramsay, "An Oration on the Advantages of American Independence," 4 July 1778, in Robert L. Brunhouse, ed., "David Ramsay, 1749–1815, Selections from His Writings," *Transactions of the American Philosophical Society*, n.s., 55, no. 4 (1965): 185; George Mason to John Mason, 31 July 1789, *PGM*, 3:1166; Joseph Coolidge to Nicholas Trist, 3 March 1826, FLDA.

22. George Mason to Thomas Marshall, 16 October 1789, *PGM*, 3:1175; *PHC*, 2:200–201.

23. Boykin, *To the Girls and Boys*, 180; George Washington to George Washington Parke Custis, 7 January 1798, *PGW (Retirement)*, 2:4–5; Thomas Jefferson to Francis Eppes, 21 May 1816, FLDA.

24. John Wayles Eppes to Francis Eppes, 28 June 1819, John Wayles Eppes Letters, DUL; George Washington to Samuel Washington, 22 September 1799, *PGW (Retirement)*, 4:319.

25. Thomas Jefferson, *Notes on the State of Virginia*, ed. William Peden (New York: W. W. Norton, 1972), 162.

26. John B. Peachy to Robert Anderson, 31 July 1825, quoted in Jan Ellen Lewis, *The Pursuit of Happiness: Family and Values in Jefferson's Virginia* (Cambridge: Cambridge University Press, 1983), 156.

27. George Washington to George Steptoe Washington, 23 March 1789, *PGW (Presidential)*, 1:438.

28. John Locke, *Some Thoughts Concerning Education* (1693), in *The Educational Writings of John Locke: A Critical Edition with Introduction and Notes*, ed. James L. Axtell (Cambridge: Cambridge University Press, 1968). See also Smith, *Inside the Great House*, 46–54; Fliegelman, *Prodigals and Pilgrims*, ch. 1; C. Dallett Hemphill, *Bowing to Necessities: A History of Manners in America, 1620–1860* (New York: Oxford University Press, 1999), ch. 5; and Philip Greven, *The Protestant Temperament: Patterns of Child-Rearing, Religious Experience, and the Self in Early America* (New York: Random House, 1978), pt. 4. Some of these childrearing ethics transcended America. For France, see Lynn Hunt, *The Family Romance of the French Revolution* (Berkeley: University of California Press, 1992).

29. Margaret Bayard Smith, 1809 visit to Monticello, in *Visitors to Monticello*, ed. Merrill D. Peterson (Charlottesville: University Press of Virginia, 1989), 53; George Morgan, *The True Patrick Henry* (Philadelphia: J. B. Lippincott, 1907), 242; *PHC*, 2:518.

30. John Wayles Eppes to Francis Eppes, 9 February 1813, FLDA; George Mason to George Mason Jr., 8 January 1783, *PGM*, 2:759, 761.

31. Thomas Jefferson to Thomas Jefferson Randolph, 14 March 1810, in Betts and Bear, *Family Letters*, 396.

32. Thomas Jefferson to Ellen Randolph Coolidge, 27 August 1825, ibid., 458. For higher education in Virginia, see Rex Bowman, *Rot, Riot, and Rebellion: Mr. Jefferson's Struggle to Save the University That Changed America* (Charlottesville: University of Virginia Press, 2013); Richard Beale Davis, *Intellectual Life in Jefferson's Virginia, 1790–1830* (Knoxville: University of Tennessee Press, 1972); Kevin J. Hayes, *The Road to Monticello: The Life and Mind of Thomas Jefferson* (New York: Oxford University Press, 2008), chs.

41–42; Jennings L. Wagoner Jr., *Jefferson and Education* (Chapel Hill: University of North Carolina Press, 2004); Mark R. Wenger, "Thomas Jefferson, the College of William and Mary, and the University of Virginia," *VMHB* 103 (1995): 339–374; and Garry Wills, *Mr. Jefferson's University* (Washington, DC: National Geographic Society, 2002).

33. For the riot, see Thomas Jefferson to Ellen Randolph Coolidge, 14 November 1825, in Betts and Bear, *Family Letters*, 460; and Thomas Jefferson to Joseph Coolidge, 13 October 1825, FLDA.

34. David Stuart to George Washington, 22 August, 26 January 1798, *PGW (Retirement)*, 2:557–558, 49.

35. Patrick Henry to unknown, 2 June 1793, *PHC*, 1:20.

36. Thomas Jefferson to Anne Cary Randolph, Thomas Jefferson Randolph, and Ellen Wayles Randolph, 2 March 1802, in Betts and Bear, *Family Letters*, 218; James Madison to Richard D. Cutts, 4 January 1829, LC.

37. John Wayles Eppes to Francis Eppes, 6 August 1818, FLDA.

38. George Washington to George Steptoe Washington, 23 March 1789, *PGW, (Presidential)*, 1:440; George Washington to Samuel Stanhope Smith, 24 May 1797, *PGW (Retirement)*, 1:153–154.

39. David Stuart to George Washington, 22 August 1798, *PGW (Retirement)*, 2:558. For fathers' limited control, see also Kathleen M. Brown, *Good Wives, Nasty Wenches, and Anxious Patriarchs: Gender, Race, and Power in Colonial Virginia* (Chapel Hill: University of North Carolina Press, 1996), 342–350; and Rhys Isaac, *Landon Carter's Uneasy Kingdom: Revolution and Rebellion on a Virginia Plantation* (New York: Oxford University Press, 2005), ch. 11.

40. Thomas Jefferson to Martha Jefferson Randolph, 5 January 1808, in Betts and Bear, *Family Letters*, 320.

41. Patrick Henry to Thomas Madison, 19 September 1792, *PHC*, 2:479.

42. Thomas Jefferson to James Madison, 8 May 1784, *PJM (Congressional)*, 8:31 (quotation); James Madison to Thomas Jefferson, 25 November 1786, ibid., 9:178; misc. corres., *PGM*, 2:489–490.

43. Samuel Hanson to George Washington, 18 November 1787, *PGW (Confederation)*, 5:443.

44. For changing inheritance patterns, see Holly Brewer, *By Birth or Consent: Children, Law, and the Anglo-American Revolution in Authority* (Chapel Hill: University of North Carolina Press, 2005); and Carole Shammas, *A History of Household Government in America* (Charlottesville: University of Virginia Press, 2002).

45. George Washington to Fielding Lewis Jr., 27 February 1784, *PGW (Confederation)*, 1:161; George Washington to Marquis de Lafayette, 8 October 1797, *PGW (Retirement)*, 1:390.

46. Francis Eppes to Thomas Jefferson, 23 February 1826, in Betts and Bear, *Family Letters*, 471.

47. James Madison to Dolley Madison, 19–20 November 1805, in *The Selected Letters of Dolley Payne Madison*, ed. David B. Mattern and Holly C. Shulman (Charlottesville: University of Virginia Press, 2003), 76; Mary Custis Lee Memoir, in George Washington Parke Custis, *Recollections and Private Memoirs of Washington, by His Adopted Son, George Washington Parke Custis, with a Memoir of the Author, by His Daughter; and Illus-*

trative and Explanatory Notes, by Benson J. Lossing (New York: Derby and Jackson, 1860; reprint, 1999), 38.

48. Archibald Blair to Patrick Henry, 13 January 1799, *PHC*, 3:427; Thomas Jefferson to John Adams, 5 July 1814, in *The Domestic Life of Thomas Jefferson*, ed. Sarah N. Randolph (1871; Charlottesville: University Press of Virginia, 1994), 359. See also Gordon S. Wood, *The Radicalism of the American Revolution* (New York: Knopf, 1992), 358–359.

49. Dolley Madison to Anna Cutts, 16 July 1804, in Mattern and Shulman, *Letters of Dolley Payne Madison*, 58.

50. Dolley Madison to Anna Cutts, 6 June 1829, ibid., 279. See also John Payne Todd Memorandum Book, LC.

51. George Mason to John Mason, 5 July, 10 September 1792, *PGM*, 3:1269, 1274. Tom Mason (1770–1800) should not be confused with his dutiful older brother, Thomson Mason (1759–1820).

52. Willard J. Webb, "John Mason of Analostan Island," *Arlington Historical Magazine* 5 (1976): 21–35; Papers of John Mason (1766–1849), Gunston Hall Library and Archives.

53. George Washington to David Stuart, 13 August 1798, *PGW (Retirement)*, 2:525.

54. Thomas Jefferson Encyclopedia, www.monticello.org.

Chapter 5. A "Natural Aristocracy"

1. Thomas Jefferson to John Adams, 28 October 1813, in *The Adams-Jefferson Letters: The Complete Correspondence Between Thomas Jefferson and Abigail and John Adams*, ed. Lester J. Cappon (New York: Simon and Schuster, 1971), 388.

2. Thomas Jefferson to Anne Willing Bingham, 11 May 1788, *PTJ*, 13:151.

3. For the brief New Jersey exception, see Judith Apter Klinghoffer and Lois Elkis, "'The Petticoat Electors': Women's Suffrage in New Jersey, 1776–1807," *Journal of the Early Republic* 12 (1992): 159–193. There was, however, no sustained gender critique of the Revolution before the antebellum era. For women's roles in colonial Virginia, see esp. Kathleen M. Brown, *Good Wives, Nasty Wenches, and Anxious Patriarchs: Gender, Race, and Power in Colonial Virginia* (Chapel Hill: University of North Carolina Press, 1996), pt. 3; and Terri L. Snyder, *Brabbling Women: Disorderly Speech and the Law in Early Virginia* (Ithaca, NY: Cornell University Press, 2003).

4. Thomas Jefferson to Anne Cary Randolph, Thomas Jefferson Randolph, and Ellen Wayles Randolph, 2 March 1802, in *The Family Letters of Thomas Jefferson*, ed. Edwin Morris Betts and James Adam Bear Jr. (Columbia: University of Missouri Press, 1966), 218.

5. Quoted in Cynthia A. Kierner, *Martha Jefferson Randolph, Daughter of Monticello: Her Life and Times* (Chapel Hill: University of North Carolina Press, 2012), 105.

6. Margaret Bayard Smith, in *To the Girls and Boys: Being the Delightful, Little-Known Letters of Thomas Jefferson to and from His Children and Grandchildren*, ed. Edward Boykin (New York: Funk and Wagnalls, 1964), 120 (quotation); Ellen Wayles Randolph to Thomas Jefferson, 12 December 1806, ibid., 123; Thomas Jefferson to Ellen Wayles Randolph, 29 June 1807, ibid., 127–128.

7. Ellen Wayles Randolph to Martha Jefferson Randolph, 18 July 1819, FLDA.

8. Ibid. For the Randolph sisters' educations, see Kierner, *Martha Jefferson Randolph*, 136–140. For Jefferson's relationships with women, see Jon Kukla, *Mr. Jefferson's Women* (New York: Knopf, 2007); and Virginia Scharff, *The Women Jefferson Loved* (New York: HarperCollins, 2010).

9. For refinement, see Richard Bushman, *The Refinement of America: Persons, Houses, Cities* (New York: Knopf, 1992); Jay Fliegelman, *Declaring Independence: Jefferson, Natural Language, and the Culture of Performance* (Stanford, CA: Stanford University Press, 1993); and Charlene M. Boyer Lewis, *Ladies and Gentlemen on Display: Planter Society at the Virginia Springs, 1790–1865* (Charlottesville: University of Virginia Press, 2001).

10. For coming-of-age advice, see Lorri Glover, *Southern Sons: Becoming Men in the New Nation* (Baltimore: Johns Hopkins University Press, 2007); Harvey J. Graff, *Conflicting Paths: Growing Up in America* (Cambridge, MA: Harvard University Press, 1995); Joseph F. Kett, *Rites of Passage: Adolescence in America, 1790 to the Present* (New York: Basic Books, 1977); Steven M. Stowe, *Intimacy and Power in the Old South: Ritual in the Lives of the Planters* (Baltimore: Johns Hopkins University Press, 1987). For letter writing, see William Merrell Decker, *Epistolary Practices: Letter Writing in America Before Telecommunications* (Chapel Hill: University of North Carolina Press, 1998); Konstantin Dierks, *In My Power: Letter Writing and Communications in Early America* (Philadelphia: University of Pennsylvania Press, 2009); and Tamara Plakins Thornton, *Handwriting in America: A Cultural History* (New Haven: Yale University Press, 1996).

11. Thomas Jefferson to Martha Jefferson, 28 March 1787, in Boykin, *To the Girls and Boys*, 26–27; Thomas Jefferson to Peter Carr, 11 December 1783, *PTJ*, 6:379.

12. Thomas Jefferson to Thomas Jefferson Randolph, 24 November 1808, in Boykin, *To the Girls and Boys*, 184. For additional examples, see Thomas Jefferson to Ellen Wayles Randolph, 27 November 1801, ibid., 110; Patrick Henry to Betsy Aylett, 20 August 1796, *PHC*, 2:571; and George Mason to Thomas Jefferson, 26 May 1788, *PGM*, 3:1044.

13. Dolley Madison to Mary Allen, 25 February 1834, in *The Selected Letters of Dolley Payne Madison*, ed. David B. Mattern and Holly C. Shulman (Charlottesville: University of Virginia Press, 2003), 304; Martha Washington to Fanny Bassett Washington, c. summer 1789, in *"Worthy Partner": The Papers of Martha Washington*, ed. Joseph E. Fields (Westport, CT: Greenwood, 1994), 217.

14. George Washington to Harriot Washington, 30 October 1791, *PGW (Presidential)*, 9:130–131.

15. Thomas Jefferson to Maria Jefferson, 25 July 1790, in Betts and Bear, *Family Letters*, 62; Thomas Jefferson to Martha Jefferson, 28 November 1783, 6 March 1786, in Boykin, *To the Girls and Boys*, 9, 21; Thomas Jefferson to Maria Jefferson, 20 September 1785, ibid., 66.

16. Martha Jefferson Randolph to Thomas Jefferson, 22 January 1798, in Betts and Bear, *Family Letters*, 154. For Martha Jefferson Randolph's life, see Kierner, *Martha Jefferson Randolph*.

17. Abigail Adams to Thomas Jefferson, 26 June 1787, in Cappon, *Adams-Jefferson Letters*, 178; Thomas Jefferson to Maria Jefferson, 11 April 1790, in *The Domestic Life of*

Thomas Jefferson, ed. Sarah N. Randolph (1871; Charlottesville: University Press of Virginia, 1994), 181.

18. Thomas Jefferson to Martha Jefferson Randolph, 12 May 1793, in Betts and Bear, *Family Letters,* 117.

19. Ellen Randolph Coolidge to Henry Randall, 15 January 1856, in Randolph, *Domestic Life of Jefferson,* 302.

20. *PHC,* 2:502. For analyses of southern gender and family values, see esp. Brown, *Good Wives, Nasty Wenches;* Kierner, *Beyond the Household;* Jan Ellen Lewis, *The Pursuit of Happiness: Family and Values in Jefferson's Virginia* (Cambridge: Cambridge University Press, 1983); Stephanie McCurry, *Masters of Small Worlds: Yeomen Households, Gender Relations, and the Political Culture of the Antebellum South Carolina Lowcountry* (New York: Oxford University Press, 1995); Daniel Blake Smith, *Inside the Great House: Planter Family Life in Eighteenth-Century Chesapeake Society* (Ithaca, NY: Cornell University Press, 1980); and Brenda Stevenson, *Life in Black and White: Family and Community in the Slave South* (New York: Oxford University Press, 1996).

21. Mason Family Bible, in Kate Mason Rowland, *The Life of George Mason, 1725–1792, Including His Speeches, Public Papers, and Correspondence,* 2 vols. (New York: G. P. Putnam's Sons, 1892), 1:163.

22. Martha Washington to Sally Cary Fairfax, 17 May 1798, in Fields, *"Worthy Partner,"* 314–315.

23. Thomas Jefferson to Thomas Jefferson Randolph, 24 November 1808, in Boykin, *To the Girls and Boys,* 184.

24. Thomas Jefferson to Maria Jefferson, 13 June 1790, in Randolph, *Domestic Life of Jefferson,* 185; Thomas Jefferson to Maria Jefferson, 25 July 1790, 30 May 1791, in Betts and Bear, *Family Letters,* 62, 84.

25. For women's roles, see Catherine Allgor, *Parlor Politics: In Which the Ladies of Washington Help Build a City and a Government* (Charlottesville: University Press of Virginia, 2000); Cynthia A. Kierner, *Beyond the Household: Women's Place in the Early South, 1700–1835* (Ithaca, NY: Cornell University Press, 1998); Linda Kerber, *Women of the Republic: Intellect and Ideology in Revolutionary America* (Chapel Hill: University of North Carolina Press, 1980); Jan Ellen Lewis, "Motherhood and the Construction of the Male Citizen in the United States, 1750–1850," in *Constructions of the Self,* ed. George Levine (New Brunswick, NJ: Rutgers University Press, 1992), 143–163; Mary Beth Norton, *Liberty's Daughters: The Revolutionary Experience of American Women, 1750–1800* (Boston: Little, Brown, 1980); Joan Hoff Wilson, "The Illusion of Change: Women and the American Revolution," in *The American Revolution: Explorations in the History of American Radicalism,* ed. Alfred F. Young (DeKalb: Northern Illinois University Press, 1976), 385–431; and Rosemarie Zagarri, *Revolutionary Backlash: Women and Politics in the Early American Republic* (Philadelphia: University of Pennsylvania Press, 2007). For reproductive practices, see Susan E. Klepp, *Revolutionary Conceptions: Women, Fertility, and Family Limitation in America, 1760–1820* (Chapel Hill: University of North Carolina Press, 2009).

26. Thomas Jefferson to Nathaniel Burwell, 14 March 1818, in Boykin, *To the Girls and Boys,* 178.

27. Quoted in Richard Beale Davis, *Intellectual Life in Jefferson's Virginia, 1790–1830* (Knoxville: University of Tennessee Press, 1972), 66. For Jefferson and education, see

Rex Bowman, *Rot, Riot, and Rebellion: Mr. Jefferson's Struggle to Save the University That Changed America* (Charlottesville: University of Virginia Press, 2013); Dumas Malone, *Jefferson and His Time: The Sage of Monticello* (Boston: Little, Brown, 1970); Kevin J. Hayes, *The Road to Monticello: The Life and Mind of Thomas Jefferson* (New York: Oxford University Press, 2008), chs. 41–42; Jennings L. Wagoner Jr., *Jefferson and Education* (Chapel Hill: University of North Carolina Press, 2004); and Garry Wills, *Mr. Jefferson's University* (Washington, DC: National Geographic Society, 2002). For women's education, see esp. Catherine Kerrison, *Claiming the Pen: Women and Intellectual Life in the Early American South* (Ithaca, NY: Cornell University Press, 2005).

28. Thomas Jefferson to Elizabeth Eppes, 28 July 1787, in Randolph, *Domestic Life of Jefferson*, 127.

29. George Washington to Harriot Washington, 30 October 1791, *PGW (Presidential)*, 9:131. For additional examples, see Benedict Calvert to George Washington, 8 April 1773, *PGW (Colonial)*, 9:215; and Lawrence Augustine Washington to George Washington, 23 August 1797, *PGW (Retirement)*, 1:317–318. For Washington's relationships with women, see Don Higginbotham, "George Washington and Three Women," in *George Washington's South*, ed. Tamara Harvey and Greg O'Brien (Gainesville: University Press of Florida, 2004), 121–142; and Thomas A. Foster, "On Sex and the Founding Fathers: America's Fascination with the Intimate Lives of the Political Leaders of the American Revolution," ch. 1, unpublished ms in author's possession.

30. George Washington to Burwell Bassett, 23 May 1785, www.gwpapers.virginia.edu.

31. Quoted in Scharff, *Women Jefferson Loved*, 242.

32. George Washington to Lund Washington, 20 September 1783, www.gwpapers.virginia.edu. For divorce, see Norma Basch, *Framing American Divorce: From the Revolutionary Generation to the Victorians* (Berkeley: University of California Press, 1999); Thomas E. Buckley, *The Great Catastrophe of My Life: Divorce in the Old Dominion* (Chapel Hill: University of North Carolina Press, 2002); and Glenda Riley, *Divorce: An American Tradition* (New York: Oxford University Press, 1991).

33. Martha Washington to Fanny Bassett Washington, 29 September 1794, in Fields, *"Worthy Partner,"* 276; George Washington to Burwell Bassett, 23 May 1785, www.gwpapers.virginia.edu.

34. Martha Washington to Sally Cary Fairfax, 17 May 1798, in Fields, *"Worthy Partner,"* 315; Patrick Henry to Anne Christian, 20 October 1786, *PHC*, 3:380. For southern courtship and marriage traditions, see Brown, *Good Wives, Nasty Wenches*, 334–342; Jane Turner Censer, *North Carolina Planters and Their Children, 1800–1860* (Baton Rouge: Louisiana State University Press, 1984), ch. 4; Anya Jabour, *Marriage in the Early Republic: Elizabeth and William Wirt and the Companionate Ideal* (Baltimore: Johns Hopkins University Press, 1998); Smith, *Inside the Great House*, ch. 4; Stevenson, *Life in Black and White*, chs. 2–3; and Stowe, *Intimacy and Power in the Old South*, ch. 2.

35. George Washington to Eleanor Parke Custis, 16 January 1795, in George Washington Parke Custis, *Recollections and Private Memoirs of Washington, by His Adopted Son, George Washington Parke Custis, with a Memoir of the Author, by His Daughter; and Illustrative and Explanatory Notes, by Benson J. Lossing* (New York: Derby and Jackson, 1860; reprint, 1999), 42–43.

36. Martha Washington to Fanny Bassett Washington, 29 September 1794, in Fields, *"Worthy Partner,"* 276–277; George Washington to Lund Washington, 20 September 1783, www.gwpapers.virginia.edu; Eleanor Parke Custis to Elizabeth Bordley Gibson, 4 November 1799, in *George Washington's Beautiful Nelly: The Letters of Eleanor Parke Custis Lewis to Elizabeth Bordley Gibson, 1794–1851,* ed. Patricia Brady (Columbia: University of South Carolina Press, 2006), 61.

37. Thomas Jefferson to Thomas Mann Randolph Sr., 4 February 1790, *PTJ,* 16:154.

38. Thomas Jefferson to Maria Jefferson, 14 June 1797, in Betts and Bear, *Family Letters,* 148; Thomas Jefferson to Martha Jefferson Randolph, 8 June 1797, ibid., 146. For kinship in southern families, see Lorri Glover, *All Our Relations: Blood Ties and Emotional Bonds Among the Early South Carolina Gentry* (Baltimore: Johns Hopkins University Press, 2000); Allan Kulikoff, *Tobacco and Slaves: The Development of Southern Cultures in the Chesapeake, 1680–1800* (Chapel Hill: University of North Carolina Press, 1986); and Darrett B. Rutman and Anita H. Rutman, *A Place in Time: Middlesex County, Virginia, 1650–1750* (New York: W. W. Norton, 1986).

39. Thomas Jefferson to Martha Jefferson Randolph, 4 April 1790, in Boykin, *To the Girls and Boys,* 48; Thomas Jefferson to Maria Jefferson Eppes, 7 January 1798, ibid., 94. See also Jan Lewis, "'The Blessings of Domestic Society': Thomas Jefferson's Family and the Transformation of American Politics," in *Jeffersonian Legacies,* ed. Peter S. Onuf (Charlottesville: University Press of Virginia, 1993), 109–146, esp. 135.

40. Patrick Henry to Betsy Aylett, 12 December 1787, *PHC,* 2:330; Thomas E. Buckley, ed., "The Duties of a Wife: Bishop James Madison to His Daughter, 1811," *VMHB* 91 (1983): 98–104 (quotation on 100–101).

41. Thomas Jefferson to Martha Jefferson Randolph, 17 July 1790, in Randolph, *Domestic Life of Jefferson,* 188.

42. Martha Jefferson Randolph to Thomas Jefferson, 16 January 1791, in Betts and Bear, *Family Letters,* 68.

43. Eleanor Parke Custis to Elizabeth Bordley Gibson, 3 February, 4 November 1799, in Brady, *Beautiful Nelly,* 59, 61–62.

44. Eleanor Parke Custis Lewis to Elizabeth Bordley Gibson, 23 March 1806, 4 July 1817, in Brady, *Beautiful Nelly,* 68, 82.

45. Brady, *Beautiful Nelly,* 11–15.

46. Martha Jefferson Randolph to Thomas Jefferson, 25 April 1790, 27 February 1793, in Betts and Bear, *Family Letters,* 52–53, 112.

47. Martha Jefferson Randolph to Thomas Jefferson, 25 April 1790, in Betts and Bear, *Family Letters,* 53. For Randolph's life, see William H. Gaines Jr., *Thomas Mann Randolph: Jefferson's Son-in-Law* (Baton Rouge: Louisiana State University Press, 1966).

48. Martha Jefferson Randolph to Thomas Jefferson, 18 November 1801, in Betts and Bear, *Family Letters,* 213.

49. Ellen Wayles Randolph to Martha Jefferson Randolph, 14 December 1821, 3 April 1822, FLDA.

50. Nicholas Trist to Martha Jefferson Randolph, 18 September 1818, FLDA; Martha Jefferson Randolph to Nicholas Trist, c. 19 September 1818, ibid. Randolph assured

Trist that she thought highly of him and would give identical advice if "it would have been in the case of one of my own sons." The couple married at Monticello six years later.

51. For deputy husbands, see Laurel Thatcher Ulrich, *Good Wives: Image and Reality in the Lives of Women in Northern New England, 1650–1750* (New York: Knopf, 1982), ch. 2. The most notable exception to this general pattern was Abigail Adams.

52. Thomas Jefferson to Anne Willing Bingham, 11 May 1788, *PTJ*, 13:151; Thomas Jefferson to George Washington, 21 December 1788, in Randolph, *Domestic Life of Jefferson*, 158. See also Kukla, *Mr. Jefferson's Women;* and John Steele, "Thomas Jefferson's Gender Frontier," *Journal of American History* 95 (2008): 17–42.

53. Eleanor Parke Custis to Elizabeth Bordley, 23 November 1797, in Brady, *Beautiful Nelly*, 40–41; Patrick Henry to Betsy Aylett, 20 August 1796, *PHC*, 2:570; George Mason to John Mason, 18 December 1788, *PGM*, 3:1136.

54. Allgor, *Parlor Politics;* Catherine Allgor, *A Perfect Union: Dolley Madison and the Creation of the American Nation* (New York: Henry Holt, 2006). For Martha Washington, see Harlow Giles Unger, *The Unexpected George Washington: His Private Life* (Hoboken, NJ: John Wiley and Sons, 2006); and Patricia Brady, *Martha Washington: An American Life* (New York: Penguin, 2005). For women's political engagement, see also Susan Branson, *These Fiery Frenchified Dames: Women and Political Culture in Early National Philadelphia* (Philadelphia: University of Pennsylvania Press, 2001).

55. Quoted in Allgor, *Parlor Politics*, 84.

56. Ibid., ch. 2.

57. John Dandridge to Martha Washington, 6 September 1791, in Fields, *"Worthy Partner,"* 234 (first quotation); Martha Washington to John Dandridge, 20 April 1789, ibid., 213 (second quotation); Martha Washington to Fanny Bassett Washington, 23 October 1789, ibid., 220 (last quotation).

58. Martha Washington to Mercy Otis Warren, 26 December 1789, 12 June 1790, in Fields, *"Worthy Partner,"* 223, 226.

59. Margaret Bayard Smith, *The First Forty Years of Washington Society,* ed. Galliard Hunt (New York: Charles Scribner's Sons, 1906), 80 (first quotation); Thomas Jefferson to Maria Cosway, 27 December 1820, in Randolph, *Domestic Life of Jefferson*, 374 (second quotation). For Jefferson's retirement, see Alan Pell Crawford, *Twilight at Monticello: The Final Years of Thomas Jefferson* (New York: Random House, 2008); and Malone, *Jefferson and His Time: The Sage of Monticello.*

60. For example, Thomas Jefferson to Martha Jefferson Randolph, 15 January 1791, in Randolph, *Domestic Life of Jefferson*, 208. For the affectionate family, see Rhys Isaac, *Landon Carter's Uneasy Kingdom: Revolution and Rebellion on a Virginia Plantation* (New York: Oxford University Press, 2005); Jabour, *Marriage in the Early Republic;* Lewis, *Pursuit of Happiness;* and Smith, *Inside the Great House.*

61. Thomas Jefferson to Martha Jefferson Randolph, 9 February 1791, in Randolph, *Domestic Life of Jefferson*, 192; Thomas Jefferson to Elizabeth Eppes, 15 May 1791, ibid., 201.

62. Margaret Bayard Smith, 1809 visit to Monticello, in *Visitors to Monticello*, ed. Merrill D. Peterson (Charlottesville: University Press of Virginia, 1989), 53 (first quota-

tion); Virginia Randolph Trist Reminiscence, in Randolph, *Domestic Life of Jefferson*, 347 (second quotation). For "our children," see Thomas Jefferson to Martha Jefferson Randolph, 3 December 1804, 28 January 1805, in Betts and Bear, *Family Letters*, 265, 267.

63. Virginia Randolph Trist Reminiscence, in Randolph, *Domestic Life of Jefferson*, 345–346; Ellen Randolph Coolidge Reminiscence, ibid., 344.

64. Thomas Jefferson to Ellen Wayles Randolph, 27 November 1801, in Boykin, *To the Girls and Boys*, 110.

65. Ellen Wayles Randolph to Nicholas Trist, 30 March 1824, FLDA. For antebellum feminism, see Sylvia D. Hoffert, *When Hens Crow: The Women's Rights Movement in Antebellum America* (Bloomington: Indiana University Press, 1995); Nancy Isenberg, *Sex and Citizenship in Antebellum America* (Chapel Hill: University of North Carolina Press, 1998); and Mary Kelley, *Learning to Stand and Speak: Women, Education, and Public Life in America's Republic* (Chapel Hill: University of North Carolina Press, 2006).

CHAPTER 6. "ALL OTHER PERSONS"

1. Thomas Jefferson to Ellen Randolph Coolidge, 27 August 1825, in *The Family Letters of Thomas Jefferson*, ed. Edwin Morris Betts and James Adam Bear Jr. (Columbia: University of Missouri Press, 1966), 458.

2. For the Hemings family, see Annette Gordon-Reed, *The Hemingses of Monticello: An American Family* (New York: W. W. Norton, 2008). For slave families at Monticello, see Lucia Stanton, *Free Some Day: The African-American Families of Monticello* (Charlottesville, VA: Thomas Jefferson Foundation, 2000); and Lucia Stanton, *"Those Who Labor for My Happiness": Slavery at Thomas Jefferson's Monticello* (Charlottesville: University of Virginia Press, 2012). See also Jack McLaughlin, *Jefferson and Monticello: The Biography of a Builder* (New York: Henry Holt, 1988), ch. 4; Lucia Stanton, "'Those Who Labor for My Happiness': Thomas Jefferson and His Slaves," in *Jeffersonian Legacies*, ed. Peter S. Onuf (Charlottesville: University Press of Virginia, 1993), 147–180; William M. Kelso, *Archaeology at Monticello: Artifacts and Everyday Life in a Plantation Community* (Charlottesville, VA: Thomas Jefferson Memorial Foundation, 1997), ch. 3. For slaves at Mount Vernon, see Scott E. Casper, *Sarah Johnson's Mount Vernon: The Forgotten History of an American Shrine* (New York: Hill and Wang, 2008).

3. Thomas Jefferson to Ellen Randolph Coolidge, 14 November 1825, in Betts and Bear, *Family Letters*, 461.

4. Ibid., 461–462.

5. "Declaration of Independence Desk," www.monticello.org; Thomas Jefferson, *Notes on the State of Virginia*, ed. William Peden (New York: W. W. Norton, 1972), 163.

6. The scholarship on slavery in this era is extensive. Foundational works include Ira Berlin, *Many Thousands Gone: The First Two Centuries of Slavery in North America* (Cambridge, MA: Harvard University Press, 1998); Ira Berlin and Ronald Hoffman, eds., *Slavery and Freedom in the Age of the American Revolution* (Urbana: University of Illinois Press, 1986); Kathleen M. Brown, *Good Wives, Nasty Wenches, and Anxious Patriarchs: Gender, Race, and Power in Colonial Virginia* (Chapel Hill: University of North Carolina Press, 1996); Allan Kulikoff, *Tobacco and Slaves: The Development of Southern Cultures in the Chesapeake, 1680–1800* (Chapel Hill: University of North Carolina Press,

1986); and Edmund S. Morgan, *American Slavery, American Freedom: The Ordeal of Colonial Virginia* (New York: W. W. Norton, 1975).

7. Patrick Henry, "Liberty or Death," in David A. McCants, *Patrick Henry, the Orator* (Westport, CT: Greenwood, 1990), 125. Francois Furstenberg argued that this speech conveyed the widespread conviction that only those willing to sacrifice their lives could earn freedom, which afforded slaveholders a new rationale for perpetuating slavery. *In the Name of the Father: Washington's Legacy, Slavery, and the Making of a Nation* (New York: Penguin, 2006), 193–195.

8. James Madison, "Motion on Slaves Taken by the British," 10 September 1782, *PJM (Congressional)*, 5:111–112.

9. George Mason essay, 23 December 1765, *PGM*, 1:61–62.

10. *PGM*, 1:277, 287–289; Robert Allen Rutland, *The Birth of the Bill of Rights: 1776–1791* (New York: Collier Books, 1966), 45. For drafts of and deliberations on the Virginia Declaration of Rights, see *PGM*, 1:274–291. See also Richard R. Beeman, *Patrick Henry: A Biography* (New York: McGraw-Hill, 1974), 101–102; and John E. Selby, *The Revolution in Virginia, 1775–1783* (Williamsburg, VA: Colonial Williamsburg Foundation, 1988), 106–110.

11. George Mason, Virginia Ratification Debates, 11 June 1788, in *The Documentary History of the Ratification of the Constitution*, ed. John P. Kaminski et al., 26 vols. (Madison: State Historical Society of Wisconsin, 1976–present), 9:1161. See also Debates in the Federal Convention, 22 August 1787, in *The Debates in the Several State Conventions, on the Adoption of the Federal Constitution*, ed. Jonathan Elliot, 5 vols. (Philadelphia: J. B. Lippincott, 1901), 5:457–461; Virginia Ratification Debates, 17 June 1788, in Kaminski et al., *Documentary History of the Ratification*, 10:1338–1344; and George Mason to Thomas Jefferson, 26 May 1788, *PGM*, 3:1045. For Virginia's ratification debates, see also Pauline Maier, *Ratification: The People Debate the Constitution, 1787–1788* (New York: Simon and Schuster, 2010), chs. 9–10.

12. James Madison to Jedidiah Morse, 28 March 1823, quoted in Elizabeth Dowling Taylor, *A Slave in the White House: Paul Jennings and the Madisons* (New York: Palgrave Macmillan, 2012), 96. See also James Madison to Noah Webster, 17 July 1792, *PJM (Congressional)*, 14:343.

13. Patrick Henry, 18 January 1773, *PHC*, 1:152; James Madison, 6 June 1787, in Elliot, *Debates in the Several State Conventions*, 5:162; James Madison, "Notes for Essays," 19 December 1791–3 March 1792, *PJM (Congressional)*, 14:163; George Washington to Tobias Lear, 6 May 1794, in *The Writings of George Washington from the Original Manuscript Sources*, ed. John C. Fitzpatrick, 39 vols. (Washington, DC: Government Printing Office, 1931–1944), 33:358. For Madison's views on slavery, see also Drew R. McCoy, *The Last of the Fathers: James Madison and the Republican Legacy* (Cambridge: Cambridge University Press, 1989). Madison raised nearly all of his concerns in private, as did Washington. Jack Rakove, *James Madison and the Creation of the American Republic*, 3rd ed. (New York: Pearson, 2007), 229; Dorothy Twohig, "'That Species of Property': Washington's Role in the Controversy over Slavery," in *George Washington Reconsidered*, ed. Don Higginbotham (Charlottesville: University of Virginia Press, 2001), 116.

14. George Mason, 22 August 1787, *PGM*, 3:965–966; George Mason essay, 23 December 1765, in Kate Mason Rowland, *The Life of George Mason, 1725–1792, Includ-*

ing His Speeches, Public Papers, and Correspondence, 2 vols. (New York: G. P. Putnam's Sons, 1892), 1:378; Patrick Henry essay, *PHC*, 1:114, 116.

15. George Mason, 22 August 1787, *PGM*, 3:966; Jefferson, *Notes on the State of Virginia*, 162.

16. Taylor, *Slave in the White House*, 2; Virginia Scharff, *The Women Jefferson Loved* (New York: HarperCollins, 2010), 70–71.

17. George Mason runaway slave advertisement, 20 September 1786, *PGM*, 2:855–856; George Washington to George Lewis, 13 November 1797, *PGW (Retirement)*, 1:469; George Washington to Lawrence Lewis, 4 August 1797, ibid., 288.

18. James Madison to William Bradford, 26 November 1774, *PJM (Congressional)*, 1:129–130; *Virginia Gazette*, 25 November 1775. See also Alan Taylor, *The Internal Enemy: Slavery and War in Virginia, 1772–1832* (New York: W. W. Norton, 2013).

19. Thomas Jefferson to St. George Tucker, 28 August 1787, quoted in Paul Finkelman, "Jefferson and Slavery: 'Treason Against the Hopes of the World,'" in Onuf, *Jeffersonian Legacies*, 185.

20. George Mason, 22 August 1787, *PGM*, 3:966; Jefferson, *Notes on the State of Virginia*, 163.

21. Richard Beeman, *Plain, Honest Men: The Making of the American Constitution* (New York: Random House, 2009), 335 (delegate quotations). James Madison similarly explained the intentional avoidance of the words in James Madison to Robert Walsh Jr., 27 November 1819, *PJM (Retirement)*, 1:553–558. See also David Waldstreicher, *Slavery's Constitution: From Revolution to Ratification* (New York: Hill and Wang, 2009); and Morgan, *American Slavery, American Freedom*, bk. 4. For early sectional tensions over slavery, see Linda Kerber, *Federalists in Dissent: Imagery and Ideology in Jeffersonian America* (Ithaca, NY: Cornell University Press, 1970), ch. 2; Joyce Appleby, *Inheriting the Revolution: The First Generation of Americans* (Cambridge, MA: Harvard University Press, 2000), ch. 7; and Jack P. Greene, "The Constitution of 1787 and the Question of Southern Distinctiveness," in *Imperatives, Behaviors, and Identities: Essays in Early American Cultural History* (Charlottesville: University Press of Virginia, 1992), 327–347.

22. Marquis de Lafayette to George Washington, 5 February 1783, in *Lafayette in the Age of the American Revolution: Selected Letters and Papers, 1776–1790*, ed. Stanley J. Idzerda et al., 5 vols. (Ithaca, NY: Cornell University Press, 1977–1983), 5:90–93; Robert Pleasants to James Madison, 6 June 1791, *PJM (Congressional)*, 14:30; Edward Coles to James Madison, 8 January 1832, in "Letters of Edward Coles," *WMQ*, 2nd ser., 7 (1927): 37. Coles made similar appeals to Thomas Jefferson. Edward Coles to Thomas Jefferson, 31 July 1814, 26 September 1813, in *Governor Edward Coles*, ed. Clarence W. Alvond, Collections of the Illinois State Historical Library, vol. 15 (Springfield: Illinois State Historical Society Library, 1920), 22–29. See also Alan Pell Crawford, *Twilight at Monticello: The Final Years of Thomas Jefferson* (New York: Random House, 2008), 99–104; and Philip D. Morgan, "'To Get Quit of Negroes': George Washington and Slavery," *Journal of American Studies* 39 (2005): 403–429.

23. Gordon S. Wood, *Revolutionary Characters: What Made the Founders Different* (New York: Penguin, 2006), 38. See also Joanne Pope Melish, *Disowning Slavery: Gradual Emancipation and "Race" in New England, 1780–1860* (Ithaca, NY: Cornell University Press, 1998); and Beverly C. Tomek, *Colonization and Its Discontents: Emancipation, Emi-*

gration, and Antislavery in Antebellum Pennsylvania (New York: New York University Press, 2011).

24. James Madison to James Madison Sr., 8 September 1783, *PJM (Congressional)*, 7:304; George Washington to Tobias Lear, 12 April 1791, in Tobias Lear, *Letters and Recollections of George Washington* (New York: Doubleday, Page, 1906), 38.

25. James Madison to Robert Evans, 15 June 1819, *PJM (Retirement)*, 1:468–470. See also Ralph Ketcham, *The Madisons at Montpelier: Reflections on the Founding Couple* (Charlottesville: University of Virginia Press, 2009), 39–45; and McCoy, *Last of the Fathers*, 260–286.

26. James Madison to Edmund Randolph, 26 July 1785, *PJM (Congressional)*, 8:328; Patrick Henry, 18 January 1773, *PHC*, 1:152; Thomas Jefferson to Thomas Cooper, 10 September 1814, *PTJ (Retirement)*, 7:652; Thomas Jefferson to John Holmes, 22 April 1820, in *The Writings of Thomas Jefferson*, ed. Paul L. Ford, 10 vols. (New York: G. P. Putnam's Sons, 1899), 10:157. For the centrality of race in the early national era, see Lacy K. Ford, "Making the 'White Man's Country' White: Race, Slavery, and State-Building in the Jacksonian South," *Journal of the Early Republic* 19 (1999): 713–737.

27. Thomas Jefferson to Edward Coles, 25 August 1814, in *The Portable Thomas Jefferson*, ed. Merrill D. Peterson (New York: Viking, 1975), 547; James Madison to Robert Pleasants, 30 October 1791, *PJM (Congressional)*, 14:92; Patrick Henry, 18 January 1773, *PHC*, 1:153.

28. George Mason, Virginia Ratification Debates, 11 June 1788, in Kaminski et al., *Documentary History of the Ratification*, 9:1161; Dolley Madison to Anna Cutts, c. 23 July 1818, in *The Selected Letters of Dolley Payne Madison*, ed. David B. Mattern and Holly C. Shulman (Charlottesville: University of Virginia Press, 2003), 231; James Madison, 6 June 1787, in Elliot, *Debates in the Several State Conventions*, 5:162.

29. Jefferson used this phrasing to describe an illness spreading "in our family, both in doors and out." Thomas Jefferson to Mrs. M. B. Jefferson, 2 August 1815, in *Thomas Jefferson's Farm Book*, ed. Edwin Morris Betts (1953; reprint, Charlottesville, VA: Thomas Jefferson Memorial Foundation, 1999), 39. For another example, see Rhys Isaac, *Landon Carter's Uneasy Kingdom: Revolution and Rebellion on a Virginia Plantation* (New York: Oxford University Press, 2005), 59.

30. Spencer Roane, *PHC*, 2:515–516; Edmund Winston, ibid., 516.

31. John Mason Recollection, transcribed by Terry Dunn, Papers of John Mason (1766–1849), Gunston Hall Library and Archives.

32. Thomas Fleming, *The Intimate Lives of the Founding Fathers* (New York: Smithsonian/HarperCollins, 2009), 321; George Washington Parke Custis, *Recollections and Private Memoirs of Washington, by His Adopted Son, George Washington Parke Custis, with a Memoir of the Author, by His Daughter; and Illustrative and Explanatory Notes, by Benson J. Lossing* (New York: Derby and Jackson, 1860; reprint, 1999), 454; Recollection of Reverend Ashbel Green, ibid., 436 (quotation).

33. John Mason Recollection; Morgan, "'To Get Quit of Negroes,'" 422. Slaves knew their owners so intimately that they could expose their darkest secrets. See, e.g., Cynthia A. Kierner, *Scandal at Bizarre: Rumor and Reputation in Jefferson's Virginia* (New York: Palgrave Macmillan, 2004).

34. Paul Jennings, *A Colored Man's Reminiscences of James Madison, by Paul Jennings*

(Brooklyn, NY: George C. Beadle, 1865); Taylor, *Slave in the White House*. For Sawney, see Ketcham, *Madisons at Montpelier*, 7. For Gardner, see James Madison to James Madison Sr., 8 September 1783, *PJM (Congressional)*, 7:304–305.

35. For Jefferson's earliest memories, see *The Domestic Life of Thomas Jefferson*, ed. Sarah N. Randolph (1871; Charlottesville: University Press of Virginia, 1994), 23. For his death, see Gordon-Reed, *Hemingses of Monticello*, 650–651. See also Scharff, *Women Jefferson Loved*, 77, 91; and Stanton, *Free Some Day*, 18–27.

36. Gordon-Reed, *Hemingses of Monticello*, 130; Kierner, *Martha Jefferson Randolph*, 15, 125; Stanton, *Free Some Day*, 22–23; Scharff, *Women Jefferson Loved*, 179, 358.

37. Gordon-Reed, *Hemingses of Monticello*, 125; Beeman, *Plain, Honest Men*, 35, 43; Joseph J. Ellis, *His Excellency: George Washington* (New York: Knopf, 2004), 269.

38. Jennings, *Reminiscences of Madison*, 11–15. For slavery in Jefferson's White House, see Stanton, *"Those Who Labor for My Happiness,"* ch. 3.

39. Betts, *Jefferson's Farm Book*, 27. See also Stanton, *"'Those Who Labor for My Happiness,'"* in Onuf, *Jeffersonian Legacies*, 148.

40. George Washington to Tobias Lear, 21 September 1792, in Lear, *Letters and Recollections of Washington*, 59. See also George Washington to Tobias Lear, 19 June 1791, ibid., 45; Thomas Jefferson to James Madison, 17 August 1809, in *The Republic of Letters: The Correspondence Between Thomas Jefferson and James Madison, 1776–1826*, ed. James Morton Smith, 3 vols. (New York: W. W. Norton, 1995), 3:1599; and James Madison to James Madison Sr., [29] March 1777, *PJM (Congressional)*, 1:190–191.

41. Philip D. Morgan, "Interracial Sex in the Chesapeake and the British Atlantic World, c. 1700–1820," in *Sally Hemings and Thomas Jefferson: History, Memory, and Civic Culture*, ed. Jan Ellen Lewis and Peter S. Onuf (Charlottesville: University of Virginia Press, 1999), 52–55, 64–65. For the Washington story, see Patricia Brady, *Martha Washington: An American Life* (New York: Penguin, 2005), 256.

42. Ellen Randolph Coolidge to Joseph Coolidge, 24 October 1858, FLDA. The historical profession has moved considerably since the critiques leveled at Fawn Brodie when she published *Thomas Jefferson: An Intimate History* (New York: W. W. Norton, 1974). Though the 1998 *Nature* article presenting DNA evidence became national news, Annette Gordon-Reed had already convinced many scholars in *Thomas Jefferson and Sally Hemings: An American Controversy* (Charlottesville: University Press of Virginia, 1997). For debates on the nature of the Jefferson-Hemings relationship, see Thomas A. Foster, "On Sex and the Founding Fathers: America's Fascination with the Intimate Lives of the Political Leaders of the American Revolution," ch. 2, unpublished ms in author's possession; Jon Kukla, *Mr. Jefferson's Women* (New York: Knopf, 2007), ch. 6; Lewis and Onuf, *Sally Hemings and Thomas Jefferson*; Joshua D. Rothman, *Notorious in the Neighborhood: Sex and Families Across the Color Line in Virginia, 1787–1861* (Chapel Hill: University of North Carolina Press, 2003), ch. 1; Scharff, *Women Jefferson Loved*, pt. 3; Stanton, *"Those Who Labor for My Happiness,"* ch. 6; and Clarence E. Walker, *Mongrel Nation: The America Begotten by Thomas Jefferson and Sally Hemings* (Charlottesville: University of Virginia Press, 2009).

43. James Callender, *Richmond Recorder*, 1 September 1802. See also Michael Durey, *"With the Hammer of Truth": James Thomson Callender and America's Early National Heroes* (Charlottesville: University of Virginia Press, 1990).

44. Over time, Savage's image was revised to erase slavery from Washington's domestic life. For a thoughtful analysis, see Furstenberg, *In the Name of the Father*, 76–78, 90–92.

45. James Madison to Mordecai Collins, c. 8 November 1790, *PJM (Congressional)*, 13:303; George Washington to William Stuart, Hiland Crow, and Henry McCoy, 14 July 1793, *PGW (Presidential)*, 13:225; Stanton, "'Those Who Labor for My Happiness,'" in Onuf, *Jeffersonian Legacies*, 150; Stanton, *Free Some Day*, 144.

46. Thomas Jefferson to Martha Jefferson Randolph, 5 February 1792, in Betts and Bear, *Family Letters*, 94; George Washington to Howell Lewis, 4 August 1793, *PGW (Presidential)*, 13:341–344.

47. Mason runaway slave advertisement; Robert F. Dalzell, Jr., and Lee Baldwin Dalzell, *George Washington's Mount Vernon: At Home in Revolutionary America* (New York: Oxford University Press, 1998), 131; Jefferson, *Notes on the State of Virginia*, 140.

48. George Washington to Tobias Lear, 22 November 1790, in Lear, *Letters and Recollections of Washington*, 31. For African American families and cultures in Virginia, see esp. Philip D. Morgan, *Slave Counterpoint: Black Culture in the Eighteenth-Century Chesapeake and Lowcountry* (Chapel Hill: University of North Carolina Press, 1998); and Brenda Stevenson, *Life in Black and White: Family and Community in the Slave South* (New York: Oxford University Press, 1996), part 2.

49. Dalzell and Dalzell, *Washington's Mount Vernon*, 133; Thomas Jefferson to Jeremiah Goodman, 6 January 1815, in *Thomas Jefferson's Garden Book*, ed. Edwin Morris Betts (1944; reprint, Charlottesville, VA: Thomas Jefferson Memorial Foundation, 1999), 540; James Madison to Jedidiah Morse, March 1823, *JM Writings*, 9:132.

50. George Washington to Charles Washington, 14 February 1787, *PGW (Confederation)*, 5:28–29.

51. Dolley Madison to Henry W. Moncure, 12 August 1844, in *Life and Letters of Dolley Madison*, ed. Allen C. Clark (Washington, DC: W. F. Roberts, 1914), 342; Sarah Steward to Dolley Madison, 5 July 1844, in Mattern and Shulman, *Letters of Dolley Payne Madison*, 373.

52. Mary Randolph to Ellen Randolph Coolidge, 25 January 1827, FLDA; *Central Gazette*, 13 January 1827; Stanton, "'Those Who Labor for My Happiness,'" in Onuf, *Jeffersonian Legacies*, 147.

53. Inventory of Daniel Parke Custis Estate, in *"Worthy Partner": The Papers of Martha Washington*, ed. Joseph E. Fields (Westport, CT: Greenwood, 1994), 61–75; Taylor, *Slave in the White House*, 26.

54. Martha Washington to Fanny Bassett Washington, 24 May 1795, in Fields, *"Worthy Partner,"* 287; James Madison to James Madison Sr., 27 December 1795, *PJM (Congressional)*, 16:174.

55. Martha Jefferson Randolph to Thomas Jefferson, 30 January 1800, in Betts and Bear, *Family Letters*, 182–183; Thomas Jefferson to Martha Jefferson Randolph, 11 February 1800, ibid., 183; Thomas Jefferson to Maria Jefferson Eppes, 12 February 1800, ibid., 185. For their relationship, see also Stanton, *"Those Who Labor for My Happiness,"* 107–113.

56. John Mason Recollection.

57. Dolley Madison to Mary Cutts, 1 August 1833, in Mattern and Shulman, *Letters of Dolley Payne Madison*, 300; Edmund Bacon Reminiscence, in Hamilton W. Pierson,

Jefferson at Monticello: The Private Life of Thomas Jefferson, from Entirely New Materials (New York: Charles Scribner, 1862), 124–125.

58. Thomas Jefferson to Maria Jefferson, 14 June 1797, in Betts and Bear, *Family Letters*, 148.

59. James Madison to Thomas Jefferson, 30 July 1793, in Smith, *Republic of Letters*, 2:798.

60. Martha Jefferson Randolph quoted in Henry S. Randall, *The Life of Thomas Jefferson*, 3 vols. (New York: Derby and Jackson, 1858), 1:64–65. For Brown's likely trip, see Gordon-Reed, *Hemingses of Monticello*, 114. For Jupiter, see Scharff, *Women Jefferson Loved*, 77, 91.

61. George Washington to Tobias Lear, 31 July 1797, in Lear, *Letters and Recollections of Washington*, 120.

62. Thomas Jefferson to John Page, June 1804, in Randolph, *Domestic Life of Jefferson*, 302; poem to Martha, ibid., 429; Thomas Jefferson to Thomas Jefferson Randolph, 8 February 1826, in *To the Girls and Boys: Being the Delightful, Little-Known Letters of Thomas Jefferson to and from his Children and Grandchildren*, ed. Edward Boykin (New York: Funk and Wagnalls, 1964), 191.

63. Ellen Randolph Coolidge to Thomas Jefferson, 1 August 1825, in Betts and Bear, *Family Letters*, 454. For the Missouri crisis, see Robert Pierce Forbes, *The Missouri Compromise and Its Aftermath: Slavery and the Meaning of America* (Chapel Hill: University of North Carolina Press, 2007).

64. Thomas Jefferson, *Autobiography of Thomas Jefferson, 1743–1790* (New York: G. P. Putnam's Sons, 1914), 77.

65. Quoted in Catherine Allgor, ed., *The Queen of America: Mary Cutts's Life of Dolley Madison* (Charlottesville: University of Virginia Press, 2012), 64.

66. Patrick Henry, 18 January 1773, *PHC*, 1:153.

67. Custis, *Recollections*, 158; Adams quoted in Furstenberg, *In The Name of the Father*, 74.

CHAPTER 7. "OURSELVES AND OUR POSTERITY"

1. George Mason to George Mason Jr., 1 June 1787, *PGM*, 3:892–893. Patriot leaders had begun to think in these terms as early as 1776. See, e.g., Richard Henry Lee to Patrick Henry, April 1776, *PHC*, 1:378. For the Constitutional Convention, see Richard Beeman, *Plain, Honest Men: The Making of the American Constitution* (New York: Random House, 2009).

2. Preamble to US Constitution.

3. Patrick Henry, Virginia Ratification Debates, 4 June 1788, in *The Documentary History of the Ratification of the Constitution*, ed. John P. Kaminski et al., 26 vols. (Madison: State Historical Society of Wisconsin, 1976–present), 9:930–931. See also Pauline Maier, *Ratification: The People Debate the Constitution, 1787–1788* (New York: Simon and Schuster, 2010), chs. 9–10; and Kaminski et al., *Documentary History of the Ratification*, vols. 8–10.

4. For sovereignty and constitutionalism, see Gordon S. Wood, *The Creation of the American Republic, 1776–1787* (Chapel Hill: University of North Carolina Press, 1969); Lance Banning, *Conceived in Liberty: The Struggle to Define the New Republic, 1789–1793*

(Lanham, MD: Rowman and Littlefield, 2004); Jack Rakove, *Original Meanings: Politics and Ideas in the Making of the Constitution* (New York: Viking, 1996); and Bernard Bailyn, *Ideological Origins of the American Revolution* (Cambridge, MA: Harvard University Press, 1967). For Antifederalists, see Saul Cornell, *The Other Founders: Anti-Federalism and the Dissenting Tradition in America, 1788–1828* (Chapel Hill: University of North Carolina Press, 1999).

5. The wide-ranging and extensive work on early national politics includes Lance Banning, *The Jeffersonian Persuasion: Evolution of a Party Ideology* (Ithaca, NY: Cornell University Press, 1978); Stanley Elkins and Eric McKitrick, *The Age of Federalism* (New York: Oxford University Press, 1993); Joanne B. Freeman, *Affairs of Honor: National Politics in the New Republic* (New Haven: Yale University Press, 2001); Jeffrey L. Pasley, *"The Tyranny of Printers": Newspaper Politics in the Early American Republic* (Charlottesville: University Press of Virginia, 2001); and David Waldstreicher, *"In the Midst of Perpetual Fetes": The Making of American Nationalism, 1776–1820* (Chapel Hill: University of North Carolina Press, 1997).

6. Hugh Blair Grigsby, *The History of the Virginia Federal Convention of 1788*, vol. 1, ed. R. A. Brock (Richmond: Virginia Historical Society, 1890), 42.

7. Spencer Roane Memorandum, in George Morgan, *The True Patrick Henry* (Philadelphia: J. B. Lippincott, 1907), 449.

8. James Madison to William Bradford, 23 August 1774, *PJM (Congressional)*, 1:121; James Madison to Thomas Jefferson, 16 April 1781, in *The Republic of Letters: The Correspondence Between Thomas Jefferson and James Madison, 1776–1826*, ed. James Morton Smith, 3 vols. (New York: W. W. Norton, 1995), 1:186–187.

9. James Madison, "Vices of the Political System of the United States," April 1787, *PJM (Congressional)*, 9:348–358. For Madison's views, see Lance Banning, *The Sacred Fire of Liberty: James Madison and the Founding of the Federal Republic* (Ithaca, NY: Cornell University Press, 1995); Richard Labunski, *James Madison and the Struggle for the Bill of Rights* (New York: Oxford University Press, 2006); Drew R. McCoy, *The Last of the Fathers: James Madison and the Republican Legacy* (Cambridge: Cambridge University Press, 1989); Jack Rakove, *James Madison and the Creation of the American Republic*, 3rd ed. (New York: Pearson, 2007); and Gordon S. Wood, *Revolutionary Characters: What Made the Founders Different* (New York: Penguin, 2006), ch. 5.

10. James Madison, Federalist No. 14; James Madison, c. 15 October 1788, *PJM (Congressional)*, 11:286.

11. James Madison to Robert Walsh, 27 November 1819, *PJM (Retirement)*, 1:557 (first quotation); James Madison, Federalist No. 37 (second quotation).

12. Patrick Henry, Virginia Ratification Debates, 4 June 1788, in Kaminski et al., *Documentary History of the Ratification*, 9:929.

13. Richard R. Beeman, *Patrick Henry: A Biography* (New York: McGraw-Hill, 1974), 126. See also Henry Mayer, *A Son of Thunder: Patrick Henry and the American Republic* (New York: Franklin Watts, 1986); Kevin J. Hayes, *The Mind of a Patriot: Patrick Henry and the World of Ideas* (Charlottesville: University of Virginia Press, 2008); and Thomas S. Kidd, *Patrick Henry: First Among Patriots* (New York: Basic Books, 2011).

14. Patrick Henry, Virginia Ratification Debates, 5 June 1788, in Kaminski et al., *Documentary History of the Ratification*, 9:951.

15. Ibid., 960.

16. Patrick Henry to Henry Lee, 14 July 1794, *PHC*, 2:547 (quotation); Patrick Henry to Edmund Randolph, 14 September 1794, ibid., 548.

17. Patrick Henry to George Washington, 16 October 1795, *PHC*, 2:558; Mayer, *Son of Thunder*, 466 (second quotation).

18. George Mason to Richard Henry Lee, 4 June 1779, *PGM*, 2:507. See also Helen Hill Miller, *George Mason, Gentleman Revolutionary* (Chapel Hill: University of North Carolina Press, 1975), 334.

19. George Mason to Thomas Jefferson, 27 September 1781, *PGM*, 2:697 (first quotation); George Mason to Edmund Randolph, 19 October 1782, ibid., 753 (second quotation).

20. James Madison, 31 August 1787, in *The Debates in the Several State Conventions, on the Adoption of the Federal Constitution*, ed. Jonathan Elliot, 5 vols. (Philadelphia: J. B. Lippincott, 1901), 5:502. See also Peter Wallenstein, "Flawed Keepers of the Flame: The Interpreters of George Mason," *VMHB* 102 (1994): 229–260; and Jeff Broadwater, *George Mason, Forgotten Founder* (Chapel Hill: University of North Carolina Press, 2006), 207–215.

21. George Mason to John Mason, 13 March 1789, *PGM*, 3:1142. See also Peter R. Henriques, "An Uneven Friendship: The Relationship Between George Washington and George Mason," *VMHB* 97 (1989): 185–204.

22. George Washington to David Stuart, 19 November 1786, *PGW (Confederation)*, 4:387. See also Joseph J. Ellis, *His Excellency: George Washington* (New York: Knopf, 2004); and Don Higginbotham, *George Washington: Uniting a Nation* (Lanham, MD: Rowman and Littlefield, 2002).

23. George Washington to David Stuart, 1 July 1787, *PGW (Confederation)*, 5:240.

24. Ibid., 241; George Washington to Bushrod Washington, 9 November 1787, *PGW (Confederation)*, 5:421–422.

25. For their relationship, see Stuart Leibiger, *Founding Friendship: George Washington, James Madison, and the Creation of the American Republic* (Charlottesville: University Press of Virginia, 1999).

26. George Washington Will, 9 July 1799, *PGW (Retirement)*, 4:482–483.

27. Thomas Jefferson, Second Inaugural Address, 4 March 1805, in *The Writings of Thomas Jefferson*, ed. Paul L. Ford, 10 vols. (New York: G. P. Putnam's Sons, 1899), 8:344. For Jefferson's later views, see Gordon S. Wood, "The Trials and Tribulations of Thomas Jefferson," in *Jeffersonian Legacies*, ed. Peter S. Onuf (Charlottesville: University Press of Virginia, 1993), 410–414; and Susan Dunn, *Dominion of Memories: Jefferson, Madison, and the Decline of Virginia* (New York: Basic Books, 2007), 65.

28. Patrick Henry, Virginia Ratification Debates, 5 June 1788, in Kaminski et al., *Documentary History of the Ratification*, 9:959.

29. For the persistence of local interests, see Richard Beeman, *The Old Dominion and the New Nation, 1788–1801* (Lexington: University Press of Kentucky, 1972), 239 (quotation). For continued elite control, see John E. Selby, *The Revolution in Virginia, 1775–1783* (Williamsburg, VA: Colonial Williamsburg Foundation, 1988); Charles Sydnor, *Gentleman Freeholders: Political Practices in Washington's Virginia* (Chapel Hill: University of North Carolina Press, 1952); and Brent Tarter, *The Grandees of Government: The Origins and Persistence of Undemocratic Politics in Virginia* (Charlottesville: University

of Virginia Press, 2013). For non-elite influences, see Woody Holton, *Forced Founders: Indians, Debtors, Slaves, and the Making of the American Revolution in Virginia* (Chapel Hill: University of North Carolina Press, 1999); and Michael A. McDonnell, *The Politics of War: Race, Class, and Conflict in Revolutionary Virginia* (Chapel Hill: University of North Carolina Press, 2007).

30. Draft of Washington's First Inaugural Address, *PGW (Presidential)*, 2:162.

31. Patrick Henry, Virginia Ratification Debates, 4 June 1788, in Kaminski et al., *Documentary History of the Ratification*, 9:931; Smith, *Republic of Letters*, 2:1140.

32. George Washington Parke Custis, *Recollections and Private Memoirs of Washington, by His Adopted Son, George Washington Parke Custis, with a Memoir of the Author, by His Daughter; and Illustrative and Explanatory Notes, by Benson J. Lossing* (New York: Derby and Jackson, 1860; reprint, 1999), 394; George Washington to Benjamin Franklin, 2 June 1784, *PGW (Confederation)*, 1:414; Joseph E. Fields, ed., *"Worthy Partner": The Papers of Martha Washington* (Westport, CT: Greenwood, 1994), xxix–xxx; Martha Washington to Fanny Bassett Washington, 29 September 1794, ibid., 276; Martha and George Washington to Tobias Lear, 30 March 1796, ibid., 291.

33. Betty Washington Lewis to George Washington, 14 May 1792, *PGW (Presidential)*, 10:383; George Washington to Charles Carter, 19 May 1792, ibid., 398. For another example, see George Washington and Martha Washington to Tobias Lear, 30 March 1796, in Fields, *"Worthy Partner,"* 291; and Martha Washington to Mary Stillson Lear, 4 November 1796, ibid., 293.

34. See George Green Shackelford, *Jefferson's Adoptive Son: The Life of William Short, 1759–1848* (Lexington: University Press of Kentucky, 1993).

35. William Grayson to James Madison, 22 March 1786, *PJM (Congressional)*, 8:510; Caleb Wallace to James Madison, 12 July 1785, ibid., 321.

36. Dolley Madison to James Madison, 5 December 1826, in *The Selected Letters of Dolley Payne Madison*, ed. David B. Mattern and Holly C. Shulman (Charlottesville: University of Virginia Press, 2003), 266; James Madison to Dolley Madison, 14 December 1826, ibid., 268. For Dolley Madison's political contributions, see Catherine Allgor, *Parlor Politics: In Which the Ladies of Washington Help Build a City and a Government* (Charlottesville: University Press of Virginia, 2000); and Catherine Allgor, *A Perfect Union: Dolley Madison and the Creation of the American Nation* (New York: Henry Holt, 2006).

37. For more on their fluid household, see Allgor, *Perfect Union;* Ralph Ketcham, *The Madisons at Montpelier: Reflections on the Founding Couple* (Charlottesville: University of Virginia Press, 2009); and Elizabeth Dowling Taylor, *A Slave in the White House: Paul Jennings and the Madisons* (New York: Palgrave Macmillan, 2012).

38. Charles Pinckney to James Madison, 16 March 1801, *PJM (State)*, 1:23.

39. Paul Jennings, *A Colored Man's Reminiscences of James Madison, by Paul Jennings* (Brooklyn, NY: George C. Beadle, 1865), 19.

40. Thomas Jefferson Randolph, ed., *Memoirs, Correspondence, and Private Papers of Thomas Jefferson, Late President of the United States*, 4 vols. (London: Henry Colburn and Richard Bentley, 1829), 1:35. For the Jefferson-Madison relationship, see "An Intimate Relationship," in Smith, *Republic of Letters*, 1:1–35; Lance Banning, *Jefferson and Madison: Three Conversations from the Founding* (Madison, WI: Madison House, 1995); and Andrew Burstein and Nancy Isenberg, *Madison and Jefferson* (New York: Random House, 2010).

41. Thomas Jefferson to James Monroe, 18 February 1808, in Randolph, *Memoirs, Correspondence, and Private Papers of Jefferson*, 4:108; Harlow Giles Unger, *The Last Founding Father: James Monroe and a Nation's Call to Greatness* (New York: Da Capo, 2009), 83.

42. Albert Gallatin to James Madison, 30 July 1810, *PJM (Presidential)*, 2:455; Thomas Macon to James Madison, 13 June 1810, ibid., 376; Henry Clay to James Madison, 10 October 1828, in *The Papers of Henry Clay*, ed. Robert Seager II, vol. 7 (Lexington: University Press of Kentucky, 1982), 487. For another example, see Martha Jefferson Randolph to Dolley Madison, 15 January 1808, in Mattern and Shulman, *Letters of Dolley Payne Madison*, 83; and Mary Randolph to Dolley Madison, 10 February 1808, ibid., 84.

43. Kierner, *Martha Jefferson Randolph*, 135.

44. Isaac Coles to James Madison, 29 December 1809, *PJM (Presidential)*, 2:150–151; James Madison to Thomas Jefferson, 11 December 1809, ibid., 125; Alfred Madison to James Madison, 24 November 1809, ibid., 83–84; James Madison to Benjamin Rush, 29 October 1810, ibid., 600; Benjamin Rush to James Madison, 30 January 1811, ibid., 3:141; Frances Madison Rose to James Madison, 20 March 1813, ibid., 6:138 (quotation). For Madison's presidency, see Rakove, *James Madison*, chs. 14–15; and J. C. A. Stagg, *Mr. Madison's War: Politics, Diplomacy, and Warfare in the Early American Republic, 1783–1830* (Princeton, NJ: Princeton University Press, 1983).

45. Philadelphia Arch Street Quaker Meeting Minutes, 27 February 1789, in *The Queen of America: Mary Cutts's Life of Dolley Madison*, ed. Catherine Allgor (Charlottesville: University of Virginia Press, 2012), 48 (quotations); Allgor, *Queen of America*, 49; *PJM (Presidential)*, 3:200–201, n. 1; Lucy Washington Todd to Dolley Madison, 18 April 1812, in Mattern and Shulman, *Letters of Dolley Payne Madison*, 162. John Payne worked for a long period after James Madison's retirement on Madison's papers. He never fully overcame his alcoholism and eventually moved to Illinois, where he struggled financially. Ibid., 346–347, n 1.

46. Dolley Madison to John Payne Todd, 2 December 1824, in Mattern and Shulman, *Letters of Dolley Payne Madison*, 257–258; Dolley Madison to John Payne Todd, 22 January 1844, in Allgor, *Queen of America*, 187. See also John Payne Todd Memorandum Book, LC.

47. Dolley Madison to Lucy Payne Washington Todd, 23 August 1814, in Mattern and Shulman, *Letters of Dolley Payne Madison*, 193. For the War of 1812, see Donald R. Hickey, *The War of 1812: A Forgotten Conflict, Bicentennial Issue* (Urbana: University of Illinois Press, 2012); Alan Taylor, *The Internal Enemy: Slavery and War in Virginia, 1772–1832* (New York: W. W. Norton, 2013); and Steven Watts, *The Republic Reborn: War and the Making of Liberal America, 1790–1820* (Baltimore: Johns Hopkins University Press, 1987).

48. Thomas Jefferson to Martha Jefferson Randolph, 15 January 1792, in *The Domestic Life of Thomas Jefferson*, ed. Sarah N. Randolph (1871; Charlottesville: University Press of Virginia, 1994), 208. For public and private, see esp. Allgor, *Parlor Politics*; Cynthia A. Kierner, *Beyond the Household: Women's Place in the Early South, 1700–1835* (Ithaca, NY: Cornell University Press, 1998); and Rosemarie Zagarri, *Revolutionary Backlash: Women and Politics in the Early American Republic* (Philadelphia: University of Pennsylvania Press, 2007).

49. Thomas Jefferson to Martha Jefferson Randolph, 8 June 1797, in *The Family Letters of Thomas Jefferson*, ed. Edwin Morris Betts and James Adam Bear Jr. (Columbia: University of Missouri Press, 1966), 146; Thomas Jefferson to Martha Jefferson Randolph, 31 May 1798, in Randolph, *Domestic Life of Jefferson*, 250. See also Dunn, *Dominion of Memories*, 18–19; Jan Lewis, "'The Blessings of Domestic Society': Thomas Jefferson's Family and the Transformation of American Politics," in Onuf, *Jeffersonian Legacies*; and Jon Kukla, *Mr. Jefferson's Women* (New York: Knopf, 2007).

50. George Washington to Marquis de Lafayette, 1 February 1784, *PGW (Confederation)*, 1:88; George Washington to Samuel Hanson, 10 January 1789, *PGW (Presidential)*, 1:241; George Washington to Marquis de Lafayette, 19 March 1791, ibid., 7:596–597.

51. For the emergence of separate spheres, see Nancy Cott, *The Bonds of Womanhood: "Woman's Sphere" in New England, 1780–1835* (New Haven: Yale University Press, 1977); and Kierner, *Beyond the Household*.

52. Thomas Jefferson to George Washington, spring 1789, in Randolph, *Domestic Life of Jefferson*, 147; James Madison to George Washington, 6 December 1786, *PJM (Congressional)*, 9:199.

53. Patrick Henry to Henry Lee, 27 June 1795, in *Patrick Henry in His Speeches and Writings and in the Words of His Contemporaries*, ed. James M. Elson (Lynchburg, VA: Warwick House, 2007), 166; George Mason to George Mason Jr., 27 May 1787, *PGM*, 3:884.

54. George Washington to Henry Knox, 2 March 1797, LC; Thomas Jefferson to Martha Jefferson Randolph, 27 February 1809, in Betts and Bear, *Family Letters*, 385; Ralph L. Ketcham, ed., "An Unpublished Sketch of James Madison by James K. Paulding," *VMHB* 67 (1959): 435.

55. Thomas Jefferson to John Holmes, 22 April 1820, in Ford, *Writings of Jefferson*, 10:157. Gordon Wood argued that this was the unintended result of the founding generation's republican ideals put into action. *The Radicalism of the American Revolution* (New York: Knopf, 1992), 365–369.

Chapter 8. Reputation

1. Patrick Henry Will, 20 November 1798, www.redhill.org.

2. *PHC*, 2:632.

3. For character, see Gordon S. Wood, *Revolutionary Characters: What Made the Founders Different* (New York: Penguin, 2006). For Washington, see esp. Richard Brookhiser, *Founding Father: Rediscovering George Washington* (New York: Free Press, 1996), 131–136; and Paul K. Longmore, *The Invention of George Washington* (Berkeley: University of California Press, 1988). For Jefferson, see esp. Francis D. Cogliano, *Thomas Jefferson: Reputation and Legacy* (Charlottesville: University of Virginia Press, 2006). See also Douglass Adair, "Fame and the Founding Fathers," in *Fame and the Founding Fathers: Essays by Douglass Adair*, ed. Trevor Colbourn (Indianapolis, IN: Liberty Fund, 1998); Joanne B. Freeman, *Affairs of Honor: National Politics in the New Republic* (New Haven: Yale University Press, 2001); and John P. Kaminski, *The Great Virginia Triumvirate: George Washington, Thomas Jefferson, and James Madison in the Eyes of Their Contemporaries* (Charlottesville: University of Virginia Press, 2010).

4. George Washington to Josiah Quincy, 24 March 1776, in Josiah Quincy, *Memoir of the Life of Josiah Quincy, Jr.* (Boston: Little, Brown, 1875), 416; George Washington to David Stuart, 19 November 1786, *PGW (Confederation)*, 4:387–388; Thomas Jefferson to George Washington, spring 1789, in *The Domestic Life of Thomas Jefferson*, ed. Sarah N. Randolph (1871; Charlottesville: University Press of Virginia, 1994), 148.

5. Thomas Jefferson to James Madison, 8 December 1784, in *The Republic of Letters: The Correspondence Between Thomas Jefferson and James Madison, 1776–1826*, ed. James Morton Smith, 3 vols. (New York: W. W. Norton, 1995), 1:354; Thomas Jefferson to William Wirt, misc. corres., in Stan V. Henkels, ed., "Jefferson's Recollections of Patrick Henry," *PMHB* 34 (1910): 385–418. See also Richard R. Beeman, *Patrick Henry: A Biography* (New York: McGraw-Hill, 1974), 132–133; and Andrew Burstein, *America's Jubilee* (New York: Knopf, 2001), ch. 2.

6. Cynthia A. Kierner, *Martha Jefferson Randolph, Daughter of Monticello: Her Life and Times* (Chapel Hill: University of North Carolina Press, 2012), 202; Thomas Jefferson to James Madison, 17 February 1826, in Smith, *Republic of Letters*, 3:1967.

7. James Madison to George Tucker, 27 June 1836, LC; Douglass Adair, ed., "James Madison's Autobiography," *WMQ*, 3rd ser., 2 (1945): 199.

8. George Washington to John Augustine Washington, 15 June 1783, quoted in Wood, *Revolutionary Characters*, 57.

9. George Washington, First Inaugural Address, 30 April 1789, *PGW (Presidential)*, 2:175.

10. Edward Fontaine, "Patrick Henry, Corrections of biographical mistakes, and popular errors in regard to his character. Anecdotes and new facts illustrating his religious and political opinions; & the style & power of his eloquence. A brief account of his last illness & death" (1872), ed. Mark Couvillon (Brookneal, VA: Patrick Henry Memorial Foundation, 1996), 32.

11. Anonymous to George Washington, 3 January 1792, *PGW (Presidential)*, 9:369–370 (quotation). For these events, see Leonard L. Richards, *Shays's Rebellion: The American Revolution's Final Battle* (Philadelphia: University of Pennsylvania Press, 2002); Thomas P. Slaughter, *The Whiskey Rebellion: Frontier Epilogue to the American Revolution* (New York: Oxford University Press, 1986); Paul Douglas Newman, *Fries's Rebellion: The Enduring Struggle for the American Revolution* (Philadelphia: University of Pennsylvania Press, 2004); Jay Winik, *The Great Upheaval: America and the Birth of the Modern World, 1788–1800* (New York: HarperCollins, 2007); Frank Lambert, *The Barbary Wars: American Independence in the Atlantic World* (New York: Hill and Wang, 2005); Edward J. Larson, *A Magnificent Catastrophe: The Tumultuous Election of 1800, America's First Presidential Campaign* (New York: Free Press, 2007); John Ferling, *Adams vs. Jefferson: The Tumultuous Election of 1800* (New York: Oxford University Press, 2004); Thomas J. Fleming, *Duel: Alexander Hamilton, Aaron Burr and the Future of America* (New York: Basic Books, 1999); and esp. Freeman, *Affairs of Honor*. For overviews of the era, see Gordon S. Wood, *Empire of Liberty: A History of the Early Republic, 1789–1815* (New York: Oxford University Press, 2009); and Stanley Elkins and Eric McKitrick, *The Age of Federalism* (New York: Oxford University Press, 1993).

12. Thomas Jefferson to John Holmes, 22 April 1820, in *The Writings of Thomas*

Jefferson, ed. Paul L. Ford, 10 vols. (New York: G. P. Putnam's Sons, 1899), 10:157–158; James Madison to Jared Sparks, 1 June 1831, in Smith, *Republic of Letters*, 3:1991. See also Ralph Ketcham, *The Madisons at Montpelier: Reflections on the Founding Couple* (Charlottesville: University of Virginia Press, 2009), 65–73.

13. Quoted in Susan Dunn, *Dominion of Memories: Jefferson, Madison, and the Decline of Virginia* (New York: Basic Books, 2007), 23.

14. Martha Jefferson Randolph to Ellen Randolph Coolidge, 15 September 1833, FLDA. For the movement of the Randolphs, see Kierner, *Martha Jefferson Randolph*, 279. For another prominent Virginia family's decline, see Philip Hamilton, *The Making and Unmaking of a Revolutionary Family: The Tuckers of Virginia, 1752–1830* (Charlottesville: University of Virginia Press, 2003).

15. Herbert E. Sloan, *Principle and Interest: Thomas Jefferson and the Problem of Debt* (New York: Oxford University Press, 1995), 26–27; Charles Royster, *Light-Horse Harry Lee and the Legacy of the American Revolution* (New York: Knopf, 1981), 183, 231.

16. Thomas Jefferson, "Report of the Commissioners for the University of Virginia," in *Thomas Jefferson: Writings*, ed. Merrill D. Peterson (New York: Library of America, 1984), 459–460. For his retirement, see also Alan Pell Crawford, *Twilight at Monticello: The Final Years of Thomas Jefferson* (New York: Random House, 2008).

17. Smith, *Republic of Letters*, 3:1919–1920 (first quotation); Thomas Jefferson to Joseph C. Cabell, 7 February 1826, in Ford, *Writings of Jefferson*, 10:373–374 (second quotation); Dunn, *Dominion of Memories*, 66. For southern college students, see Lorri Glover, *Southern Sons: Becoming Men in the New Nation* (Baltimore: Johns Hopkins University Press, 2007), pt. 2; and Robert F. Pace, *Halls of Honor: College Men in the Old South* (Baton Rouge: Louisiana State University Press, 2004).

18. For Wythe's murder, see Julian P. Boyd, "The Murder of George Wythe," *WMQ*, 3rd ser., 12 (1955): 513–542. For Randolph's resignation, see Mary Bonsteel Tachau, "George Washington and the Reputation of Edmund Randolph," *Journal of American History* 73 (1986): 15–34. For the infanticide case, see Cynthia A. Kierner, *Scandal at Bizarre: Rumor and Reputation in Jefferson's Virginia* (New York: Palgrave Macmillan, 2004).

19. Henry Mayer, *A Son of Thunder: Patrick Henry and the American Republic* (New York: Franklin Watts, 1986), 468; Martha Washington to Fanny Bassett Washington, 6 April 1795, in *"Worthy Partner": The Papers of Martha Washington*, ed. Joseph E. Fields (Westport, CT: Greenwood, 1994), 284; *PJM (State)*, 2:125–126, 197, 268; George Washington to David Stuart, 22 January 1798, *PGW (Retirement)*, 2:37–38.

20. Catherine Allgor, *A Perfect Union: Dolley Madison and the Creation of the American Nation* (New York: Henry Holt, 2006), 95, 251. For the partisan press, see Jeffrey L. Pasley, *"The Tyranny of Printers": Newspaper Politics in the Early American Republic* (Charlottesville: University Press of Virginia, 2001).

21. Spencer Roane Memorandum, in George Morgan, *The True Patrick Henry* (Philadelphia: J. B. Lippincott, 1907), 436; Mayer, *Son of Thunder*, 473.

22. Martha Jefferson Randolph to Elizabeth Trist, 31 May 1815, FLDA (first quotation); Martha Jefferson Randolph to Thomas Jefferson, 20 November 1816, in *The Family Letters of Thomas Jefferson*, ed. Edwin Morris Betts and James Adam Bear Jr.

(Columbia: University of Missouri Press, 1966), 417 (second quotation). See also Virginia Scharff, *The Women Jefferson Loved* (New York: HarperCollins, 2010), 344–347, 366–367; Kierner, *Martha Jefferson Randolph*, 168–169.

23. Mary Jefferson Randolph to Ellen Randolph Coolidge, 23 October 1825, FLDA (first quotation); Cornelia Randolph to Ellen Randolph Coolidge, 24 November 1825, FLDA (second quotation); Thomas Jefferson to Thomas Jefferson Randolph, 8 February 1826, in *To the Girls and Boys: Being the Delightful, Little-Known Letters of Thomas Jefferson to and from his Children and Grandchildren*, ed. Edward Boykin (New York: Funk and Wagnalls, 1964), 191 (last quotation). See also Marc Leepson, *Saving Monticello: The Levy Family's Epic Quest to Restore the House That Jefferson Built* (New York: Free Press, 2001), ch. 1; Sloan, *Principle and Interest*.

24. Ellen Randolph Coolidge Reminiscence, in Randolph, *Domestic Life of Jefferson*, 344; Virginia Randolph Trist Reminiscence, ibid., 345–346.

25. George Washington Parke Custis, *Recollections and Private Memoirs of Washington, by His Adopted Son, George Washington Parke Custis, with a Memoir of the Author, by His Daughter; and Illustrative and Explanatory Notes, by Benson J. Lossing* (New York: Derby and Jackson, 1860; reprint, 1999), 175.

26. Thomas Jefferson to William Wirt, 4 August 1805, in Henkels, "Jefferson's Recollections of Patrick Henry," 395. See also Norine Dickson Campbell, *Patrick Henry: Patriot and Statesman* (New York: Devin-Adair, 1969); Kevin J. Hayes, *The Mind of a Patriot: Patrick Henry and the World of Ideas* (Charlottesville: University of Virginia Press, 2008), 1–28; Burstein, *America's Jubilee*, ch. 2.

27. Eleanor Parke Custis Lewis to Elizabeth Bordley, 23 March 1806, in *George Washington's Beautiful Nelly: The Letters of Eleanor Parke Custis Lewis to Elizabeth Bordley Gibson, 1794–1851*, ed. Patricia Brady (Columbia: University of South Carolina Press, 2006), 67; Thomas Jefferson to William Wirt, 14 August 1814, in Henkels, "Jefferson's Recollections of Patrick Henry," 402. See also Cogliano, *Thomas Jefferson*, ch. 2.

28. Sketch of George Mason, in Kate Mason Rowland, *The Life of George Mason, 1725–1792, Including His Speeches, Public Papers, and Correspondence*, 2 vols. (New York: G. P. Putnam's Sons, 1892), 2:367–368; Samuel Meredith Statement, in Morgan, *True Patrick Henry*, 433. See also Edmund Randolph Reminiscence, *PHC*, 1:260.

29. Thomas Jefferson to James Madison, 17 February 1826, in Smith, *Republic of Letters*, 3:1966–1967; James Madison to Thomas Jefferson, 24 February 1826, ibid., 1968.

30. John Mason Recollection, transcribed by Terry Dunn, Papers of John Mason (1766–1849), Gunston Hall Library and Archives; Eleanor Parke Custis to Elizabeth Bordley, 19 October 1795, in Brady, *Beautiful Nelly*, 21; Thomas Jefferson Randolph Reminiscence, in Henry S. Randall, *The Life of Thomas Jefferson*, 3 vols. (New York: Derby and Jackson, 1858), 3:671.

31. Edward Coles to William C. Rives, 21 January 1856, "Letters of Edward Coles," *WMQ*, 2nd ser., 7 (1927): 163–164; Martha Jefferson Randolph to Ellen Randolph Coolidge, c. 22 October 1826, FLDA.

32. Ellen Randolph Coolidge to Nicholas Trist, 27 September 1826, FLDA (quotation); Martha Jefferson Randolph to Ellen Randolph Coolidge, c. 22 October 1826, FLDA; Kierner, *Martha Jefferson Randolph*, ch. 7.

33. Ellen Randolph Coolidge to Joseph Coolidge, 24 October 1858, FLDA. See also

Fawn Brodie, *Thomas Jefferson: An Intimate History* (New York: W. W. Norton, 1974); Annette Gordon-Reed, *The Hemingses of Monticello: An American Family* (New York: W. W. Norton, 2008); Scot A. French and Edward L. Ayers, "The Strange Career of Thomas Jefferson: Race and Slavery in American Memory, 1943–1993," in *Jeffersonian Legacies*, ed. Peter S. Onuf (Charlottesville: University Press of Virginia, 1993), 418–456.

34. Ellen Randolph Coolidge to Henry Randall, 1857, in Randolph, *Domestic Life of Jefferson*, 392.

35. Fontaine, "Patrick Henry, Corrections of biographical mistakes," 3, 31.

36. William Wirt Henry, "The Causes Which Produced the Virginia of the Revolutionary Period," 1891 AHA Presidential Address, www.historians.org/info/aha_history/wwhenry.htm.

37. For the fascinating history of Jefferson's papers, see Cogliano, *Thomas Jefferson*, ch. 3. For Washington's papers, see W. W. Abbot, "An Uncommon Awareness of Self: The Papers of George Washington," in *George Washington Reconsidered*, ed. Don Higginbotham (Charlottesville: University of Virginia Press, 2001), 275–286.

38. George Washington to Lund Washington, 10–17 December 1776, *PGW (War)*, 7:291; Joseph J. Ellis, *His Excellency: George Washington* (New York: Knopf, 2004), 151–152; Kaminski, *Great Virginia Triumvirate*, 47, 30.

39. Custis, *Recollections*, 373–374, 436–437 (quotation on 436).

40. Thomas Jefferson to John Adams, 10 August 1815, in *The Adams-Jefferson Letters: The Complete Correspondence Between Thomas Jefferson and Abigail and John Adams*, ed. Lester J. Cappon (New York: Simon and Schuster, 1971), 452.

41. Thomas Jefferson to William Johnson, 4 March 1823, quoted in Cogliano, *Thomas Jefferson*, 44; Thomas Jefferson to Virginia Delegates and George Washington, 10 May 1781, *PJM (Congressional)*, 3:119. For Jefferson's zeal for a legacy, see Cogliano, *Thomas Jefferson*, chs. 2–3; R. B. Bernstein, *Thomas Jefferson* (New York: Oxford University Press, 2003), ch. 10; Jack P. Greene, "The Intellectual Reconstruction of Virginia in the Age of Jefferson," in Onuf, *Jeffersonian Legacies*, 225–253.

42. Dumas Malone, *Jefferson and His Time: The Sage of Monticello* (Boston: Little, Brown, 1970), 489.

43. *PJM (Congressional)*, 5:232–233; Ketcham, *Madisons at Montpelier*, 102.

44. Dolley Madison to Sarah Coles Stevenson, c. February 1820, in *The Selected Letters of Dolley Payne Madison*, ed. David B. Mattern and Holly C. Shulman (Charlottesville: University of Virginia Press, 2003), 238–239; C. C. Proctor, ed., "After-Dinner Anecdotes of James Madison: Excerpt from Jared Sparks' Journal of 1829–1831," *VMHB* 60 (1952): 255–256 (quotation on 264).

45. Patrick Henry to Henry Lee, 27 June 1795, in *Patrick Henry in His Speeches and Writings and in the Words of His Contemporaries*, ed. James M. Elson (Lynchburg, VA: Warwick House, 2007), 165.

46. Jeff Broadwater, *George Mason, Forgotten Founder* (Chapel Hill: University of North Carolina Press, 2006), 245. For Mason's priorities, see George Mason to John Mason, 12 June, 18 December 1788, *PGM*, 3:1072, 1138.

47. James Madison to George Mason, 29 December 1827, *JM Writings*, 9:293.

48. Custis, *Recollections*, 437; Jefferson quoted in Malone, *Jefferson and His Time: The Sage of Monticello*, 214; James Madison Will, 15 April 1835, *JM Writings*, 9:549.

49. Quoted in Cogliano, *Thomas Jefferson*, 82.

50. Mary Cutts, Memoir II, in *The Queen of America: Mary Cutts's Life of Dolley Madison*, ed. Catherine Allgor (Charlottesville: University of Virginia Press, 2012), 189; James Madison Will, 15 April 1835, *JM Writings*, 9:549.

51. Mattern and Shulman, *Letters of Dolley Payne Madison* (quotation on 318); Allgor, *Perfect Union*, 378–380; *PJM (Congressional)*, 1:xv–xvii; John Payne Todd Memorandum Book, LC. See also Holly C. Shulman, "'A Constant Attention': Dolley Madison and the Publication of the Papers of James Madison, 1836–1837," *VMHB* 118 (2010): 40–70.

52. Cogliano, *Thomas Jefferson*, 78–79.

53. George Washington to Marquis de Lafayette, 1 February 1784, *PGW (Confederation)*, 1:88.

54. For reactions to Washington's death, see Gerald Kahler, *The Long Farewell: Americans Mourn the Death of George Washington* (Charlottesville: University of Virginia Press, 2008); Edward G. Lengel, *Inventing George Washington: America's Founder, in Myth and Memory* (New York: HarperCollins, 2011), esp. 11–14; Longmore, *Invention of Washington*, ch. 17; Andrew Burstein, "Immortalizing the Founding Fathers: The Excesses of Public Eulogy," in *Mortal Remains: Death in Early America*, ed. Nancy Isenberg and Andrew Burstein (Philadelphia: University of Pennsylvania Press, 2003), 91–107; and "A Concert of Mourning," http://gwpapers.virginia.edu/project/exhibit/mourning/index.html.

55. Tobias Lear, 14 December 1799, in Tobias Lear, *Letters and Recollections of George Washington* (New York: Doubleday, Page, 1906), 131–134.

56. Tobias Lear, "occurrences not noted in the previous narrative," December 1799, in Lear, *Letters and Recollections of Washington*, 135–136; James Craik and Elisha Dick, 21 December 1799, *Virginia Herald* (Fredericksburg), 31 December 1799. See also Peter R. Henriques, "The Final Struggle between George Washington and the Grim King: Washington's Attitudes Toward Death and an Afterlife," *VMHB* 107 (1999): 73–97.

57. Martha Washington to Jonathan Trumbull, 15 January 1800, in Fields, *"Worthy Partner,"* 339.

58. Henry Lee to Martha Washington, 10 April 1800, ibid., 374; Martha Washington to John Adams, 31 December 1799, ibid., 332; John Augustine Washington to Lawrence Lewis, 14 February 1832, quoted in Jean B. Lee, "Historical Memory, Sectional Strife, and the American Mecca: Mount Vernon, 1783–1853," *VMHB* 109 (2001): 274. See also Frances W. Saunders, "Equestrian Washington: From Rome to Richmond," *Virginia Cavalcade* 25 (1975): 4–13.

59. George Dabney to William Wirt, 14 May 1806, in Elson, *Patrick Henry in His Speeches*, 187. For a "good death," see Gary Laderman, *The Sacred Remains: American Attitudes Toward Death, 1799–1883* (New Haven: Yale University Press, 1996); and Isenberg and Burstein, *Mortal Remains*.

60. Patrick Henry Fontaine, *PHC*, 2:625–626; *Virginia Gazette*, 14 June 1799, ibid., 627.

61. Thomas Jefferson Randolph, in Randolph, *Domestic Life of Jefferson*, 426–427.

62. Ibid., 428.

63. Paul Jennings, *A Colored Man's Reminiscences of James Madison, by Paul Jennings*

(Brooklyn, NY: George C. Beadle, 1865), 20–21. George Mason is the only member of this cohort for whom there is no surviving death story.

64. James Madison to Nicholas Trist, 6 July 1826, LC.

65. Adams quoted in Adair, "Fame and the Founding Fathers," 29. For Virginians' looking backward, see Dunn, *Dominion of Memories;* and Richard Beeman, *The Old Dominion and the New Nation, 1788–1801* (Lexington: University Press of Kentucky, 1972).

66. John Wayles Eppes to Francis Eppes, John Wayles Eppes Letters, DUL; www .fsu.edu/~fsu150/history.

67. *Lynchburg Virginian,* 26 January 1854, transcribed by Edith Poindexter, Red Hill Patrick Henry National Memorial.

68. *Alexandria Gazette,* 21 March 1849, Gunston Hall Library and Archives.

69. Brodie, *Thomas Jefferson,* 281; William H. Gaines Jr., *Thomas Mann Randolph: Jefferson's Son-in-Law* (Baton Rouge: Louisiana State University Press, 1966), 186–187.

70. "In Memoriam: William Wirt Henry," *VMHB* 8 (1901): xiii. See also *New York Times,* 19 September 1893.

71. Mary Custis Lee Memoir, in Custis, *Recollections,* 71.

EPILOGUE

1. *The Pilgrimage to Monticello, The Home and Tomb of Thomas Jefferson, by the Jefferson Club of Saint Louis, Missouri, October 10 to 14, 1901* (St. Louis: Curran, 1902), 18, 65. Replicating the familial rhetoric often employed in the 1760s–1770s, Missouri's lieutenant governor proclaimed: "Virginia has been called the mother of States and Missouri is proud to bear testimony to the maternity of Virginia and to appear here to-day as a daughter, coming home to receive a mother's welcome and blessing." Speech by John A. Lee, ibid., 14.

2. George Washington to Samuel Vaughan, 5 February 1785, *PGW (Confederation),* 2:326.

3. For examples, see Robert F. Dalzell and Lee Baldwin Dalzell, *George Washington's Mount Vernon: At Home in Revolutionary America* (New York: Oxford University Press, 1998); Robert F. Dalzell, Jr., "Constructing Independence: Monticello, Mount Vernon, and the Men Who Built Them," *Eighteenth-Century Studies* 26 (1993): 543–580; Francis D. Cogliano, *Thomas Jefferson: Reputation and Legacy* (Charlottesville: University of Virginia Press, 2006), 106–126; Helen Hill Miller, *George Mason, Gentleman Revolutionary* (Chapel Hill: University of North Carolina Press, 1975), 47–54; and Jack McLaughlin, *Jefferson and Monticello: The Biography of a Builder* (New York: Henry Holt, 1988).

4. George Washington to Marquis de Lafayette, 1 February 1784, *PGW (Confederation),* 1:87–88.

5. Martha Jefferson Randolph to Ann Cary Morris, 8 August 1825, FLDA; Custis, *Recollections,* 166–167; Julian Ursyn Niemcewicz, 1798 visit to Mount Vernon, in *Experiencing Mount Vernon: Eyewitness Accounts, 1784–1865,* ed. Jean B. Lee (Charlottesville: University of Virginia Press, 2006), 82. See also Myron Magnet, *The Founders at Home: The Building of America, 1725–1817* (New York: W. W. Norton, 2013).

6. Samuel I. Prime, "A Pilgrimage to the Tomb of Washington," *New York Ob-*

server, 27 June 1846, in Lee, *Experiencing Mount Vernon*, 179. For fame, see Douglass Adair, "Fame and the Founding Fathers," in *Fame and the Founding Fathers: Essays by Douglass Adair*, ed. Trevor Colbourn (Indianapolis, IN: Liberty Fund, 1998).

7. Chevalier de Chastellux, 1782 visit to Monticello, and Margaret Bayard Smith, 1809 visit to Monticello, in *Visitors to Monticello*, ed. Merrill D. Peterson (Charlottesville: University Press of Virginia, 1989), 13, 52; Henning W. Prentis, 1901 speech, in *Pilgrimage to Monticello*, 18.

8. Thomas Jefferson to Thomas Cooper, 10 September 1814, *PTJ (Retirement)*, 7:652 (quotation). For the centrality of slaves to these estates, see Robert L. Self and Susan R. Stein, "The Collaboration of Thomas Jefferson and John Hemings: Furniture Attributed to the Monticello Joinery," *Winterthur Portfolio* 33 (1998): 231–248; William M. Kelso, *Archaeology at Monticello: Artifacts and Everyday Life in a Plantation Community* (Charlottesville, VA: Thomas Jefferson Memorial Foundation, 1997), ch. 3; and Scott E. Casper, *Sarah Johnson's Mount Vernon: The Forgotten History of an American Shrine* (New York: Hill and Wang, 2008).

9. *The Selected Letters of Dolley Payne Madison*, ed. David B. Mattern and Holly C. Shulman (Charlottesville: University of Virginia Press, 2003), 325.

10. John H. B. Latrobe, 1832 visit to Monticello, and David M. R. Culbreath, 1872 visit to Monticello, in Peterson, *Visitors to Monticello*, 120, 153.

11. Benjamin Brown French, 1834 visit to Mount Vernon, and L. Osgood, 1839 visit to Mount Vernon, in Lee, *Experiencing Mount Vernon*, 143, 152–154.

12. "A Visit to Mount Vernon," *Daily National Intelligencer*, 14 June 1850, in Lee *Experiencing Mount Vernon*, 181–182.

13. Unnamed Sailor, 1861, in Lee, *Experiencing Mount Vernon*, 207; Edmund Bacon Reminiscence, in Hamilton W. Pierson, *Jefferson at Monticello: The Private Life of Thomas Jefferson, from Entirely New Materials* (New York: Charles Scribner, 1862), 131. See also Casper, *Sarah Johnson's Mount Vernon*, 79–106; McLaughlin, *Jefferson and Monticello*, 375–385; and Marc Leepson, *Saving Monticello: The Levy Family's Epic Quest to Restore the House That Jefferson Built* (New York: Free Press, 2001).

14. David M. R. Culbreath, 1872 visit to Monticello, and Fiske Kimball, 1924 visit to Monticello, in Peterson, *Visitors to Monticello*, 153, 192.

15. Jean B. Lee, "Historical Memory, Sectional Strife, and the American Mecca: Mount Vernon, 1783–1853," *VMHB* 109 (2001): 256, 280 (first quotation); "House of Patrick Henry to Become National Shrine," www.redhill.org/memorialfoundation.htm (second quotation).

16. Leepson, *Saving Monticello*; Patricia West, *Domesticating History: The Political Origins of America's House Museums* (Washington, DC: Smithsonian Institution Press, 1999), 100 (quotation); James Silk Buckingham, 1841 visit to Monticello, in Peterson, *Visitors to Monticello*, 134.

17. For women's leadership, see esp. Lee, "Historical Memory, Sectional Strife, and the American Mecca," 293–299; West, *Domesticating History*, chs. 1, 3.

18. See Evelyn Bence, ed., *James Madison's Montpelier: Home of the Father of the Constitution* (Montpelier Foundation, 2008), ch. 3; and Bryan Clark Green, Ann L. Miller, and Conover Hunt, *Building a President's House: The Construction of James Madison's Montpelier* (Montpelier Foundation, 2007). See also James L. Nolan Jr. and Ty F. Buck-

man, "Preserving the Postmodern, Restoring the Past: The Cases of Monticello and Montpelier," *Sociological Quarterly* 39 (1998): 253–269; Peter J. Hatch, "Restoring the Monticello Landscape, 1923–1955," *Magnolia: Publication of the Southern Garden Society* 23 (Fall 2009–Winter 2010): 1–8; Susan R. Stein and John B. Rudder, "Lighting Jefferson's Monticello: Considering the Past, Present, and Future," *Association for Preservation Technology International Bulletin* 31 (2000): 21–26; Frank Sagendorph Welsh, "Restoring the Colors of Thomas Jefferson: Beyond the Colors of Independence," in *Architectural Finishes in the Built Environment*, ed. Mary A. Jablonski and Catherine R. Matsen (London: Archetype, 2009).

19. Fairfax County Militia Plan, February 1775, *PGM*, 1:216 (first quotation); Thomas Jefferson to John Holmes, 22 April 1820, in Ford, *Writings of Jefferson*, 10:157 (second quotation).

Index